THE ROLE OF THE STATE IN TAIWAN'S DEVELOPMENT

Political and Economic Development/Asia

"Though long neglected, except by those concerned with its still unresolved security and national identity status vis-à-vis mainland China, Taiwan is increasingly recognized as a developmental model in its own right. Among the world's most successful 'NICs,' with an average annual growth rate of some 9.3% (1961–1988), Taiwan now faces many of the problems of a maturing industrial democracy. *The Role of the State in Taiwan's Development* is among the first books to deal with many of these problems (e.g., the recent shift to an emphasis on private-sector initiative). With a general concern with the interaction between market and plan in Taiwan's industrial policy, this collection of sophisticated and topical analyses focuses successively on various leading economic sectors (foreign trade, finance, semi-conductors, fiscal policy, the role of women), contributing substantially to our understanding of both the country's outstanding success stories (e.g., export-oriented growth) and its occasional failures (e.g., automobiles)."

—Lowell Dittmer,
University of California, Berkeley

This book is sponsored by the Center for Pacific Rim Studies, University of California, Los Angeles.

THE ROLE OF THE STATE IN TAIWAN'S DEVELOPMENT

Yu-Hsia Chen
Chia-Lin Cheng
Lucie Cheng
Yun-han Chu
Stephan Haggard
Ping-Chun Hsiung
Chen-Kuo Hsu
Chun-chieh Huang
Fa-Chin Liang
Kuo-yuan Liang

Cheng-hung Liao
Liang-Yn Liu
Wei-Lin Mao
Constance Squires Meaney
Chien-Kuo Pang
Jia-Dong Shea
Chu-Wei Tseng
Fang-Yi Wang
Wing Thye Woo
Ya-Hwei Yang

JOEL D. ABERBACH, DAVID DOLLAR,
and KENNETH L. SOKOLOFF
Editors

An East Gate Book

M.E. Sharpe

Armonk, New York
London, England

An East Gate Book

Copyright © 1994 by M. E. Sharpe, Inc.

Library of Congress Cataloging-in-Publication Data

The Role of the state in Taiwan's development / edited by Joel D. Aberbach,
David Dollar, Kenneth L. Sokoloff.
p. cm.—(Taiwan in the modern world)
"An East gate book."
Includes bibliographical references and index.
ISBN 1-56324-325-3.—ISBN 1-56324-326-1 (pbk.)
1. Industrial promotion—Taiwan.
2. Industry and state—Taiwan.
3. Taiwan—Economic policy—1975–
I. Aberbach, Joel D.
II. Dollar, David.
III. Sokoloff, Kenneth Lee.
IV. Series.
HC430.5.Z9I536   1993
338.95124´9—dc20
93–33071
CIP

Printed in the United States of America

MV (c)   10   9   8   7   6   5   4   3   2   1
MV (p)   10   9   8   7   6   5   4   3   2   1

In memory of John C. Ries

Contents

About the Contributors

JOEL D. ABERBACH, Professor, Department of Political Science, and Director, Center for American Politics and Public Policy, University of California, Los Angeles

YU-HSIA CHEN, Associate Professor, Department of Economics, Soochow University, Taipei

CHIA-LIN CHENG, Professor, Department of Economics, Soochow University, Taipei

LUCIE CHENG, Professor, Department of Sociology, University of California, Los Angeles

YUN-HAN CHU, Associate Professor, Department of Political Science, National Taiwan University, Taipei

DAVID DOLLAR, Ph.D., Senior Economist, The World Bank, Washington, D.C.*

STEPHAN HAGGARD, Professor, Center for International Affairs, Harvard University, Cambridge, Massachusetts

PING-CHUN HSIUNG, Assistant Professor, University of Toronto, Scarborough, Ontario, Canada

CHEN-KUO HSU, Associate Professor, Department of Political Science, Soochow University, Taipei

CHUN-CHIEH HUANG, Professor, Department of History, National Taiwan University, Taipei

FA-CHIN LIANG, Professor, Graduate Institute of Economics, National Chung Hsing University, Taipei

KUO-YUAN LIANG, Professor, Department of Economics, National Tsing Hua University, Hsin Chu, Taiwan

CHENG-HUNG LIAO, Professor, Department of Agricultural Extension, National Taiwan University, Taipei

LIANG-YN LIU, Research Associate, Pacific Rim Studies Program, University of California, Davis, and Research Specialist, Texas Commission on Alcohol and Drug Abuse

WEI-LIN MAO, Associate Professor, Graduate Institute of Economics, National Chengchi University, Taipei

---

*Views expressed by David Dollar are his own and do not necessarily reflect official positions of The World Bank or its member countries.

CONSTANCE SQUIRES MEANEY, Assistant Professor, Department of Government, Mills College, Oakland, California

CHIEN-KUO PANG, Associate Professor, Department of Sociology, National Taiwan University, Taipei

JIA-DONG SHEA, Research Fellow, Institute of Economics, Academia Sinica, Taipei

KENNETH L. SOKOLOFF, Professor, Department of Economics, University of California, Los Angeles

CHU-WEI TSENG, Associate Professor, Graduate Institute of Public Finance, National Chengchi University, Taipei

FANG-YI WANG, Ph.D., The World Bank, Washington, D.C.*

WING THYE WOO, Professor, Department of Economics and Pacific Rim Studies Program, University of California, Davis

YA-HWEI YANG, Research Fellow, Chung-Hua Institution for Economic Research, Taipei

*Views expressed by Fang-Yi Wang are her own and do not necessarily reflect official positions of The World Bank or its member countries.

Introduction

Joel D. Aberbach, David Dollar, and Kenneth L. Sokoloff

The economic growth of Taiwan over the past four decades has been little short of remarkable. Real GNP growth per year, one of the authors in this volume reports, averaged 7.3 percent in the period from 1953 to 1960, 10.2 percent from 1961 to 1970, 9.1 percent from 1971 to 1980, and 9.0 percent from 1981 to 1987 (Liang: 231). Inflation was kept under control during this period and unemployment was always below 4 percent, averaging as low as 1.6 percent during the decade from 1971 to 1980.

This volume examines the nature of Taiwan's successful development, with an emphasis on the role of the state in stimulating and shaping Taiwan's economic growth. The book is divided into two parts. The first covers sources of economic growth, both international and domestic. The second focuses on social and political aspects of Taiwan's economic development.

Many countries are interested in attaining Taiwan's record of growth and in using it as a model, but there is surprisingly little agreement about which policies, if any, have been the keys to the rapid economic development that has taken place. Readers of this volume should come away with a better understanding of why and how growth has occurred and of its consequences for the lives of the people of Taiwan.

Part I, "Sources of Economic Growth," starts with five chapters analyzing the relationship of technology, international trade, and economic growth.

David Dollar and Kenneth Sokoloff look at industrial policy, productivity growth, and structural change in manufacturing industries in both Taiwan and South Korea. They conclude that a rapid accumulation of

xi

physical capital, human capital, and technology explain the rapid industrialization in both countries. Private initiative, they argue, was key to the
accumulation in both countries, although the governments of both nations played a key supporting role in providing a sound environment for
saving and investing (and also in supporting education). Dollar and Sokoloff are skeptical about the impact of industrial targeting, seeing its main
effect in Korea as a mechanism for providing benefits to particular firms
and as a contributing factor to Korea's comparatively lower wages and
less equitable distribution of income.

Fang-Yi Wang is concerned with the sources of the extremely rapid
growth in manufacturing productivity that has powered the ascent of the
Taiwanese economy. Employing a sample of firm-level data that allows
her to observe firms over time, she finds that firms in export-oriented industries not only realized more rapid productivity growth than those in
other industries, but that the more export-oriented firms outperformed
their counterparts in the same industry. As she notes, this provides
stronger evidence than any previously available in support of the hypothesis that access to the competitive and vast export markets helps
stimulate a faster pace of technical change.

Stephan Haggard and Chien-Kuo Pang ask why the political leadership of Taiwan was willing to experiment with unproven reform measures and to sustain reform, particularly in light of the fact that the
Kuomintang (KMT) was historically committed to support of state-
owned enterprises rather than to the development of the private sector.
They find the answers to their questions in the peculiar political position
of the KMT after its failure on the mainland. The leadership was pain-
fully aware that inattention to economic development had been a major
contributor to its defeat. It was determined not to fail again, and it was
willing to change its policies to ensure that it did not. This, combined
with the government's distance from the institutions and interests of the
Taiwanese society it governed and the fear that American assistance was
finite, made for a flexible and relatively pragmatic regime.

Wing Thye Woo and Liang-Yn Liu look at the role of underdeveloped
financial markets in producing Taiwan's persistent trade surplus and argue that the banking system must be reformed in order to provide a
smooth channel for domestic savings into domestic investment. Kuo-
yuan Liang examines the impact of Taiwan's export strategy in producing rapid economic growth, but he also considers the problems that have
accompanied this strategy including pollution, unbalanced internal development, and the difficulties that a huge trade surplus brings.

The second section of Part I focuses on government policy and the development of economic institutions and endowments.

Yun-Han Chu presents a comparative analysis of the role of the state in the development of the automobile industry in South Korea and Taiwan. State policy clearly played an important role in influencing the very different routes traveled by the automobile industries in the two countries (Korea as a major producer of finished cars and Taiwan of auto parts), but the author believes that the current analytic tools available to economists do not allow a definitive assessment of the merits and faults of specific patterns of industrial targeting as practiced by the two countries.

Constance Meany's case study of state policy and the development of Taiwan's semiconductor industry concludes that the state was a decisive actor in the development of enterprises in this area. She further stresses the role of overseas Chinese as advisers and key personnel in the emergence of Taiwan's successful semiconductor industry. Additional study of the role of overseas Chinese capital and expertise in the economic development of the mainland as well as of Taiwan should clearly be high on the research agendas of scholars and policymakers.

Jia-Dong Shea and Ya-Hwei Yang present an analysis and critique of Taiwan's financial system. They expect that reforms the authorities have made in the areas of interest rate control, restrictions on the operation of foreign banks, and the development of a private banking system will aid future economic development in Taiwan.

Following an analytic overview of monetary policy in Taiwan by Fa-Chin Liang, Chu-Wei Tseng and Wei-Lin Mao examine fiscal policy and economic development, with an emphasis on the effects of taxation on income distribution. They conclude that while income distribution improved during Taiwan's rapid economic development, taxation policy was not the cause of the reduction in income inequality.

Chia-Lin Cheng and Yu-Hsia Chen report on the efficiency of government investment in higher education in Taiwan through an examination of the income levels and occupations of public and private university graduates. Taiwan has a universal and constantly expanding system of formal education, and the demand for higher education is higher than the supply. The Cheng and Chen analysis indicates that the effects of a public or private university education on the income and job prestige of graduates is about the same, although private universities in Taiwan spend less per capita than public institutions. The two scholars recommend that the state ease the restrictions it places on private universities and redirect some of its subsidies to them in order to increase competition and elevate the overall quality of higher education in Taiwan.

An interesting implication of several of the essays in the first part of the book is that the secret of Taiwan's rapid and effective development lies as much in governmental restraint as in the many effective policies Taiwan's regime has employed to develop human capital and nurture the

development of physical capital. We will return to this point in the After-
word.

Part II of the book focuses on political and social aspects of economic
development in Taiwan.

Chen-Kuo Hsu's analysis of the changing ideology of the KMT rein-
forces the political analysis in Part I of the volume by Haggard and Pang.
Sitting on Taiwan, with no realistic hope of regaining the mainland, the
Nationalists began to define the development of Taiwan within the
framework of for-profit enterprises as the fundamental way in which the
KMT could express its resistance to the communist government of China.

Lucie Cheng and Ping-Chun Hsiung, in a scathing paper, argue that
Taiwan's rapid development was and is dependent on the exploitation of
women as low-wage workers in industrial enterprises and unwaged family workers. They believe that the export-oriented growth strategy in Taiwan is related to a system of male domination that gives firms and
families a license to exploit women's labor.

Cheng-hung Liao and Chun-chieh Huang look at attitudinal changes
among the farming population of Taiwan. They argue that following the
land reform carried out by the KMT in the 1950s, farmers were eager to
adopt innovations. The agricultural reform thus helped to create a surplus for use in the takeoff of local industries. This is apparently an instance where a governmental initiative had a clear and significant impact
on Taiwan's economic development.

The editors hope that these essays will improve understanding of the
causes and consequences of Taiwan's rapid economic development, and
particularly of the state's role in the process. Obviously, the writers of the
essays do not take a single view on these complex subjects, but we believe that their analyses add significantly to what is known and will
stimulate additional work on a subject that has profound implications for
policymakers around the world.

* * *

Many people played important roles in making this volume possible.

We want to acknowledge in particular the contribution of our late col-
league John C. (Chuck) Ries, who initiated UCLA's series of conferences
on the role of the state in economic development. He developed a fatal ill-
ness before the project was completed, but his vision, energy, and commitment were keys to the entire enterprise.

This volume had its origin in a long-term research project begun in
1986 at the University of California, Los Angeles, on the role of government intervention in the growth of Pacific Rim economies. Two segments
of the study were completed, one on South Korea in 1986 and 1987, and

the work presented here on Taiwan's development pattern. Both studies were marked by close collaboration between U.S. and Asian economists and political scientists. This cooperative research was facilitated by linkages with Asian institutions of higher learning established by the UCLA Center for Pacific Rim Studies. The Center provided important staff support for the project. Major funding for both the Korea and Taiwan studies was made possible by a grant from the University of California systemwide Pacific Rim Research Program.

Our work on the role of the state in Taiwan's development began with a planning workshop held at UCLA on January 27-28, 1989. The workshop led to a conference held in Taipei, Taiwan, on December 4-5, 1989, jointly sponsored by Soochow University and the Center for Pacific Rim Studies. The faculty and staff at Soochow were generous hosts who provided a conference environment that made for an unforgettable experience.

The editors thank both institutions for their support and also are grateful to Soochow University for providing funds to facilitate the publication of this volume.

We also wish to express our appreciation to Elwin Svenson, who as vice-chancellor of UCLA ably served as official representative of the university at the Taiwan conference and to Sue Fan of the UCLA Center for Pacific Rim Studies, who handled much of the administrative work for the project.

Finally, we thank Leslie Evans of the Pacific Rim Center, who had the difficult job of editing a manuscript by many authors for whom English is not a first language. Only those who have worked on conference volumes of this sort can fully understand his contribution. He also designed and typeset the volume.

August 1993

Part I:
Sources of Economic Growth

A. Technology, Growth, and International Trade

1

Industrial Policy, Productivity Growth, and Structural Change in the Manufacturing Industries: A Comparison of Taiwan and South Korea

David Dollar
Kenneth L. Sokoloff

Introduction

W hen policymakers in developing countries concern themselves with promoting industrialization, they generally have two things in mind. First, they want to increase industry's share of total output and the industrial labor force's share of total employment; and, second, they want to see a shift within industry toward higher value-added activities (meaning activities with higher average labor productivity). The former can be referred to as "widening" the industrial sector, the latter as "deep-

Views expressed are those of the authors and do not necessarily reflect the positions of the World Bank. The authors would like to thank Fang-Yi Wang for excellent research assistance.

ening" the sector. In general, widening industry is more important in the early stages of industrialization, and deepening it in the later stages.

Widening and deepening the industrial structure both require that the economy generate additional supplies of factors of production. Industry is more capital intensive than agriculture or services, and more skill intensive as well. Furthermore, within industry, the higher value-added activities require more physical and human capital than the lower value-added activities. Thus the economy needs to accumulate physical and human capital if industrialization is to proceed. Most economists would identify accumulation of factors as the fundamental *cause* of industrialization. As successful industrialization occurs, we will generally observe structural change in the economy, with resources shifting in relative terms out of agriculture into industry, and within industry, from labor-intensive, low-technology activities toward more capital-intensive, higher-technology activities. Such structural change is the *result* of industrialization.

Government policies to promote industrialization can be divided into two types: those that act directly on the cause of industrialization, and attempt to encourage the accumulation of factors, without prejudging where in the economy these factors become employed; and those that focus on the end result of industrialization—structural change—and attempt to encourage the growth of particular industries. We will refer to the former as "general" or "functional" incentives, and the latter as "industrial targeting." Examples of general incentives are tax measures that encourage saving, subsidization of research and development (provided the subsidies are available to all sectors and industries), and public investment in education. Industrial targeting might involve import protection, subsidized credit, or public investment, provided these are targeted to specific industries.

The basic hypothesis of our essay can be stated as follows: South Korea and Taiwan have followed very similar policies concerning general incentives to accumulate factors, and these policies have been quite successful in promoting industrialization. In the area of industrial targeting, on the other hand, the policies have been quite different, and in neither country have they been successful in accelerating industrialization. Some targeted policies have failed completely. Others have been successful in the narrow sense that the industries targeted have in fact grown, but they have failed to accelerate overall industrialization. In other words, industrial targeting has displaced growth from one industry to another, but has not increased growth in the aggregate.

Clearly this kind of hypothesis cannot be definitively proved or disproved. Instead we will attempt to marshal some empirical evidence concerning industrialization in South Korea and Taiwan that provides general support for the hypothesis. To this end, Section I briefly reviews the experiences of the two economies with general incentives and industrial targeting. Sections II and III then demonstrate that the records of productivity growth, structural change, and export success in Taiwan and South Korea are very similar, despite their different practices of industrial targeting.

I. Policies to Promote Industrialization in Taiwan and South Korea

A. General Incentives to Accumulate Factors

The important general incentives in South Korea and Taiwan in the 1960s and 1970s concerned the trade regime, interest rate and monetary policy, and education. These policies have been widely discussed, and need be mentioned only briefly here.[1]

In the area of trade policy, both economies maintained stable real exchange rates at levels that encouraged exports. Other general policies to promote exports were duty drawback schemes for imported inputs and credit allocation systems that favored exporters. In the 1960s these incentives in both South Korea and Taiwan were not targeted, but rather were available to all industries. Whatever their intention, these incentives to export had the effect of encouraging the accumulation of factors, particularly skills and technology. There is a growing body of empirical evidence that an export-oriented trade regime leads to rapid technological development of labor-intensive industries; that is, the process of exporting leads firms to acquire new technical expertise and facilitates the acquisition of new skills by workers.[2] Hence maintaining a relatively open trade regime can be viewed as a general incentive that accelerates the accumulation of human capital and technology.

Monetary and interest rate policies were conducted so that real deposit

---

1. On Taiwan's development, see Ho 1978; Kuo, Ranis, and Fei 1981; and Wu 1971; on Korea's development, see Mason et al. 1980.

2. Empirical studies of the relationship between exporting and technical advance, conducted at a more macro level, include Dollar and Sokoloff 1990 and Nishimizu and Robinson 1984. Examinations of the relationship at a more micro level can be found in Dahlman, Ross-Larson, and Westphal 1987 and Westphal, Rhee, and Pursell 1984.

rates were generally significantly positive, in contrast to many other developing countries where real deposit rates in the formal banking system have been frequently negative. High real interest rates encourage savings, and domestic savings are the primary source of capital formation. The high savings rates in East Asian economies are often attributed to cultural factors. While there may be some truth in that argument, it is worth noting that in both South Korea and Taiwan the savings rate increased significantly after interest rate reform in the late 1950s or early 1960s dramatically raised the return to saving.

Both South Korea and Taiwan made major public commitments to provide universal education, at times when these countries were still relatively poor. Combined public and private investment in education is now extremely high in these societies. In addition to providing basic, primary education, the state has been involved in designing training programs aimed at upgrading the skills of the workforce.

B. Experiences with Industrial Targeting

In the 1960s the main government interventions in both South Korea and Taiwan were of the general kind, as described above. While some of these policies continued into the 1970s, the distinctive feature of that decade is that both countries moved away from general incentives toward industrial targeting of specific industries. Both governments made an effort to build up heavy industry, and in both cases the motives were similar: a sense that the potential of labor-intensive industries would soon be exhausted and that there would be a need for a deepening of the industrial structure, combined with growing political and military insecurity that was the result, in part, of the U.S. defeat in Vietnam.

At this point it is worth noting two important differences in the underlying endowments of these econonmies. South Korea is about twice as large as Taiwan, in terms of population, and has a larger domestic market. Taiwan in the 1950s and 1960s had a countervailing advantage, however, in that it began the industrialization process with a larger stock of entrepreneurs. Entrepreneurs from the mainland—most notably the Shanghai textile entrepreneurs—came to Taiwan in large numbers around 1950. The nature of Japanese colonialism was somewhat different in Taiwan and South Korea, as well, so that there may have been relatively more indigenous entrepreneurs in Taiwan.

As a result of these differences in endowments, Taiwan's economy right from the start of industrialization was composed of many small firms and tended to remain that way. In Korea, on the other hand, a handful of very large conglomerates (*chaebul*) began to dominate the economy in the 1960s. Some aspects of government policy in the 1960s may have further encouraged these underlying tendencies. In Taiwan, for instance, the tax code favored the starting up of new firms by allowing a five-year tax holiday for new firms, and by having a fairly steep, progressive corporate income tax.[3] If you took a typical Korean family-held business group and shifted it to Taiwan, it would greatly reduce its total tax burden by dividing up into many small firms owned by different family members.

When similar notions of industrial targeting were introduced into these different environments in the 1970s, the end results were very different. In Korea, some large chaebul were already planning to invest in certain heavy industries, such as shipbuilding and motor vehicles, and hence these firms were very open to government programs to support heavy industry. Private firms in Taiwan, on the other hand, smaller to begin with and facing a smaller domestic market, had no interest in the government's plan to develop heavy industry. Consequently, Taiwan's industrial targeting had to proceed through the medium of state-owned corporations.

In Korea, industrial targeting was carried out under the "Heavy and Chemical Industry" (HCI) policy launched by President Park Chung-hee in 1973. The program operated primarily through tax breaks, subsidized credit, and import protection for certain industries. The investments by and large were carried out by private firms. The favored industries were iron and steel, nonferrous metals, shipbuilding, general machinery, chemicals, electronics, and motor vehicles. The incentives to shift resources into these industries were very large. A study by KDI estimated that in the late 1970s the marginal tax rate was below 20% for HCI industries, and around 50% for non-HCI industries (Kwack 1985). Real interest rates for investment in the favored industries were consistently negative, whereas other sectors had to pay much higher rates for the use of capital. Furthermore, rates of import protection were increased during the 1970s for industries such as steel, machinery, and motor vehicles.

The results of this ambitious program in Korea were quite mixed. Certain investments in chemicals and machinery were disastrous. The investment in steel was successful in the sense that the industry became technically efficient and began to export. However, the financial return to investment in steel was very poor.[4] The greatest success was realized in motor vehicles and electronics. Aside from the mixed nature of the direct

---

3. Biggs and Lorch (1989) examine the factors behind the dominance of small and medium firms in Taiwan and the emergence of large firms in Korea.

4. Auty (1988) estimates the real return to investment in the Korean steel industry to be *negative*.

results of the program, there were also some negative side effects. Bad loans through the HCI program, for instance, threatened the bankruptcy of the whole banking system around 1980. The tremendous capital cost of the program was also the main reason that the country built up a burdensome external debt. Furthermore, most of the targeted credit had gone to a small number of chaebul, and as a result their share of total output increased dramatically during the 1970s. By 1983, total sales of the ten largest business groups in Korea amounted to US$47.1 billion, compared to $7.4 billion for the ten largest groups in Taiwan (Biggs and Lorch 1989). Small and medium industry in Korea, on the other hand, was starved for capital during this period, so that a dualistic industrial structure emerged, with large firms operating with the most modern techniques, and small firms lagging far behind in terms of technology and productivity. As a result of these problems, the Korean government moved away from industrial targeting in the 1980s.[5]

In Taiwan, the government effort to build up heavy industry was not as ambitious as in Korea. As noted, the private sector essentially refused to cooperate, and the program had to proceed through public enterprises. The state set up the country's only integrated steel mill, and expanded businesses that it had taken over in the 1940s (mining, aluminum, fertilizer, etc.). Some of this was undertaken under the rubric of the "Ten Major Development Projects." Nevertheless, the government's program to develop heavy industry was on a much smaller scale than in Korea. Taiwan's experience with its smaller program was not much better than Korea's. The public enterprises have had difficulty operating efficiently, and a recent study has found that total factor productivity is considerably lower in public enterprises than in private enterprises (Wang 1989).

The Taiwan government also set up public research institutes, and decided to target integrated circuits as an important technology for Taiwan to develop. Not only the research, but also eventual production, was carried out by public enterprises. This targeted research program was largely unsuccessful. In terms of mass production of integrated circuits, Taiwan has always lagged behind the major producers, especially Japan, though it has had some success in the area of custom-made computer chips. The program was very costly, not only in financial terms, but also because it drained off some of the best university graduates into a program with low returns (Biggs and Lorch 1989).

In addition to its own investment program in heavy and high-tech industry, the government in Taiwan has also tried indirect measures to get

---

5. The successes and problems of the HCI program are examined at length in a World Bank report, Leipziger et al. 1987.

private industry to shift into heavy activities. For instance, it tried to encourage the development of larger firms by creating tax incentives for existing firms to merge (a two-year, 15 percent reduction in corporate tax after merger). The incentives were not very strong, however, and did little to run against the preference for small firms. Only eighteen combinations were registered during the period 1971-85.

One general lesson from the experiences of South Korea and Taiwan is that it is difficult to implement an industrial targeting policy that is not basically in line with where the private sector is planning to go anyway. We are concerned here with the *economic effect* of these policies, and hence we cannot go into detail on the *political origin* of the policies. But it is worth noting that in Korea, where there were large firms interested in developing heavy industry behind protective tariffs, the HCI program became very large and absorbed more than half of all the industrial investment for several years. The large chaebul benefited very much from the program. In Taiwan, on the other hand, the nature of the private sector was such that protected development of heavy industry was not financially attractive, and the extent of this kind of program was quite limited. It seems quite plausible that differences in basic endowments in South Korea and Taiwan can explain not only the different results of the targeting of heavy industry, but also why the Korean government chose to undertake such a large and costly program, while the program in Taiwan was much more modest.

II. Productivity Growth in Manufacturing

In the previous section we reviewed the experiences of Taiwan and South Korea with industrial targeting. There were three important differences in the approaches taken by the two governments: the specific industries targeted were somewhat different; South Korea created strong incentives for the private sector to move into targeted areas, whereas Taiwan proceeded through the medium of public enterprises; and the overall scope of the Korean program was much larger, involving more than half of all investment in industry by the end of the 1970s (Kwack 1985). Despite these differences in targeted industrial policy, however, we show in the next two sections that the *overall development of manufacturing has been quite similar in these two economies,* in terms of productivity growth, structural change, and export success. The specific industries that have developed differ in the two economies, no doubt partly as a result of the Korean HCI policy. The similarity in productivity growth, structural

TABLE 1   Labor Productivity and Value-Added Growth in Manufacturing,
Taiwan and South Korea, 1961-79 (%)

	Growth of Value Added (per annum)		Growth of Labor Productivity (per annum)		Average % of Value Added	
	Korea (63-79)	Taiwan (61-79)	Korea (63-79)	Taiwan (61-79)	Korea (63-79)	Taiwan (61-79)
Heavy Industries[a]	19.6	16.4	9.6	6.9	37.0	37.0
Basic metals	23.9	21.2	12.5	11.6	6.1	4.4
Pottery and glass	17.1	11.4	9.4	6.6	5.4	4.6
Chemicals and plastics	17.7	15.7	8.1	4.7	16.8	18.8
Transportation equipment	22.0	18.7	10.9	10.0	5.37	5.6
Machinery, n.e.c.	21.8	16.7	10.1	8.5	3.0	3.6
Light Industries[a]	20.4	18.5	7.9	6.0	43.1	45.3
Paper and printing	14.4	12.1	6.9	6.5	4.5	4.1
Textiles	17.7	13.6	9.0	4.3	14.8	10.9
Wood products/ furniture	14.5	12.4	6.1	5.6	3.0	3.9
Electrical machinery	28.5	22.8	7.1	5.4	7.4	11.1
Metal products, n.e.c.	20.7	15.9	9.6	3.6	2.8	2.9
Rubber products	20.7	17.3	8.1	6.8	2.6	1.3
Clothing	22.6	19.5	5.7	6.0	4.6	4.2
Leather and footwear	30.3	28.6	8.4	7.5	0.7	1.2
Other industries	22.7	27.1	9.0	10.9	2.7	5.7
Food Products	15.4	7.6	10.0	7.7	19.6	17.8
All Manufacturing[a]	19.1	15.8	8.9	6.6	99.7	100.1

a. Weighted average, using employment weights.

Note: Value added has been deflated with wholesale price indexes.

change, and export success in the aggregate, however, suggests that industrial policy has not been an important *cause* of industrialization in
either of these economies.

As is well known, both Taiwan and South Korea realized rapid growth
in manufacturing output and labor productivity during the 1960s and
1970s. In Table 1, we directly compare their performance across specific
industries over roughly the same periods—1963 to 1979 for Korea and
1961 to 1979 for Taiwan. Overall, the records of aggregate growth are
very similar, with manufacturing value added increasing at a 19.1% per
annum rate in Korea as opposed to 15.8% in Taiwan. The respective figures for value added per worker, or labor productivity, are also reasonably close: 8.9% per annum for Korea and 6.6% in Taiwan. Given that
Taiwan had begun to industrialize somewhat before Korea and was at a
more advanced stage of development at the beginning of the 1960s, it is

perhaps not surprising that the latter appears to have registered slightly more rapid progress. It is possible, however, that problems arising from our having to rely on wholesale price indexes (in order to provide a consistent basis for comparison) to deflate value added may account for the relatively small discrepancies between the two economies.

The pattern of Korea realizing somewhat higher rates of growth extended across all three subsectors of manufacturing—heavy (as identified by their greater capital intensity), light, and food products industries. Moreover, it was rather robust across the individual industries specified, with Korean labor productivity advance leading in thirteen of fifteen industries and Korean output growth higher in fourteen of them. The divergence in performance was somewhat larger on average for the heavy industries than for the light, but it was only in food products that the gap in the rates of growth of value added could not be entirely explained by the difference in the rates of labor productivity increase. The implication is that whereas employment in the heavy and light industries grew rapidly and at nearly the same rates in both countries, the congruence broke down in food products. In these industries, the Korean labor force grew by 5.4% per annum while Taiwanese employment actually fell in absolute numbers.

Despite the small but rather consistent edge in the measured performance of Korean manufacturing industries, the dominant impression gathered from these estimates is that the two countries were on quite similar paths of industrial development. Even though they differed in food products labor force growth, their compositions of manufacturing outputs exhibited the same trends. In each of the economies, the light industries grew somewhat more rapidly than the heavy, which in turn grew faster than food products. Indeed, the resemblance extends to the individual industries, with only 2 of the 14 heavy and light industries having growth paths of value added that differed by more than 20% between the two countries. Food products was the only industry classification in which there was a major contrast in experience. There are also parallels in labor productivity growth. Although the rates of advance were similar across the three subsectors within each of the countries, with the Korean case being slightly faster (in 13 of 15 industries as well), the heavy industries on average managed better records than their light counterparts.

Perhaps the most striking evidence of the correspondence between Korean and Taiwanese industrial development, however, comes from the figures on the distribution of value added across industries. They indicate that the heavy industries accounted for 37.0% of manufacturing value added in both Korea and Taiwan over the respective periods. Although not identical, the 43.1% (Korea) and 45.3% (Taiwan) shares of the light industries are equally impressive in their reflection of remarkably similar

TABLE 2   Shares of Value Added in Manufacturing, Taiwan and South Korea, Early 1960s and 1978

	Korea		Taiwan	
	1963	1978	1961	1978
Heavy Industries[a]	27.4	37.1	27.1	38.6
Basic metals	3.4	6.6	3.1	6.0
Pottery and glass	6.0	5.0	7.2	4.7
Chemicals and plastics	12.4	14.8	12.6	18.1
Transportation equipment	3.3	6.8	2.1	6.3
Machinery, n.e.c.	2.3	3.9	2.0	3.5
Light Industries[a]	41.0	44.8	31.0	47.1
Paper and printing	7.8	4.0		
Textiles	17.4	13.8		
Wood products/furniture	4.1	2.8	25.8	23.6
Rubber products	2.9	2.7		
Clothing, leather, footwear	2.8	6.2		
Electrical machinery	2.4	8.9	1.8	12.5
Metal products, n.e.c.	2.3	3.6	2.3	3.1
Other industries	1.3	2.8	1.1	7.9
Food Products	31.6	18.0	42.1	14.2

a. Weighted average, using employment weights.
Note: % of manufacturing value added.

industrial compositions. This display of congruence is not an artifact of excessive aggregation. Examination of the shares for 15 manufacturing industries yields the same conclusion. The clear implication is that although the manufacturing sector composed a smaller fraction of the national economy in Korea than in Taiwan, its composition varied little. Granted that the two economies have similar factor endowments, most observers will likely judge this finding to be surprising in light of the different institutional and policy environments of the two economies.

In Table 2, we present the shares of manufacturing value added for 1963-78 and 1961-78 in Korea and Taiwan respectively. Again, with the outstanding exception of the food products industrial classification (which was much larger in Taiwan at the outset and collapsed in relative size over time), the figures suggest that the trends in industrial composition were similar in the two countries. In the early 1960s, heavy industry accounted for 27% of manufacturing value added in both economies. By 1978 the heavy industry share had increased to 37.1% in Korea and 38.6% in Taiwan. Hence both at the beginning and at the end of the period examined, the structure of the manufacturing sector in these two economies was very similar. The argument is sometimes made, however, that while the investments in the HCI program were made in the 1970s, the fruits of the program were not fully realized until the 1980s. It is thus useful to compare industrial structure in the mid-1980s, as is done in the next section.

III. Structural Change in Manufacturing

In the previous section we compared productivity *growth rates* in South Korean and Taiwanese manufacturing. In this section we compare the *levels* of certain variables in a recent year, 1983. The variables are labor productivity, capital intensity, and hourly wages. We also examine the distribution of value added, employment, and exports across manufacturing industries to investigate the extent of structural adjustment in these two economies in the 1980s.

The year 1983 was chosen because that is the most recent year for which industry-level capital stock data are available for both South Korea and Taiwan. In order to compare levels of variables denominated in domestic currency, we have chosen to convert domestic currency into U.S. dollars using the purchasing power parity exchange rates calculated by Summers and Heston (1984). It was necessary first to deflate 1983 data to 1978 prices using each country's own wholesale price index, and then to use 1978 PPP exchange rates.

Table 3 shows labor productivity (value added per hour) for manufacturing disaggregated into 14 industries. Food products have been separated out, and the other 13 industries have been divided into three groups of manufactures: heavy, high-skill light, and traditional light. In the heavy category we have placed the four industries with the greatest capital intensity in Korea. In the high-skill light category, we have tried to create a grouping that includes industries with high value added but relatively low capital intensity. The general characteristic of the industries chosen for this category is that in Taiwan they have lower capital intensity but higher productivity than textiles. The traditional light industries have low productivity and low capital intensity. The bulk of this grouping is textiles and clothing. It should be noted that it is difficult to devise a categorization that is ideal for both economies. For instance, "Other Industries" is clearly a high-skill category in Taiwan, where it includes precision instruments, musical instruments, and photographic equipment. In Korea, on the other hand, this category is primarily composed of the toy industry and is relatively low productivity. We use this categorization, which is different from that employed in the previous sec-

TABLE 3   Labor Productivity in Manufacturing, Taiwan and South Korea, 1983

| | Value Added Per Workhour (In 1978 US$) | | |
	Taiwan	Korea	Korea Relative to Taiwan
Heavy industries[a]	5.37	8.71	1.62
Basic metals	9.70	17.91	1.85
Pottery and glass	4.29	6.37	1.48
Chemicals and plastics	4.24	7.10	1.57
Transportation equipment	7.13	5.87	0.82
High-Skill Light Manufactures[a]	4.26	3.89	0.91
Machinery, n.e.c.	4.45	4.21	0.95
Electrical machinery	4.30	4.48	1.04
Metal products, n.e.c.	2.64	3.30	1.25
Other industries	5.89	3.01	0.51
Traditional Light Manufactures[a]	3.53	3.23	0.92
Paper and printing	4.75	5.87	1.24
Textiles	2.88	3.30	1.15
Wood products/furniture	2.22	3.68	1.66
Rubber products	3.55	3.05	0.86
Clothing, leather, footwear	4.73	2.24	0.47
Food Products	6.11	6.93	1.13
All Manufacturing[a]	5.04	5.19	1.03
Mean	4.78	5.52	1.15
Coefficient of variation	0.40	0.68	1.70

a. Weighted average, using employment weights.

tion, because it enables a number of important differences between Taiwan and Korea in the 1980s to show up clearly.

The (weighted) average labor productivity for the whole manufacturing sector is very similar in the two economies, $5.04 in Taiwan and $5.19 in Korea (in 1978 dollars).[6] This similarity in the aggregate disguises the fact that Korea has a substantial labor productivity advantage in the heavy industries ($8.71 to $5.37), whereas Taiwan has an advantage in

6. The fact that the *level* of productivity was virtually the same in the two manufacturing sectors in 1983, whereas the *growth rate* of productivity was higher in Korea during the 1960s and 1970s, demonstrates that Taiwan was at a higher level of development circa 1960.

TABLE 4   Capital Intensity in Manufacturing, Taiwan and South Korea, 1983

| | Net Capital Stock Per Workhour (In 1978 US$) | | |
	Taiwan	Korea	Korea Relative to Taiwan
Heavy Industries[a]	9.81	19.99	2.03
Basic metals	27.06	62.79	2.32
Pottery and glass	8.69	10.61	1.22
Chemicals and plastics	7.38	9.75	1.32
Transportation equipment	6.83	8.55	1.25
High-Skill Light Manufactures[a]	4.00	4.27	1.07
Machinery, n.e.c.	5.44	7.01	1.29
Electrical machinery	3.95	4.21	1.07
Metal products, n.e.c.	4.29	4.02	0.94
Other industries	2.83	2.26	0.80
Traditional Light Manufactures[a]	4.56	3.61	0.79
Paper and printing	6.99	5.71	0.82
Textiles	6.07	4.81	0.79
Wood products/furniture	3.97	4.72	1.19
Rubber products	3.35	3.42	1.02
Clothing, leather, footwear	1.74	1.17	0.67
Food Products	11.27	8.14	0.72
All Manufacturing[a]	6.68	6.88	1.03
Mean	7.13	9.80	1.37
Coefficient of variation	0.85	1.52	1.79

a. Weighted average, using employment weights.

the light industries, both traditional ($3.53 to $3.23) and high-skill ($4.26 to $3.89). Consequently, the dispersion in average labor productivity is much greater across Korean industries than across Taiwan's industries (the coefficient of variation is 0.68 in Korea, 0.40 in Taiwan). These data reflect the dualistic nature of industry in Korea: productivity is eight times as great in basic metals as in clothing, whereas in Taiwan the differential is only twofold.

Table 4 indicates that these differences in labor productivity can be largely explained by the distribution of the capital stock across industries. Once again, the economies are very similar in the aggregate: capital stock per hour is $6.68 in Taiwanese manufacturing, and $6.88 per hour in Korean manufacturing. There is much more dispersion across Korean industries, however. Heavy industry in Korea is twice as capital intensive as heavy industry in Taiwan. The extreme example is basic metals, employing $62.79 of capital stock per hour in Korea, and $27.06 in Taiwan. These data also indicate that total factor productivity (TFP) for heavy industry is somewhat lower in Korea than in Taiwan. In earlier work we estimated the capital elasticity in Korean heavy industry to be around 0.75; with such an elasticity, Korea's 103% advantage in capital per hour should generate a 77% advantage in productivity. The measured productivity differential of 62% implies that TFP is relatively low in Korea.

The high-skill light manufacturing industries are interesting in that Taiwan has a productivity advantage of around 10% *but uses less capital per hour than Korea.* Clearly in this area Taiwan firms have a TFP advantage that could reflect superior skills in the labor force and/or superior technology. The traditional light industries in Taiwan, however, employ more capital per hour than their counterparts in Korea. In Korea, basic metals has 54 times as much capital stock per hour as clothing; in Taiwan, the differential is 16-fold.

This concentration of the capital stock in a small group of industries in Korea can create a number of distortions, such as low marginal product of capital in heavy industries relative to the marginal product in light industries. Subsidizing the use of capital in heavy industries could also reduce the demand for labor below what it would otherwise be. Evidence that this has in fact happened is provided in Table 5 on page 19, which compares real hourly wages in the two economies. For the whole manufacturing sector, the (weighted) average wage was almost 25% higher in Taiwan than in Korea in 1983, despite the fact that manufacturing labor productivity was essentially the same (actually, 3% higher in Korea). Only in heavy industries, in which the Korean productivity advantage was 103%, were wages higher in Taiwan, and then only by 7%. In both high-skill and traditional light manufactures, the Taiwan wage advantage was over 30%.

Such evidence suggests that the absence of an industrial policy targeting heavy industry in Taiwan has resulted in more balanced development of the manufacturing sector, with capital intensity and labor productivity increasing more evenly across sectors. Without the distorting influence of subsidized use of capital in heavy industries, wages have reached a higher real level in Taiwan.

One still might ask, however, whether or not the Korean policy has led to more rapid structural adjustment of manufacturing out of low value-added activities. Table 6 on page 20 indicates the distribution of value added among manufacturing industries in 1983. It can be seen that Korea has somewhat more value added arising in the heavy industries, 37.6% compared to Taiwan's 34.3%. Taiwan in turn has more value added in high-skill light industries, 30.5% compared to Korea's 24.3%. Korea has

TABLE 5   Hourly Wages in Manufacturing, Taiwan and South Korea, 1983

	Taiwan	Korea	Korea Relative to Taiwan
	Wages Per Workhour (In 1978 US$)		
Heavy Industries[a]	1.82	1.94	1.07
Basic metals	2.22	3.21	1.45
Pottery and glass	1.61	1.69	1.05
Chemicals and plastics	1.69	1.39	0.82
Transportation equipment	2.17	1.83	0.84
High-Skill Light Manufactures[a]	1.65	1.24	0.75
Machinery, n.e.c.	1.93	1.40	0.73
Electrical machinery	1.59	1.20	0.76
Metal products, n.e.c.	1.79	1.23	0.69
Other industries	1.44	1.19	0.83
Traditional Light Manufactures[a]	1.56	1.19	0.76
Paper and printing	1.96	1.74	0.89
Textiles	1.59	1.13	0.71
Wood products/furniture	1.49	1.40	0.94
Rubber products	1.72	1.41	0.82
Clothing, leather, footwear	1.35	0.95	0.70
Food Products	1.71	1.59	0.93
All Manufacturing	1.68	1.37	0.82
Mean	1.73	1.53	0.88

a. Weighted average, using employment weights.

slightly more value added in traditional light industries and food processing, but the difference with Taiwan is not great.

Alteration in the distribution of value added is not the only measure of structural change. Table 7 on page 20 shows the distribution of manufacturing employment in 1983. Here, surprisingly, it is Taiwan that has the larger share in heavy industry. That finding may seem paradoxical, but it is the result of the fact that Korean heavy industries are so capital intensive that they employ relatively few workers. Taiwan also has a greater share of its labor force in the high-skill light industries. As a result, the labor force remaining in traditional light industries is much larger in Korea (44.6% of manufacturing workers) than in Taiwan (34.7%). It seems fair to conclude, then, that Taiwan's strategy has been more successful in shifting labor out of low-productivity industries.

It should also be noted that moving to higher value-added activities does not necessarily require shifting resources from one industry to an-

TABLE 6   Distribution of Value Added Among Manufacturing Industries, Taiwan and South Korea, 1983

| | Percent of Manufacturing Value Added | |
	Taiwan	Korea
Heavy Industries	34.3	37.6
Basic metals	7.2	9.4
Pottery and glass	4.7	5.7
Chemicals and plastics	14.7	12.8
Transportation equipment	7.7	9.7
High-Skill Light Manufactures	30.5	24.3
Machinery, n.e.c.	4.1	4.7
Electrical machinery	13.8	11.6
Metal products, n.e.c.	4.4	4.8
Other industries	8.2	3.2
Traditional Light Industries	28.5	30.0
Paper and printing	4.4	5.7
Textiles	9.7	12.4
Wood products/furniture	2.6	2.1
Rubber products	2.0	2.9
Clothing, leather, footwear	9.8	6.9
Food Products	6.8	8.3

TABLE 7   Distribution of Employment Among Manufacturing Industries, Taiwan and South Korea, 1983

| | Percent of Manufacturing Employment | |
	Taiwan	Korea
Heavy Industries	28.2	22.4
Basic metals	3.3	4.4
Pottery and glass	4.8	4.6
Chemicals and plastics	15.3	6.7
Transportation equipment	4.8	6.7
High-Skill Light Manufactures	32.1	26.3
Machinery, n.e.c.	4.2	4.6
Electrical machinery	14.4	11.0
Metal products, n.e.c.	7.2	5.4
Other industries	6.3	5.3
Traditional Light Industries	34.7	44.6
Paper and printing	3.9	4.5
Textiles	14.4	17.8
Wood products/furniture	4.9	3.0
Rubber products	2.5	5.7
Clothing, leather, footwear	9.0	13.6
Food Products	5.1	6.7

other. Within each industry there is also a process of shifting to higher value-added activities, so that average labor productivity tends to rise over time in every single industry. It appears that this type of structural change has also been accomplished more successfully in Taiwan than in Korea. For instance, in the clothing industry, which in 1983 still employed 9.0% of manufacturing employees in Taiwan and 13.6% in Korea, labor productivity was more than two times higher in Taiwan than in Korea. (In fact, based on Taiwan data, clothing should really be included as a high-skill light industry.)

Another measure of structured change is alterations in the pattern of trade. The trade data are reported in slightly different categories than those employed in tables 1-7, but we have made an effort to group industries into the same broad categories. Table 8 shows the distribution of Taiwan's exports across industries in 1970, 1979, and 1986. There is virtually no change over this period in the share of exports accounted for by heavy industrial products. (Within the heavy category, though, there has been a noticeable decline of steel exports, matched by an equivalent increase in transport equipment.)

There has nevertheless been considerable alteration in Taiwan's pattern of exporting. The share of primary products declined from 23.3% in 1970 to 8.7% in 1986. Also declining was the share of traditional light manufactures (particularly textiles and wood products) from 38.8% to 29.7% of exports. The industries in which the relative share of exports has increased are those in the "High-Skill Light" category. The share of exports accounted for by machinery (electrical and nonelectrical) rose from 15.8% in 1970 to 24.8% in 1986. The export share of Other Industries almost doubled (from 12.8% to 23.4%), as firms rapidly increased their exports of precision instruments, musical instruments, photographic equipment, etc.

The structural change observed in Taiwan's exports during the 1970s and 1980s hence can be characterized as a shift out of primary products and traditional light manufactures, into products that require skilled labor, but not a lot of capital.

The shift in the pattern of exports in Korea has been somewhat different, as can be seen in Table 9. During the 1970s, no doubt partly as a result of the HCI program, Korea's exports of heavy products increased from 4.7% to 18.2% of total exports. As in Taiwan, there were decreases in export shares for primary products and traditional light manufactures. There was, however, no large increase in exports of high-skill light manufactures. Thus during the 1970s the structural change occurring in Taiwan and South Korea was quite different. Since 1979, on the other hand, Korea has moved away from the explicit support of heavy industry, and the changes in the pattern of trade for these two economies in the 1980s

TABLE 8   Distribution of Taiwan's Exports, 1970, 1979, and 1986

	Percent of Total Exports		
	1970	1979	1986
Heavy Manufactures	7.5	8.7	8.4
Iron and steel	3.5	3.2	1.4
Nonferrous metals	0.7	0.3	0.3
Chemicals and plastics	2.4	2.4	2.8
Transportation equipment	0.9	2.8	3.9
High-Skill Light Manufactures	30.4	45.1	53.1
Machinery, n.e.c.	3.4	4.8	9.7
Electrical machinery	12.4	15.2	15.1
Metal products, n.e.c.	1.8	4.1	4.9
Other industries	12.8	21.0	23.4
Traditional Light Manufactures	38.8	33.5	29.7
Textiles	13.9	9.8	7.7
Wood products, paper	7.2	5.5	2.5
Rubber products	0.4	0.8	0.7
Leather products	0.4	0.4	0.6
Clothing, footwear	16.9	17.0	18.2
Primary Products	23.3	12.7	8.7

Source: UN Trade System

TABLE 9   Distribution of Korea's Exports, 1970, 1979, and 1986

	Percent of Total Exports		
	1970	1979	1986
Heavy Manufactures	4.7	18.2	20.9
Iron and steel	1.6	7.4	5.7
Nonferrous metals	0.7	0.3	0.4
Chemicals and plastics	1.4	3.5	3.3 '
Transportation equipment	1.0	7.0	11.5
High-Skill Light Manufactures	22.7	28.5	37.6
Machinery, n.e.c.	1.0	2.0	4.7
Electrical machinery	5.3	11.3	15.1
Metal products, n.e.c.	1.0	4.0	4.0
Other industries	15.4	11.2	13.8
Traditional Light Manufactures	49.8	42.6	33.7
Textiles	10.2	12.2	9.2
Wood products, paper	11.3	3.9	0.9
Rubber products	0.4	2.3	1.6
Leather products	0.1	0.2	0.3
Clothing, footwear	27.8	24.0	21.7
Primary Products	22.7	10.7	7.6

Source: UN Trade System

are more similar. Between 1979 and 1986 Korea's exports of traditional light products continued to decline (in relative terms), and the large increase was in the area of high-skill light manufactures. Exports of heavy products grew only slightly during the 1980s.

What we observe in the value added, employment, and export data, then, is that both economies have undergone substantial structural change in the past two decades. Relatively speaking, Korea has shifted more into capital-intensive products, and Taiwan into more skill- and technology-intensive areas. Clearly the differences in industrial policy played a role in the particular *form* that structural change took in each society, though underlying endowments also predisposed each economy in the direction that it went. It is difficult to avoid the conclusion, however, that *industrial policy is not an underlying cause of rapid economic growth and the resulting structural change*. South Korea and Taiwan had very different policies regarding industry-specific incentives, and nevertheless their overall growth and rates of structural change are quite similar. The best single measure of overall structural change is value added per hour in all manufacturing; that measure indicates the extent to which labor has been shifted from low- to high-productivity industries, as well as the extent to which productivity has increased in existing industries. As noted earlier, value added per hour was remarkably similar in the two economies in 1983. Hence it is difficult to make a case that industrial targeting—either Korea's highly activist policy or Taiwan's more limited one—has been an important *cause* of industrial growth or structural change, though certainly targeting affects the specific *form* that the structural change takes.

Conclusions

R apid industrialization in Taiwan and Korea can be explained by rapid accumulation of productive factors—physical capital, human capital, and technology. Underlying the accumulation of productive factors are high savings rate, strong investment in education, and an outward-oriented trade regime that accelerated technological development. This accumulation has mostly resulted from private initiative, though there are a number of important government policies that have played a supporting role. In both economies, government ensured a relatively stable price level and regulated the formal banking system in an effective manner, providing a sound environment for saving and investing. Policymakers generally avoided two crucial mistakes common to developing economies: maintaining negative real interest rates in the formal banking system and overvaluing the exchange rate.

Policies in Taiwan and South Korea have been quite similar in the areas of monetary policy, interest rates, education, and the exchange rate. Concerning incentives targeted to specific industries, on the other hand, policies in the two economies have been quite different, especially in the 1970s. Despite Korea's much more ambitious industrial targeting program, however, the aggregate performance of the two economies—in terms of GDP growth or growth of industry—has been remarkably similar. This outcome is consistent with the hypothesis that *industry-specific interventions have not been an important cause of growth in either economy.*

It also appears that industrial targeting in Korea has not *retarded* growth in any major way. Nevertheless, the Heavy and Chemical Industry program in Korea has created some serious distortions, and a good argument can be made because of these distortions that Taiwan's shift to higher value-added activities has been more successful than Korea's. One indication of this is that a much larger share of the manufacturing labor force has been left in traditional, low-productivity industries in Korea than in Taiwan. The channeling of investment funds to a few highly capital-intensive industries appears to have retarded the upgrading of other manufacturing sectors in Korea. Subsidizing capital-intensive sectors also seems to have held back the growth of wages, which remain considerably lower in Korea than in Taiwan.

Finally, the main benefit of the industrial targeting in Korea accrued to firms and their owners, and this likely contributed to the deteriorating income distribution there. In Taiwan, on the other hand, the shift to higher value-added activities has occurred more uniformly across manufacturing industries, leading to higher wages and a more equitable distribution of income than is found in Korea.

Bibliography

Auty, R. M. 1988. The Financial Performance of South Korean HCI/RBI: Steel and Petrochemicals. Working Paper, Lancaster University.

Biggs, T., and K. Lorch. 1989. Small Enterprise and Market Transactions in Taiwan: The Role of Government Policy. Paper presented at the Association for Asian Studies, Washington, D.C., March.

Dahlman, C., B. Ross-Larson, and L. Westphal. 1987. Managing Technological Development: Lessons from the Newly Industrializing Countries. *World Development* 15 (6).

Dollar, D., and K. Sokoloff. 1990. Patterns of Productivity Growth in South Korean Manufacturing Industries, 1963-1979. *Journal of Development Economics* 33 (2): 309-27.

Ho, Samuel P. S. 1978. *Economic Development of Taiwan, 1860-1970*. New Haven: Yale University Press.

Kuo, S. W. Y., G. Ranis, and J. C. H. Fei. 1981. *The Taiwan Success Story: Rapid Growth with Improved Distribution in the Republic of China, 1952-1979*. Boulder, Colorado: Westview Press.

Kwack, Taewon. 1985. *Depreciation and Taxation of Income from Capital*. Seoul: Korea Development Institute. (In Korean.)

Leipziger, D. M., Y. J. Cho, F. Iqbal, P. Petri, and S. Urata. 1987. *Korea: Managing the Industrial Transition*. Washington, D.C.: The World Bank.

Mason, E. S., M. J. Kim, D. H. Perkins, K. S. Kim, and D. C. Cole. 1980. *The Economic and Social Modernization of the Republic of Korea*. Cambridge: Harvard University Press.

Nishimizu, M., and S. Robinson. 1984. Trade Policies and Productivity Change in Semi-Industrialized Countries. *Journal of Development Economics* 16.

Summers, R., and A. Heston. 1984. Improved International Comparisons of Real Product and Its Composition, 1950-80. *Review of Income and Wealth* 30: 207-62.

Wang, Fang-Yi. 1989. The Role of Manufactured Exports in Technological Improvement and Economic Growth: Evidence from Taiwanese Manufacturing Industries. Mimeo.

Westphal, L., W. Rhee, and G. Pursell. 1984. Sources of Technological Capability in South Korea. In *Technological Capability in the Third World*, edited by M. Fransman and K. King.

Wu, Rong-I. 1971. *The Strategy of Economic Development: A Case Study of Taiwan*. Louvain: Vander.

2

Reconsidering Export-Led Growth: Evidence from Firm Performance, Taiwan, 1983-1987

Fang-Yi Wang

Introduction

The remarkable success of East Asian economies has attracted much attention in recent years. Based on the aggregate data, a considerable volume of research has sought to establish the relationship between export growth and output growth. What has emerged from these studies is rather strong and largely replicable correlations between these two variables across countries and over time. This finding has led many to con-

This chapter draws on the author's Ph.D. dissertation, "Reconsidering the 'East Asian Model of Development'—The Link Between Exports and Productivity Enhancement: Evidence from Taiwan, 1950-1987," completed at the University of California, Los Angeles, in December 1990. The author gratefully acknowledges the comments and suggestions received form Kenneth Sokoloff, Edward Leamer, David Dollar, Howard Pack, Carl Dahlman, Mark Haberman, and Geng Xiao. Earlier versions of this work were presented at UCLA and at the Hoover Institute Workshop for Advanced Research in the Republic of China and Taiwan Studies, March 1991. She also wishes to acknowledge financial support for this work from the Earhart Foundation Fellowship.

clude that trade and exchange rate policies have played a crucial role in determining economic growth in the underdeveloped world.

However, the issues of how and why this occurred remain in dispute. Neoclassical trade theory places emphasis on allocative efficiency under relatively open trade regimes. Others hold that a closed trade regime, or an import-substitution one, tends to facilitate "directly unproductive rent-seeking and profit-seeking activities," incurring significant loss to the society (Krueger 1974; Bhagwati 1982). Researchers in recent years have also noted several dynamic effects of an export promotion strategy such as more rapid technology transfer and domestic innovations at the firm level (Krueger 1984; Westphal, Rhee, and Pursell 1984; Dahlman and Westphal 1982). These effects may result in continued productivity improvement and therefore long-term economic growth.

Although there is no shortage of theories linking trade regimes to economic growth, and certainly no lack of empirical studies at the aggregate level, there has been virtually no systematic examination on the subject with disaggregated or micro data. Without utilizing firm data to delineate stylized facts, fundamentally microeconomic issues such as technology transfer remain unanswered.

This chapter will examine the role that exports of manufactured goods have played in improving productivity in one of the high export economies—Taiwan—by utilizing a recently compiled firm-level data set. This data set pertains to the output, employment, and capital stock of the one thousand biggest firms in Taiwan from 1983 to 1987. Among the first studies to use firm data, the present research contributes to the existing knowledge by offering evidence quite consistent with the hypothesis on export-spurred productivity advancement.

In addition to the micro data, industry-level data over a longer time span (1952-86) are employed to shed some light on the issue of long-term economic growth beyond the (one-time) allocative efficiency gains highlighted in trade theory.

This chapter proceeds as follows: Section I examines changes in trade regimes in Taiwan since the early 1950s. Dramatic shifts in economic structure emanating from the 1960 reform are documented. Section II explores the role of export activity by employing firm data. Various issues such as technology diffusion, scale economies, and export-spurred productivity change are pursued on the basis of this data set. A summary draws together the results of the present study.

I. Structural Shifts: the 1950s to the 1980s

Perhaps the most straightforward way to examine gains from allocative efficiency under different trade regimes is to see how economic
structural shifts emanated from regime change. In Taiwan the decade of
the 1950s was characterized by heavy import and foreign-exchange controls and a multiple and overvalued exchange rate system. Starting from
a small base, the economy experienced remarkable growth in the first
half of the decade, reaching an annual growth of GNP per capita of 6 percent. However, as home markets became saturated in the second half of
the 1950s, output growth slowed down dramatically, with GNP per capita growing at a meager 3.7 percent per annum during the late 1950s (Lin
1973). In the face of economic stagnation, the government embarked on a
series of liberalization programs and export promotion measures in 1960.

The strong reaction of the economy to the change in policy is mani-
fested in profound structural shifts. As Table 1 shows, the agricultural
sector shrank dramatically while the industrial and service sectors expanded at a rapid rate between 1952 and 1986. This process began under
the import-substitution era of the 1950s. Its pace accelerated in the export-oriented reforms of the early 1960s. From Table 1, we see that the agricultural sector's share in employment decreased moderately from 55%
in 1952 to 50% in 1962, and dropped sharply to 33% in 1972. The manu-

TABLE 1   Distribution of Employment among Sectors, and Changes over Time
in Taiwan, 1952-86 (%)

	1952	1962	1972	1986	1952-62	1962-72	1972-86	1952-86
Total	100.0	100.0	100.0	100.0				
Agriculture	54.8	49.7	33.0	17.0	-5.1	-16.7	-16.0	-37.8
Secondary:	17.7	21.0	31.8	41.5	3.3	10.8	9.8	23.8
Manufacturing	12.9	15.1	24.6	33.8	2.2	9.5	9.2	20.9
Others	4.8	5.9	7.2	7.7	1.1	1.3	0.5	2.9
Tertiary:	27.5	29.3	35.2	41.5	1.8	5.9	6.3	14.0
Commerce	10.2	9.8	14.0	17.9	-0.4	4.2	3.9	7.7
Transportation	3.8	4.5	5.2	5.2	0.7	0.7	0.0	1.4
Others	13.5	15.0	16.0	18.4	1.5	1.0	2.4	4.9

Source: *Taiwan Statistical Data Book*, 1988, and *Monthly Bulletin of Earnings and Productivity
Statistics in Taiwan*, March 1988.
Notes: (1) The item "Others" in the secondary sector includes mining, construction, and
utilities. (2) The period from 1952 to 1960 was characterized by the
implementation of import-substitution polices. Since 1961 export promotion has
been the main theme.

TABLE 2   Distribution of Employment and Changes over Time, Manufacturing
Industries in Taiwan, 1954-86 (%)

	1954	1961	1972	1986	1954-61	1961-72	1972-86
K-intensive industries:	29.97	29.48	29.64	32.73	-0.48	0.15	3.09
Basic metals	2.06	2.45	2.55	2.94	0.39	0.11	0.39
Nonmetals	9.65	8.82	5.09	4.30	-0.82	-3.73	-0.79
Chemicals	8.13	8.22	13.75	16.99	0.08	5.54	3.24
Transport equipment	5.92	6.29	3.39	4.70	0.38	-2.90	1.31
Machinery	4.21	3.71	4.85	3.80	-0.51	1.14	-1.05
L-intensive industries:	47.84	47.46	59.99	61.64	-0.38	12.53	1.65
Paper & printing	5.51	5.98	4.22	3.74	0.47	-1.75	-0.48
Textiles & apparel	21.92	20.91	25.27	20.23	-1.01	4.36	-5.04
Wood products	7.76	8.54	6.50	4.12	0.78	-2.04	-2.38
Electronics	1.67	2.93	11.83	15.91	1.26	8.90	4.08
Metal products	4.62	4.53	4.32	6.74	-0.10	-0.20	2.42
Rubber products	1.74	1.51	2.13	2.39	-0.23	0.62	0.26
Misc. products	4.15	2.74	4.76	6.55	-1.41	2.01	1.80
Leather products	0.47	0.33	0.96	2.26	-0.14	0.63	1.30
Food industries	22.19	23.06	10.37	5.63	0.87	-12.69	-4.74
All manufacturing	100.0	100.0	100.0	100.0			

Sources and Notes: See Table 1.

facturing sector, on the other hand, increased its employment share from
13% in 1952 to 15% in 1962 and reached a height of 25% by the end of the
1960s. In fact, on a per annum basis, the 1960s was certainly the decade of
most rapid change.

Similar observations can be made within the manufacturing sector (see
Table 2). During the 1954-61 period, or the second half of the import-
substitution era, the distribution of employment across manufacturing industries was virtually unchanged. The stable pattern reflects the slowly
shifting tastes and preferences in the domestic economy as severely limited foreign trade made international specialization through foreign demand almost impossible.

Following the regime change, the share of labor-intensive industries
jumped dramatically from 47 percent to 60 percent between 1961 and

1972.[1] The overall pattern suggests Taiwan's strong comparative advantage in the labor-intensive industries. Among them, textiles and electronics realized the most substantial expansion in the 1960s. These two industries either possessed abundant local entrepreneurship with considerable experience in industry[2] or benefited from strong support of MNCs in technology, management, finance, and marketing.[3]

Unlike the labor-intensive sectors, the capital-intensive industries as a whole maintained an almost constant employment share of 29 percent in the 1960s.[4] Except for chemicals,[5] the labor shares of some industries such as basic metals and machinery were virtually unchanged during the 1960s. Others, such as nonmetal and transport equipment, suffered from declines. The slow progress of the capital-intensive industries relative to the labor-intensive ones was probably due to the difficulty for the former

---

1. L-intensive industries are referred to as those with lower capital-labor ratios. They are represented by paper and printing, textiles, wood products, electrical machinery, metal products, rubber products, clothing, leather, and miscellaneous manufactures.

2. The significant expansion of the textile industry can be attributed to the experienced Shanghai entrepreneurs fleeing to Taiwan as a result of the defeat of the Nationalists in the Chinese Civil War in 1949. Foreign technology transferred by the Japanese trading companies also played an important role in the development of Taiwan's textiles industry during the 1960s. As documented in Kojima and Ozawa (1984), production facilities were moved in large scale from Japan to Taiwan in that period.

3. The extremely rapid growth of the electronics industry was attributed mainly to the big inflow of foreign direct investment (FDI) in the 1960s, most of which concentrated on low-end electronics assembly activities (Dahlman and Sananikone 1990). According to the official estimates, electronics accounted for 41.1 percent of total FDI in manufacturing at the end of 1976. More than half (59.8 percent) of the workers in the electronics industry were hired by multinational corporations (MNCs), and close to three quarters (71.5 percent) of the total production was exported. See various issues of *An Analysis of the Operations and Economic Effects of Foreign Enterprises*, Ministry of Economic Affairs, Investment Commission.

4. The K-intensive industries refer to basic metals, nonmetals, chemicals, transportation equipment, and machinery.

5. The labor share of the chemical industry rose from 8.2% to 13.8% in the 1960s. The increase in the chemical industry came mainly from the expansion of plastic production. In fact, workers engaged in plastic production accounted for 17.7% of total workers in the chemical industry in 1961. This ratio sharply increased to 50% in 1971. The expansion of plastic production was probably due to the increase in exports. According to Lin (1973, 213-16), the export-output ratio in this subsector was 12.0% in 1961 and 44.2% in 1969.

in entering foreign markets. Their growth during this period depended largely on domestic demand.

The expansion rate of the capital-intensive industries, however, surpassed that of the labor-intensive ones in the 1970s and 1980s, although the magnitude of change was much smaller in comparison with what the labor-intensive industries had experienced in the previous decade. Specifically, several capital-intensive industries either increased their share more rapidly (basic metals by 0.39%; transportation equipment by 1.31%) or stopped dropping as fast (nonmetals from -3.73% in 1961-72 to -0.79% in 1972-86). The anomaly is machinery, which suffered from a reduced share of employment in the 1970s and 1980s, after expanding in the 1960s. There is little doubt that the expansion of the capital-intensive industries was related to changes in factor endowment—the accumulation of human and physical capital over time and the exhaustion of unskilled labor.

At the same time, some traditional labor-intensive industries such as textiles and wood products began to stagnate as labor costs increased in the 1970s and 1980s. They were replaced gradually by the high-skill industries such as electronics and metal products. Table 2 shows that between 1972 and 1986 the labor shares of textiles and wood products decreased by 5.0% and 2.4% respectively, while electronics gained 4.9% and metal products 2.4%.

From the above discussion, it is clear that export-promotion policies stimulated resource reallocation, causing significant structural change in Taiwan's economy. This reallocation process was most extreme in the 1960s, or the first decade of the export-oriented regime. The outstanding shift in the 1960s in comparison with the stagnant situation in the late 1950s demonstrates Taiwan's huge potential in the labor-intensive industries. The gain from specializing in these industries was immediately realized, as indicated by the sharp increase in the growth rate of per capita income in the 1960s.

However, after a decade of radical shifts in resources, only modest changes in employment shares among industries were observed in the 1970s and 1980s. In this period, high-skill industries emerged while traditional, low-skill ones declined in the face of changed endowments. This pattern seems to suggest that resource reallocation might have been critical in the early stage of Taiwan's economic growth, but it might not have been the main factor in sustained economic growth throughout the whole period, as the continued high growth in the 1970s and 1980s is not likely to be explained by the moderate structural shifts in this period.

Another important aspect of structural shift is the change in firm size. From Table 3, the average size of firms was only 8.8 workers at the end of the import substitution period (1961). It increased rapidly to 21.3 workers

TABLE 3   Distribution of Number of Firms among Size Groups, 1961-86 (%)

	1961	1966	1971	1986	1961-66	1966-86
Number employed	100.0	100.0	100.0	100.0		
1-9	89.49	72.11	64.15	63.32	-17.38	-8.79
10-29	7.51	13.45	23.63	22.04	5.94	8.59
30-49	1.43	8.94	4.44	5.85	7.51	-3.09
55-99	0.83	2.72	3.51	4.78	1.89	2.06
100-499	0.62	2.31	3.57	3.59	1.69	1.28
>500	0.13	0.47	0.70	0.42	0.34	-0.05
Average firm size (persons)	8.8	21.3	26.3	24.3	12.5%	3.0%

Source: *Economic Development of Taiwan, 1860-1970* (Ho 1978), and *General Report of Industry and Commerce Census of Taiwan,* 1986.

in the first five years of the export-oriented regime. The distribution of employment among size groups also shows a substantial drop in the share of labor employed by very small firms since 1961 (Table 4). Specifically, almost one third (31 percent) of the workers in manufacturing were employed by firms with fewer than ten workers in 1961. This dropped quickly to around 13 percent in 1966.

This pattern is consistent with substantial gains in efficiency from increasing returns to scale in the early stage of industrialization (Sokoloff 1984). Increasing returns to scale in this situation were probably due to the transition from the traditional artisan shops to the plants catering to international markets because enlarged market size permits finer division

TABLE 4   Distribution of Employment among Size Groups in Taiwanese Manufacturing Industries (%)

	1961	1966	1971	1986	1961-66	1966-86
Number employed	100.0	100.0	100.0	100.0		
1-9	31.07	12.82	9.45	10.37	-18.25	-2.45
10-29	14.09	8.53	10.52	15.01	-5.56	6.48
30-49	6.04	12.69	6.43	9.10	6.65	-3.59
50-99	6.40	8.68	9.22	13.63	2.28	4.95
100-499	14.03	22.52	28.25	28.17	8.49	5.65
>500	28.39	34.77	36.13	23.71	6.38	-11.06

Source: *Economic Development of Taiwan, 1860-1970* (Ho 1978), and *General Report of Industry and Commerce Census of Taiwan,* 1986.

of labor, which renders the latter more efficient than the former even in the absence of new machinery or technology.

Nonetheless, the gain from increasing returns to scale was soon exhausted. The average firm size and the percentage of labor employed by firms with fewer then ten workers have remained almost unchanged since 1966. The almost constant average firm size is consistent with Ho's finding (1980) of unimportant increasing returns to scale in Taiwan's economy during the 1970s. His estimates of scale parameter range from 1.06 for the chemical industry to 0.80 for the food processing industry. Our estimation using firm data for 1983-87 generated similar results, as will be discussed in the next section.

II. Export Orientation and Productivity Performance: Hypothesis Testing Using Firm-Level Data

The Data

The firm-level data are compiled from special issues of *Commonwealth Magazine* published between September 1984 and July 1988. Each year the magazine provides data on the largest manufacturing firms in the country. In 1983 and 1984, the five hundred largest firms in terms of sales were reported. Since 1985, the one thousand largest firms have been listed every year. The data set contains information on output, capital stock, and the number of employees for each of these manufacturing firms.

In addition to the quantitative information, some qualitative characteristics are also reported. For example, firms are classified as foreign, state-owned, or domestic according to their ownership structure. Foreigner (state)-owned firms are those with foreign (state) ownership exceeding 50 percent of total. Domestic firms are those that are neither foreigner- nor state-owned. Firms' export performance is also indicated. Although export volume is not available, the data source identifies those which are selected and honored by the government every year for their excellent performance in terms of export volume.

Finally, this data set distinguishes firms located in export processing zones (EPZs). The EPZs were first established in 1965 with the purpose of promoting exports. Firms located in them are granted various preferen-

TABLE 5   Representativeness of the Firm-Level Data: Distribution of Sales and
Labor among Taiwanese Manufacturing Industries, 1986

	Sales (%)			Labor (%)		
	Pop.	Sample	Ratio	Pop.	Sample	Ratio
Food industry	9.4	12.8	68.6	5.57	8.8	40.0
Textiles	9.8	11.5	58.8	10.5	14.4	35.0
Clothing	3.2	2.7	41.2	5.6	5.8	26.3
Leather products	1.6	2.1	66.9	2.1	4.8	57.7
Wood products	3.4	1.4	20.6	4.8	3.3	17.4
Paper & printing	3.8	2.7	34.9	4.1	2.3	14.3
Chemicals	24.4	26.7	54.8	18.7	14.2	19.3
Nonmetals	3.2	2.6	40.4	4.1	2.1	13.1
Metal products	12.3	9.1	36.9	11.7	5.3	11.5
Machinery	3.2	1.2	19.0	4.3	1.6	9.3
Electronics	15.3	19.6	64.3	16.6	30.0	46.1
Transport equip.	5.7	6.3	55.9	4.7	5.2	28.2
Miscellaneous prod.	4.7	1.3	13.7	7.2	2.3	8.2
All manufactures	100.0	100.0	50.1	100.0	100.0	25.5
Sales (NT$ million)	3,481	1,742		—	—	
Labor (1,000s))	—	—		2,790	711	

Source: Same as Table 4.
Notes: The ratio is calculated as Sample divided by population (Pop.) times 100.

tial treatment, such as tax holidays and very low import duties, with the
condition that all or most of the production output must be exported.

Table 5 indicates that in 1986[6] firms in this sample together produced
50.1 percent of the total gross output of manufacturing and absorbed one
quarter of the total manufacturing employees. Moreover, the industry
distribution of the sample in terms of sales and labor is close to the population with the exception of machinery, miscellaneous manufacturing,
and wood products. These underrepresented industries usually account
for a rather small share in total manufacturing and therefore the consequence of their underrepresentation is less serious. The leading industries, on the other hand, are generally well represented in the sample. For
example, the sample covers around 59 percent of total sales and 35 percent of the employees in the textile industry, and 64 percent of total sales
and 46 percent of employees in the electronics industry.

---

6. Since the data on total manufacturing can only be obtained from the
Industry and Commerce Census, which is conducted every five years, the
comparison of the sample and the population is made only for 1986. It is assumed
that the representativeness of the firms in 1986 can be generalized to the rest of
the sample in the other years (1983 to 1985, and 1987).

TABLE 6 Representativeness of the Firm-Level Data: Number of Firms in Different Size Groups in Taiwanese Manufacturing Industries, 1986

Size of firms (# employed)	Population (1)	Sample (2)	Sample (%) (3)	Ratio (%) (2)/(1)
< 5	46,656	0	0.00	0.00
5-9	26,112	0	0.00	0.00
10-19	17,910	0	0.00	0.00
20-29	7,422	2	0.02	0.03
30-39	4,140	7	0.71	0.17
40-49	2,580	12	1.22	0.47
50-99	5,497	61	6.21	1.11
100-199	2,763	157	15.97	5.68
200-299	811	138	14.04	17.02
300-499	553	218	22.18	39.42
500-999	296	220	22.38	74.32
>1,000	184	168	17.09	91.30
	114,924	983	100.00	0.86

Source: *Commonwealth Magazine*, August 1987, and *General Report of Industry and Commerce Census in Taiwan*, 1986.

In terms of firm size, the sample covers 91.3 percent of the firms with more than 1,000 employees and 74.32 percent of the firms with between 500 and 999 employees. Only 0.21 percent of the firms with fewer than 40 employees are included in the sample (see Table 6). Containing mainly the large and medium firms, the results drawn from this sample therefore must be interpreted in the context of the large and medium firm spectrum.

Although the absence of information on tiny firms handicaps this sample, preventing systematic study of many interesting issues on their behavior, and rendering predictions of population parameters unreliable, the sample does provide sufficient variation in firm size, permitting sufficient degrees of freedom to do interesting statistical work on firm size. Specifically, 8% of the firms in the sample are those that employ fewer than 100 persons; 16.0%, between 100 and 199; 14.0%, 200-299 persons; 22.2%, 300-499; 22.4%, 500-999. Firms with more than 1,000 persons account for another 17.1% of the sample.

The Methodology

The conventional method to measure productive efficiency is to calculate the index of total factor productivity (TFP). Due to the absence of information on intermediate inputs, production output is estimated as value added rather than gross output and the composite input as the geometric weighted average of labor and physical capital, with the weights equal to the respective labor and capital shares. Mathematically,

$$\text{TFP} = V/F \tag{1}$$

where TFP and V are total factor productivity and output, respectively. F, the composite input, can be expressed as

$$F = L^{wL/C} K^{rK/C} \tag{2}$$

where C, w, r, L, and K are total cost, wage rate, interest rate, labor, and capital, respectively.

Under the assumption of producer equilibrium and constant returns to scale, wL/C and rK/C are equal to output elasticity of labor (α_L) and capital (α_K), respectively. In the case of nonconstant returns to scale, wL/C is equal to $\alpha_L/(\alpha_L + \alpha_K)$, and rK/C to $\alpha_K/(\alpha_L + \alpha_K)$.

Note that TFP, defined as above, comprises two elements: (1) the scale economies, which are determined by $\alpha_L + \alpha_K$, and (2) the neutral technological parameter, which is specified in the production function. Under the condition of constant returns to scale, the change in total factor productivity is equal to the neutral technological parameter, while in the case of increasing returns to scale, TFP differentials among firms are due to technological (dis)advantage and increasing returns, as the latter can help large firms generate proportionally higher output for the increase of production scale.

As the first step toward computation of TFP, the weights can be estimated through either the output elasticities or the distributional shares. In principle, both methods will generate the same estimates given a perfect data set and the correct specification of production functions. However, to the extent that comprehensive data on labor compensation are not available for the calculation of distributional shares, the construction of the TFP index requires the estimation of the output elasticities from production functions. The basic model to be estimated is the modified Translog production function without the restriction of constant returns to scale:

$$1n \ Y/L = r_0 + s \ 1n \ L + r_1 \ 1n \ K/L + r_2 \ (1n \ K/L)^2 + \Sigma_i \ D_i + \Sigma_t \ D_t + u \tag{3}$$

where Y, K, and L stand for value added, physical capital stock, and labor, respectively; s is the scale coefficient. The intercept r_0 can be interpreted as a technology parameter. D_i and D_t are the industry dummy and the year dummy, respectively; u is the error term.

Since different types of firms may utilize different technologies, and there may be measurement problems associated with the types of firms, it is necessary to combine qualitative information on firm characteristics for more accurate estimation of output elasticity.

The qualitative information to be included in the regressions are:

$G = 1$ if firms are state-owned

   0 otherwise

$F = 1$ if firms are foreign-owned

   0 otherwise

$E = 1$ if firms are top exporters

   0 otherwise

$Z = 1$ if firms are located in the EPZs

   0 otherwise

Under this specification of production function, the output elasticities are the function of capital-labor ratio:

$$\alpha_K = r_1 + 2r_2 \ln K/L \tag{4}$$

$$\alpha_L = (s + 1 - r_1) - 2r_2 \ln K/L \tag{5}$$

Table 7 summarizes the regression results. The scale coefficient is rather small ($s = 0.040$), but is significantly positive, implying mildly increasing returns to scale in Taiwanese manufacturing. This result is largely consistent with the general record on firm size discussed in the previous section. The scale parameters are found to be more significant in the capital-intensive industry group than in the labor-intensive one (s is 0.058 for the former, and 0.035 for the latter), reflecting the importance of scale economies in the capital-intensive industries.

According to (4), the calculated output elasticity with respect to capital (α_K) is 0.34 for an average manufacturing firm. It is 0.55 and 0.23 for an average firm in the capital-intensive and labor-intensive industry group, respectively. Following (1), the index of total factor productivity is then computed for each individual firm in the sample and regressed upon various qualitative variables such as dummies for state-owned firms, foreign firms, top exporters, and firms located in the export processing zone.[7]

TABLE 7   Estimation of Modified Translog Production Functions for Taiwanese Manufacturing, 1983-87

Dependent variable: Log(value added/labor)

Independent variables	(1) Total	(2) K-intensive industries	(3) L-intensive industries
Intercept	-3.032*	-2.592*	-3.998*
	(-15.243)	(-8.406)	(-14.220)
Log(labor)	0.040*	0.058*	0.035*
	(3.633)	(2.818)	(2.758)
Log(capital/labor)	1.177*	1.272*	0.818*
	(15.455)	(9.548)	(7.742)
Log(capital/labor)^2	0.087*	0.089*	0.057*
	(11.210)	(6.007)	(5.570)
Qualitative variables:			
Dummy for G	-0.312*	-0.708*	0.283*
	(-4.506)	(-6.921)	(2.826)
Dummy for F	0.147*	0.275*	0.089*
	(5.125)	(4.979)	(2.787)
Dummy for E	0.051*	0.017	0.063*
	(2.551)	(0.488)	(2.619)
Dummy for Z	-0.052	0.292	-0.044
	(-1.009)	(1.405)	(-0.8644)
R^2	0.417	0.458	0.328
Number of observations	3,234	1,174	2,060
α_K	0.340	0.550	0.230
α_L	0.700	0.508	0.805
s	0.040	0.058	0.035

Notes: (1) The industry and year dummies are omitted from this table. (2) t-statistics are reported in parentheses. (3) *Significant at 5 percent

Since the data set contains no direct information on export orientation, in order to investigate the effects of export orientation by utilizing the information on top exporters, the sales variable is included in the regression. By controlling for the sales variable, a top exporter will then have a higher export-sales ratio than a non-top exporter.

In addition to the qualitative variables, export volume at the industry

---

7. Because of some typographical errors, firms with some specific characteristics are assumed to be so throughout the whole period. For example, if a firm were reported to be foreign-owned in 1984 and 1986, but not in 1983, 1985, and 1987, then it is assumed to be foreign-owned also in these three years. The assumption that the categorical effects won't disappear overnight is justified for the relatively short time span covered by the sample.

level is introduced as an additional explanatory variable. The purpose of including this variable is to explore the effect of export-related technology diffusion within industries. The magnitude and direction of the coefficient on this variable indicate how an increase in industry exports may affect TFP performance of an average firm within this industry. Given that an individual firm is generally too small to affect the entire industry, causality in this regression may run from industry export expansion to firm's productivity change.

Finally, the year dummies and the industry dummies are added to the regressions. Year dummies are used to control for TFP change over time, while industry dummies are included to reduce ambiguities of interpretation when very different industries are pooled together in the regression.

Table 8 reports the regression results. Regression (1) shows that the coefficient of the export dummy is significantly positive (0.036), suggesting that export orientation, regardless of firm size, has some effect on TFP performance. To investigate the effect of firm size, regression (2) includes an interaction term between the dummy for export orientation and the size of firm measured by the weighted average of labor and capital stock.[8] It is found that the coefficient on the dummy for export-oriented firms is significantly positive (about 0.355) and the coefficient on the interaction term is significantly negative (about -0.074)

These two coefficients together suggest that in this sample smaller firms orienting toward export markets are more productive than their counterparts orienting toward domestic markets, but the gaps between large export-oriented firms and their domestic counterparts are narrower.[9] This result seems to suggest that when firms grow, market orientation becomes less crucial as a source of productivity improvement. One possible explanation is that big firms tend to have a large capability of doing R&D and transferring technology from abroad without relying solely on foreign buyers for productivity improvement. It is also possible that the finding of declining importance of market destination with the size of firms is due to the measurement of export "orientation." For large firms, the ratio of exports to sales may not be high, despite their large export volume. Such large export volume will still enable these firms to en-

---

8. The weights are the labor and capital shares, respectively.

9. These coefficients can be used to calculate the threshold. It turns out that for 60 percent of the firms in the sample which reported their inputs below this threshold, market orientation is an important determinant of productivity performance.

TABLE 8   Regression with the TFP Level as Dependent Variable for Taiwanese Manufacturing, 1983-87

Independent variables	(1)	(2)	(3)	(4)
Intercept	-5.633*	-5.617*	-10.791	-18.306*
	(-85.663)	(-85.232)	(-13.152)	(-20.066)
Industrial variables:				
Log (export volume)			0.422*	
			(6.353)	
Qualitative variables				
Dummy for G	-0.445*	-0.527*	-0.612*	-0.875*
	(-6.651)	(-7.704)	(-7.451)	(-7.551)
Interaction, G and year				0.155*
				(3.515)
Dummy for F	0.147*	0.143*	0.132*.	0.202*
	(5.117)	(5.018)	(3.830)	(3.756)
Interaction, F and year				-0.029
				(-1.391)
Dummy for Z	-0.009	0.010	0.040	0.141
	(-0.172)	(0.195)	(0.665)	(1.384)
Interaction, Z and year				-0.056
				(-1.414)
Log (sales)	0.092*	0.134*	0.158*	0.155*
	(8.000)	(9.390)	(9.141)	(11.074)
Dummy for E	0.036*	0.355*	0.552*	0.509*
	(1.820)	(5.587)	(7.211)	(6.882)
Interaction between E and log (composite inputs)		-0.074*	-0.114*	-0.083*
		(-5.278)	(-6.640)	(-5.868)
Interaction, E and year				-0.054*
				(-3.863)
Year dummies				
1987	0.485*	0.476*		
	(15.897)	(15.680)		
1986	0.333*	0.330*	0.187*	
	(10.989)	(10.953)	(4.795)	
1985	0.130*	0.129*	0.147	
	(4.211)	(4.226)	(1.367)	
1984	0.156*	0.152*	0.084*	
	(4.513)	(4.415)	(2.217)	
Year				0.151*
				(14.250)
R^2	0.737	0.737	0.695	0.738
Number of observations	3,234	3,234	2,450	3,234

Notes: (1) In the third regression, the 1987 firm-level data are excluded because the available industry-level data do not encompass 1987. (2) In the fourth regression, the year variable is used to replace year dummies to capture the technical change over time. The year variable is normalized such that the year 1983 is represented by 0; 1984 by 1; ... ; 1987 by 4. (3) The industry dummies are omitted from this table. (4) t-statistics are reported in parentheses. (5) * Significant at 5 percent.

joy the beneficial externalities from exports even though they are not "export-oriented."

The finding that smaller export-oriented firms are more productive lends some support to the causality from exports to productivity improvement. Since small firms, unlike large firms, are generally not able to commit their own resources to R&D, the interpretation that international technical advancement leads to the expansion of exports appears weaker. This evidence is especially critical to the explanation of economic growth in Taiwan, where small and medium firms dominate.

When whole industries become more export-oriented, they tend to be more dynamic and to diffuse technology more quickly. Given that small-exporting firms largely concentrate on high-exporting industries (e.g., electronics), it is possible that their high productivity may derive from industry-wide dynamism. To capture this effect, the industry exports variable is included in regression (3). The significantly positive coefficient on the industry export variable suggests that whether export-oriented or not, firms in the high-exporting industries are on average more productive than their counterparts in the low-exporting ones, confirming greater dynamism inherent in a high-exporting industry. According to this coefficient, a 1 percent increase in industry export volume will bring about almost a 0.42 percent increase in the TFP level.

Interestingly, the coefficients on the export dummy and the interaction term between the export dummy and firm size are not affected by the inclusion of the industrial variables. This finding suggests that small exporting firms realize higher TFP levels than their domestic counterparts, regardless of the market orientation of the whole industry.

The question of how exports can facilitate productivity advancement has been widely discussed in recent literature. One explanation is that in order to meet higher international standards, exporting firms must incorporate the latest technology and pay much attention to the fine points of production engineering. Competition among MNCs and large buying houses to reduce production costs also leads them to invest in and transfer technology to receptive developing countries committed to exporting. Moreover, contact with sophisticated buyers and investors from industrial economies and supervision under them encourage information flow and incremental improvement. Finally, international quota systems may help as well since they tend to bias output toward more sophisticated higher valued production. Benefits of exportation accrue not only to actively exporting firms but to nonexporting firms as well. This is because even without direct competition in goods markets, the nonexporting sectors must compete for scarce inputs with the exporting sector.

Other categorical effects are also reported in Table 8. The coefficient on the dummy for state-owned firms is significantly negative. Its magnitude indicates that on average state-owned firms are about 50 percent lower in TFP level than their private counterparts in this sample. Although the gaps might be somewhat exaggerated, this finding is largely consistent with the widely recognized poor management of the state-owned firms and their restructuring efforts in recent years.

In contrast to the state-owned firms, foreign firms exhibit significantly 14 percent higher productivity than the average domestic firm. Their high productivity is probably due to the fact that most of the foreign direct investment (FDI) in Taiwan came from the United States and Japan, known for their advanced technologies and organizational skills. This result suggests that FDI is important to the developing countries not only because of foreign capital inflows, but also because of their superior technology and management. Such superior performance of foreign firms provides another channel of technological improvement for the domestic firms as the latter can copy or imitate the visible example of a high standard.

Another categorical effect concerns export-processing zones. Firms located inside the zones are shown to be no more productive than those outside. This finding reflects the declining importance of the zones over time as more and more firms outside the zones were engaged in export activity without added incentives.

Given these results, an important question arises. If subject to the discipline of market forces, why are the less productive firms observed to coexist with the more productive ones? A common explanation is market imperfections such as local monopoly. In this situation, profitability is only loosely associated with productivity. This problem is exacerbated by government subsidization to priority areas. State-owned firms are a case in point.

In addition, under subcontracting, foreign and domestic firms may produce highly complementary rather than substitutable goods. Since they do not compete directly with each other, it is possible to observe productivity differentiation among them.

But even for firms producing exactly the same products, economics of technical change and diffusion has found that firms generally do not adopt an innovation simultaneously and therefore will not exhibit a uniform productivity index. The cumulative number of adopters of innovation usually follows a logistic growth path (S-shaped curve) over time (Griliches 1957, Mansfield 1961), and the diffusion rate is largely determined by the expected profitability, the perceived risk reduction, and the size of the investment to install it.

Insofar as there is no detailed data, only an indirect test of productivity convergence is possible. The last regression of Table 8 includes the interaction terms between qualitative variables and the year dummy to exam-

ine changes in relative TFP over time. State-owned firms are found to improve their productivity relative to private firms and thus narrow the
productivity gap between them over time. Nonexporting firms experience similar narrowing of the gaps with exporting ones. These firms appear to undergo a selection process, through which inefficient firms are
either scrapped or forced to improve their efficiency. In fact, as the sample shows, of the 1,000 largest firms, 28 were state-owned firms in 1985,
25 in 1986, and the number further reduced to only 20 in 1987. In contrast
to the state-owned firms and exporting firms, foreign firms seem able to
maintain an advantageous position against domestic firms. The coefficient on the interaction term between foreign dummy and time suggests
insignificant shrinkage of the gaps between them. Separate regressions
for each year also show no tendency to narrow the gaps between foreign
and domestic firms. This result is plausible, considering the still unchal-
lenged position in the technology owned by the U.S. and Japanese
MNCs.

The problem of autocorrelation arises from pooling time series and
cross section data together. In this situation, least-square estimators, although still defined, linear, unbiased, and consistent, no longer exhibit
minimum variance, rendering the t-tests of significance invalid. To investigate this problem, separate regressions for each year from 1983 to 1987
are estimated. It is found that the direction and significance of various
categorical effects are quite robust to these specifications.

Summary

This study empirically examined the relationship between export activity and productivity improvement at the firm level in one of the
high-export economies—Taiwan. The results show that high-exporting
industries tend to facilitate faster productivity progress of an individual
firm than low-exporting industries. In addition, high-exporting firms, especially when they are not large, exhibit higher productivity than their
low-exporting counterparts. Considering these firms' limited internal capacity to do R&D, this finding is consistent with the hypothesis of export-
spurred productivity improvement.

Other results, that state-owned firms are less productive than private
ones and foreign firms are more productive than domestic ones, suggest
that economic dynamism lies primarily in the private sector and that FDI
is important not only because of capital inflow but also because of the ad-

vanced skills and technology it brings to the host countries. Export Processing Zones, on the other hand, have little effect on productivity improvement, reflecting the declining importance of EPZs as "enclaves." In other words, export-led prosperity is not confined to EPZs only. It extends to the entire economy.

The impact of exportation on the whole economy can be better appreciated by noting that the ratio of exports to output in the manufacturing sector increased dramatically from 1.7% in 1954 to 10.5% in 1961, then to 30.5% in 1974 and 40.3% in 1985. Since manufactured exports appear to have a direct impact on TFP improvement for smaller firms, they could be a very important source of labor productivity growth in an economy such as Taiwan where small firms prevail.

The present research provides useful information to distinguish several interpretations of "export-led" growth. Allocative efficiency à la trade theory was gained as the economy experienced dramatic structural change in favor of labor-intensive industries in the 1960s, or the first decade of the export-oriented regime. Thereafter, the economy evolved slowly, as is shown in the rather stable distribution of employment in the manufacturing sector during the 1970s and 1980s. Given this pattern, it is clear that the increased efficiency resulting from resource reallocation to industries having comparative advantages cannot explain adequately the growth beyond the 1960s.

On the other hand, while the scale economies, largely associated with the transition from a craft to a modern labor-intensive production method, must have contributed to the efficiency gains in the early 1960s, the average size of firms and their distribution across size groups have remained virtually unchanged from the mid-1960s to the end of the 1980s. The scale parameters estimated in Ho (1980) for the 1970s and in the present study for the 1980s also suggest "unimportance" of scale economies in Taiwan's economic growth. Again, this source of efficiency gain proves insufficient to account for the sustained economic growth over the past decades.

What factors, then, generated the "export-led" growth in this East Asian economy? The evidence presented here suggests that manufactured exports contributed significantly to productivity progress in the 1980s. Considering that the 1980s was a period when the static gains mentioned above subsided, we might interpret "export-led growth," at least in Taiwan, to mean growth created by continuous improvement in production method facilitated to a large extent by manufactured exports.

Given this interpretation, the recent confusion surrounding the export-oriented development strategies can be at least partly clarified. Rising protectionism and a slowdown in economic activity in the 1980s raise serious doubt as to the extent to which the East Asia model can be generalized (Cline 1982). The export pessimists base their arguments on the difficulty in increasing the share of exports in GNP in the 1980s and 1990s, contending that high exports experienced in East Asia in the 1960s and 1970s can no longer be replicated for today's developing countries. Our findings, however, suggest that exports can lead to productivity advancement through integration into the world market. Therefore, despite slower growth of world trade, the growth potential of developing countries pursuing relatively open trade regimes will still be larger than that of those sticking to closed trade regimes.

Bibliography

Bhagwati, J. 1978. *Anatomy and Consequences of Exchange Control Regimes.* Cambridge, Mass.: Ballinger.

———. 1982. Directly Unproductive, Profit-Seeking (DUP) Activities. *Journal of Political Economy* (Oct.).

———. 1988. Export-Promoting Trade Strategy: Issues and Evidence. *World Bank Research Observer* 3 (1).

Chen, T., and D. Tang. 1990. Export Performance and Productivity Growth: The Case of Taiwan. *Economic Development and Cultural Change* 38.

Cline, W. R. 1982. Can the East Asia Model of Development Be Generalized? *World Development* 10 (2).

Commonwealth Magazine. Taipei. Special issues dated Sept. 1984, Aug. 1985, Aug. 1986, Aug. 1987, and July 1988.

Council for Economic Planning and Development. 1988. *Taiwan Statistical Data Book.* The Republic of China.

Dahlman, C. J., and L. Westphal. 1982. Technological Effort in Industrial Development: A Survey. In *The Economics of New Technology in Developing Countries,* edited by F. Steward and J. James. London: Frances Pinter.

Dahlman, C. J., and O. Sananikone. 1990. *Technology Strategy in the Economy of Taiwan: Exploiting Foreign Linkages and Investing in Local Capability.* Washington, D.C.: World Bank, International Economics Department.

Directorate-General of Budget, Accounting, and Statistics in Taiwan. *Industry and Commerce Census of Taiwan.* Various issues, 1966-86.

Directorate-General of Budget, Accounting, and Statistics in Taiwan. 1988. *Monthly Bulletin of Earnings and Productivity Statistics in Taiwan* (Mar.).

Directorate-General of Budget, Accounting, and Statistics in Taiwan. 1987. *National Income in Taiwan.*

Griliches, Z. 1957. Hybrid Corn: An Explanation in the Economics of Technological Change. *Econometrica* (Oct.).

Ho, Samuel P. S. 1978. *Economic Development of Taiwan, 1860-1970*. New Haven: Yale University Press.

Ho, Yhi-Min. 1980. The Production Structure of the Manufacturing Sectors and Its Distribution Implication: The Case of Taiwan. *Economic Development and Cultural Change* 28.

Jorgenson, D. W., and Z. Griliches. 1967. The Explanation of Productivity Change. *Review of Economic Studies* 34.

Kojima, K., and T. Ozawa. 1984. *Japan's General Trading Companies: Merchants of Economic Development*. Paris: Development Center of the OECD.

Krueger, A. 1974. The Political Economy of the Rent-Seeking Society. *American Economic Review* (June).

———. 1978. *Foreign Trade Regimes and Economic Development: Liberalization Attempts and Consequences*. Cambridge: Ballinger for NBER.

———. 1984. Comparative Advantage and Development Policy: Twenty Years Later. In *Economic Structure and Performance*, edited by M. Syrquin, L. Taylor, and L. E. Westphal. Orlando: Academic Press.

Krueger, A., and B. Tuncer. 1982. Empirical Test of the Infant Industry Argument. *American Economic Review* 72: 1142-52.

Lin, Ching-Yuan. 1973. *Industrialization in Taiwan, 1946-1972*. New York: Praeger Publishers.

Mansfield, E. 1961. Technical Change and the Rate of Imitation. *Econometrica* 29 (4).

Nelson, R. R. 1973. Recent Exercises in Growth Accounting: New Understanding or Dead End? *American Economic Review* 63 (3).

———. 1981. Research on Productivity Growth and Productivity Differences: Dead Ends and New Departures. *Journal of Economic Literature* 19.

Nishimizu, M., and S. Robinson. 1984. Trade Policies and Productivity Change in Semi-Industrialized Countries. *Journal of Development Economics* 16.

Sokoloff, K. 1984. Was the Transition from the Artisanal Shop to the Nonmechanized Factory Associated with Gains in Efficiency? Evidence from the U.S. Manufacturing Census of 1820 and 1850. *Explorations in Economic History* 21.

Wade, R. 1990. *Governing the Market: Economic Theory and the Role of Government in East Asian Industrialization*. Princeton, N.J.: Princeton University Press.

Westphal, L., W. Rhee, and G. Pursell. 1984. Sources of Technological Capability in South Korea. In *Technological Capability in the Third World*, edited by M. Fransman and K. King. London: Macmillan.

3

The Transition to Export-Led Growth in Taiwan

Stephan Haggard
Chien-Kuo Pang

The standard interpretation of Taiwan's postwar economic history identifies a relatively sharp break in policy and economic structure in the early 1960s. Prior to that time, the government had pursued a more or less typical strategy of import-substituting industrialization (ISI). There were, to be sure, several peculiarities of the Taiwan case that set it off sharply from other developing countries, including land reform and particular attention to agricultural development. Yet the defining characteristic of Taiwan's economic development has clearly been the expansion of manufactured exports in labor-intensive industries that began in the 1960s.

This transition to export-led growth resulted from a series of policy reforms launched between 1958 and 1961 that included a gradual unification of the exchange rate at a realistic level and a battery of new incentives to investment and exports. Prior to that time, and equally if

We would like to thank Greg Noble, Robert Wade, Ed Winckler, and Joe Yager for comments on earlier versions of this chapter. This essay draws on Stephan Haggard, "The Transition to Export-Led Growth in Taiwan," chapter five of *Pathways from the Periphery: The Politics of Growth in the Newly Industrializing Countries* (Cornell University Press, 1990); and Chien-Kuo Pang, *The State and Economic Transformation: The Taiwan Case* (New York: Goodend Publishing, 1992).

not even more fundamental to subsequent success, the government had committed itself both to macroeconomic stability and to the development of the private sector.

From the perspective of political economy, these reforms raise a host of intriguing puzzles. Why was the political leadership willing to experiment with unproven reform measures? Why were the reforms undertaken in the sequence they were, and why were they sustained? Why did a political leadership with a strong commitment to state-owned enterprise come to support the development of an indigenous private sector?

The answers to these questions must be sought, first, in the peculiar political position of the Kuomintang (KMT). On moving from the mainland to Taiwan, the party quickly established its dominance over a society with which party elites had few organic social connections. Resembling a Leninist party in organization and strategy, the KMT acted swiftly to neutralize contending centers of societal power. This political autonomy permitted the government to pursue policies, such as stabilization, land reform, and reform of the exchange rate regime, that would have been beyond the capabilities of other governments. Within the party, Chiang Kai-shek also eliminated or reduced the power of contending factions. The "leaderist" political system that resulted permitted resolute decision-making once the interest of the president was engaged.

KMT power was accompanied, however, by a relatively coherent ideological perspective that championed an interventionist state and showed skepticism toward the development of the private sector. The party's stance toward the private sector on the mainland had been predatory as much as developmental. The transition to export-led growth was thus intertwined with a more basic shift toward support for local Taiwanese capital. Any explanation of the transition to export-led growth must account for this fundamental change in orientation.

Examining an individual case necessarily draws attention to explanatory factors particular to that case. In Taiwan, the legacy of past policy weighed very heavily on the top political leadership. The KMT leadership was aware that inattention to the economy had been a major factor in the political debacle on the mainland. The KMT was committed not to repeat the mistakes on which the Communists had capitalized: inattention to the countryside; inflationary monetary and fiscal policies; the squelching of productive economic activity.

The year 1958 also marked a turning point in Taiwan's security relations that affected economic policy. It is probable that Chiang Kai-shek had abandoned any real hope of recapturing the mainland long before then. The resolution of the Taiwan Straits crisis resulted in a definitive restatement of U.S. policy on the question. Party ideology and rhetoric continued to pay obeisance to the goal of retaking the mainland, but the

KMT's political strategy shifted decisively in a "domesticist" direction, emphasizing economic development and welfare considerations.

There are several other features of the Taiwan case that are of broader comparative and theoretical significance, however. The first was the development of a particularly insulated group of technocrats, working closely with American aid officials. The government's autonomy from Taiwanese society facilitated the development of bureaucratic structures that, while dependent on executive support, were largely freed from the demands of social clienteles. Because of the policy instruments available to them, these segments of the bureaucracy played an important role in developing the private sector in the 1950s, particularly in such commodities as textiles.

While these "developmentalist" portions of the bureaucracy were important advocates of private-sector led growth, they were also the first groups within the government to become aware of the economic limitations of import-substitution, including the tendency to the creation of rent-seeking groups. Freed from the pull of what Mancur Olson has called "distributional coalitions" (1983), however, the economic bureaucracy was politically and institutionally positioned to take a long-term perspective on the country's economic development.

The case of Korea demonstrates clearly that technocratic reformers cannot be successful unless they enjoy support from the political leadership; Syngman Rhee consistently undermined the organizationally scattered reformers in his administration in the late 1950s (see Haggard, Kim, and Moon 1989). Yet once the reform decision was taken, both the bureaucratic and political capacity to move swiftly in instituting the desired policies was in place. Thus discrete policy reforms rested critically on prior institutional reforms and capabilities.

This brings us to the second general factor that helps explain the reforms: the incentives provided by foreign-exchange difficulties. These have, of course, operated in a number of other settings with little effect, but in Taiwan they were particularly severe because of the heavy dependence on U.S. aid and the absence of other alternatives, such as those later provided to other developing countries by the emergence of the Eurocurrency markets. From very early after the relocation to Taiwan, the United States warned that there were limits on American largesse over the long run, though additional funds were forthcoming to assist particular reform efforts. In the most important reforms, including the stabilization of the early 1950s, the exchange rate reform, and new incentives to exports and foreign investment, both short-term and longer-run foreign-exchange constraints played a critical role both in engaging Chiang Kai-shek directly, and in tipping the political balance within the bureaucracy and political leadership in the reform direction.

Our political analysis of the reform process also sheds light on the debate about the relative role of market-oriented reforms and state intervention in the export-led growth strategies of the East Asian newly industrializing countries.[1] For at least four reasons, the reform process proved an eclectic mix of macrolevel reforms of incentives with ongoing state interventions of various sorts. First, the concern with foreign exchange and the government's dependence on trade taxes limited the speed of import liberalization. Second, though substantial, the victory of the "liberalizers" within the government was not complete, and involved tacit or explicit compromises with bureaucratic and political factions favoring a more statist economic strategy. Third, the economic views of the reformers have frequently been misread. While there were a small group of economists who argued a radical laissez-faire position, this view never dominated within the economic bureaucracy, where strong commitments to industrial policy remained intact.

Finally, the neoclassical portrait of export-led growth has underplayed the critical role of the state in easing the transition into world markets. Various interventions served the function of reducing the risk of shifting capital into the export sector by providing premia to exporters, by providing information, and reducing transactions costs. A full picture of the "developmentalist state" must pay close attention to the provision of such public goods.

Two Legacies: The Mainland
and the Japanese Colonization

Before turning to economic policy in the 1950s, it is useful to review both the evolution of the KMT and developments under the Japanese in Taiwan prior to 1949. These two legacies, one on the mainland, the other on Taiwan, established the political and economic context within which the KMT operated in the 1950s.

The KMT was formally reorganized along Leninist lines in 1923-24, but the Nationalist government of the Nanking Decade (1927-37) is generally considered weak. (The following draws on Bedeski 1981, Coble 1980, Eastman 1974, Tien 1972, Wilbur 1983, and Gold 1990.) Despite the much celebrated Northern Expedition of 1926, the government's territo-

---

1. For a review of some of these issues, see Deyo 1988; on Taiwan in particular, Wade n.d. and Gold 1986.

rial reach was limited. Internal party factionalism combined with the centrifugal pull of regional warlords to undermine any social-revolutionary aspirations the party had once maintained. Gradually, the center of authority shifted away from the party and state altogether, and toward Chiang Kai-shek and the military. With the militarization of the party, "the Nationalist regime tended...to be neither responsible nor responsive to political groups or institutions outside the government. It became, in effect, its own constituency" (Eastman 1974, 286).

This political insulation extended to relations with the Shanghai capitalists. Parks Coble shows that relations between the state and Chinese capital were "characterized by government efforts to emasculate politically the urban capitalists and to milk the modern sector of the economy" (Coble 1980, 3). State control over banking became a means for establishing a favored "state-capitalist" sector of semigovernmental corporations and agencies, which became an important locus of economic and political power. This model was extended to confiscated Japanese properties on Taiwan in the immediate postwar years.

These actions were justified by an ideology that sanctioned state intervention in the economy. The third of Sun Yat-sen's "three principles of the people" has been translated variously as "people's livelihood" and "socialism." Sun expressed a concern with equity, an aversion to the concentration of economic power, and the need to regulate and even restrict capitalism (Sun 1924, 10). At the same time, however, he also placed limits on the range of state activity, arguing that "all matters that can be and are better carried out by private enterprise should be left to private hands which should be encouraged and fully protected by liberal laws" (Sun 1922, 9). KMT ideology thus combined private ownership and central planning in a flexible mix. While there were conflicts in the 1950s over the precise balance between state and market, Sun's writings allowed room for a pragmatic interpretation.

Despite the generally negative assessment of the KMT's economic policy during the Nanking Decade, there were substantial accomplishments toward the creation of a national economy. Programs for industrial and infrastructural development, as well as monetary, fiscal, and institutional reforms were pushed by reformers who saw economic development and closer cooperation with the private sector as a prerequisite for the effective exercise of political power. This view would ultimately triumph on Taiwan, but in the 1930s it suffered at the hands of the military, which saw territorial control as the top priority. With the coming of war and revolution, all possibilities of pursuing a rational economic course were lost. Between 1945 and 1949, the military's claims on the budget were increasingly financed by printing money. National finances fell into complete disarray. Following an abortive currency reform in 1948, prices reached hyperinflationary levels, contributing to the KMT's declining political fortunes.[2]

On Taiwan, economic development under the Japanese had been substantial. Japan's interest in extracting an "export surplus" led to the economic transformation of the rural sector, even if the pre-existing social structure remained largely intact. Unlike Korea, Japan's interest was not limited to rice, but included development of the island's comparative advantage in a number of tropical products linked to processing industries, the most important of which was sugar. Investments in rural infrastructure, expanded agricultural inputs, and the fixing of property rights all contributed to the creation of a commercialized agricultural sector. An extension system and network of farmers' associations assisted the Japanese in rural surveillance, but also hastened the adoption of new technologies; these associations were revived and strengthened under KMT rule.

Japanese *zaibatsu* and locally established Japanese firms dominated the modern enclave. Until 1924, Taiwanese were prohibited from forming corporations without Japanese participation. Thereafter Taiwanese were largely restricted to small-scale industry, commerce, and land development, though a small number of collaborating families became rich through these activities, banking, and commercial monopolies extended them by the Japanese (Gold 1986, 39-40). As in Korea, the industrial structure was diversified after the mid-1930s to include several war-related industries and the development of raw materials needed by Japanese industry. As Japan mobilized the Taiwan economy for the drive to the south, many Taiwanese concerns were merged with Japanese ones, weakening, but not destroying, a nascent Taiwanese bourgeoisie.

The Consolidation of State Power on Taiwan

Key to understanding subsequent economic policy in Taiwan is the concentration of political power in the hands of the KMT and conversely, the political and organizational weakness of indigenous social forces. This peculiar political outcome was the result of the KMT's defeat in civil war and retreat to Taiwan. According to the Cairo Declaration, Taiwan was to return to the Republic of China after the war. In September 1945, Chiang Kai-shek appointed a military governor to extend Na-

---

2. See Chou 1963, 15-17, which underlines the distributional consequences of the inflation.

tionalist administration to the island. This first group of Nationalists established a relatively independent provincial administration. Since most of the modern industry had been developed or taken over by the Japanese, the early KMT administrators inherited almost complete control of the island's economy.

The tasks of reconstruction were daunting. In 1946, industrial and agricultural production stood at less than half their 1937 levels (Lin 1973, 37). The repatriation of the Japanese, including numerous technicians, managers, entrepreneurs, and administrators contributed to the economic confusion. The economic system was further strained by the first influx of refugees from the mainland. Between 1946 and 1950, more than one-and-a-half million persons from the mainland, principally servicemen and civil servants, arrived on Taiwan, an island with a population of approximately six million at the end of the war.

As during the 1930s on the mainland, however, economic problems were compounded by mismanagement and corruption.[3] The relationship between public and private was quickly blurred. New and established public entities were run as private enterprises by officials formed into boards of directors. Capital was siphoned out of going concerns in the form of inflated salaries, dividends, and nepotism, and the tradition of financing unprofitable public enterprises through money creation continued, contributing to the general economic disruption caused by the war.

The provincial government's mismanagement of the economy went hand in hand with a disregard for the interests of the indigenous Taiwanese.[4] Hoping to participate in the Japanese spoils, the Taiwanese faced a government worse than its predecessor in monopolizing industrial opportunities through control of inputs, credit, and transport. A small conflict over licensing triggered a spontaneous islandwide uprising on the last day of February, 1947, an event subsequently known as the Two Twenty-Eight Incident. Taiwanese leaders appeared to be in a position to press the provincial government for greater participation in both politics and the economy. With the arrival of military support from the mainland, however, the governor opted for a military solution, Key Formosan nationalists were killed, driven into exile, or silenced; the number of victims remains unclear, but some estimates range as high as 20,000 (Kerr 1965, 310).

---

3. Though clearly partisan, one of the few accounts of this early period remains Kerr 1965, chaps. 5 and 6. See also Gold 1986, 47-55, and Riggs 1952.

4. For example, a statute on the confiscation of Japanese properties allowed joint enterprises with 50 percent or more Taiwanese capital to be taken over by the Taiwanese, but others were either nationalized or sold off. See Kerr 1965, 122.

By late 1948, it was clear that Chiang's military position on the mainland was untenable. In December, he dispatched his son Chiang Ching-kuo to the island, as well as a new governor, Ch'en Ch'eng. Ch'en Ch'eng was extremely close to Chiang Kai-shek, and had previous administrative experience as governor of Hupeh province from 1938 to 1944, where he had undertaken some efforts at land reform. Throughout his political career he placed particular emphasis on the link between economic development and political power and legitimacy, and was the key political supporter of the group of technocrats who shaped Taiwan's development strategy.[5]

In the short run, however, the war footing and the aim of ultimately recapturing the mainland provided the rationale for the imposition of martial law and the incarceration and execution of politically suspect Taiwanese and refugees. Taiwan thus began its postwar history without any organized political left, and indeed with virtually no organized political opposition of any sort.

The problem of building a new political order in Taiwan centered as much on the government and the highly factionalized party as on society. In April 1948, Chiang Kai-shek was elected president under a new constitution, but in May, the Temporary Provisions Effective During the Period of Communist Rebellion were enacted. These gave the president a wide range of emergency powers. While formally within the bounds of the constitution, the Temporary Provisions effectively suspended any pretense of constitutional rule, and remained the legal foundation of KMT rule into the 1980s.

Following a series of disastrous military and diplomatic defeats, and under increasing pressure from dissidents within the party, Chiang retired from the presidency in January 1949, but established an "alternative government" on Taiwan on 1 August, and resumed the presidency in March 1950. Drawing on the loyalty and organization of the military's "Whampoa Clique," Chiang reestablished his dominance over the party through a "reform" launched in July 1950. Through June 1952, Chiang worked through a Central Reform Committee, the forerunner to the Central Standing Committee, to centralize decision-making.

The main objective of the reform was the elimination of the debilitating factionalism that had plagued the party on the mainland. The effort was also no doubt aimed at an American audience as part of the ongoing effort to woo American assistance. Domestic economic considerations

---

5. On Ch'en Ch'eng's career and his crucial relationship with both Chiang Kai-shek on the one hand and the technocrats on the other, see Yang 1986; *China Yearbook 1963-64*, 722; and Chou 1982, 8.

also played a role, however.[6] The reform plan is worth quoting at some length, since it suggests the links that Chiang drew publicly between the party's economic failures on the mainland and the need for decisive action:

> Almost every one of our comrades knows that our failure in the anti-Communist struggle is due to our neglect of the *min-sheng* principle on the mainland. Every comrade also knows that henceforth in our anti-Communist struggle we must rely on this principle. However, let me ask: during the past four years in the mainland, did any of our party branches in the villages ever carry out land surveys? Did any city party office conduct any labor surveys? Did any provincial party office submit any report based on systematic social and economic investigation? We should realize the *min-sheng* principle through practical action, not theoretical discussion. (*Chung-hua min-kuo nien-chien* 1950, 123)

While some of this can no doubt be dismissed as political rhetoric, the underlying concern of strengthening the economic capabilities of the government was undoubtedly genuine.

The KMT retained a complicated multilevel governmental structure. The national level was made up of five branches, including a directly elected Legislative Yuan and an indirectly elected Control Yuan that maintained the pretense of governing all of China. An elected Provincial Assembly played an advisory role, and county and municipal governments were opened to electoral contestation after 1950, albeit under close party surveillance. Nonetheless, the KMT was relatively unconstrained by these institutions. The party structure paralleled that of the government at all levels, permitting a thorough penetration of both society and bureaucracy, and all important decisions were taken within the upper councils of the party, if not personally by Chiang Kai-shek.

Important social groups were also incorporated into party organizations. State-controlled youth corps preempted independent student organization. Labor, which had been an important force in undermining the KMT's power on the mainland, was also brought under control, albeit preemptively. Ironically, workers first had to be organized, as labor organization had been prohibited under the Japanese. State-created labor unions, penetrated by KMT cadres, were forced on both private and public sector enterprises. A special law, promulgated in 1947 entitled "Measures for Handling of Labor Disputes during the Period of National Mobilization and Suppression of Rebellion," gave priority to the prompt settlement of disputes and was in effect until the political liberalization of

---

6. On the factionalism in the party, see Tucker 1980.

the mid-1980s. The law eliminated the right to strike and gave local governments extensive powers in mediation and arbitration (Djang 1977).

Both the political autonomy of the KMT and the party's interest in preemptive reform are perhaps most in evidence in the extensive land reforms carried out between 1949 and 1953. Landlord-tenant relations on Taiwan were not exactly analogous to those on the mainland, and the Two Twenty-Eight Incident had been largely an urban phenomenon. Nonetheless, perhaps one half of Taiwan's farm workers in the 1940s were tenant sharecroppers (Ho 1978, 160). Ch'en Ch'eng subsequently linked the initiation of the first stage of the reform, a rent reduction, with events on the mainland:

> [Communist infiltration of the villages] was one of the main reasons why the mainland fell into Communist hands. On the eve of the rent reduction in Taiwan, the situation on the Chinese mainland was becoming critical and the villages on the island were showing signs of unrest and instability. It was feared that the Communists might take advantage of the rapidly deteriorating situation. (Chen 1978, 131)

Support from rural elites had blunted the KMT's support for land reform on the mainland; no such constraints now operated. When the Provincial Assembly raised objections to the 1952 reform, the KMT attacked the body as a tool of the landlords (National Archives RG 59 1953). The reform proceeded in three stages: a rent reduction program in 1949; the sale of public land acquired from the Japanese; and a Land to the Tiller program begun in 1953 that constituted an assault on the rural power of landlords through strict limits on holdings.[7]

Landlords were compensated by a combination of land bonds (70 percent) and stock shares in four government enterprises (30 percent).[8] While the rural reforms undercut the basis of landlord power in the countryside, the compensation in the state-controlled industrial sector only increased the dependence of the new owners on the good will of the regime. As the landlords recognized, stock ownership was divorced from effective control over the enterprises, in which the government retained the major share. Not only were land prices undervalued, but interest rates on the bonds were low, and their value declined even further in panic selling. Martin Yang's survey of 500 landlords found that more

---

7. Taiwan's land reform has been extensively studied, but there is little on the politics of the process. See Yang 1970, Ch'en 1961, Hsiao 1981, and Yager 1989.

8. The companies were Taiwan Cement Corporation, Taiwan Pulp and Paper Corporation, and two holding companies, Taiwan Agriculture and Forestry Corporation and Taiwan Industrial and Mining Corporation.

than 90 percent sold their shares to the government enterprises (Yang 1970). While these funds may, in turn, have been invested in industrial ventures, it is clear that the new state-owned enterprises did not spawn the new generation of industrial capital.

The KMT's stance toward the countryside defies a simple characterization. On the one hand, government policy aimed at extraction of resources.[9] The new class of smallholders created by the reforms was also tied to the regime by the extension of the KMT's organizational presence in the countryside. The government monopolized inputs and credit, creating powerful levers for control. To meet the needs of the swollen urban population and to feed military personnel and civil servants, the government controlled the marketing of rice through a rice-fertilizer barter system. Not only were the terms of exchange disadvantageous to the farmers, but the Food Bureau was empowered to collect rice as payment for taxes, inputs, land sold to farmers, and rents on publicly held lands.

On the other hand, the government invested heavily in agricultural development and sought to rebuild the rural organizations that had ceased to operate after the war. Credit cooperatives, farmers' associations, and community organizations were consolidated into a Farmers' Association that served as an extension service, provider of credit and inputs. This reorganization displaced rural moneylenders and served as a channel for the expression of rural interests, as did the opening of municipal elections. Thus extraction was coupled with various forms of government investment, suggesting that the nature of the tradeoff between industry and agriculture under ISI can be offset by other policies where the government has an interest in doing so. Politically, the reforms drove a wedge between landlords and the rural Taiwanese poor, and created a new class of smallholders that provided the KMT with at least a tacit support base.

By the end of 1950, crucial features of the KMT system were beginning to crystallize. First, the pretext of constitutional rule was dropped under the exigencies of civil war. Organizational "reforms" created a "leaderist" political system in which Chiang Kai-shek headed the army, the political system, and an increasingly centralized party apparatus. Alternative centers of political power in Taiwan—leftist and Formosan nationalist forces, labor, students, and landlords—were either crushed, displaced, or drawn into state-controlled organizational networks. The shock of past events on the mainland, however, created a strong political current within the government, of which Ch'en Ch'eng was exemplary, that linked eco-

---

9. For interpretations emphasizing this extractive side of the reforms, see Chen 1978, Apthorpe 1979, and Amsden 1985.

nomic reform to the consolidation and maintenance of political power and legitimacy. It is to the exact shape of that reform program over the 1950s that we now turn.

The Sequence of Reform: Stabilization First

One of the distinctive features of Taiwan's economic development, particularly when compared with Latin America, is that the country established price stability quite early, and managed to maintain it. The first problem the KMT faced on relocating to Taiwan was to manage the spillover of hyperinflation from the mainland. Despite a rapid appreciation of the local currency, the *taipi*, in relation to the yuan, the provincial authorities were unable to wholly neutralize the effect of inflation imported from the mainland in 1947 and 1948 (Lundberg 1979, 282-83).

On 15 June 1949 the New Taiwan Dollar Reform was put into effect in an effort to slow inflation that had reached 3,000 percent for the first half of the year. The old currency was devalued and fixed and an extremely conservative system of monetary management instituted. This involved 100 percent backing for the currency in gold, foreign exchange, and commodities and a limit on the amount of currency in circulation. This program could be entertained because of the shipment of the assets of the Bank of China to Taiwan beginning in the fall of 1948, which totalled roughly US$350 million in gold, U.S. and British banknotes, and other items.

Given the chaotic economic situation, this effort at a constitutional solution to stabilization did not last. The provincial Bank of Taiwan was obligated to finance large budget deficits, associated mostly with military expenditures and the investment expenditures of the state-owned enterprises. United States officials in Taiwan estimated in April 1950 that Chiang had 600,000 ounces of gold, but expenditures were running at 120,000 to 140,000 ounces a month. The government was reduced to a series of stopgap revenue measures, including the sale of Japanese houses, "patriotic" bonds, a lottery, and the sale of stockpiled commodities (National Archives RG 59 1950a, 1950b). This was clearly an unsustainable position, and with serious shortages and a rapid devaluation of the currency, inflationary pressures remained strong.

Stabilization involved a mix of factors, about which there is still some debate. These included a gradual move toward more conservative fiscal and monetary policies, the imposition of controls, and increases in supply, but two factors appear central: an innovative interest rate policy and the resumption of U.S. aid.

Monetarists emphasize the role of the preferential savings program introduced in March 1950 that provided positive real interest rates to savers.[10] The idea of price-index-escalated savings certificates, advanced by S. C. Tsiang, an American-trained economist, as early as 1947, represented a sharp departure from the current development orthodoxy which emphasized the developmental advantages of low interest rates. It is a telling sign of the difficult situation in which the government found itself that it was willing to experiment by adopting a similar proposal for high nominal-interest deposits.

The reform had an important stabilizing effect by drawing excess liquidity into the financial system. The high interest rate policy had effectively halted the inflation *prior* to the resumption of American aid that came following the outbreak of the Korean War. Monthly inflation rates that averaged 10.3 percent in the first quarter of 1950 dropped to 0.4 percent in the second quarter.

Encouraged by this success, and fearful that interest rates of 7 percent per month would be a crippling burden, the government reversed the policy in the second half of the year. Prices immediately resumed their upward march, and the trend toward financial intermediation reversed itself. In March 1951, once again faced with rising prices and a deteriorating external position, deposit rates were once again raised, and only gradually lowered in line with expectations concerning future inflation.

Interest rate policy also had an important institutional consequence. The commercial banks received more deposits than they could lend under conservative credit standards, and the excess deposits were increasingly redeposited with the Bank of Taiwan. This permitted the Bank of Taiwan to bring credit expansion by the commercial banks under its control, to play the role of Central Bank, and to mesh credit policy with other objectives. As interest rates were controlled, however, they did not reflect market rates, implying a strict rationing of credit on the part of the banks. For example, in July 1954 the rate on one-month deposits was cut to 1 percent a month and the loan rate to 1.95 percent, but rates on the unorganized market ranged from 3.5 to 4.5 percent. These gaps narrowed somewhat over the 1950s, but the control of interest rates remained a consistent feature of Taiwan's financial system into the 1980s.

The effect of interest rate policy on stabilization appears compelling, but is difficult to disentangle from other factors. The most important of

---

10. S. C. Tsiang naturally places particular emphasis on the interest rate reforms in achieving stabilization. See Tsiang 1984; 1985, 65–95.

these was the resumption of U.S. aid in July 1950 following the outbreak of the Korean War and a redefinition of American interests in the Western Pacific. In the words of K. Y. Yin (Yin Chung-jung), the great economic reformer of the 1950s, "the timely arrival of U.S. aid was no less than a shot of stimulant to a dying patient" (Yin 1961, 17).

Under a previous aid agreement, the New Taiwan Dollar equivalent to the sales value of aid commodities delivered would be deposited at the Bank of Taiwan. As Lundberg points out, the stabilizing effect of aid thus worked on both the demand and supply sides (Lundberg 1979, 283). The increase in counterpart funds deposited with the Bank of Taiwan reduced the availability of high-powered money. The counterpart funds were used in part to cover productive investment and the government budget deficit in a noninflationary way. A large portion of the funds were, in effect, impounded as deposits which by 1954 equaled 40 percent of the money supply then in circulation. On the supply side, increased commodity imports through the aid program also dampened prices and speculation, both immediately and through their contribution to increases in overall production and productivity.

Throughout the 1950s, the United States was a constant source of pressure on the government for a variety of fiscal reforms, including tax increases, reform of the tax structure, and limits on military spending. The state-owned enterprises were also a bete-noire of American aid officials, since they were off-budget and engaged in costly subsidies through their employment and pricing policies.[11] As early as March 1951, the State Department warned Wellington Koo that "the United States must proceed from the assumption that it will be possible in the foreseeable future for the Government of the United States to reduce, and then to eliminate, what now amounts to an economic subsidy to Taiwan." This promise was coupled with an implicit threat that were economies not forthcoming, the aid relationship would be reconsidered (National Archives RG 59 1951).

Given the redefinition of American security interests, this threat was not wholly credible. In part through the mechanism of the counterpart fund, though, the government did commit itself to a relatively stable monetary course. By 1953, the country had achieved a modicum of price stability, a crucial prerequisite for the success of subsequent reforms.

---

11. See National Archives RG 59 1954 for a typical assessment.

The Politics of Production:
The Institutional Machinery of ISI

In order to cope with the extraordinary situation in the early years of Taiwan's postwar development and to maintain relations with the U.S. aid machinery, the KMT created a number of relatively autonomous economic agencies. These ad hoc organs maintained direct links with the top political leadership, and gave key economic officials an organizational base and the policy instruments to operate amid the confusion created by a large state-owned enterprise sector and the preservation of a complex and overlapping national and provincial political structure (Lin 1973, 40). It is important to understand the broad organizational structure of the economic bureaucracy, since it played a key role both in initiating the import-substitution process and in generating the reform proposals that propelled Taiwan toward export-oriented development. It is also particularly important to understand because the main sources of resistance to reform came not from civil society, but from within the government itself.

For the purpose of analyzing the development of ISI, the economic bureaucracy may be divided into three parts.[12] First were the agencies for economic planning. A series of bureaucracies performed similar functions, yet held different hierarchical positions and power during different periods.

As early as June 1949, before the central government moved to Taiwan, it authorized the provincial government to create a Taiwan Production Board to oversee the state enterprises that were relocated to Taiwan as well as properties inherited from the Japanese. The board was in charge of planning of production and supply for the companies, financing, export arrangements, and the disposal of Japanese indemnities. The TPB was nominally chaired by the governor of Taiwan (Ch'en Ch'eng, June to December 1949; Wu Kuo-cheng, December 1949 to April 1953; O. K. Yui, April to July 1953), but was actually directed by the vice chairman of the board, K. Y. Yin, a crucial figure in economic policy over the 1950s.

The Taiwan Production Board was absorbed into the Economic Stabilization Board (ESB) in July 1953. Before the merger, a special committee

---

12. A fourth important area was the organizations for agricultural development, the most interesting of which was the Joint (i.e., Chinese-American) Commission on Rural Reconstruction, which had virtual plenary powers in the agriculture reform area.

on economic and financial affairs had been formed in March 1951 to review and coordinate trade, payments, and monetary and fiscal policies in
the interest of stabilization. The ESB was an enlargement of that committee. The board consisted of five divisions: the first was responsible for industrial development planning; the second was in charge of utilizing U.S.
aid; the third assumed responsibility for controlling fiscal policy, including the state-owned enterprises; the fourth undertook planning for agriculture, forestry, and fishing; and the fifth was in charge of making
policies for controlling the price level.

The first division of the ESB was a key player in the evolution of ISI in
Taiwan, and assumed an important role in establishing relations with the
Taiwanese private sector. An Industrial Development Commission was
established as a subsidiary of the first division to implement the industrial parts of the first Four-Year Economic Development Plan, 1953-56,
which were drawn up by the ESB.

A second institutional complex was the agency for administering U.S.
aid, the Council for United States Aid (CUSA). CUSA was established in
1948 when the U.S. Congress passed a $500 million aid bill for China's re-
construction. This aid was suspended in 1949, but CUSA resumed operations in 1950. The functions of CUSA included the selection of aid
projects, oversight of the local currency or counterpart program, and
maintaining a liaison with the U.S. AID mission. In September 1958, the
Economic Stabilization Board was dissolved. On the one hand, inflation
had been curbed and its raison d'etre seems to have passed; on the other
hand, the ESB was considered as too powerful, with functions that over-
lapped with those of the regular ministries. These functions were for the
most part decentralized into the ministries of Economic Affairs and Communications, but the functions of macroeconomic planning and the utilization of aid, as well as the Industrial Development Commission, were
shifted into CUSA, which became the new superministry for overall economic planning.

A third organizational complex that deserves mention was the agencies for controlling foreign exchange and trade. To balance foreign trade
and payments, an Industrial Finance Committee was set up in June 1949
under the Taiwan Production Board. When the Taiwan Production Board
was merged into the Economic Stabilization Board, however, this committee was reorganized into an independent Foreign Exchange and Foreign Trade Committee, attached to the Taiwan provincial government
and supervised by the Ministry of Economic Affairs and Ministry of Finance. In 1955, an independent Foreign Exchange and Trade Control
Commission (FETCC) was established, which had a wide range of functions concerning the setting of the exchange rate, determining import re-

quirements, screening foreign exchange applications, and coordinating U.S. aid, all of which gave it tremendous power.

There are several features of this organizational structure that are important for understanding the nature of policy-making. First, the apparent complexity of the organizational structure and the constant changes they appeared to undergo was offset by a system that resembled interlocking directorates. For example, in 1955 the members of the Economic Stabilization Board included the governor of Taiwan (chair), the ministers of Finance, Economic Affairs, Communications, and National Defense, the chairman of the Joint Committee on Rural Reconstruction (JCRR), the secretary-general of CUSA, the commissioner of finance of the Taiwan provincial government, the chairman of the board of the Bank of Taiwan, and the chairman of the Industrial Development Commission. A similar story can be told for CUSA. Such overlaps created greater cohesion in the economic bureaucracy than might be apparent at first.

A second feature of this economic policy structure was its unusual organizational independence. With their budgets supported by U.S. aid, the institutions analyzed here all enjoyed a degree of financial independence. The one exception was the FETCC, and it, interestingly, had a particular reputation for patronage. Not only were the agencies financially independent; they were also exempted from normal civil service regulations, and were thus able to pay much higher salaries; in the early 1950s, as much a five times as high. This enabled the agencies to recruit and train highly competent staff, to attract talent, and to maintain an organizational esprit de corps.

This organizational autonomy had operational consequences that are summarized by Neil Jacoby in a discussion of CUSA:

> Being free of the need to obtain legislative approval of its expenditures, the Council was able to act speedily on developmental projects.... Whereas the top councils of the Chinese government were preoccupied with political and military problems of security and "return to the mainland," the Council could concentrate upon the development of Taiwan.... Had U.S. aid been part of the Chinese government's budget, and administered through the regular departments of government, its developmental effects would have been greatly diminished. (Jacoby 1966, 61)

A third feature of this structure was its surprising openness to penetration by American aid officials. American officials sat in on the meetings of the Economic Stabilization Board, Council on United States Aid, Joint Committee on Rural Reconstruction, and the Foreign Exchange and Trade Commission. Chinese officials actually had to hold meetings in English for the benefit of American advisers, who would make their case formally and informally for particular reforms (Gold 1986, 68-69). The re-

TABLE 1   Personnel Evolution of Key Economic Policymakers, 1949-63

Agency or Position and Date	Chairman	Vice Chairman	Secretary-General
Agencies for Economic Planning*			
6/49	Ch'en Ch'eng	K. Y. Yin	
12/49	Wu Kuo-cheng	K. Y. Yin	
4/53	O. K. Yui		
6/54	K. Y. Yin		
9/58	Ch'en Ch'eng	K. Y. Yin	K. T. Li
1/63	Ch'en Ch'eng	C. K. Yen	K. T. Li
Council for United States Aid			
(Prior to 9/58)			
3/50	Ch'en Ch'eng		
6/54	O. K. Yui		
8/57	C. K. Yen		
7/58	Ch'en Ch'eng		
Foreign Exchange and Trade			
Control Commission			
2/55	Hsu Peh-yuan		
3/58	K. Y. Yin		
1/63	Hsu Peh-yuan		
Minister of Economic Affairs			
2/50	C. K. Yen		
3/50	Cheng Tao-ju		
5/52	Chang Tse-k'ai		
6/54	K. Y. Yin		
12/55	Chiang Piao		
3/58	Yang Chi-tseng		
1/65	K. T. Li		
Minister of Finance			
3/50	C. K. Yen		
6/54	Hsu Peh-yuan		
3/58	C. K. Yen		
12/63	Ch'en Ch'ing-yu		
Bank of Taiwan and Central Bank			
of China (from 7/60)			
1951	Hsu Peh-yuan		
1952	O. K. Yui		
1953	Chang Tse-k'ai		
1960	K. Y. Yin		
7/60	Hsu Peh-yuan		

* Taiwan Production Board, 6/49-7/53; Economic Stabilization Board, 7/53-9/58; Council for United States Aid, 9/58-9/63.

sult was a particularly strong transnational alliance among aid donors and portions of the host government.

Table 1 reveals a final feature of the economic bureaucracy: the surprising continuity in personnel among a limited number of key individuals. The career paths of C. K. Yen and K. Y. Yin are particularly striking.

Thanks to a recent study by Alan Liu, we have a statistical comparison between forty-four economic policymakers and bureaucrats in the major economic policy-making institutions in the 1950s and 1960s with the 1957 members of the Central Standing Committee of the KMT (Liu 1989, 89-91). About 75 percent of the planners came from the coastal areas of China, particularly the three main centers of Western influence, Kwangtung, Chekiang, and Kiangsu provinces. Only 47 percent of the CSC members were born in the coastal provinces. Some 98 percent of the planners had a university education, while the proportion for the party members was a still high 70 percent; 52 percent of the planners had studied in the United States, as compared with 28 percent of the CSC members. These data suggest that the top planning staff, though often educated in engineering and science rather than economics (Yang 1984, 161-63), had a more cosmopolitan and liberal outlook than their political counterparts.

The Politics of ISI: Contending Policy Currents[13]

In general, there was a broad consensus among the Chinese planners and the Americans on the basic thrust of policy. As already discussed, the disastrous consequences of the great inflation on the mainland had a conservatizing effect on the KMT's macroeconomic policy, even if disagreements continued to persist about military spending and the state-owned enterprise sector. There was also broad consensus between the Americans and the Chinese on the importance of rural development. Through the JCRR, the United States was a vigorous advocate of land reform, not only for economic reasons, but on the political grounds that it was likely to promote stability and political development (see Simon 1988, and Montgomery, Hughes, and Davis 1964). The combination of the commission's joint Chinese-American structure, the high rank and political independence of the Chinese commissioners, and the concentration of technocratic expertise within its ranks made the JCRR suited to formulating and implementing reforms.

The Americans also concurred with their Chinese counterparts on the necessity of an import-substituting strategy. As in most developing countries, this policy regime initially emerged primarily as a result of severe

---

13. We have borrowed the term "policy currents" from Sylvia Maxfield.

external constraints. In April 1951, in response to the deteriorating external accounts position, strict import controls were imposed along with a multiple exchange rate system. High tariffs and full advance payment and licensing of all imports established the bias toward import-substitution. Export pessimism was widely accepted within the government, however, and buttressed the initial policy stance. Protected or preferential markets for Taiwan's sugar and tropical products were now closed—China's abruptly, Japan's as a result of its own reconstruction efforts—and ISI held powerful sway within the development policy community.

In the summer of 1954, an advisory mission headed by S. C. Tsiang and T. C. Liu, both then working at the IMF, advocated wide-ranging reforms, including the adoption of an exchange surrender certificate system that would allow the certificates to be traded freely on the market, an abolition of quantitative restrictions, and a flexible exchange rate for the available export earnings of foreign exchange (Tsiang 1980). These reforms were not adopted at that time, despite a dramatic decline in exports in 1954 and a recognition within the government itself that some action should be taken.

The reasons have to do with competing "policy currents" that combined ideological and institutional differences within the state with different social clienteles. These conflicts concerned the share of resources to be devoted to the military, the priority to be given to economic versus military objectives, the nature of the industrial policy regime, and the balance between the public and private sectors. Though the exact nature of the bureaucratic cleavages over policy remain somewhat obscure, the Bank of Taiwan, provincial political authorities, the managers of state-owned enterprises, and the members of the FETCC fell into the "conservative" camp. The military also was in this group, since it was the largest recipient not only of budget outlays, but of various subsidies and patronage through the state-owned enterprise sector as well. This camp was also supported by conservative elements within the party who gave priority to the task of recapturing the mainland and for whom the main "economic" priority was thus guaranteeing the maintenance of the military machine.

This group accepted the need for monetary stability and a balanced budget, but was reluctant to use financial instruments for the purpose of expanding private industry. Multiple exchange rates and trade controls were seen as instruments for limiting the flow of imports and maintaining a current account balance rather than as a way of fostering the growth of the private sector. Devaluation was opposed on the grounds that it would be inflationary, though the opportunities for rent-seeking provided by the FETCC's control over the allocation of foreign exchange were also no doubt important.[14]

Devaluation was also opposed on grounds of the export pessimism then prevalent. S. C. Tsiang recalls a debate in 1954 with a "well-informed" minister, who argued that exports of Taiwan's two major commodities, sugar and rice, were fixed by international agreement and bilateral negotiations with Japan respectively, and as a result were independent of the exchange rate. Tsiang, in turn, argued that devaluation would reveal those firms whose comparative advantage was hidden by an overvalued rate. K. T. Li recalls a similar "heated debate" in 1955 in the Economic Stabilization Board. Arguing that Taiwan should seek to exploit its comparative advantage by exporting textiles, he met the argument that "our textile industry could never compete successfully with Japanese manufacturers" (Tsiang 1980, 322; Li 1976, 100).

A central component of the conservative line was support for the state-owned enterprise sector. U.S. aid officials first became embroiled in this issue in connection with the compensation program of the land reform. In 1953, a Statute for Transferring Public Corporations to Private Ownership was passed, but the United States feared that without adequate government support, the aim of turning landlords into capitalists would not be realized. According to Dennis Fred Simon, T. K. Chang, the minister of Economic Affairs, was actually willing to turn all of the five corporations over to the landlords and to let them fail in order to make the point that private enterprise could not function without state support (Simon 1988). While the conservatives admitted that state businesses had been inefficient, they argued that this was not necessarily the case. Given the weakness of indigenous entrepreneurial talent, the state should be prepared to take a direct role in production by creating new enterprises and forming joint ventures with the private sector.[15] In the formulation of the second four-year plan in 1956, for example, an ambitious proposal for a steel mill using Philippine ore was elaborated, only to be shelved as a result of U.S. objections.

Underneath support for the state's control of the commanding heights was an unspoken (and thus necessarily speculative) political issue. Private sector growth would inevitably mean a strengthening of native Tai-

---

14. For an impressionistic account, see *Asian Survey* 1967.

15. A good introduction to this debate is the forum in *Industry of Free China* 1 (5) 1954, including particularly Shih-cheng Liu, "On the Development of Taiwan's Industry"; Fong Chang, "An Intermediate Course between Private Enterprise and Government Control"; and K. Y. Yin, "A Discussion of Industrial Policy in Taiwan."

wanese, who then might use their economic power for political ends. The United States, on the other hand, and the reformers as well, saw the strengthening of the private sector contributing to long-run political stability by co-opting the Taiwanese into the political system.[16]

This more conservative policy current was opposed by a "developmentalist" one. The "industrializing reformers" were headed politically by Ch'en Ch'eng, but their moving spirit was K. Y. Yin, who held a variety of key posts (see Table 1) and was head of the Industrial Development Commission from 1953 through 1955. The IDC was responsible for industrial planning and developing the island's industrial capacity. It was split into a number of sections, the most important of which was the General Industry Section. The IDC believed in strengthening the productive elements of the private sector, and maintained close relations with refugee capitalists from Shanghai and some of the larger Taiwanese capitalists. Through these direct connections, it sought to encourage investment in designated sectors, including plastics, glass, and plywood, but most importantly textiles.

The textile industry demonstrates clearly that the difference between the "conservatives" and the "developmentalist reformers" was not between state intervention and free markets, but over the *nature* of government intervention. As early as 1950, sectoral plans had been launched by the Taiwan Production Board for the revival of the textile industry with technical assistance from an American engineering firm, imported power looms from Japan, and U.S. aid in the form of raw cotton. CUSA's textile subcommittee, cooperating later with the IDC, acted directly to promote linkages between different segments of the industry by allocating raw cotton and yarn through industry associations.[17]

Through the state-owned Central Trust of China, the government intervened in the weaving stage. The Central Trust engaged in advance purchases and distributed yarn through a quota system to the textile guilds and their member mills, guaranteeing repurchase of the final product. Loans were available for plant expansion through CUSA. Applications were evaluated by J. G. White, an American consulting firm that operated as an arm of the aid mission and cooperated closely with the IDC in project evaluation. As K. Y. Yin explained, "while desiring to re-

---

16. The goal of politically strengthening the Taiwanese is implicit in the JCRR's work; see for example Montgomery, Hughes, and Davis 1964.

17. This draws on Thomas Gold, Dependent Development in Taiwan (unpublished Ph.D. dissertation, Harvard University 1980), 96ff. Gold's thesis is an indispensable source, containing fascinating information not available in his *State and Society in the Taiwan Miracle.*

store the free market for textiles, [the subcommittee] has not overlooked the possibility of such a free market being taken advantage of by speculators and profiteers" (1954a, 26).

The comment is suggestive. While Yin was a reformer who championed the development of the private sector, he was by no means in favor of laissez-faire. Like many of Taiwan's leading economic policymakers, Yin had an engineering background and combined arguments for liberalization with a defense of a significant role for the state in planning and allocating resources. The ultimate aim of industrialization, he argued, was to reduce dependence on American aid. This vision required a careful designation of those industries that were viable and in which Taiwan had a comparative advantage. Yin argued for protection from the "menace of unfair competition from abroad," government rationing of credit, foreign exchange, and raw materials, and licensing control over the investment decision-making process itself. Yin also underlined that state-owned industries would continue to have a place in an economy with a larger private sector.

The Incentives to Reform

Through the 1950s, the two policy currents described above coexisted. Intermediate goods industries developed by the Japanese such as fertilizer and chemicals continued to be run by the government, and public sector enterprises expanded, though not at the rate of the overall economic growth. At the same time, a significant battery of controls on trade, the allocation of foreign exchange, and the licensing of industrial activity remained in place, which contributed to high rates of substitution by private consumer goods manufacturers. The planners were frequently ahead of the private sector; larger projects that were included in government plans as highly promising had to be postponed because private capital was not forthcoming.[18] Nonetheless, the growth of the private sector is impressive.

Some sense of this process can be gathered from Table 2, which shows changes in the ratios of domestic supply to total supply. The nature of the data make it somewhat suspect, and suggest that these are best seen as estimates. Nonetheless, it is clear that import-substitution was not only

---

18. K. T. Li describes the difficulty of getting private investment in synthetic fibers, though these later became the fastest growing segments in the country (1976, 99).

TABLE 2   Changes in Ratios of Domestic Production to Total Supply
(By major subsectors of manufacturing, 1937, 1954, and 1961)

Manufacturing Subsector	Domestic Production as Percent of Total Supply		
	1937	1954	1961
Textiles and apparel	35.9	94.4	91.7
Wood and furniture	42.9	92.7	100
Paper and pulp	33.8	85.8	91.5
Leather goods	37.4	73.3	95.3
Rubber products	37.4	70.4	61.1
Chemical fertilizers	37.4	59.0	80.8
Pharmaceuticals	37.4	59.0	48.6
Plastics and products	37.4	59.0	80.2
Other chemicals	37.4	59.0	63.2
Petroleum products	52.0	87.9	94.3
Cement	52.0	87.9	100
Other nonmetallic mineral products	52.0	87.9	94.3
Iron and steel products	66.1	63.9	70.6
Aluminum and products	66.1	63.9	99.1
Other metal and metal products	66.1	63.9	49.9
Machinery	66.1	32.9	28.2
Household and electrical appliances	66.1	41.8	42.5
Communication equipment	66.1	41.8	42.5
Transport equipment	66.1	55.7	68.0
Total	40.4	77.0	75.7

Source: Lin 1973, 66.

quite far advanced in the consumer goods sectors, but in several intermediate goods as well. Also striking is the increasing dependence on imported machinery, an indication of the increased investment that was
taking place over the 1950s.

What, then, accounts for the change in policy course? Clearly, a major
factor is an evolution in both the views and political position of the "developmentalists" within the bureaucracy, who in turn were influenced by
changes in the economy. By the mid-1950s, the economy was experiencing a number of difficulties typically associated with ISI. The first was
market saturation and slowed growth. GNP growth rates dropped every
year from 1952 through 1956. Per capita consumption did not increase at
all in 1956, and only marginally in 1957. K. Y. Yin and others also began
to recognize the bias against exports, driven home by the sluggish performance of the mid 1950s and the ongoing problem of foreign exchange
(Yin 1973, vol. 2, 29-35).

As elsewhere, the overvaluation of the exchange rate also encouraged
arbitrage at the expense of productive activity. In 1954, K. Y. Yin already

complained about the "profiteers" who "in the name of factories they have founded with negligible capital and symbolic or make-believe equipments, scramble for the privilege of obtaining foreign currency allocation or import quota" (Yin 1954c, 2). The concern with inefficiency, corruption, and the growth of a rent-seeking complex figure in a number of the reform debates.

Finally, there were important changes in the international environment that altered the possibilities for reform. These came both from the overall security and aid contexts, but both ultimately had to do with positions taken by the United States.

The question of Taiwan's security was by no means a settled one in the mid-1950s. In 1954, the PRC attacked the offshore island of Tachen; one observer argues that this may explain the sluggishness of investment from 1954 through 1958 (Jacoby 1966, 89). On 23 August 1958 the PRC began a massive bombardment of Quemoy, apparently on the assumption that the United States would not intervene. This proved mistaken. The United States quickly deployed both naval and air forces to the area, and sharply warned Beijing that it would not hesitate to use force in defense of Quemoy and Matsu. The U.S. Navy began to escort Nationalist supply ships, even if they stayed clear of the three-mile zone, and Taiwan acquired new military hardware from the United States. By the end of September 1958, the bombardment slowed.

Though weathering the crisis was a foreign policy success for the KMT, it also highlighted conflicts of interest between Washington and Taipei over the importance of the offshore islands for the future of Taiwan. Even those who supported defense of Taiwan questioned intervention in support of Quemoy and Matsu. Seeking to counter criticism of his policies at home, Secretary of State Dulles argued that the United States would favor a reduction of Nationalist forces on the islands, and reiterated that the United States had no commitment to help the KMT retake the mainland.[19]

Chiang Kai-shek reacted to Dulles's pronouncements by rejecting any reduction of the forces on the offshore islands. To mediate the emerging conflict between Washington and Taipei, Dulles visited Taiwan on 21 October. Dulles obtained Chiang's agreement to a reduction of forces on the islands by 15,000 in exchange for an increase in weaponry. In a joint communiqué issued on 23 October, the two governments recalled that the Mutual Defense Treaty of 2 December 1954 was defensive, and that unification would not be achieved by forceful means. This strengthened those

---

19. For a review of this incident, see Clough 1978, 18–20.

advocating greater attention to economic development, and weakened somewhat the claims of the conservatives and the military establishment.

The second international change concerned aid policy. Partly as a result of budgetary and balance of constraints, partly as a result of new thinking about the relationship between economic growth and political stability, U.S. aid policy began to pay greater attention to purely developmental objectives. On the one hand, United States aid policy advanced the goal of making aid recipients self-sufficient over the longer run, gradually weaning them from aid. At the same time, however, there was a willingness to provide increased amounts of aid in the short run for the purpose of supporting particular policy reforms. Both the short-term carrot and the longer-term stick of reduced commitments accelerated the reform process.

The operation of these factors can be seen in more detail by examining the course of three reform efforts: those affecting the exchange rate and trade regime; the passage of the Nineteen-Point Program; and the passage of the Statute for the Encouragement of Investment.

The Politics of Reform 1: Foreign Exchange and Trade Reform

We have already noted that prevailing economic ideas and models of the economy constituted one barrier to trade and exchange rate reform. Given the inelasticity of world demand for Taiwan's exports and the country's dependence on imports, it was argued that devaluation and trade liberalization could result in a deterioration of the country's terms of trade and a return of inflationary pressures.

The ideas of T. C. Liu and S. C. Tsiang, advanced initially in their 1954 consulting mission, constituted an intellectually coherent counter to these claims. As the balance of payments situation worsened, their ideas began to attract increasing attention within the bureaucracy.[20] They had particular appeal because of the growing problems of corruption on the part of the exchange control agencies and the collusive practices on the part of business. In a lecture in June 1954, K. Y. Yin had already advocated a series of reforms that included the following measures:

---

20. See, for example, Liu 1957 and Hsing 1954, which advocated the exploitation of comparative advantage and influenced K. Y. Yin.

1. Auctioning imported raw materials, or if that proved impractical, allocating them preferentially to the most cost-competitive firms;
2. Easing restrictions on the establishment of new firms, though with continued limits on minimum size and quality;
3. Limiting protection to prespecified periods;
4. Making greater efforts to expand manufactured exports;
5. Passing an antitrust law with import liberalization used selectively to counter local monopolistic arrangements. (Yin 1973, vol. 2, 30-35.)

In July 1955, however, Yin was forced to resign all of his posts because of a court case involving a local firm that had defaulted on a loan from the Central Trust of China, which Yin headed. The case was triggered by a member of the Legislative Yuan who questioned Premier O. K. Yui in a session about the suspicion of collusion in the loan. In part because of personal rivalries over policy-making jurisdictions, O. K. Yui did not come vigorously to Yin's defense. Yin's enemies both within and outside the bureaucracy took advantage of the opportunity to attack him, and the pace of reform slowed (see Shen 1972, 264; Hu 1964, 398-400).

In September 1956, the court cleared Yin. He returned to the government in August 1957 as the secretary-general of the Economic Stabilization Board. Shortly thereafter he was promoted to a variety of other posts, including chairman of the FETCC in March 1958, vice chairman of CUSA in September 1958, and chairman of the board of the Bank of Taiwan in July 1960. While it is wrong to attribute too much to any one individual, Yin's powers came to include oversight of U.S. aid use; foreign exchange, trade, and monetary policy; and overall economic planning!

As the reaction to Yin's alleged involvement in the China Trust case showed, however, the issue was not merely one of ideas or individual bureaucratic positions. Certainly, the beneficiaries of preferential access to foreign exchange and high levels of protection could be expected to resist liberalizing reforms, even though there was a growing recognition that some new measures were required. In 1957, the Provincial Assembly of Industries appealed to the Ministry of Economic Affairs to permit firms to organize on a cartel basis to limit competition. According to K. T. Li, the government was "pestered" by business with "requests to restrict the construction of new plants in their fields on the grounds that production had already saturated the domestic market" (Li 1976, 99). Among the planners, there was a search for new secondary import-substituting industries, including chemicals, rayon fiber, urea, plastics, and even autos, an approach championed in particular by those supporting the state-owned enterprise sector.

If the KMT as a whole was quite autonomous from local capital, particular portions of the government had their own institutional interests.

The trade and exchange controls instituted in the early 1950s resulted in a steadily growing set of bureaucratic structures to manage them. These structures became the center of an important rent-seeking "complex" built on a predictable set of practices, including excessive regulation, red tape, and licensing, which resulted in administrative corruption. When K. Y. Yin sought to reform and simplify the system, he encountered resistance from officials in the FETCC (Liu 1980, 51).

At the end of 1957, when foreign-exchange problems worsened, Chiang Kai-shek personally nominated a nine-man group to address the problem. The involvement of the head of state in the issue was a signal of its importance, and reflected the growing awareness that the problem was not merely a short-term cyclical one, but was tied to the probability that aid would decline in the medium run (Yin 1959, 2-21).

Headed by Ch'en Ch'eng, the group included O. K. Yui (premier), Hsu Peh-yuan (chairman of the FETCC and minister of Finance), K.Y Yin (secretary-general of the ESB), and C. K. Yen (chairman of CUSA). The meetings reflected the general splits described above, with Hsu Peh-yuan in particular arguing that the existing system contributed to stability and that the overemphasis on the market would hurt, rather than help, the development of Taiwan's industry. K. Y. Yin argued that the system had triggered both inefficiency and corruption, and, perhaps crucially, that the reforms would not prove inflationary. The liberal line was backed by the top political leadership. As a result, Hsu and several other conservatives resigned, Yin quickly submitted his proposal for exchange and trade reform, and it was passed in a meeting of the Central Standing Committee on 9 April 1958.

The reform aimed at simplifying the exchange rate system, loosening import restrictions, and encouraging exports. The unification of the exchange rates was executed in several steps. In April 1958 the multiple rates were first consolidated into two buying rates in parallel with two selling rates. Further simplifications were made during following years, and by October 1963 a foreign-exchange system with a single exchange rate was instituted.

Even more significant was the devaluation. Before the reform, the average rate of the New Taiwan dollar was about 25 to one U.S. dollar. In November 1958 the rate was adjusted to about 36 to 1, and finally in July 1960 to 40 to 1, at which point the difference between the official exchange rate and the black market rate was virtually eliminated.

In the wake of these reforms, exports began to expand rapidly, and the success of the reform quickly became self-reinforcing. While the exchange rate reform certainly played a central role in this process, it is important to underline a variety of complementary measures that were of a decidedly more interventionist sort. These interventions served the function of reducing the risk of shifting into the export business by providing various premia to exporters and reducing information and transactions costs; they also call into question an interpretation that emphasizes solely the role of market-oriented reforms.

Taiwan has not used the financial system as an instrument of industrial policy to the same extent that Korea has (Liang and Skully 1982). Dominated by state-owned banks, Taiwan's financial system remained underdeveloped. Interest rates have been set by the government, reliance on collateral has been typical, and over the 1950s a strong public-sector bias operated, with state-owned enterprises absorbing more than half of the outstanding loans and discounts. In July 1957, however, the Bank of Taiwan launched an export loan program under which short-term loans were extended to exporters to finance the entire production chain of their export operations. Firms were granted credit lines on the basis of past export performance and future plans. The effective subsidy could be substantial. Loans repayable in foreign currencies carried a 6 percent interest rate, those in local currencies 12 percent. By contrast, loans available through the financial system to private sector borrowers ranged between 20 and 22 percent. Though the interest differentials narrowed over time, they remained large into the 1970s.

The close association that developed between the government and private sector associations in Korea is not as prominent in Taiwan. Nonetheless, several important sectoral associations performed functions supportive of export activity, effectively cartelizing trade in some sectors (Lin 1973, 108-9). These groups collected dues from members to be placed into a cooperative fund, out of which bonuses were paid to exporters. Firms were allocated export targets, and made to pay penalties for falling short. In the case of the cotton textile industry, only 40 percent of total output could be sold on the home market, with excesses subject to penalty. These arrangements were overseen by government agencies, and covered significant sectors of Taiwan's export industry over the 1960s, including cotton and woolen textiles.

There are reservations about the extent of import liberalization even in neoclassical accounts of Taiwan's growth.[21] The tariff system coupled high rates with various offsetting packages. Import liberalization did not, therefore, become a divisive political issue until the late 1970s (Chou 1985). While the government did reduce duties on those raw materials and intermediates required by exporters, it "financed" this decrease in

---

21. Studies of import liberalization include Lee et al. 1975, and Lee and Liang 1982, both of which find a number of redundant and high tariffs, particularly in the "import-competing" category. See the review of these studies in Wade 1988.

critical customs revenues with increases on the rates of duty on finished goods. An additional offsetting package was the rebate of both customs duties and commodity taxes on imported raw materials, without which the export of many categories of products would not have been possible. Exporters were also allowed to use a portion of their foreign exchange earnings to import raw materials for sale to other end users, in effect granting local monopoly rents as a reward to export performance. Though this premium declined over the 1960s, and was finally abolished under IMF pressure in 1970, it provided additional windfalls to the early exporters. Chou refers to this administratively complex system as one of "import tariffs-cum-export rebates" or "domestic sales subsidizing export sales," a system in which the domestic consumer bears the ultimate cost and the government exercises significant discretion (ibid.).

The removal of quantitative restrictions (QRs) was not dramatic either (Wade 1988). In addition to luxury goods, goods produced by state monopolies, and goods affecting national security, domestic producers were allowed to apply to limit the import of other items. These items had to meet the following criteria: first, local producers had to be able to satisfy domestic demand; second, quality had to be reasonable; and third, the price, inclusive of tariffs, could not exceed a certain margin above the price of comparable imports. In 1960, this margin was 25 percent, lowered only gradually over the 1960s.

In sum, the "liberalization" of the trade and exchange rate regime was focused primarily on the exchange rate, and was driven by two considerations: both short-term and longer-run concerns about foreign exchange, and concerns about the growth of a corrupt, rent-seeking complex around the foreign-exchange control system. While this did result in some losses for those with preferential access to foreign exchange, and weakened the exchange control portions of the bureaucracy, it was not accompanied by substantial liberalization except in those categories of goods required by exporters. The critical conflicts both within and outside the bureaucracy that might have arisen around import liberalization were effectively sidestepped.

The Politics of Reform 2:
The Nineteen-Point Program
of Economic and Financial Reform

The formulation of the Nineteen-Point Program was tied more immediately to American influence than the exchange rate reform, though that influence was achieved by positive inducements. By 1956, Taiwan had regained its prewar level of per capita GNP, and the American aid mission felt that greater attention should be given to sustaining growth through institutional and legal reforms. In early 1955 AID's presentation of the 1956 aid program for Taiwan to the U.S. Congress already had proposed various policy reforms (Jacoby 1966, 33). Congress, however, continued to define aid policy in the context of cold war objectives: defense support, direct forces support, and surplus agricultural commodities continued to be the dominant instruments of policy. AID thus had to rationalize assistance for economic development within the loose statutory definition of "defense support."

In 1958, with the inauguration of the Development Loan Fund, Congress began to appropriate aid for developmental purposes. In the same year, an Office of Private Enterprise was established within AID as well. These changes brought the long-standing objectives of the AID mission in Taiwan into closer alignment with U.S. policy.

The parallel change within the KMT toward a more "domesticist" and developmental orientation was signaled in February 1958 when Chiang Kai-shek ordered the organization of an ad hoc Administrative Reform Committee to examine the issues of organization, personnel, budgeting, and regulations of the entire state machinery. Modeled on the Hoover Committee in the United States, the committee presented eighty-eight proposals for reform, many of which concerned economic management. There is still some debate about the importance of this reform effort, in part because the combined effect of institutional reforms is difficult to measure.[22] The Administrative Reform Proposal did signal the government's commitment to organizational and institutional changes, however, and fed into the comprehensive Nineteen-Point Program that followed shortly thereafter.

In the area of public finance, the committee recommended an improvement in the tax structure and administration by eliminating regressive and indirect taxes and increasing the income tax, while improving the independence of local governments by expanding their access to revenues. Regarding the monetary system, the proposals focused on the development of a modern credit system by reactivating the Central Bank of China and some other public banks, setting up a stock market, opening a life insurance industry, and increasing the flow of loans to the private

---

22. K. T. Li and Ch'en Mu-tsai argue that the reforms had a powerful influence on subsequent developments (1987, vol. 1, 188). Wang Tso-jung, by contrast, argues that the committee was not effective, and by disbanding the ESB and other measures actually reduced state capacity to intervene (1978, 56-57). The following account of the reform measures draws on Li and Ch'en, pp. 182-88.

sector. A variety of measures aimed at increasing national savings and capital formation, including raising interest rates, shortening depreciation periods, reducing business taxes, and lowering tariffs for the import of capital goods.

Other reforms aimed at restructuring the system of economic management. The laws governing the state enterprise sector were revised in order to strengthen the evaluation of their performance. Various regulations that had hampered the operations of the private sector were to be abolished, and the utilization of American aid was to be coordinated in such a way as to expand the benefits flowing to the private sector.

The emphasis on economic issues was naturally interrupted by the Taiwan Straits crisis. In 1959, however, Under Secretary of State C. Douglass Dillon and Deputy Director of AID Leonard Saccio visited Taiwan in October and December respectively. Both of them indicated that the United States was willing to render increased assistance to the government if a program for accelerated economic growth was advanced by the government (Liu and Tso 1980, 6). This was the first signal of the change in U.S. aid policy, which was now offering positive inducements to model recipients.

On 20 December 1959 Wesley C. Haraldson of the AID mission sent an outline of an Accelerated Development Program to the CUSA. In the outline, Haraldson underlined Taiwan's advantages, while also noting the advantages of reform for the country's foreign-exchange position:

> [By] maximizing sound economic growth for the next four or five years, thereby attaining a condition where the needed future growth will be self-generated, [Taiwan will eliminate] the need for foreign aid except for heavy items of military equipment and some surplus agricultural commodities. It is expected that in this process Taiwan will prove increasingly attractive to foreign investors and will also be able to establish an enviable international credit rating. (Quoted from an official file in the Council for Economic Planning and Development)

To accomplish these objectives, Haraldson proposed an eight-point program of action:

1. A "firm decision" to reduce the amount of resources for military purposes;
2. Noninflationary fiscal and monetary policies;
3. Tax reforms to remove disincentives to business;
4. A uniform and realistic exchange rate, a process that had already begun;
5. Liberalized exchange controls;
6. Establishment of a utilities commission to give public utility management the freedom necessary to operate efficiently;

7. Establishment of banking machinery with simplified investment rules to attract more capital from the public;

8. Sale of state enterprises to the private sector.

Ten days later, a meeting was held in Ch'en Ch'eng's official residence to discuss the outline. In addition to Ch'en and Haraldson, C. K. Yen, K. Y. Lin, and K. T. Li, three of the most prominent technocratic reformers, were also present. At the meeting, Haraldson explained that while U.S. aid was declining globally due to recession and balance of payments considerations, the government had decided to showcase a number of countries, both for the purpose of accelerating their growth and for demonstrating the superiority of the market system over a Communist one. Taiwan was on the list because of its previous performance, but in order to convince Congress a concrete reform plan was required. Urgency was needed if the plan was to be included in the foreign aid program for 1961.

Ch'en Ch'eng, long a supporter of a "domesticist" approach, was positive on the reforms, though he expected divergent opinions in the Legislative Yuan, and some resistance to the creation of a utilities commission, particularly since it was likely to result in an upward revision of rates. He agreed to the program in principle and promised a formal government response.

On 4 January a memorandum together with the minutes of the meeting were submitted to Chiang Kai-shek, and a meeting convened with the president on 7 January, attended by the same trio of leading economic policymakers. Ch'en Ch'eng emphasized that the reform measures would be advantageous for the economy regardless of the availability of additional assistance. While the exact reasons for Chiang's support cannot be known precisely, K. T. Li has emphasized the importance of arguments concerning Taiwan's independence. According to Li, Chiang supported the reforms primarily because they would enable Taiwan to give up American aid and to become self-reliant (Li and Ch'en 1987, 189).

Among the eight proposals, the reduction of military expenditures and utility rates presented the biggest potential problems; the military budget, which the Americans wanted to cut quite drastically, was anticipated to generate the sharpest resistance.

On a suggestion by C. K. Yen, the planners advanced the proposal that national defense expenditures be frozen in 1961 at their 1960 level, implying a real reduction. Surprisingly, Chiang accepted this, a change in posture that would have been impossible prior to the positive outcome of the Taiwan Straits crisis.

At the meeting, it was also decided to establish a public utility commission outside the Legislative Yuan. The commission would be attached to the Executive Yuan and in charge of drafting a formula for calculating rates. The Legislative Yuan would have input into the formula, but not set prices per se. Once the formula was determined, the commission had the ability to adjust the price automatically on the basis of changes in the components of the indicator. This proposal constituted a particularly clear example of the ability of the technocrats to devise institutional solutions for insulating themselves from political pressures.

After receiving a positive response from the top political leadership, K. Y. Yin was charged with drafting a formal response. At that point, a number of economic policymakers argued that the program was not comprehensive enough and that the moment could be exploited to enlarge the scope of the program. Drawing on the recommendations of the Administrative Reform Committee and the Foreign Exchange and Trade Reform, Yin extended the program to cover nineteen points, adding measures that would encourage savings, establish central banking, liberalize trade selectively, fully utilize government production, adjust salary payments, and diminish hidden subsidies to government employees.

On 14 January a formal document—the Accelerated Economic Growth Program—was sent to Haraldson from K. Y. Yin, summarizing the goals of the third Four-Year Economic Plan period (1961-64) and listing the Nineteen-Point Program. Haraldson was particularly interested in clarifying the commitment to reduced military expenditures, but his interpretation of the document was accepted by the KMT government, and the program was passed by the Central Standing Committee on 23 March.

Because the program had been presented as an internal administrative reform, despite its extensive scope, it did not have to be sent to the Legislative Yuan for approval, though the party did solicit the views of legislators through a Policy Coordination Commission. In the legislature, a committee was set up to monitor the program, and a formal report was issued in June 1961 covering its implementation. According to the report, every measure was implemented to a certain degree. An Industrial Development and Investment Center was established, headed by K. T. Li. A China Development Corporation, with financing from the party, was set up and all of the other reforms—salary adjustments, the launching of a stock market, and so forth—were undertaken.

Two measures were not taken on schedule, however, and they were the ones on which some resistance was anticipated. Probably influenced by the disastrous outcome of the Great Leap Forward, which appeared to present military opportunities for the KMT, expenditures in 1961 were not kept to 1960 levels; indeed, increases even exceeded the rise in prices. Electricity rate adjustments also lagged, partly as a result of resistance from the legislature, partly due to fears of fueling inflation.

The application of American pressure appears to have played an important role in overcoming resistance to these measures. American advisers had initially promised an additional loan of US$20-30 million in support of the program. The promised amount was reduced to US$20 million as a penalty for the failure to reduce military expenditures. Military spending was subsequently brought under control. A mission threatening to withhold assistance was also used to secure compliance with the electricity rate change. With the promise to approve proposed aid to construct new power plants, AID obtained compliance with the rate realignment in 1962 (Jacoby 1966, 135).

It is an interesting indicator of the relationship between the government and the private sector that the opinions of business leaders regarding the reforms were only solicited *after* the program had been drafted. Major business leaders were invited to attend a conference in 1961, where they were asked to air their views of economic policy. This conference was significant in allowing local industrialists to express opinions, but was not institutionalized.

It has been argued that the Nineteen-Point Program, like its predecessor, the Administrative Reform Committee, was less successful than is often maintained (Wang 1978, 61-62). As an internal document, it lacked the same status as a law, while many officials did not fully understand its implications or even opposed it as a product of CUSA, which was viewed with some suspicion. Moreover, the reform process slowed somewhat following the death of K. Y. Yin in January 1963. Nonetheless, even critics agree that the program initiated institutional reforms that had significant longer-term effects.

The Politics of Reform 3:
The Statute for the Encouragement
of Investment

We have suggested that the central change in KMT strategy toward the economy over the 1950s was increasing attention to the role of the private sector. In the early 1950s, "developmentalists" were able to use the preferential allocation of foreign exchange, access to U.S. aid, and preferential loans to advance industrial development. While these did result in both economic and political distortions, they also contributed to the creation of a domestic capitalist class. As inflation came down, access to inputs was improved through selective import liberalization and the gap between official and black market rates was reduced, the scope for policy intervention narrowed. Indicative of the continuing dirigisme within the planning bureaucracy was the effort to meet the new situation through the promulgation of new incentives.

The government had passed two investment laws over the 1950s, the Statute for the Encouragement of Foreign Investment (July 1954) and the Statute for the Encouragement of Overseas Chinese Investment (November 1955). Both statutes allowed investors to use foreign exchange freely to import capital goods and raw materials in connection with investments. The dim political and economic prospects of the island in the mid-1950s overwhelmed the effects of these new incentives, and, given the American aid commitment, the need to attract foreign capital was not pursued vigorously. This perspective changed with the recognition that aid was going to decline.

Three problems deterred both local and foreign investment in the late 1950s: the tax burden; the complexity of the procedures governing investment licensing; and the acquisition of plant sites. While the first two are self-evident, the third is less so. To prevent weakening the land reform and the reconcentration of rural assets, the government laid down extremely strict regulations limiting land alienation. Though measures had been drafted to deal with each of these three problems, such as tax exemptions and tariff rebates for exporters, planners favored a special law that would include comprehensive measures to address all three problems simultaneously.

Again, this approach was typical of the particular autonomy that CUSA enjoyed, both within the government and vis-à-vis civil society. Ch'en Ch'eng assigned CUSA the major role in drafting the statute precisely because he wished to avoid the interference, conflicting goals, and resistance from particular interests that would have affected the course of the law in other organizational settings. Similarly, the Industrial Development and Investment Center, set up to consolidate the investment application process, was placed in CUSA rather than elsewhere specifically at Ch'en Ch'eng's command.

An example of the conflicts that plague such comprehensive efforts was the measures governing tax reductions. Tax exemptions and deductions naturally affected the authority of the Ministry of Finance, which, institutionally, took a conservative stance toward incentives and tried to reduce their scope. The minister of finance, however, was none other than C. K. Yen, who, unlike his subordinates, favored action for improving the investment climate, in effect, shifting resources from the public to the private sectors (Chou 1982, 15).

The salient points of the statute included an income tax holiday, a preferential business income tax rate, tax exemptions for undistributed profits, tax deductions for exports, and various other exemptions and reductions. The effects of the statute were quite significant. Total refunds of income, stamp, and commodity taxes, and customs duties totalled 5.1 percent in 1958, jumped to 11.5 percent in 1960 following the institution of a rebate on customs duties for exporters, but jumped again to 23.2 percent in 1962 following the passage of the statute (Kuo, Ranis, and Fei 1981, 76).

Conclusion

The reform process in Taiwan was facilitated by a peculiar political system, one in which the top political leadership and the economic bureaucracy were relatively unconstrained by entrenched social forces. Under the ISI regime pursued in the early 1950s, firms evolved that benefitted from protection and preferential access to foreign exchange, but business had little political power and was restricted in its ability to move capital out of the country. In any case, the reform process never directly confronted the new firms in the consumer goods sector because import liberalization was quite limited.

The major political story has to do with the contending policy currents within the bureaucracy itself. Economic performance, corruption, and a changed security environment were all important in reducing the influence of what we have called the "conservative" line. A recurrent pressure for reform, however, was concern over foreign exchange, whether in the form of particular foreign exchange shortages, such as in late 1950 and early 1951, short-term manipulation of aid flows, as in 1960-61, or the expectation over the longer run that aid would be curtailed.

In all of the important reform episodes, the interest of the president was directly engaged, and reformers were thus able to secure backing from the highest political levels. While we emphasize that the organizational design of the policy-making bureaucracy was important in maintaining the autonomy of the planners, it is important to underscore that this autonomy ultimately rested on the broader structure of political power within and outside the KMT.[23]

These points can be demonstrated by comparing Taiwan's transition to export-led growth with Korea's. The origins of ISI in both countries are quite similar. Both countries faced severe problems of reconstruction from war and a severing of traditional export markets. Both countries

---

23. This important point concerning the nature of bureaucratic "autonomy" is a theme of Eliza Willis, The Politicized Bureaucracy: Regimes and Presidents in Brazilian Development (1989).

were tightly integrated into the American security orbit as a result of the Korean War. Both became dependent to roughly equal degrees on aid for the financing of ISI. In both countries, ISI policies fostered the growth of an indigenous private sector (Haggard, Kim, and Moon 1989).

At a general level, there are also interesting similarities in the configuration of social forces in the two countries. In both countries, the power of rural elites was broken early; there was no rural counterweight to the government's interest in industrialization, no sectoral conflict such as that seen in many Latin American countries. Partly because of their external political situations—divided countries facing Communist adversaries—little ideological or organizational space was allowed for socialist, leftist, or populist forces, nor was labor allowed much of an independent voice. ISI was therefore not a child of populist political forces, and when the transition to export-led growth was launched, both systems had weak labor movements.

There are, however, interesting differences between the two countries in state structure and political history that date to the period of decolonization and account for differences in their respective development trajectories. The most obvious is the nominally democratic nature of the Korean political system imposed by the Americans, compared to the one-party structure in Taiwan. Rhee's need to build political support contributed to a particular inconsistency in policy. Efforts to develop a planning capacity were overridden or neglected by central political authorities, and technocratic resources were therefore scattered, and lacked political support or an organizational base. On Taiwan, by contrast, both political control and planning capacities were more highly developed.

These differences in political and institutional structure affected the ability of the United States to exercise policy leverage. In Taiwan, close working relationships developed between Chinese and Americans operating in relatively insulated fora. In Korea, by contrast, the influence over policy was closely guarded at the top with little delegation to technocrats.

In both cases, the combination of foreign exchange constraints and the manipulation of aid played some role in the reform process. The extent of dependence in the two countries was virtually unprecedented, but it was only when the United States began to link aid to policy reform that leverage was effective. In Korea, Park Chung Hee attempted to resist by pursuing other channels of funding, including Japanese aid and commercial borrowing. In Taiwan, the transition was smoother, but in both cases, political leaderships were ultimately sold on the grounds that they would increase independence; ironically, a strategy depending heavily on world markets had the attraction of increasing self-reliance.

The comparison between Taiwan and Korea demonstrates that external pressures are not enough to explain reform; distinctive institutional and political capabilities also mattered. Pressured to change course, facing annual stabilization programs and declining growth, Rhee failed to respond. In both Taiwan and Korea, the policy transition was preceded by centralizing administrative reforms that reflected an alliance between high-level political authority and reformist technocrats. In Korea, these reforms came in the wake of a change of regime by the military. In Taiwan, they were more gradual, but organizational similarities are clear.

While these capabilities allowed for comprehensive policy reform, they also modified its nature in a statist direction. The government in both cases relied on a variety of microlevel interventions that had the effect of reducing risk to exporters operating for the first time in uncertain international markets. The "liberalization" in the two East Asian NICs thus came to have a distinctly mercantilist cast.

Bibliography

Amsden, Alice. 1985. The State and Taiwan's Economic Development. In *Bringing the State Back In*, edited by Peter Evans, Dietrich Rueschemeyer, and Theda Skocpol. Cambridge: Cambridge University Press.

Apthorpe, Raymond. 1979. The Burden of Land Reform in Taiwan. *World Development* (April-May).

Asian Survey. 1967. The Political Roles of Taiwanese Entrepreneurs. *Asian Survey* 7 (September): 645-54.

Bedeski, Robert. 1981. *State-Building in Modern China: The Kuomintang in the Pre-War Period.* Berkeley: Institute of East Asian Studies, Center for Chinese Studies.

Chang, Fong. 1954. An Intermediate Course between Private Enterprise and Government Control. *Industry of Free China* 1 (5).

Ch'en, Ch'eng. 1961. *Land Reform in Taiwan.* Taipei: China Publishing Co.

Chen, Yu Hsi. 1978. Rural Transformation in Mainland China and Taiwan: A Comparative Study. *Social Praxis* 5 (1-2).

China Yearbook, 1963-64. 1964. Taipei: China Publishing Co.

Chou, Shun-hsin. 1963. *The Chinese Inflation.* New York: Columbia University Press.

Chou, Tien-Chen. 1985. The Pattern and Strategy of Industrialization in Taiwan: Specialization and Offsetting Policy. *The Developing Economies* 23 (2) (June): 138-57.

Chou, Yu-kou. 1982. Hsi-shu t'sai-ching shou-chang ti pei-ching (A detailed account of the backgrounds of the leading economic officials). In *Ch'eng-chang ti t'ung-k'u* (Growing pains). Taipei: Commonwealth Publishing Co.

Chung-hua min-kuo nien-chien 1950 (Yearbook of the Republic of China 1950). 1951. Taipei: Chung-hua min-kuo nien-chien she.

Clough, Ralph. 1978. *Island China.* Cambridge: Harvard University Press.

Coble, Jr., Parks M. 1980. *The Shanghai Capitalists and the Nationalist Government, 1927-1937.* Cambridge: Harvard University Press.

Deyo, Fred, editor. 1988. The Political Economy of the New Asian Industrialism. Ithaca: Cornell University Press.

Djang, T. K. 1977. *Industry and Labor in Taiwan.* Nankang, Taipei: Academica Sinica.

Eastman, Lloyd. 1974. *The Abortive Revolution: China Under Nationalist Rule, 1927-1937.* Cambridge: Harvard University Press.

Gold, Thomas. 1980. Dependent Development in Taiwan. Unpublished Ph.D. dissertation, Harvard University.

——. 1986. *State and Society in the Taiwan Miracle.* Armonk, New York: M. E. Sharpe.

——. 1990. Origins of Development Strategies: The Nationalist Chinese State on the Mainland and Taiwan. In *Development Strategies in Latin America and East Asia,* edited by Gary Gereffi and Dony Wyman. Princeton: Princeton University Press.

Haggard, Stephan, Byung-kook Kim, and Chung-in Moon. 1989. The Transition to Export-Led Growth in Korea, 1954-1966. Cambridge: Harvard University, Committee for Research on Political and Social Organization Working Paper.

Ho, Samuel. 1978. *Economic Development in Taiwan, 1895-1970.* New Haven: Yale University Press.

Hsiao, Hsin-Huang Michael. 1981. *Government Agricultural Policies in Taiwan and South Korea.* Nankang, Taipei: Academica Sinica.

Hsing, Mo-huan. 1954. Ching-chi chiao-lian yu ching-chi chen-ch'e (Economic comparison and economic policy). *Industry of Free China* (October).

Hu, Kuang-piao. 1964. *P'o-chu liu shih nien* (An age of drifting with the current). Hong Kong: Hsin-wen t'ien-ti she.

Jacoby, Neil. 1966. *U.S. Aid to Taiwan: A Study of Foreign Aid, Self-Help, and Development.* New York: Praeger.

Kerr, George. 1965. *Formosa Betrayed.* Boston: Houghton Mifflin.

Kuo, Shirley W. Y., Gustav Ranis, and John C. H. Fei. 1981. *The Taiwan Success Story: Rapid Growth with Improved Distribution in the Republic of China, 1952-1979.* Boulder, Colorado: Westview Press.

Lee, T. H., K. S. Liang, Chi Schive, and R. S. Yeh. 1975. The Structure of Effective Protection and Subsidy in Taiwan. *Economic Essays* (Taipei) 6 (November).

Lee, T. H., and K. S. Liang. 1982. Taiwan. In *Development Strategies in Semi-Industrial Countries,* edited by Bela Balassa. Baltimore: Johns Hopkins.

Li, K. T. 1976. *The Experience of Dynamic Economic Growth on Taiwan.* Taipei: Mei Ya Publications, Inc.

Li, K. T., and Ch'en Mu-tsai. 1987. *Chung-kuo ching-chi fa-chan ch'e-lueh tsung-lun* (Introduction to the development policies of the Chinese economy), vol. 1. Taipei: Lien-ching Publishing.

Liang, C., and M. Skully. 1982. Financial Institutions and Markets in Taiwan. In *Financial Institutions and Markets in the Far East: A Study of China, Hong Kong, South Korea and Taiwan*, edited by M. Skully. London: Macmillan.

Lin, Ching-yuan. 1973. *Industrialization in Taiwan, 1946-1972: Trade and Import-Substitution Policies for Developing Countries*. New York: Praeger.

Liu, Alan P. L. 1989. *Phoenix and the Lame Lion: Modernization in Taiwan and Mainland China, 1950-1980*. Stanford: Hoover Institute Press.

Liu, Feng-wen. 1957. Kai-shan wai-hui chih-tu ch'u-i (My humble view for the improvement of the foreign-exchange system). Unpublished ms.

———. 1980. *Wai-hui mao-i cheng-ts'e yu mao-i k'uo-chan* (Foreign exchange, trade policies, and trade expansion). Taipei: Lien-ching.

Liu, Min-ch'eng, and Hung-t'au Tso. 1980. *Kai-shan t'ou-tzu huan-ching* (Improvement of the investment climate). Taipei: Lien-ching.

Liu, Shih-cheng. 1954. On the Development of Taiwan's Industry. *Industry of Free China* 1 (5).

Lundberg, Erik. 1979. Fiscal and Monetary Policies. In *Economic Growth and Structural Change in Taiwan*, edited by Walter Galenson. Ithaca: Cornell University Press.

Montgomery, John, Rufus Hughes, and Raymond H. Davis. 1964. Rural Improvement and Political Development: the JCRR Model. AID Survey Report, unpublished.

National Archives RG (Record Group) 59. 1950a. Taiwan Monthly Economic Report, March 1950. RG 59, 894A.00/4-1250. National Archives, Washington.

———. 1950b. Telegram, Taipei to Secretary of State #565, 8 April 1950. RG 59, 894A.00/4-850.

———. 1951. Dean Rusk to Dr. V. K. Wellington Koo, 13 March 1951. RG 59, 794A.5MAP/3-751.

———. 1953. Embassy dispatch, 14 September 1953, RG 59, 794A.00/9-1453.

———. 1954. Summary Analysis of Formosa's Major Economic Problems, FS Dispatch #397, 11 January 1954. RG 59, 894A.00/1-1154.

Olson, Mancur. 1983. *The Rise and Decline of Nations*. New Haven: Yale University Press.

Riggs, Fred. 1952. *Formosa Under Chinese Nationalist Rule*. New York: Macmillan.

Shen, Yun-lung. 1972. *Yin Chung-jung hsien-sheng nien-p'u ch'u-kao* (Biography of K. Y. Yin). Taipei: Cheng-chung Books.

Simon, Dennis Fred. 1988. U.S. Assistance, Land Reform, and Taiwan's Political Economy. In *Contending Approaches to the Political Economy of Taiwan*, edited by Edwin Winckler and Susan Greenhalgh. Armonk, New York: M. E. Sharpe.

Sun, Yat-sen. [1922] N.d. *The International Development of China*. Taipei: China Cultural Service.

———. [1924] N.d. *San Min Chu I* (The three principles of the people), translated by Frank Prince. Taipei: China Publishing Co.

Tien, Hung-mao. 1972. *Government and Politics in Kuomintang China, 1927-1937*. Stanford, California: Stanford University Press

Tsiang, S. C. 1980. Exchange Rate, Interest Rate, and Economic Development. In *Quantitative Economics and Development*, edited by Mark Nerlov, Lawrence Klein, and S. C. Tsiang. New York: Academic Press.

———. 1984. Taiwan's Economic Miracle: Lessons in Economic Development. In *World Economic Growth*, edited by Arnold Harberger. San Francisco: Institute for Contemporary Studies.

———. 1985. *Taiwan ching-chi fa-chan ti ch'i-shih* (Lessons from the economic development of Taiwan). Taipei: Commonwealth Publishing Co.

Tucker, Nancy Bernkopf. 1980. Nationalist China's Decline and Its Impact on Sino-American Relations, 1949-50. In *Uncertain Years: Chinese American Relations, 1947-1950*, edited by Dorothy Borg and Waldo Heinrichs. New York: Columbia University Press.

Wade, Robert. n.d. Sweet and Sour Capitalism: Industrial Policy Taiwan Style. Unpublished manuscript.

———. 1988. State Intervention in Outward-Oriented Development: Neoclassical Theory and Taiwanese Practice. In *Developmental States in East Asia*, edited by Robert Wade and Gordon White. London: Macmillan.

Wang, Tso-jung. 1978. *Wo-men ju-ho ch'uang-chao-le ching-chi ch'i-chi* (How we created the economic miracle). Taipei: China Times.

Wilbur, C. Martin. 1983. *The Nationalist Revolution in China, 1923-1928*. New York: Cambridge University Press.

Willis, Eliza. 1989. The Politicized Bureaucracy: Regimes and Presidents in Brazilian Development. Boston College, unpublished manuscript.

Yager, Joseph. 1989. *The Joint Committee on Rural Reconstruction*. Ithaca: Cornell University Press.

Yang, Chi-wei. 1986. Hsing-hsien i-lai cheng fu tsung-t'ung yu ke-k'uei ti ch'uan-li-kuan-hsi (The power relationships between president, vice president and premier since promulgation of the constitution). In *Taiwan wei-lai lin hsiu* (The leadership of Taiwan in the future). Taipei: Feng-yun lun-t'ang she.

Yang, Hsu-sheng. 1984. Taiwan ching-chi ti lin-hang-jen (The pilots of Taiwan's economy). In *T'ou-shih ching chi ch'iang-jen* (Gaining a perspective on the economic strong men). Taipei: Ching-chi-jen tsa-chi she.

Yang, Martin M. C. 1970. *Socio-Economic Results of the Land Reform in Taiwan*. Honolulu: University Press of Hawaii.

Yin, K. Y. (Yin Chung-jung). 1954a. The Development of the Textile Industry in Taiwan. *Industry of Free China* 1 (1).

————. 1954b. A Discussion of Industrial Policy in Taiwan. *Industry of Free China* 1 (5).

————. 1954c. Adverse Trend [sic] in Taiwan's Industrial Development. *Industry of Free China* 2 (2) (August).

————. 1959. A Review of Existing Foreign Exchange and Control Policy and Technique. *Industry of Free China* 12 (5) (November).

————. 1961. A Decade of U.S. Economic Aid and Economic Development in Taiwan. *Industry of Free China* 15 (6) (June).

————. 1973. *Wo-tui Taiwan ching-chi ti k'an-fa* (My views on Taiwan's economy). Taipei: Economic Planning Council.

4

Taiwan's Persistent Trade Surpluses: The Role of Underdeveloped Financial Markets

Wing Thye Woo
Liang-Yn Liu

Introduction

Taiwan's huge trade surpluses and rapid accumulation of foreign exchange reserves in the 1980s stand in sharp contrast to the trade deficits and debt crises that plague many developing countries. While Taiwan's performance is enviable, these trade surpluses do have important negative consequences. First, the current account surpluses are inflationary. In the absence of sterilized foreign exchange market interventions, the increase of net foreign assets expanded the domestic money supply and brought upward pressure on prices. Second, the large trade surpluses have fueled calls in the industrialized countries for protectionist legislation. Third, the accumulation of foreign assets is inefficient because the foreign rates of return are lower than the domestic rates of return.[1] Because of these three unforeseen effects, Taiwan's trade sur-

---

1. B. Balassa and J. Williamson (1987) assert: "It does not make sense, in terms of future development or current welfare, to place 20 percent of GDP in low-yield-

pluses are increasingly viewed as undesirable by both domestic and foreign observers.

The most commonly recommended prescription for Taiwan's trade surplus problem is appreciation of the NT$. Taiwan's biggest trade partner, the United States, has been particularly insistent on this solution as the quid pro quo for not levying discriminatory measures against Taiwan's exports. As a consequence of this standard economic advice and U.S. political pressure, Taiwan appreciated its currency 32 percent against the U.S. dollar in the 1985-88 period. But the ameliorative effects on the trade account have been extremely slow in coming. The trade account surplus continued upward from US$11 billion in 1985 to US$20 billion in 1987 before falling to US$14 billion in 1988. The United States still regards the present trade surplus as too big and is demanding further appreciation of the NT$.

While there is little doubt that further currency appreciation would eliminate the trade surpluses, our research suggests that currency appreciation alone is not the best way to solve the trade surplus problem. Our conclusion is that currency appreciation would be optimal only if the existing structure of Taiwan's economy and the present stance of Taiwan's macroeconomic policies cannot be changed. Since this is clearly not the case, Taiwan's welfare could be improved by keeping the NT$ at the level which maintains current export volume and eliminating the trade surplus through changes in the structure of Taiwan's economy and in Taiwan's fiscal policy.

Our analysis is based on two observations. The first is that Taiwan's trade account, unlike those of other countries with big surpluses, has shown a secular tendency toward accelerating surplus since 1970 (interrupted by the periods immediately after the oil price shocks). The second observation is that the trade surplus did not begin to increase rapidly until 1981, the year that the Reagan budget trade deficits began soaring upward. These observations suggest that internal factors may be responsible for a significant portion of the persistent trade surpluses, and that the swinging U.S. budget deficits are only partly responsible for the unusually large trade surpluses of the 1980s. The focus of this study is on how much of the current account surpluses of Taiwan are due to domestic fac-

---

ing foreign assets." And M. Fry (1988) confirms: "Despite the declining trend in rates of return on Taiwan's capital stock, at least until 1986, these estimates support the assumption made by Balassa and Williamson (1987) that domestic investments in Taiwan still yield rates of returns that are high relative to returns on investment opportunities available in the rest of the world."

tors. This is an important question because its answer tells us whether the inevitable (and long overdue) elimination of the U.S. budget deficits would also end the present trade tensions.

Since the current account position equals the difference between national saving[2] and domestic investment, it is thus natural to view Taiwan's burgeoning trade surplus as the result of its rising saving rate. Many analysts have alleged that Taiwan's high saving rate reflects a national psychological insecurity that demands a large financial cushion to guard against possible adversity, and a cultural penchant for sizable bequests to future generations. We do not deny the validity of these two factors in determining saving behavior, but unless we reject consumer sovereignty (private preference) as the guide to policy choices we cannot deem the resulting high saving to be economically inefficient. The high saving can be regarded as undesirable only if it is caused by distortions in the market system. We believe that such a distortion exists in Taiwan, and that a significant portion of the high saving is due to it.

Our theoretical analysis suggests that Taiwan's chronic trade surpluses have been caused by the interaction among four factors: the undeveloped state of the domestic long-term financial markets, the restrictions on capital flows, the high rates of return to domestic investment, and the lumpiness of investment goods. Since a major reason for the secular rise in Taiwan's current account balance has been the inability of its financial institutions to match the supply of saving with the demand for fixed capital, an important part of the efficient solution to Taiwan's current account balance lies in developing its long-term financial markets.

This study is organized as follows. Section I compares Taiwan's trade surpluses with those of Japan, Germany, and Korea—countries also with large trade surpluses and also the targets (except for Germany) of U.S. protectionist wrath. Section II provides an overview of the financial system to show how it has distorted saving and investment behavior. In Section III, we provide a model of private saving and investment decision-making when capital markets are highly fragmented. Section IV then presents some simulation results based on our saving-investment model. Exchange rate management is discussed in Section V. We conclude with some policy recommendations.

---

2. We follow the usual convention of using *saving* to mean the amount saved in the period and *savings* to mean the accumulation of each period's saving.

I. Taiwan's Trade Surpluses in a Comparative Perspective

To understand the role of domestic factors in generating external imbalance, we focus on the national income accounting identity:

$$X - M = (S_1 - I_1) + (S_2 - I_2) + (T - G)$$

where

X = exports of goods and services (plus net factor income from abroad)

M = imports of goods and services

S_1 = gross private saving

I_1 = gross private investment

S_2 = gross saving of public enterprises

I_2 = gross investment of public enterprises

T = total taxes

G = government expenditure

A country's current account balance (X-M) is the sum of its excess saving (i.e., saving minus investment and its government budget balance). The private sector comprises households and private businesses. Households cover both individual (worker, farmer, and nonfarm proprietor) households and private nonprofit institutions. The government sector includes the central government, the state/local government, and the social security funds. The public enterprise category is an ambiguous one. Its analytical classification depends on the degree to which public enterprises pursue objectives similar to those of private enterprises. To the extent that they have been structured toward maximizing profits for their owner (the government), they could be combined with the private sector category. However, if the public enterprises are so heavily regulated that their managers run the firms under the civil service code, they should be classified with the government sector. This is because their saving and investment behavior are so independent of market-based criteria that these decisions are effectively policy instruments.

Table 1 presents the saving-investment decomposition of the current account balance for Taiwan and Japan. In Taiwan's case, the current account surplus has tended to increase over time since 1970—a trend that has been masked by the two OPEC shocks. The current account position soared from -1 percent of GNP in 1969 to 7 percent in 1972 before being halted by the quadrupling of oil prices in 1973-74. The upward trend

TABLE 1   A Decomposition of Current Account Balance for Taiwan and Japan (percent of GNP)

			TAIWAN							JAPAN			
(1)	(2)	(3)	(4)	(5)	(6)	(7)	(8)	(9)	(10)	(11)	(12)	(13)
Year	Current Account	Private Sector Savings	Private Sector Investm't	Government Balance	Public Enterprises Investm't	Public Enterprises Investm't	Current Account	Private Sector Savings	Private Sector Investm't	Government Balance	Public Enterprises Savings	Public Enterprises Investm't
1965	-2.02	14.16	15.69	0.79	3.71	4.99	1.01	25.51	23.20	2.43	0.64	4.37
1966	0.96	16.21	13.95	0.66	3.22	5.18	1.18	26.27	23.02	1.78	1.00	4.85
1967	-1.61	16.35	15.48	0.67	3.82	6.98	-0.15	27.38	26.44	2.07	1.62	4.78
1968	-2.76	13.97	16.02	1.56	4.54	6.82	0.70	29.08	28.03	3.16	1.05	4.56
1969	-0.70	13.87	14.34	2.13	5.24	7.60	1.23	29.12	29.48	3.91	1.55	3.87
1970	0.01	17.34	15.41	0.80	4.63	7.36	0.98	32.00	31.13	2.48	1.13	3.49
1971	2.61	20.55	15.72	1.43	4.25	7.89	2.52	29.86	27.31	2.50	0.93	3.45
1972	6.54	21.66	15.64	3.99	4.07	7.54	2.19	30.74	26.13	0.44	1.06	3.92
1973	5.29	25.44	19.14	3.79	2.97	7.77	-0.03	30.83	28.58	0.36	1.18	3.82
1974	-7.77	19.82	24.46	5.07	3.50	11.70	-1.03	29.09	28.28	1.45	0.59	3.88
1975	-3.86	15.76	13.05	2.73	4.08	13.37	-0.14	28.69	23.59	-1.31	-0.00	3.92
1976	1.60	19.70	14.52	3.68	4.56	11.82	0.67	29.79	22.97	-2.77	0.36	3.74
1977	4.25	20.77	14.10	2.30	4.37	9.09	1.58	28.71	21.58	-2.36	0.56	3.75
1978	6.04	21.83	15.74	4.20	4.41	8.66	1.70	29.58	20.85	-3.86	0.76	3.92
1979	0.55	20.76	20.18	4.78	4.30	9.11	-0.86	27.72	22.45	-3.30	0.85	3.67
1980	-2.24	20.04	17.68	2.52	4.96	12.08	-1.02	26.97	22.84	-2.84	0.99	3.29
1981	1.13	19.94	15.41	1.94	5.36	10.71	0.41	26.69	21.92	-1.89	0.80	3.27
1982	4.83	19.86	11.68	0.15	5.46	8.96	0.63	26.25	21.28	-2.07	0.74	3.01
1983	8.70	21.37	11.73	1.30	5.17	7.40	1.76	26.26	20.03	-2.18	0.48	2.77
1984	12.10	21.83	12.16	1.78	6.16	5.51	2.79	26.33	20.46	-0.78	0.41	2.71
1985	15.30	22.04	9.36	1.27	5.97	4.62	3.70	26.63	21.47	0.67	0.01	2.14
1986	20.80	28.96	8.79	-0.90	4.99	3.46	4.37	27.27	21.11	0.30	-0.08	2.00
1987	16.59	30.38	11.14	-2.04	3.76	4.37	3.65	NA	NA	NA	NA	NA

Sources: Taiwan: *Taiwan Statistical Data Book, 1981-88; Financial Statistics, Taiwan District*, May 1989.
Japan: *IFS Yearbook*, 1988; *OECD National Accounts*, vol. II, 1983-88; *Japan Statistical Yearbook*, 1972-75.

soon reasserted itself. The current account surplus grew from -4 percent of GNP in 1975 to 6 percent in 1978. This trend was then interrupted by the 1979-80 doubling of oil prices.

The current account surpluses of Taiwan in the 1983-88 period are extraordinary by historical standards. The biggest surplus prior to 1983 occurred in 1972 and it was 6.5 percent of GNP. This figure is puny compared to the 15.3 percent in 1985, 20.8 percent in 1986, and 16.6 percent in 1987. The huge surpluses of the 1980s came from historically unprecedented high private saving rates and from historically unprecedented low private investment rates (see columns 3 and 4 of Table 1). The private saving rate in 1986 was 9 percentage points higher than in 1981; and the private investment rate was 7 percentage points lower. Throughout the 1965-83 period, the excess saving in the private sector and the government budget surplus were used to finance the deficits of the public enterprises (see columns 6 and 7). But public enterprise investment has declined continuously since 1984, hence contributing to the widening of the trade imbalance.

Japan's current account performance is reported in column 8 of Table 1. Japan's current account is also normally in surplus but it shows no upward trend in the pre-1983 period. While Japan's surplus did accelerate from 1983 on, the rise was proportionately much less than Taiwan's. Japan's current account surplus in 1986 was only 1.7 times larger than its pre-1983 peak, compared with 3.2 times in Taiwan. What is most interesting is that, unlike Taiwan, the main source for Japan's enlarged surplus in the 1980s was not the private sector. Japan had quite stable private saving and investment rates. The excess saving in the private sector showed little tendency to increase after 1983. The larger trade imbalances after 1983 appear to come from smaller deficits in the government and public enterprise budgets.

For Germany and Korea (see Table 2), the saving and investment data of their public enterprises are not available. Public enterprise behavior is subsumed within the private sector data. The current account of Germany, the second largest trade surplus country, did not reach historically unprecedented levels until 1986. The large surpluses in 1985 and 1986 appear to come from low investments coinciding with higher government budget surpluses. There is nothing unusual about savings, investment, and government budget behavior in these two years; all three fell within their historical ranges—see columns 3, 4, and 5 in Table 2.

Korea, unlike Taiwan, did not display a trend toward larger current account surpluses in the 1970s because its investment rate rose in line with the saving rate. The movement of the current account balance in the 1980s was dramatic. It jumped from -2.1 percent of GNP in 1983 to -1.1 percent in 1985 and then to 8.3 percent in 1987. The extraordinary per-

Wing Thye Woo and Liang-Yn Liu

TABLE 2   A Decomposition of Current Account Balance for Germany and
Korea (percent of GNP)

| (1) | (2) | GERMANY | | (5) | (6) | KOREA | | (9) |
| | | (3) Private & Public Corpora- | (4) Private & Public Corpora- | | | (7) Private & Public Corpora- | (8) Private & Public Corpora- | |
Year	Current Account	tions Savings	tions Invest't	Govern- ment Balance	Current Account	tions Savings	tions Invest't	Govern- ment Balance
1965	-1.42	21.92	24.18	0.83	0.26	7.92	11.80	4.14
1966	0.08	21.46	22.39	1.02	-2.72	11.64	17.15	2.79
1967	2.03	21.58	19.43	-0.12	-4.05	9.19	17.21	3.96
1968	2.23	22.53	20.78	0.48	-7.38	10.75	19.71	1.58
1968	1.25	21.04	22.37	2.59	-7.34	14.82	21.21	-0.95
1970	0.46	21.81	22.96	1.62	-7.07	10.43	19.90	2.40
1971	0.44	20.99	22.21	1.65	-8.72	10.44	19.87	0.71
1972	0.45	21.11	21.83	1.16	-3.42	14.21	17.61	-0.03
1973	1.48	19.93	21.40	2.94	-2.21	19.89	22.15	0.04
1974	2.78	20.32	18.03	0.49	-10.88	18.17	28.05	-1.00
1975	1.05	20.93	15.96	-3.91	-9.08	16.19	25.71	0.44
1976	0.83	20.52	18.07	-1.62	-1.09	18.81	21.81	1.91
1977	0.77	18.95	17.75	-0.43	0.03	23.20	24.14	0.97
1978	1.42	19.90	17.79	-0.69	-2.19	23.26	27.09	1.63
1979	-0.74	19.98	19.99	-0.73	-6.54	22.15	31.19	2.51
1980	-1.71	19.25	19.96	-1.00	-8.81	16.93	26.35	0.61
1981	-0.50	19.02	17.73	-1.78	-7.01	16.28	24.61	1.32
1982	0.75	19.16	16.91	-1.49	-3.82	17.90	24.01	2.30
1983	0.82	19.58	17.87	-0.89	-2.11	20.71	25.22	2.39
1984	1.55	19.62	18.05	-0.01	-1.67	23.25	27.15	2.23
1985	2.72	19.21	17.17	0.69	-1.06	23.72	26.38	1.60
1986	4.43	20.77	16.79	0.45	4.85	27.84	25.78	2.78
1987	4.02	NA	NA	NA	8.31	30.38	25.94	3.88

Sources: Germany: *IFS Yearbook*, 1988; *OECD National Accounts*, vol. II, 1983-88.
         Korea: *IFS Yearbook*, 1988; *Economic Statistics Yearbook*, 1983, 1984, 1988, The Bank
         of Korea.

formance of the current account in 1986 and 1987 came mainly from a big
surge in the private saving rate. It increased from 23 percent in 1984 to 28
percent in 1986, and then to 30 percent in 1987. The larger government
budget surplus in 1985 and 1986 also made a minor contribution toward
enlarging the trade surplus. In sum, all four countries experienced substantial current account improvements from 1983 on, but only Taiwan
displayed a trend of increasing current account surplus before that. The
reason for the rise in the current account balance and in the private saving rate of these four countries after 1983 was the Reagan budget deficits,
which were financed by foreign borrowing. The rise in the saving rates of
the four countries were the result of the common recognition that the ex-

port-driven income growth was temporary. But since Taiwan's current account balance had shown an upward tendency throughout the 1970s, it is unlikely that all of the post-1983 saving rate increase could be attributed to the U.S. budget deficit shock. It is hence necessary to explain this secular trend in terms of private saving and investment behavior.

II. The Structure of the Financial System

In this section we sketch out the features of Taiwan's financial system that have shaped domestic saving and investment. This provides the empirical basis for the theoretical model to be presented in the next section.

The financial institutions in Taiwan consist of the Central Bank of China, domestic commercial banks, local branches of foreign banks, medium and small business banks, credit cooperatives, investment and trust companies, the postal savings system, and insurance companies. The first five types of financial institution are monetary institutions because they can create money, and the last three types are nonmonetary institutions. The financial institutions are supervised by both the Ministry of Finance and the Central Bank of China.

Of the four financial markets (money market, foreign exchange market, bond market, and equity market), the money market is the best organized. This is because there are four sets of institutions competing to provide short-term working capital—the monetary institutions, the non-monetary institutions, big enterprises, and the illegal curb market.[3] It is possible that the value of transactions in the curb market may not be much smaller than that in the legal money market. The enormous size of the curb market reflects the general underdevelopment of the financial infrastructure and the absence of long-term financial markets for funds to flow to.

When Taiwan abandoned the fixed exchange rate in July 1978, a small number of banks were allowed to trade foreign exchange under tight restrictions. Short-term capital movements are officially discouraged, and this was also true of long-term capital outflows until recently. Long-term capital inflows are freely allowed only into targeted industries. The result of the official restrictions in the foreign exchange market is that the do-

---

3. See Lee and Tsai (1988) for a critical view of the operations of the legal money market, especially of the limited participation by the big enterprises.

mestic rates of return are only weakly linked with those in international financial markets.

The long-term bond market is surprisingly underdeveloped for a country at Taiwan's economic level. This is largely because almost all the domestic banks are owned and controlled by the government. The foreign bank branches, although numerous, are restricted with respect to both operations and locations. Moreover, one-half of the domestic banks were established as specialized banks for specific policy purposes with little or no competition from other financial institutions (Cheng 1986). Stringently conservative lending guidelines combined with the fact that loan officers are personally responsible for bad loans have prevented the banks from becoming a significant intermediary of investment funds to borrowers. This happens especially when the borrower is a small private firm. Bank loan officers favor large firms over small ones, and public enterprises over private ones.[4] Loans from the medium business banks and the credit cooperatives cannot fill the intermediation vacuum because they operate under even tighter restrictions.

The postal savings system has grown tremendously under preferential treatment. Its share of the total assets of all financial institutions has grown from 0.66 percent in 1961 to 11.53 percent in 1986.[5] However, the postal savings system is prohibited from extending loans to the public. All the saving deposits collected are redeposited in the Central Bank of China and in various specialized banks.

The equity market is even more underdeveloped than the bond market. Because of highly bureaucratic underwriting procedures, the equity market has relatively few listed companies. There is, however, no shortage of funds flowing into the equity market, especially in the wake of the surge in the saving rate since 1984. What is lacking is new equity issues. The result has been extraordinarily high turnover ratios (the transaction value of listed stocks divided by the market value of listed stocks) in the last few years. Taiwan's average turnover ratio during the period of 1983-87 was 1.13 compared with 0.60 in the United States and 0.49 in Japan.

As a first approximation, the fixed capital financing component of Taiwan's financial system can be described as insulated and undeveloped (fragmented). Since long-term financing is denied to most enterprises, private agents have to accumulate large savings in order to purchase lumpy capital to capture the high rates of return.

---

4. Shea and Kuo (1984) provide evidence of the second bias.

5. See the Central Bank of China (Taiwan, R.O.C.), *Financial Statistics Monthly*, various issues.

III. Saving-Investment Behavior
in the Absence of a Domestic Equity Market

In Section I we documented that most of the excess saving in Taiwan are from the private sector; and in Section II we observed the near absence of organized long-term lending to small and medium enterprises. We now impose our Section II finding upon a life-cycle model to generate the saving and current account patterns of Section I.

The life-cycle model is the central idea in the modern theory of saving because it provides the link between the microeconomics of rational individual behavior and the macroeconomics of saving rate. It hypothesizes that individuals maximize an intertemporal utility function subject to the constraint of lifetime resources. The insight is that people save during working years for consumption during retirement; that is, there is a "humped" pattern of saving over an individual's lifetime. In the standard life-cycle model, the aggregate household saving rate increases with (1) the ratio of the retirement span to the life span, (2) the rate of population growth, and (3) the rate of productivity growth (Horioka 1984).

For our purpose, we amend the standard life-cycle model in four ways. The first amendment is to consider the model in a semiopen economy setting. Semiopen in this case means that there are binding quantitative restrictions on private capital flows but not on private merchandise trade. The second amendment is that the rates of return on investment i are greater than both the regulated domestic bank deposit rate and the foreign interest rate. The third amendment is that there are no long-term bond market and equity market. The fourth amendment is that investments are lumpy, i.e., there is a minimum size for a factory. The first amendment allows the second amendment to be possible. The second, third, and fourth amendments together dictate that an investor has to accumulate a threshold amount of savings before his or her investment can be undertaken. Given the required investment amount (which equals the savings target), the labor income stream, the working span, and the life span, we can derive the person's optimal consumption/saving behavior and calculate the time (age) of the individual's investment.

We emphasize that the agents in our model have "target savings" only because investments are lumpy. Agents invest only because the high rate of return i makes investing the utility-maximizing thing to do. Our agents are *not* "target savers" in the sense that ownership of an enterprise in itself boosts utility. We interpret the great number of small- and medium-sized enterprises (SMEs) in Taiwan to be caused by the low amount of fixed capital needed for setting up low-tech industries. By the World Bank's definition of an SME, where the number of employees is fewer than 100, SMEs account for more than 98 percent of Taiwan's enterprises in the 1961-85 period. We ignore the possibility that the great number of SMEs reflect a culturally unique desire by Taiwanese to be their own bosses as far as possible.

We assume that people do not have bequest motives,[6] live for D periods, and have additive separable utility functions. Agents face the decision of whether to invest at some future date or not. Agents calculate the respective utility for the two options, and choose the higher utility option.

Option 1: Save for Investment and for Retirement

The individual's choice problem is given by

$$\text{Max} \sum_{t=0}^{D} (1 + \delta)^{-t} \left\{ \frac{1}{1-\gamma} c_t^{1-\gamma} \right\}$$

Subject to

$$\sum_{t=0}^{D} c_t (1 + r)^{-t} = \sum_{t=0}^{T_1} y_t (1 + r)^{-t} - \sum_{t=0}^{T_1} s_t (1 + r)^{-t} + iK_0 \sum_{t=T_{1+1}}^{D} (1 + r)^{-t}$$
$$+ K_0 (1 + r)^{-D} \tag{1}$$

$$\sum_{j=0}^{t} (c_j - y_j) (1 + r)^{t-j} \leq 0, \ t = 0,...,T_1 \tag{2}$$

$$c_t \geq 0, \ t = 0,...,D \tag{3}$$

where

δ = time preference rate

γ = degree of constant relative risk aversion

r = real deposit interest rate

y_t = labor income at time t

---

6. This assumption can be relaxed by presuming that the utility over time is a homogeneous function of planned bequests as well as of planned consumption. This allows us to simply add one more term in the utility function in the model.

s_t = saving *from nonbank interest income* at time t

c_t = consumption at time t

i = rate of returns on investment

T_1 = period when investment is undertaken

K_0 = minimum required amount of investment

Equation (1) is the lifetime budget constraint, the present discounted value of the consumption stream equals the present discounted value of the revenue stream. The investor receives a labor income every period before T_1 and earns the returns of investment after only T_1. The investor earns the returns of investment till she dies.

If the investor retires at time T, which is larger than T_1 and less than D, the last two terms of the right-hand side of equation (1) would be changed to

$$\ldots + iK_0 \sum_{t=T_1+1}^{T}(1+r)^{-t} + K_0(1+r)^{-T}$$

The last term on the right-hand side of equation (1) is due to the assumption of no inheritance. Equation (2) represents the constraint against borrowing on the capital market: the individual must have a non-negative net holding of liquid assets in each period before the investment time.

Since the total amount of investment is exactly the accumulation of saving plus the interest income before T_1, K_0 can be expressed as

$$K_0 = \sum_{t=0}^{T_1} s_t (1+r)^{T_1-t} \tag{4}$$

Individual's saving is defined here as nonbank interest income minus consumption

$$s_t = y_t - c_t, \quad t = 0, \ldots, T_1 \tag{5}$$

Equation (5) implies that all of the bank interest income is saved.

Substituting equations (4) and (5) into the constraint (1), we get

$$R \sum_{t=0}^{T_1} c_t (1+r)^{-t} + \sum_{t=T_1+1}^{D} c_t (1+r)^{-t} = R \sum_{t=0}^{T_1} y_t (1+r)^{-t} \qquad (6)$$

where

$$R = \frac{i(1+r)^D - i(1+r)^{T_1} + r(1+r)^{T_1}}{r(1+r)^D}$$

And R is greater than one due to the assumption of $i > y > 0$ and $D > T_1 > 0$.

Using the Lagrangean for the model, with multipliers λ and μ_t ($t = 0,...,T_1$), and solving the Kuhn-Tucker conditions, we can derive the optimal consumption stream for $0 \leq t \leq T_1$ and $T_1 + 1 \leq t \leq D$ respectively:[7]

$$c_t = \lambda^{-1/\gamma} R^{-1/\gamma} \left(\frac{1+r}{1+\delta}\right)^{t/\gamma} , \ t = 0,...,T_1 \qquad (7)$$

$$c_t = \lambda^{-1/\gamma} \left(\frac{1+r}{1+\delta}\right)^{t/\gamma} , \ t = T_1 + 1,...,D \qquad (8)$$

where

$$\lambda = \left(\frac{\beta_1}{\beta_2 + \beta_3}\right)^{-\gamma}$$

and

$$\beta_1 = R \sum_{t=0}^{T_1} y_t (1+r)^{-t} ,$$

$$\beta_2 = R^{1-1/\gamma} \sum_{t=0}^{T_1} \left(\frac{1+r}{1+\delta}\right)^{t/\gamma} (1+r)^{-t} ,$$

---

7. To simplify the optimization procedure, we can first assume for each period $y_t > c_t$, $t = 0,...,T_1$; and, such condition indicates all the μ_t, $t = 0,..., T_1$ are equal to zero. Then, if we found the optimal derived consumption is greater than the labor income for some certain periods, we would set these periods' μ_t to be nonzero and come back to reoptimize the problem.

$$\beta_3 = \sum_{t=T_1+1}^{D} \left(\frac{1+r}{1+\delta}\right)^{1/\gamma} (1+r)^{-t}$$

It is noteworthy that when the interest rate is greater than the time preference rate, the stream of consumption depends on an individual's degree of relative risk aversion. The higher the degree of relative risk aversion, the slower is consumption growth.

From (7) and (8), the optimal saving paths are:

$$s_t = y_t - \lambda^{-1/\gamma} R^{-1/\gamma} \left(\frac{1+r}{1+\delta}\right)^{1/\gamma} , \quad t = 0,...,T_1 \tag{9}$$

$$s_t = iK_0 - \lambda^{-1/\gamma} \left(\frac{1+r}{1+\delta}\right)^{1/\gamma} , \quad t = T_1 + 1,...,D \tag{10}$$

We note that the optimal consumption streams (7) and (8) are functions of the unknown value T_1. To solve for the investment time T_1, we substitute equation (9) into equation (4). We then put the T_1 solution into the equations (7), (8), (9), and (10) to get the representative individual's optimal consumption and saving streams over one's lifetime under the situation of a noncapital market. The utility level of Option 1 is obtained by substituting the optimal consumption stream into the utility function.

Option 2: Save Only for Retirement

In this case the individual maximizes her utility function subject to the constraints

$$\sum_{t=0}^{D} c_t (1+r)^{-t} = \sum_{t=0}^{T} y_t (1+r)^{-t} \tag{11}$$

$$\sum_{j=0}^{t} (c_j - y_j)(1+r)^{t-j} \leq 0 , \quad t = 0,...,T \tag{12}$$

$$c_t \geq 0 , \quad t = 0,...,D \tag{13}$$

where T is the individual's retirement time and taken to be exogenous.

Using a similar analysis in Option 1 above for the inequality constrained optimization, we have

$$c_t = \theta^{-1/\gamma}\left(\frac{1+r}{1+\delta}\right)^{t/\gamma} \quad , \quad t = 0,...,T \tag{14}$$

$$c_t = \theta^{-1/\gamma}\left(\frac{1+r}{1+\delta}\right)^{t/\gamma} \quad , \quad t = T+1,...,D \tag{15}$$

where

$$\theta = \left\{\frac{\left[\displaystyle\sum_{t=0}^{T} y_t(1+r)^{-t}\right]}{\left[\dfrac{1-\pi^{D+1}}{1-\pi}\right]}\right\}^{-\gamma}$$

and

$$\pi = (1+\delta)^{-1/\gamma}(1+r)^{1/\gamma-1}$$

The optimal saving path for the individual who does not invest becomes

$$s_t = y_t - \theta^{-1/\gamma}\left(\frac{1+r}{1+\delta}\right)^{t/\gamma} \quad , \quad t = 0,...,D \tag{16}$$

Now, the individual saves only for retirement. The utility level can be derived by substituting the optimal consumption of (14) and (15) into the utility function. The individual's choice between investment (Option 1) and noninvestment (Option 2) will depend on which yields a higher level of utility.

IV. Simulation Results

As T_1 is described by a highly nonlinear equation, an explicit analytical solution is not obtainable. Numerical methods have to be used to solve the nonlinear equation. Since it is hard to prove the prerequisite that the T_1 is non-negative, nonzero, and less than the death time, the only thing we can do is to choose reasonable values for the parameters and see if a sensible value of T_1 emerges.

We begin by simplifying the variable y_t. Suppose that y_t has followed a constant growth rate w over the working period; that is, $y_t = y_0 (1 + w)^t$ where y_0 is the labor income at time 0 (i.e., age twenty). For the parameters, the initial labor income y_0 and its growth rate, w, can be calculated from the personal income data by age group of the head of household. The individual investment amount K_0 is estimated from the total number of private small- and medium-sized firms and the aggregate operating assets of private small- and medium-sized firms. The bank deposit rate r is proxied by the one-year deposit rate minus the consumer price inflation. The rate of returns on investment is from Fry (1988). The lifespan, D,

FIGURE 1   Consumption Pattern of Individual Who Invests, with
K_0 = US$30,000

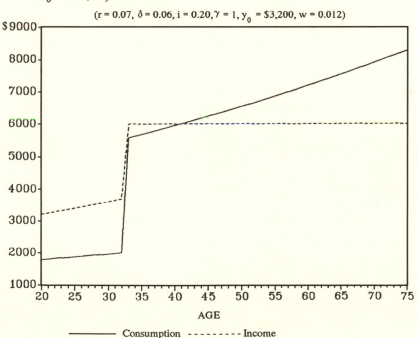

$(r = 0.07, \delta = 0.06, i = 0.20, \gamma = 1, y_0 = \$3,200, w = 0.012)$

——— Consumption --------- Income

FIGURE 2   Consumption Pattern of Individual Who Invests, with K_0 = US\$40,000

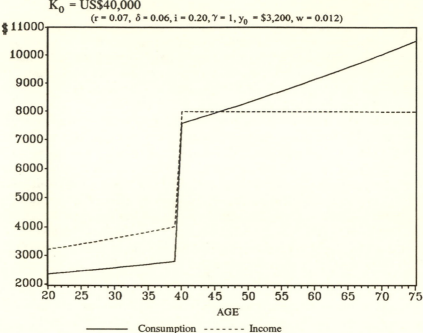

$(r = 0.07, \; \delta = 0.06, \; i = 0.20, \; \gamma = 1, \; y_0 = \$3,200, \; w = 0.012)$

AGE

——— Consumption   ------- Income

is set at fifty-five (i.e., the age of death is 75 because individuals are assumed to start life and work at 20). The retirement age for workers is set at 65. The following relationships among the parameters of the individual's optimization problem are imposed: $r > w, r > \delta, \delta > 0$ and $i \gg r$.

Figures 1 to 3 are an example of simulating Option 1, which uses parameter values that are reasonable for Taiwan's case in 1985. The values are: D = 55, y0 = US\$3,200, w = 0.012, i = 0.20, r = 0.07, d = 0.06, g = 1; and, K0 is assumed to change from US\$30,000 to US\$40,000 and to US\$50,000.[8] As we can see, the individual's age of investment becomes older (from age 32, 39, and 52 respectively) when K_0 gets bigger. Since the deposit interest rate is greater than the time preference rate, the individual's optimal consumption pattern is a two-stage upgrading trend. So,

---

8. The relevant information is inferred from the following sources. *Report on the Survey of Personal Income Distribution in Taiwan District, R.O.C.*, 1985; *Taiwan Statistics Data Book*, 1988; M. Fry 1988; *The Report on 1986 Industrial and Commercial Census, Taiwan-Fukien Area, R.O.C.*; *Small and Medium Enterprises—Statistics*, 1987; and *Small and Medium Enterprises—Overview in Taiwan*, 1986.

FIGURE 3   Consumption Pattern of Individual Who Invests, with
K_0 = US$50,000

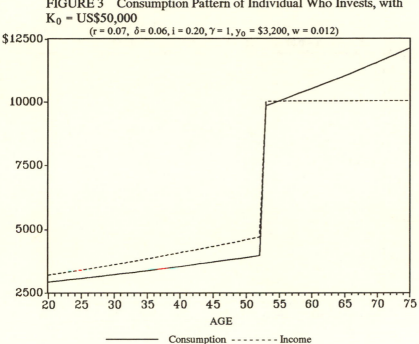

$(r = 0.07, \ \delta = 0.06, i = 0.20, \gamma = 1, y_0 = \$3,200, w = 0.012)$

Consumption ——— Income - - - - - - -

the optimal saving pattern is no longer the "humped" shape as the traditional life-cycle hypothesis showed. The utility levels also increase with
K_0: 137.26, 138.86, and 139.61 respectively.

Figure 4 shows the simulation of Option 2 with the same parameters.
The utility level for Option 2 is 139.47, which is greater than the utility
levels in Option 1 where K_0 equals US$30,000 and US$40,000, but smaller
than the third investment case of K_0 = US$50,000. Therefore, if the re-
quired investment amount is US$50,000, the individual will invest at age
52 to maximize her lifetime utility level.

The private aggregate saving, S^A, as measured by NIPA definition, depends on the population age structure. The higher the ratio of working
population to retired population, the larger aggregate saving would be.
For a particular year, the value of S^A is calculated as

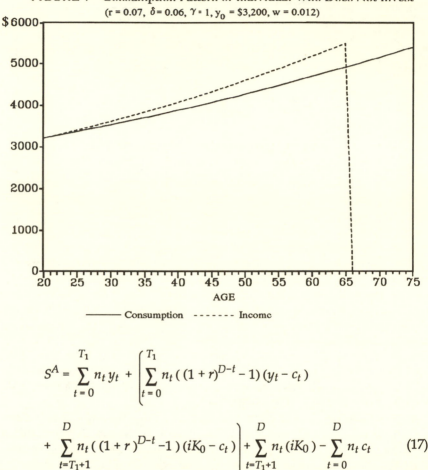

FIGURE 4   Consumption Pattern of Individual Who Does Not Invest
($r = 0.07$, $\delta = 0.06$, $\gamma = 1$, $y_0 = \$3,200$, $w = 0.012$)

——— Consumption   - - - - - - Income

$$S^A = \sum_{t=0}^{T_1} n_t y_t + \left(\sum_{t=0}^{T_1} n_t ((1+r)^{D-t} - 1)(y_t - c_t) \right.$$

$$\left. + \sum_{t=T_1+1}^{D} n_t ((1+r)^{D-t} - 1)(iK_0 - c_t) \right) + \sum_{t=T_1+1}^{D} n_t (iK_0) - \sum_{t=0}^{D} n_t c_t \qquad (17)$$

where n_t is the population number at age $t + 20$, i.e., t is interpreted in the cross-section and not time-series sense. The first term on the right-hand side of equation (17) is aggregate labor income, the second term is the bank interest income, the third term is the investment income, and the fourth term is aggregate consumption.

In the case of K_0 = US$50,000 calibrated on 1985 data, S^A is about US$39 billion (using the employed population data); and private aggregate investment is US$9.23 billion. This gives an *excess private saving* (not current account balance) of US$29.77 billion versus an actual value of US$7.62 billion. There are two good reasons why the stimulated value is so much bigger than the actual number. The first reason is the assumption that investors work and earn returns till they die. If we allow investors to retire at age 70 instead of the maximum age 75, then the value of excess savings would fall by 21.7 percent.

The second reason for the overestimation is that not everyone is unable to borrow long-term from domestic sources. The big enterprises do have privileged access to long-term banking loans.

V. Exchange Rate Management

Shiu-Tung Wang (1989) used a computable general equilibrium model to analyze Taiwan's trade flows. He found that if currency appreciation were the only policy instrument to eliminate the trade surplus, then the exchange rate required to do so would be NT$22.8 per US$. If functioning bond and equity markets had been present, the equilibrium exchange rate would have been only NT$27.6 per US$—a difference of 21 percent. Wang's finding is important because it makes clear that the reason for the still large trade surplus of today is not merely the result of slow response to the big currency appreciation that had occurred. The exchange rate of NT$25.4 per US$ in October 1989 is still undervalued for the *given* structure of the economy. The tragedy is that the fall in exports as a result of the exchange rate moving from NT$27.5 in 1988 to the 1989 value could have been avoided if Taiwan's financial institutions had functioned adequately.

We want to suggest that the use of currency appreciation to solve Taiwan's trade problem is not only inefficient but may also adversely affect its future growth rate. Our cautiousness about currency appreciation comes from our reading of the four multicountry studies conducted by Little, Scott, and Scitovsky (1970); Bhagwati (1978); Krueger (1978); and Balassa (1982). All four studies found that the countries which developed successfully were those that kept *the relative price ratios among domestically produced tradeable goods* close to international relative price ratios. The reason for the similarity in relative price ratios was *not* due to laissez-faire trade policies but to the tariffs cum export subsidies imposed by the state. The hallmark of the tariffs and export subsidies is that they apply to nearly all goods more or less equally. Targeting of specific products is seldom done. In short, the successful countries are those that have intervened to promote the production of tradeables in a market-compatible manner. Market compatible means that the government allows market forces (i.e., international prices) to determine the composition of the tradeables produced.

Why the growth of the tradeable sector has led to fast income growth in Korea, Singapore, and Taiwan is an open question. Woo (1990) speculates that the beneficial effects of these market-compatible interventionist policies come from putting these countries in an advantageous position in the international product cycle. By making conditions favorable to the production of tradeables, domestic entrepreneurs are willing to risk investing in simplifying the production techniques of new products developed in the technologically advanced countries. With simplified techniques, the less educated but lower cost labor in Korea, Singapore, and Taiwan can now produce these new products. These private efforts to hasten the product cycle ensured a steady stream of increasingly high value-added to the countries practicing market-compatible trade policies.

The removal of Taiwan's tariffs and export subsidies in the face of U.S. pressure is encouraging the production of nontradeables at the expense of tradeables. To now further appreciate the exchange rate is to discriminate against the production of tradeables. If the product cycle had indeed been the source of Taiwan's impressive growth, other policies besides currency appreciation must be considered in the effort to reduce the trade surplus.

VI. Policy Options

The efficient solution to the secular tendency of the current account toward surplus is to smoothly channel domestic savings to domestic investments. An important first step is to increase competition within the banking sector. The correct translation of this is to increase the number of banks and not to merely privatize the existing ones as usually suggested. Restrictions on branches should be relaxed for domestic banks. The recent changes in banking regulations are certainly moves in the right direction.

Since the setting up of bond and equity markets is a slow process of institution building, does this mean that the only way to appease U.S. protectionism is to appreciate the currency to NT$22 per US$? The answer is happily no. The government should run bigger budget deficits by increasing expenditure. It is important that the increased expenditure be in the development and not the routine portion of the budget. This is because a capital expenditure is a one-time affair and a routine expenditure item (e.g., salaries of state employees) would be hard to reduce after the financial sector had developed. It is also equally important that the development projects implemented use tradeables and not nontradeables intensively, otherwise inflation would be the result.

If the government is unable to improve the financial system and unable to increase development spending, it should at least appreciate the currency to NT$22 per US$ in one swoop. The present strategy of gradual revaluation is not an efficient way to facilitate structural adjustment; it is efficient only in transferring income from Taiwan's taxpayers to international speculators.

Bibliography

Balassa, B. 1982. *Development Strategies in Semi-Industrial Economies.* Baltimore: Johns Hopkins.

Balassa, B., and J. Williamson. 1987. *Adjusting to Success: Balance of Payments Policy in the East Asian NICs.* Washington: Institute for International Economics (June).

Bhagwati, J. 1978. *Anatomy and Consequences of Exchange Control Regimes.* Cambridge, MA: Ballinger.

Cheng, Hang-Sheng. 1986. Financial Policy and Reform in Taiwan, China. In *Financial Policy and Reform in Pacific Basin Countries,* edited by H. S. Cheng, 143-59. San Francisco: Federal Reserve Bank.

Fry, Maxwell J. 1988. *Should Taiwan Reduce Its Current Account Surplus?* Irvine: University of California, Irvine (November).

Horioka, Charles Y. 1984. The Applicability of the Life-Cycle Hypothesis of Saving to Japan. *Kyoto University Economic Review* 54 (October): 30-56.

Krueger, A. 1978. *Liberalization Attempts and Consequences.* Cambridge, MA: Ballinger.

Lee, Yung-San, and Tzong-Rong Tsai. 1988. Development of Financial System and Monetary Policies in Taiwan. Paper presented at Conference in Economic Development, Experiences of Taiwan. Taipei: Economic Institute, Academia Sinica, June 8-10.

Little, I., M. Scott, and T. Scitovsky. 1970. *Industry and Trade in Some Developing Countries.* Oxford.

Report on the Survey of Personal Income Distribution in Taiwan District, R.O.C. 1985.

Report on 1986 Industrial and Commercial Census, Taiwan-Fukien Area, R.O.C.

Shea, Jia-Dong, and Ping-Sing Kuo. 1984. An Analysis of the Allocation Efficiency of Bank Funds in Taiwan. In *Proceedings of the Conference on Financial Development in Taiwan.* Taipei: Economic Institute, Academia Sinica, December. In Chinese.

Small and Medium Enterprises—Overview in Taiwan. 1986.

Small and Medium Enterprises—Statistics. 1987.

Taiwan Statistics Data Book. 1988.

Wang, Shiu-Tung. 1989. Taiwan's Persistent Trade Surpluses: The Policy Choices. Ph.D. dissertation, University of California, Davis.

Woo, Wing Thye. 1990. The Art of Economic Development: Markets, Politics, and Externalities. *International Organization* 44: 403-29.

5

Foreign Trade and Economic Growth in Taiwan

Kuo-yuan Liang

Introduction

Few developing economies have been mentioned as frequently or analyzed as intensively in economic-development literature as Taiwan.
For much of the period since the early 1960s, Taiwan has demonstrated
an enviable economic performance, as rapid growth has been accompanied by stable prices, healthy trade balances, and improved income distribution. Although it is difficult to generalize about the reasons for this
remarkable achievement, a key factor is certainly Taiwan's outward-
oriented trade strategy, which has provided opportunities to industrialize the economy through trade (e.g., Lau 1986, Wheeler and Wood 1987,
Sachs and Sundberg 1988). More specifically, the process has taken the
form that expansion of exports fueled economic prosperity while the importation of raw materials and capital goods has facilitated the development of modern manufacturing industries.

It is generally agreed that the development of the trade sector in Taiwan can be divided into four stages: (1) import substitution in the 1950s;
(2) export expansion in the 1960s; (3) the so-called secondary import substitution of the 1970s; and (4) the new situation of huge trade surpluses in
the 1980s. The purpose of this paper is to sketch some aspects of Taiwan's

foreign trade and to examine the economic factors and important government policies that have influenced this process of development.

Aspects of Taiwan's Foreign Trade

A. The Importance of Foreign Trade
for Economic Growth

For an initial look, the importance of Taiwan's trade sector is summarized in Table 1. The growth rates of six crucial aggregate variables in real terms — GDP (y), private consumption (c), gross investment (i), government expenditure (g), exports (x), and imports (m) — are arranged into four periods: 1961-70, 1971-80, 1981-88, and 1961-88. From 1961 to 1988 the average annual growth of real GDP was 9.3%, an impressive performance by any reasonable standard.

The strong growth in GDP was accompanied by high growth rates in its components. Between 1961 and 1988, the average annual growth rates of real private consumption, real gross investment, real government consumption, real exports, and real imports were 8.4%, 11.7%, 6.8%, 16.7%, and 14.2% respectively. Except for real private consumption and real government consumption, growth rates of other GDP components were all higher than that of the real GDP. As a consequence, there was a dramatic change in Taiwan's GDP structure (see Table 2). For example, in nominal terms over the period 1961 to 1988, the export/GDP (x/y) ratio grew from 14% to 54.75%; the import/GDP (m/y) ratio from 21.08% to 43.72%; the gross investment/GDP (i/y) ratio from 16.20% to 20.73%. But the private consumption/GDP (c/y) ratio fell from 67.87% to 50.48%; the government consumption/GDP (g/y) ratio from 19.25% to 15.15%.

The high percentage of GDP invested is not surprising because economic development cannot be sustained if sufficiently high levels of investment are not generated. The high percentage of GDP exported and imported, however, is a rather unique characteristic of Taiwan's economy. By comparison, in 1987, the export/GDP ratios for the United States and Japan were 7.5% and 12.7% respectively, and the import/GDP ratios for these two countries in the same year were 10.8% and 8.9% (*Taiwan Statistical Data Book*, 1989).

A recent input-output analysis (*A Report on the 1981 Input-Output Tables, Taiwan Area, ROC*, 1985) based on a Chenery-type growth-accounting formula confirms this simple finding. Over the period 1971-81 (see

TABLE 1   Average Annual Change in Real GDP and Its Components (percent)

	1961-70	1971-80	1981-88	1961-88
Real GDP (y)	10.0	9.4	8.4	9.3
Real private consumption (c)	8.7	8.3	8.4	8.4
Real gross investment (i)	16.2	12.2	5.2	11.7
Real government consumption (g)	7.7	6.6	6.7	6.8
Real exports (x)	21.5	14.3	12.6	16.7
Real imports (m)	17.8	13.3	11.7	14.2

Source: *Statistical Abstract of National Income, Taiwan Area, Republic of China, 1951-1989,* 1989.

Table 3), roughly 40% of the economy's output growth came from the expansion of exports.

A third way to quantify the trade/growth relation is to construct a simultaneous equation econometric model. In doing so, special attention should be given to incorporating exports as demand components and imported capital goods and raw materials as supply components (Hickman and Lau 1976). In this spirit, I have constructed a macroeconometric model of Taiwan for the period 1961-86 and conducted six simulations dealing with three kinds of external shocks, which basically include changes in exchange rates, the volume index of world trade, and the composite price index of major export competitors (Liang 1988). The results revealed that all these external factors played a significant role affecting Taiwan's crucial macroeconomic variables—GPD, the general price level, balance of trade, etc.

TABLE 2   Composition of Nominal GDP (percent)

Year	c/y	i/y	g/y	x/y	m/y
1961	67.87	16.20	19.25	14.00	21.08
1966	61.15	19.07	17.35	21.84	21.56
1971	54.06	23.24	17.25	35.56	33.10
1976	52.10	27.66	15.19	47.51	45.36
1981	51.98	27.85	16.11	51.91	49.87
1986	47.86	18.12	14.81	58.10	38.30
1988	50.48	20.73	15.15	54.75	43.72

Source: *Statistical Abstract of National Income, Taiwan Area, Republic of China, 1951-1989,* 1989.

TABLE 3   Breakdown of Output Growth in Taiwan's Economy (percent)

Period	Due to domestic expansion	Due to export expansion	Due to import substitution	Due to technological change
1971-76	54.86	41.70	-0.01	3.45
1976-81	54.70	38.59	1.76	4.95

Source: *A Report on the 1981 Input-Output Tables, Taiwan Area, the Republic of China*, 1985.

B. Characteristics of Taiwan's Foreign Trade

In addition to the high growth rates in exports and imports (Table 1) and high trade dependence ratio (Table 2), Taiwan's foreign trade can be characterized by additional factors as follows.

1. High Import Content in Domestic Final Demand and Exports. The amount of import content is a measure of imported goods used to produce domestic final demand and exports (Kuo, Ranis, and Fei 1981). The coefficient of import content for each final demand component is the portion of imported goods directly and indirectly used to produce a dollar value of that component. A recent input-output study reports that Taiwan's coefficient of import content for exports gradually grew from 0.31 in 1971 to 0.36 in 1976 and 0.38 in 1981, which was the same as South Korea's figure for 1980 but was substantially higher than Japan's for 1980 (0.17) (see Table 4). This phenomenon clearly suggests that import prices can directly affect the prices of Taiwan's exports, and the economy can be very vulnerable to external shocks. Table 4 also reveals high levels of import content coefficients for Taiwan's other final demand components and the whole economy.

TABLE 4   Import-Content Coefficients for Taiwan, South Korea, and Japan

	TAIWAN			S. KOREA	JAPAN
	1971	1976	1981	1980	1980
Average (domestic final demand and exports)	0.25	0.30	0.32	0.30	0.13
Consumption	0.18	0.22	0.25	0.23	0.12
Investment	0.39	0.39	0.39	0.42	0.16
Exports	0.31	0.36	0.38	0.38	0.17

Source: *A Report on the 1981 Input-Output Tables, Taiwan Area, the Republic of China*, 1985.

TABLE 5   Trade with the United States and Japan

YEAR	United States			Japan		
	Exports	Imports	Balance	Exports	Imports	Balance
1961	42.8	130.8	-88.1	56.5	99.8	-43.2
	(21.9)	(40.6)		(29.0)	(31.0)	
1966	115.9	166.3	-50.5	128.8	251.4	-122.6
	(21.6)	(26.7)		(24.0)	(40.4)	
1971	859.2	408.2	451.0	245.0	827.0	-582.0
	(41.7)	(22.1)		(11.9)	(44.9)	
1976	3,038.7	1,797.5	1,241.2	1,094.8	2,451.5	-1,356.7
	(37.2)	(23.7)		(13.4)	(32.3)	
1981	8,158.4	4,765.7	3,392.7	2,454.2	5,928.6	-3,474.5
	(36.1)	(22.5)		(10.9)	(28.0)	
1986	19,006.0	5,415.8	13,590.2	4,559.1	8,254.7	-3695.6
	(47.7)	(22.4)		(11.4)	(34.2)	
1988	23,431.0	13,002.0	10,428.9	8,762.1	14,824.2	-6,062.1
	(38.7)	(26.2)		(14.5)	(29.8)	

Note: In US$ million; figures in parenthesis are percentages.
Source: *Taiwan Statistical Data Book,* 1989.

2. Triangular Trade Pattern: United States–Taiwan–Japan (see Wheeler and Wood 1987, Martson 1988, Moreno 1989). Taiwan's trade was also characterized by a geographically highly concentrated pattern, with the United States and Japan its two most important trading partners. For much of the period since 1961, these two markets have accounted for about half of Taiwan's total exports and an even higher percentage of Taiwan's total imports (see Table 5). Such a high geographical concentration clearly suggests that Taiwan's foreign trade is very sensitive to changes in the economic situations of these two giant economies, particularly the United States. Table 5 shows how essential the U.S. market is to Taiwan. Taiwan's unusually high dependence on the U.S. market for its exports (mainly consumer goods and capital goods components [Hickok and Klitgaard 1988]) coincided with uncommonly high dependence on Japan for imports (mainly capital goods). This constitutes a triangular trade relation among the three economies. Within this relationship, Taiwan has run a huge trade surplus with the United States on one hand, and a large trade deficit with Japan on the other. In addition, the third side of the triangle is closed by the United States selling securities to Japan and Taiwan.

3. Relative Importance of Income and Price Effects on Exports. Recent econometric studies have shown that foreign income levels and

TABLE 6   Major Export Products as a Percentage of Total Exports

Year	Textile Products	Chemicals, Rubber Products & Plastic Articles	Basic Metals & Metal Manu- factures	Machinery	Electrical Machinery & Apparatus
1961	15.1	6.3	5.3	0.4	0.8
1966	17.8	4.8	5.5	2.2	4.8
1971	35.4	5.2	4.7	3.2	12.9
1976	27.5	9.3	4.6	3.6	15.6
1981	22.3	10.9	6.9	4.2	18.4
1986	18.3	12.6	7.7	4.0	22.4
1988	14.8	12.7	7.9	5.3	27.5

Source: *Taiwan Statistical Data Book,* 1989.

terms of trade do play an important role in determining Taiwan's exports. For example, long-run income elasticities reported in Liang (1988) and Moreno (1989) were 2.50 and 2.87 respectively, and long-run price elasticities were estimated by the same authors at -0.76 and -0.79. Such a high level of income elasticity in Taiwan's export equation clearly indicates that changes in foreign economic situations can have a significant impact on the economy.

Factors Contributing to the Success of Taiwan's Trade Sector

Several factors lay behind the "successful" development of Taiwan's trade sector. I place this word in quotation marks only because success is a matter of assessment and involves one's point of view. Clearly, general economic development, government policy prescriptions, and special circumstances in some key trade industries all played a role. This literature is too vast to review in detail here. As a consequence, the factors discussed below are highly selective.

1. Sharp Product Transformation. Its penetration of the world market would not have been possible if Taiwan had not transformed its export composition in particular ways. Table 6 lists five types of export commodities, ranging from the traditional—textile products—to the more so-

FIGURE 1
Effective and US$ Exchange Rates

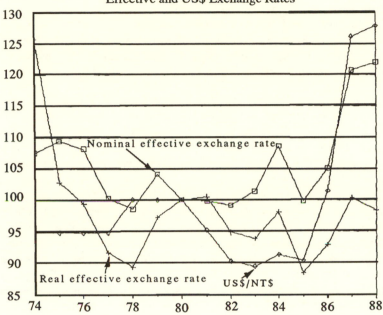

phisticated electrical machinery and apparatus. The table reveals that textile products were the most important commodities before 1980, rising steadily from 15.1% of total exports in 1961 to 35.4% in 1971, then declining gradually to 14.8% in 1988. On the other hand, electrical machinery and apparatus became the most important category in the 1980s. As also noted by Martson (1988), this product transformation process is an essential part of the Taiwan success story.

2. **Low Domestic Inflation.** Figure 1 illustrates the path of the indices (1980 = 100) of U.S. and Taiwan currency exchange rates, and of trade-weighted nominal and real effective exchange rates for the period 1974-88. The nominal effective exchange rate is computed as an arithmetic weighted average of bilateral foreign exchange rates between Taiwan and its major trade partners. Each exchange rate is defined as NT$ per foreign dollar. The weights (in each case based on an arithmetic average of bilateral trade as a percentage of Taiwan's total trade for each major trading partner over the period 1980-88) were: U.S., 48.7%; Japan, 27.1%; Hong Kong, 7.4%; West Germany, 5.3%; Australia, 4.0%; United Kingdom, 3.0%; Singapore, 2.8%; South Korea, 1.7%. The real effective exchange rate is formulated as a wholesale price, adjusting the nominal

effective exchange rate. The figures show that the nominal NT dollar fell against the U.S. dollar in the early 1980s. Then, after 1985, the NT dollar sharply appreciated against the U.S. dollar.

The low level and downward trend of the real effective exchange rate throughout most of the period since 1975 indicates that low domestic inflation appears to explain the strong competitiveness for Taiwan's products. Similar conclusions can be found in Moreno (1989).

3. Government Policies and Infrastructural Investments. There is no doubt that government policy has had a tremendous impact on Taiwan. Yet it is often difficult to quantify these effects. By all accounts, however, economists seem to agree that the comprehensive foreign exchange reform and the trade liberalization program carried out in the late 1950s and early 1960s played decisive roles in transforming Taiwan into one of the world's leading trading nations (e.g., Lin 1973). Another example of government influence on the economy was the decision to establish military defense industries at the beginning of the 1980s. Wu (1985) sees a connection between this last and the development of high technology industries in Taiwan. A third example of state intervention was the Ten Major Developments Project of the 1970s. The influence of this effort was confirmed as having speeded development in a simulation study by Liang (1984).

Conclusion

The preceding investigation has pointed out how essential foreign trade has become for Taiwan. Evidently, the expansion of this trade has made for prosperity in the Taiwan economy. It has also placed the economy in a vulnerable position, however, subject to drastic external shocks. The smooth development path Taiwan enjoyed from the early 1960s was interrupted, for example, by the 1973 oil crisis and the following world depression (1973-75). Whether future development will be smooth depends largely on Taiwan's ability to cope with such external shocks and to remain competitive in the world market.

Clearly, outward oriented trade policies are a key factor in Taiwan's economic growth. Nevertheless, overemphasis on exterior trade has produced its own problems, such as the huge trade surplus, pollution, imbalanced development between the traded and nontraded sectors, inflationary pressures, etc. Because these issues have many political and economic ramifications, ongoing research needs to be done in these areas.

Bibliography

Hickman, B. G., and L. J. Lau. 1976. Pacific Basin National Econometric Models: A Survey and Evaluation of Linkage Feasibility. *Explorations in Economic Research* 3:199-252.

Hickok, S., and T. Klitgaard. 1988. U.S. Trade with Taiwan and South Korea. *Quarterly Review* 13(3): 60-66. New York: Federal Reserve Bank of New York.

Kuo, S. W. Y., G. Ranis, and J. C. H. Fei. 1981. *The Taiwan Success Story*. Boulder, Colorado: Westview Press.

Lau, L. J. 1986. Introduction. In *Models of Development: A Comparative Study of Economic Growth in South Korea and Taiwan*, edited by L. J. Lau. San Francisco: Institute for Contemporary Studies.

Liang, K. Y. 1984. *A Macroeconometric Model of Taiwan*. Ann Arbor, Michigan: University Microfilms International.

———. 1988. *A Macroeconometric Model of Taiwan, 1961-1986*. Taipei: Council for Economic Planning and Development.

Lin, C. Y. 1973. *Industrialization in Taiwan, 1946-1972*. New York: Praeger Publishers.

Martson, R. C. 1988. Discussion. In *International Payments Imbalances in the 1980s*, edited by N. S. Fieleke, 152-56. Boston: Federal Reserve Bank of Boston.

Moreno, R. 1989. Exchange Rates and Trade Adjustment in Taiwan and Korea. *Economic Review* (Spring): 30-48. San Francisco: Federal Reserve Bank of San Francisco.

Sachs, J. D., and M. W. Sundberg. 1988. International Payments Imbalances of the East Asian Developing Economies. In *International Payments Imbalances in the 1980s*, edited by N. S. Fieleke, 103-51. Boston: Federal Reserve Bank of Boston.

Taiwan. Council for Economic Planning and Development. 1989. *Taiwan Statistical Data Book*. Taipei.

Taiwan. Directorate-General of Budget, Accounting, and Statistics. 1985. *A Report on the 1981 Input-Output Tables, Taiwan Area, the Republic of China*. Taipei.

———. 1989. *Statistical Abstract of National Income, Taiwan Area, Republic of China, 1951-1989*. Taipei.

Wheeler, J. W., and P. L. Wood. 1987. *Beyond Recrimination: Perspectives on U.S.-Taiwan Trade Tensions*. Indianapolis: Hudson Institute.

Wu, Y. L. 1985. *Becoming an Industrialized Nation: R.O.C.'s Development on Taiwan*. New York: Praeger Publishers.

B. Government Policy and the Development of Economic Institutions and Endowments

6

The State and the Development of the Automobile Industry in South Korea and Taiwan

Yun-han Chu

Introduction

No industry separates South Korea's industrialization experience from Taiwan's as much as the automobile industry. In the early 1970s, the automobile industries in these two East Asian newly industrializing countries (NICS) had an almost identical structure and had achieved comparable levels of local content. In both countries the domestic market was comparably small. The annual sales in either market in 1970 were fewer than 15,000 units. Fifteen years later, the structure of the industry in the two countries had become distinctively different. By the second half of the 1980s, the South Korean *chaebol* had made giant strides in turning automobiles into one of Korea's leading export sectors. In 1988, South Korean automakers rolled out well over one million vehicles and exported about two-thirds of them, primarily for the Canadian and U.S. markets. At home, the South Korean carmakers enjoyed a firm grip on their local market. The sale of foreign imports constituted less than 1 percent of domestic market share. Thus, within fewer than fifteen years, Korean auto producers had risen from insignificant Third World actors passively responding to the changing international competitive environment to become a new factor shaping the dynamics of the global automobile industry. In stark contrast, Taiwanese auto producers remained as uncompetitive as they had been.

In the late 1980s, even with a very high protection rate, Taiwan's automakers were barely able to compete with foreign imports in the local market. They continued to be handicapped by their small scale and dependence on the importation of major components. In 1988, with the help of an appreciated New Taiwan Dollar, the volume of imported passenger cars soared to 113,000 units and clinched 29.3 percent of the domestic passenger car market (Bank of Communication 1989, 14). Taiwanese carmakers were even threatened by low-priced Korean imports. This led to a series of negotiations between the ROC and the Korean government to conclude formal agreements to limit Korean auto exports to Taiwan.

If, however, we shift our focus from finished cars to auto parts and components, the story takes a different turn. In 1988, despite its commanding lead in exporting finished cars, South Korea was a net importer of auto parts and components while Taiwan was a net exporter. This means that Taiwan's private manufacturers in the automobile sector had also made considerable gains in increasing their presence in foreign markets while aiming at rather different market niches and going about it in a less conspicuous way. The island's myriad auto parts suppliers, in the year 1988, were making the export of minor mechanical components and miscellaneous parts a booming US$1.2 billion a year business, or roughly the equivalent of exporting 220,000 completed small cars.

For inquisitive observers, two questions come immediately to mind. First, what accounts for the striking divergence? And second, how typical is the automobile industry case? The answer to the first question is quite straightforward, but the second needs some clarification. It is my contention that the automobile industry in the two East Asian NICs traveled such diverse routes toward industrial upgrading largely as a result of differences in state policy. Divergent business strategies stemmed from differences in the state's strategy for industrial restructuring. Along this line of analysis, the automobile industry is far from exceptional and the adjustment experiences of this sector can be generalized to include the experiences of most advanced sectors that received emphatic governmental promotion during the 1970s and 1980s (Cheng and Haggard 1987; Chu 1987). Thus, the unfolding events in the automobile sector revealed the economywide patterns of private adjustment strategy. In the automobile industry, just as in many other advanced sectors, the Korean private producers were consistently more aggressive in taking up the challenge of industrial upgrading, venturing into new export markets in which Japanese transnational corporations (TNCs) still retained a competitive edge, and taking a long-term view about investment returns, demonstrating their willingness to suffer initial losses as the price of entering new markets.

It is fair to say that, on the one hand, the automobile industry exemplified the way private firms in each country responded to changing international market pressures and opportunities and to the government's insistent urging of industrial upgrading. On the other hand, the automobile industry is exceptional in the sense that the resultant difference in output performance and industry structure, as measured by international competitiveness, level of local content, production capacity, and ownership pattern, is far more dramatic than is typically the case. On these scores, we can only find a very limited number of sectors, but by no means insignificant ones, that come close to what we have witnessed in the automobile sector. These include telecommunications, shipbuilding, and the home-appliance industry. Thus, the automobile industry may misrepresent the larger picture. The overall performance of the two economies in export upgrading, as measured by increases in both volume and unit price, has been quite comparable, although the structure of their manufactured exports grew increasingly dissimilar during the 1970s and 1980s (Chu 1987).

But it is exactly its glaring contrast that makes the automobile industry case particularly interesting and significant.

First, the automobile industry makes a good case for understanding sources of divergent state adjustment strategies because it sharpens the ongoing debate in the foreign economic policy literature on the relative importance of international versus domestic sources of explanation (Lake 1984; Ikenberry 1988). The relative importance of domestic sources for state actions is better appreciated when divergent national strategies are observed in an industry that has been long dominated by transnational oligopoly and where global dynamics tend to overshadow local initiatives.

Second, the automobile sector constitutes a crucial case for comparative political economy analysis because it is right at the center of the debate between two popular views of East Asian political economy—the neoclassical and developmental state views.[1] For the neoclassical authors, the experience of Taiwan's automobile industry provides a textbook example of government failure. Taiwan's automobile industry attests to the folly of overprotection and excessive intervention under a protracted import substitution strategy, and indirectly substantiates the soundness of a market-conforming export-oriented strategy. The developmental state authors, however, can argue in just the opposite direction. They might

---

1. For a review of this debate, see Haggard and Moon 1986 and Chu 1989a.

contend, as compared to the South Korean case, that Taiwan's automobile industry failed to live up to expectations not because of overprotection or excessive state intervention but because of inadequate and untimely state intervention and an incoherent sector policy.[2] A scrutiny of policy-induced development of the industry in each country will shed some light on the debate and give us a chance to reexamine the tenets of both perspectives.

Third, our analysis elevates the theoretical stakes for a systematic understanding of domestic structure from just an important source for state strategy to an important source of a nation's international competitiveness and therefore a factor that in the long run contributes to our understanding of industrial change and economic transformation at the global level.

I. Theoretical Arguments and Research Strategy

At the center of our analysis is the state policy itself. We compare sectoral policy in terms of policy objectives—desired industry structure and output performance—as well as policy instruments and the relative priorities of particular policy objectives, e.g., trade balance and monetary stability, and we do this over time. From this we try to trace backward to their sources divergent patterns of state action and trace forward the effects of policy on private strategy. For the first part of the analysis, what I call the backward linkage part, I introduce a state-centered policy model to accentuate the explanatory power of state structure. For the second part, the forward linkage part, I base my analysis on a strategic model of the firm.

In accounting for state policy, a state-centered policy model draws attention to the strategic choices of the government elite, positioned within a distinctive state structure that constrains their ability to plan and develop programmatic national policy and limits the availability of policy instruments to intervene into the society and economy. When confronted with emerging international pressures and opportunities to make strategic choices, a state elite acts upon their own policy preferences to pursue what they perceive as the "national priority." The state is also a structure that places powerful constraints on the state elite. There are two levels to the analysis of state structure as it shapes the interests of the state elite as

---

2. Personal communication with Robert Wade.

well as the effectiveness and selectivity of government influence and control. First, there is the organizational characteristics of the state apparatus itself—the territorial and functional centralization of the executive branch; the concentration and dispersion of power and authority; the control of human, informational, and material resources by the state; and so forth. Next, there is the institutional linkage between the state and various sectors in society—the patterns and mechanisms of participation, interests intermediation, and control. Divergent motivations and approaches toward industrial upgrading are embedded in the organiza- tional characteristics of each country's economic bureaucracy and the policy network connecting the state and the national business community.

In South Korea, the economic officials in charge of industrial development avail themselves of a wide range of policy instruments and occupy a preeminent organizational position within a highly centralized and resourceful state bureaucracy. The state's direction of the industrial restructuring process is also facilitated by well-established channels of communication and a long-term exchange relationship between responsible state agencies and the large private firms. The economic officials in charge of industrial development in Taiwan, by contrast, have to compromise the coherence of their policy initiatives as they are situated in a more fragmented economic decision-making process and a less centralized economic bureaucracy. In particular, economic planning officials have little clout over the conservative financial and monetary officials who control a wide array of policy instruments. The state's influence over private business strategy is also limited by a lack of effective institutional links between the responsible state agencies and the private sector.

The characteristics of the South Korean economic bureaucracy enabled industrial planning authorities to employ a full range of policy instruments, exercise product- and firm-specific intervention, and implement programmatic plans in the area of industrial upgrading. Also, an intimate multilevel institutional linkage and a long-term exchange relationship between the Korean economic bureaucracy and the private sector facilitate coordinating their actions in carrying out the state's sectoral development goals. In Taiwan the relatively weaker organizational position of the planning technocrats in the overall economic bureaucracy limits their ability to coordinate industrial policy with other areas of economic policy and their access to important policy instruments, in particular credit policy. As a consequence, their ability to exercise high selectivity in intervening into private industry and their ability to formulate and implement coherent sectoral policy are severely constrained. The lack of a high-ranking institutional network between the state economic bureaucracy and the private sector further precludes the economic officials from cutting long-term deals with the private firms. The mode of interaction between the two, consequently, becomes dominated by mutual adjustment rather than collaboration.

From the perspective of the strategic model of firms (Caves and Porter 1977; Porter 1980), industrial upgrading is carried out by domestic firms, public or private, that initiate a strategic change and take up the risk of surmounting market entry barriers. The major sources of market entry barriers are economy of scale, product differentiation, capital requirements, stiff learning curve, and government policy (Porter 1980). The indigenous firms in the NICs that emerged during the previous export-expansion phase usually did not acquire the kind of technological and financial base to challenge the market position of transnational firms in sectors characterized by an entrenched global oligopoly. To pursue specific industrial development objectives, the state often found it imperative to supplement or alter existing market incentives to cajole national private firms to attempt a strategic change. The higher the risk of entering new foreign markets, the more dirigiste the form of state intervention necessary.

During the NICs' earlier export-expansion phase, with low capital and technology requirements, fast return to investment, and clear competitive advantage in costs of production, the local industrial capitalists, basing themselves on their accumulated experiences in the previous import-substituting, labor-intensive industrialization, could readily respond to general policy incentives for entering foreign markets. As the export-oriented industrialization deepened, with higher capital and technology requirements, slow and uncertain return to investment, and ambiguous potential competitive advantage in costs of production, administering struc- tural incentives alone became an increasingly inadequate policy instrument to influence the investment decisions of local firms. This is because, in order to help private producers to overcome stiff entry barriers, policy incentives have to be raised so high that they may not be economically viable. Blanket policy incentives would result in less efficient resource allocation because they do not discriminate among firms. Firms can be very heterogeneous in terms of resources and functional areas of deficiency in absorbing market risks, although they produce a functionally identical product. In addition, capital- and technology-intensive sectors that are nurtured under generous fiscal incentives and heavy protection might never grow into export-oriented sectors, unless the state can administer policy incentives in such a way that the allocation of rent that a firm captures in the domestic market is directly tied to its performance in improving international competitiveness. In particular, in sectors where scale economy is critical the government needs to evaluate the long-term economic viability of a suitable number of firms pursuing the same strategy and to be able to select only those firms that stand the best chance of succeeding. Hence, if the state intends to direct domestic private firms to move into markets with high entry barriers, the state needs to administer its resources in a firm-specific fashion.[3] Also, the state needs to provide private firms with a predictable business environment and a high degree of continuity in sectoral policy, on which the economic viability of private ventures in the advanced sector depends.

The aggressive moves of the South Korean automakers were brought about by the willingness and capacity of the state to establish an integrated industrial structure with dominant national control. The state modifies and alters market incentives for the firms by implementing programmatic industrial policy that is not only sector-specific but product-, function-, and firm-specific. It nurtures the growth of specific private oligopolistic economic organizations and protects them with a highly selective policy toward foreign direct investment and stringent restrictions on foreign imports.

In Taiwan, the state's push for industrial upgrading has been incremental, selective, and based more on the state-enterprise sector. Its support for private-sector industrial adjustment has been largely limited to a discretionary use of structural incentives and focused R&D support. On the other hand, the Taiwanese state has consistently opted for direct state ownership and joint-ventures with state equity participation as alternatives to large national firms.

As a result of these differences, in South Korea, leading private national firms raced to attain the official sectoral development goals, and they came to dominate the industry and challenge the Japanese TNCs in the foreign market by pursuing a strategy that promised potential long-term payoffs but involved extremely high risks in market entry. By contrast, most leading Taiwanese private firms refused to adhere to official sectoral guidelines unless these fit into their short-term business interests. They refrained from long-term, large-scale ventures, and most of them, large or small, concentrated their efforts on dividing up the existing market and exploring the emerging niches with relatively low entry barriers.

Of course, there exists considerable variation across sectors, in the de-

---

3. Of course, domestic private firms need not be the only economic agent for carrying out industrial upgrading. However, the other two options, the participation of foreign firms and state enterprises, as alternatives to national private initiative, face a number of constraints. The multinational firms maximize their profit in terms of a global strategy, not a local one. The influence the NIC states can exert over multinational corporations is always limited and indirect. State enterprises are bound to serve a set of mixed policy demands and tend to be inward-looking rather than operating according to criteria of international competitiveness (Chu 1989b).

gree to which the state is able and willing to intervene in the private sector, in the organizational properties of state agencies and policy networks, and in the dynamic nature of market entry barriers. In accounting for state actions and private business strategies at the sector level, a more precise specification and more nuanced application of the above theoretical arguments is required (Atkinson and Coleman 1989). To substantiate my theoretical arguments, a threefold analytical task is posed. First, I need to establish in the context of the automobile industry that the domestic structure is central to understanding divergent state strategies. Second, I need to demonstrate the explanatory power of a state-centered policy model in accounting for the divergent approaches taken to upgrading the automobile industry in the 1970s and 1980s. Lastly, I need to demonstrate the critical role of state sectoral policy in shaping the development of the industry over the last two decades. I will deal with the first part of the task in the following section. I will take up the second and third parts in Section III.

II. The NICs' Dynamic Comparative Advantage in the Automobile Industry

In this section, I will establish the fact that the two countries have chosen diverse routes toward industrial upgrading *not* because the global automobile industry has presented the Korean and Taiwanese governments, as well as private firms, with different sets of structural constraints and opportunities. Their diverse strategies have had little to do with the business strategies of TNCs or the commercial policies of their major trading partners. Taiwan and South Korea's choices also had little to do with certain domestic economic structural factors, such as the existing technological base, the supply of skilled and industrious workers and engineers, or the size of the domestic market. None of these factors differentiated between Taiwanese and South Korean carmakers to any appreciable degree at the outset of industrial upgrading. To this end, I will first lay out the economics and dynamics of world automobile production. This spells out the underlying forces shaping the development of the industry independent of the official intentions and governmental policies of the two NICs. Then, I will analyze the entry barriers as well as the competitive openings for the two East Asian NICs during the 1970s and early 1980s, when they began formulating and implementing sector-specific plans to develop an internationally competitive automobile industry.

The Economics and Dynamics of the
World Automobile Industry

The world automobile industry is first and foremost a highly capital-intensive one. While scale economics vary considerably among the components and steps of motor vehicle production, large economies of scale pertain to all major mechanical components, notably engines and transmissions, and all major phases of production, including final assembly. It has been estimated that the minimum efficient scale for annual output ranges from 100,000 to 250,000 units in assembly, through 500,000 in engines, to 1,000,000 in stamping. No firm could remain competitive without taking full advantage of scale economies for all component manufacture and assembly. Major world firms are able to combine these economies with economies in design and development of new models, and in marketing and distribution, and to apply all of these scale economies across a multimodel range spanning all the major market segments. It has been argued that only integrated megavolume producers can survive in this market (Altshuler et al. 1984). Scale economies have been the dominant factor that prevents the entry of new firms into the industry and drives out existing firms incapable of achieving sufficient sale volume.

Increasing concentration dictated by technological necessity has resulted in a global oligopoly that came to characterize the postwar world automobile industry. In 1960, the global automobile industry consisted of about twenty major firms, based principally in the United States and Western Europe and together accounting for about 90 percent of total world sales.[4] These firms were the survivors of a process of concentration in their respective home-country markets over the course of the preceding decades. Each has more or less been transformed into a transnational corporation with not only sales but also manufacturing operations in several different countries. The trend toward further concentration continued in the 1960s and 1970s. By 1972, two firms, Ford and General Motors, accounted for 40% of total world automobile sales, while the eight largest commanded about 85%.

Around the late 1950s and early 1960s, the TNCs began to compete for toeholds in the larger leading LDCs where they could see future growth markets. In particular, the Latin American markets had become a key competitive battleground (Bennett and Sharpe 1985). The preferred strategy of the TNCs was to supply assembled vehicles, semiknockdown

---

4. Here and throughout the rest of the chapter, world aggregate statistics do not include the former socialist bloc.

(SKD) kits, or complete knockdown (CKD) kits for local assembly rather than to undertake significant local manufacturing. But most of the larger LDCs used import restrictions and local-content requirements to cajole the TNCs to undertake local production or face the possibility of exclusion. Most well-established TNCs responded by increasing investment in local manufacturing facilities, and their investment strategy was largely defensive. Rather than ceding the emerging markets to their competitors, they responded by setting up suboptimal-size plants in each of these economies.

Around the early 1970s, just as the world automobile industry began to settle down to a pattern of stable global oligopoly based on about a dozen major firms, new raveling factors were emerging to bring about a further shakeout in the industry. The first factor was the saturation of the industrialized markets, which accounted for 80 percent of world demand in the early 1980s.[5] A direct consequence was that competition among the major auto firms was sharpened. A second factor was the proliferation of inefficient manufacturing subsidiaries in leading LDCs. This led to severe global overcapacity. This also prompted the auto TNCs to find ways to rationalize their global production. A third factor was a new wave of process technology innovation introduced by the late-coming Japanese automakers. By introducing such techniques as zero defect quality control and just-in-time inventory systems, Japanese automakers shifted the focus of productivity improvement from the costs of the factors of production to how efficiently they are combined into an integrated sequence of production operations. They have established a new standard of organizational efficiency and worker productivity for everyone else in the industry to catch up with. This competitive advantage was reinforced by a worldwide demand shift to smaller cars following the 1973 and, especially, the 1979 oil crises.

In response to the new competitive environment, all major TNCs began to pursue new strategies to cut costs. Many of them, especially among the smaller producers, entered into a complex web of joint-production arrangements to exchange new production technology, share costs, and minimize risks. Others, especially Ford and GM, began to rationalize their worldwide production network by reducing the duplication of facilities and parceling out the production of major components and subassemblies among the various subsidiaries so that production could be

---

5. During the 1970s, the demand in markets of North America, Western Europe, and Japan grew at only 1.5% per annum (and much of this in the peripheral European countries such as Spain). More than 70% of sales were now for replacement purposes (OECD 1984).

integrated on a regional or worldwide basis while each subsidiary would continue to retain a substantial level of manufacturing activity. The new global sourcing strategy created trade-offs for the host LDCs. It created limited opportunities for export production that these LDCs had previously lacked, but ran counter to their goal of fully local production.

For the automobile TNCs, however, none has been able to adopt a full-blown strategy of foreign sourcing in low-wage areas for supplying their home production sites. This is true even for the less automated and efficient U.S. automakers. The reason is that the number of components and parts suitable for foreign low-cost sourcing is limited. The production of major mechanical components is kept at home, close to the firm's centralized R&D capability, because these require heavy initial investments and their manufacture is highly automated with a low amount of direct labor. Among auto components that do require substantial labor inputs, many—for example, finish parts such as exterior body stampings, seats, and dashboard moldings—are bulky to ship and must fit very precisely. Producing them at various remote locations creates formidable quality control problems and achieves insignificant savings after shipping and additional inventory costs are taken into account. As of the early 1980s, 95 percent of a typical U.S.-made car's parts were still manufactured in North America (*Fortune*, 10 December 1984, 172). Among the auto TNCs, the Japanese firms have had the least to gain by offshore sourcing. Their capital investment has been concentrated at home. As a matter of fact, neither Nissan nor Toyota, the principal Japanese-based firms, established manufacturing subsidiaries in LDCs during the 1970s. The just-in-time production operation adopted by the Japanese auto firms creates strong incentives for shortening the supply line and centralizing production at the final point of manufacture. They also have been the first to utilize robots and other forms of automation on a large scale.

The U.S.-based auto firms were most vulnerable to the new challenge as they traditionally neglected the small car segment. Despite wage concessions from labor unions, massive new investments in automation, and intensive efforts to downsize their vehicles, the Big Three—GM, Ford, and Chrysler—have been unable to eliminate the commanding lead the Japanese automakers have continued to enjoy in the production of small cars. Many of the new process techniques have been slow to diffuse to U.S. auto plants because they are embedded in a specific kind of industrial organization and its larger socioeconomic structure (Jones and Womack 1985, 400-401). It is the combination of cross-ownership links between auto firms and their suppliers, membership in the *Keiretsu* groups and the domestic competitive environment created by the fierce rivalry among Keiretsu, and the corporate union system that enabled the

Japanese auto firms to become the leading innovators in production organization in the 1970s.

The Japanese first captured the small car market in the United States, then penetrated Europe, and came to dominate the world automobile trade by 1980 (Jones and Womack 1985, 399). By 1981, this led to some type of formal or informal arrangement to restrain or control Japanese imports in all the major industrial nations. Since then the Japanese producers have begun establishing production facilities or joint-ventures in North America and in some European countries, and usually they have brought along their Japanese part and component suppliers. Meanwhile, instead of abandoning that segment of the market, all major U.S. automakers have signed their own agreements with Japanese affiliates, primarily the second-tier Japanese automakers,[6] to produce finished small cars and major components for them.

The NICs' Competitive Advantage in the Industry

Not until the early 1970s were Korean and Taiwanese producers able to identify emerging export market niches in the automobile industry. The area where they could readily turn their low-wage and existing technological base into a clear competitive advantage was in the production of minor mechanical components, such as starters, radiators, springs, and wiring harnesses, for the replacement market. The production of those components requires moderate initial capital and simple manufacturing techniques, which the local manufacturers and their suppliers had already acquired over the 1960s. In addition, the market for replacement components in both developing and developed countries tends to be price-sensitive rather than quality-sensitive. The market is also relatively easy to penetrate. In most LDCs the effective protection rate for auto parts is much lower than for completed cars, and in the developed countries the regulations on replacement parts are much less restrictive or nonexistent.

The prospects for East Asian NICs to become OEM suppliers to the major auto firms or be selected as the prime production site for TNCs' offshore low-cost sourcing, however, were not very promising throughout the 1970s. First, in South Korea and Taiwan, no U.S. or European TNC subsidiaries were established before the 1970s. And through the end of that decade neither GM nor Ford, given the NICs' very limited domestic markets and the existing severe global overcapacity facing the auto

---

6. GM owns 34% of Isuzu Motors, Chrysler has 15% of Mitsubishi Motors, and Ford has a 25% stake in Mazda Motors.

TNCs, was interested in investing in large-scale manufacturing facilities in either of the two countries. Thus these two NICs were simply not part of the new global or region-based sourcing strategies adopted by U.S. and European automotive TNCs throughout most the 1970s. Furthermore, the East Asian NICs' comparative advantage in a limited number of auto parts and components did not provide big enough savings for the auto TNCs to justify a far-flung low-wage sourcing strategy. Among suitable low-wage locations, Mexico rather than Korea or Taiwan was considered the choice site for delivery to Detroit.

Finally, the entry barriers would be the highest if the two NICs attempted a strategy to promote the export of finished motor vehicles by indigenous producers. As a matter of fact, since World War II no independent firms had risen to be internationally competitive and challenge the existing firms except in Japan.[7] First, the two NICs faced a formidable barrier in the area of scale economy. Even toward the end of the 1970s, their respective domestic market was not big enough to support even a single producer to achieve the minimal efficient scale (about 300,000 units per year). During the period 1977-80, the average annual domestic sale was 106,185 units in Taiwan, and 116,792 units in South Korea (Chen 1981). In comparative terms, these figures were about half the production capacity of a typical GM assembly plant or about one-third of Mexican domestic auto production in 1976 (Bennett and Sharpe 1985, 193). New entrants also have to meet the capital requirement of marketing and servicing capability, a price tag too high even for many Japanese automakers. Most of them, except for the largest such as Nissan and Toyota, had to either take advantage of their existing affiliation with the Big Three or enter new joint-venture agreements to lower the barriers against entering U.S. markets. But the NICs' indigenous producers had little to offer, in terms of home market share or production technology, for such exchanges with the TNCs.

Other factors have not favored the NICs' competitive advantage in the finished motor vehicle market either. First, the entry barriers of the developed markets have actually gone up since the early 1970s because of their increasingly higher standards of emission and fuel efficiency. Second, most potential developing-country markets were all highly protected and typically dominated by local TNC subsidiaries. Third, the competition in world auto export was intensified during the 1970s. Specifically, in the subcompact market, the segment most suitable for new entrants, they would have to challenge the dominance of the Japanese TNCs, the most

---

7. Of course, this is no longer true after the ascendancy of the South Korean automakers around the early 1980s.

efficient, innovative, and most highly automated automakers in the world. Japanese firms' competitive advantage in scale economy and worker productivity could offset whatever cost advantage the NICs have in wage level (Jones and Womack 1985, 400). The Japanese automakers are also best equipped to maintain this overall cost leadership strategy, as they are financially strong and tend to pursue an aggressive long-term pricing strategy in gaining and/or defending market share.

To sum up, the economics and dynamics of the global automobile industry imposed rather restrictive constraints on Taiwan and South Korea. The underlying rational division of labor implied by the emerging global production structure is that global terminal producers take full advantage of scale economies through a high degree of internal sourcing and oligopolize the world finished-car market. This in turn creates an extremely high barrier for the NICs' automakers wishing to enter the finished-car market. The competitive opening for the NICs is in the production of parts and minor mechanical components, initially for foreign replacement markets and gradually for OEM markets.

III. The NICs' Divergent Upgrading Strategies Toward the Automobile Industry

In this section, I will establish the case that although the two economies faced a comparable set of structural constraints and opportunities in terms of the competitive opening and market entry barriers in the automobile industry, each government has taken a distinctive approach toward industrial upgrading, with predictable differences in outcomes. Policy divergences can be explained by the differences in organizational characteristics of the state economic bureaucracy and the policy network between state agencies and private automakers in each country. I will first examine to what extent those institutional arrangements for the automobile sector resemble or deviate from the macrolevel characteristics I specified earlier. Then I will trace the formation of sectoral policy and policy-induced development and adaptation in production organization and technology in the automobile sector of the two NICs at four sequential phases: the early development as an infant industry in the 1950s and 1960s, the emphatic promotion of industry upgrading in the 1970s, the restructuring effort in the first half of the 1980s, and the impact of economic and political liberalization in the late 1980s.

Institutional Arrangements for Industrial Policy in the Automobile Sector

In South Korea, the formulation of automobile sectoral policies involved the entire machinery of economic planning. This was because the sectoral plan for the industry, as established standard procedure, is incorporated into overall economic planning, embodied in a series of five-year and other special long-term plans, such as the Heavy and Chemical Industry Plan (Kwack 1984). Sectoral plans were always the building blocks of the macroeconomic development plans (Kim 1983).

The point agency responsible for industrial development is the Ministry of Trade and Industry (MTI). The MTI took on many functions of Japan's MITI (Johnson 1982) and was influential in decisions on tariff and credit policies. The MTI typically regulated market entry and terms of domestic competition, imposing sectoral reorganization or market order on private firms. Firms with a proven track record of past performance were selected and nurtured. MTI's analytical capacity was enhanced by its affiliated industrial policy think-tank, the Korean Institute of Economics and Technology (KIET),[8] which, along with an official trade promotion agency, KOTRA, surveyed the world for needed market and technology and assisted in formulating sector-specific development plans.

The other powerful arm of the planning machinery is the Ministry of Finance (MOF). The MOF supervised the entire financial sector, controlled foreign-exchange rationing, and implemented fiscal policy. The MOF in South Korea, much like its Japanese counterpart, has been a stronghold of prodirigiste officials (Economist Intelligence Unit, 1982, no. 3). While the structure and control of the banking system is very similar to Taiwan's,[9] all Korean banks, including commercial and specialized banks, have functioned as development resources to finance government-initiated industrial projects. The banks followed a list of instructions, drawn up each year by the MOF, on how much to lend to

---

8. Formerly, the Korean Institute of International Economics.

9. From 1961, when the military government repossessed those shares of the commercial banks in private hands, until the partial denationalization in 1980-83, the government had virtually complete control over the entire financial system, excepting the (informal) curb market. The banking system includes five nationwide commercial banks; several state-run special banks, notably the Korea Development Bank for long-term financing, the Export-Import Bank of Korea for long-term export financing, and the Korea Exchange Bank for short-term trade financing; and ten regional banks, one for each of the ten provinces. Access to foreign borrowers required explicit authorization by the government. The state-run specialized banks are the main conduit for the inflow of foreign savings.

each type of borrower and to each category among the industrial sectors (Cole and Park 1983). Each business group used a single bank as its main lender, which gave the bank a firm grip on the financial structure and business operations of its client business groups.

At the apex of the economic planning machinery is the Economic Planning Board (EPB), a supraministerial planning agency.[10] The EPB supervises both the development and the implementation of planning. With its budgetary control over the ministries and authority over the development and implementation of economic planning, the EPB has enjoyed the institutional power to carry out its function of coordinating fiscal, monetary, trade, and industrial policy (Kim 1983).

Within the MTI, the Machinery Industry Bureau is responsible for the entire machinery industry, of which automobiles are a part. Various sectoral plans, both the five-year and other long-term plans, for the industry are deliberated at the level of director-general officials and coordinated by the Industrial Policy Bureau. Then these plans are subject to appraisal by the officials at EPB. The EPB coordinates industrial policy among the concerned ministries through the industrial screening committee, which is attended by ministers of MTI, MOF, and other concerned ministries and chaired by the deputy premier, the head of the EPB. The implementation of industry policy is subject to the same annual review procedure that the EPB has established for the five-year plans.

South Korean private automobile producers have been directly involved in the formulation and implementation of sectoral policies. As with other state-sponsored industrial associations and trade organizations, the Korean Automobile Industry Association (KAIA) functions as more than an intermediary. The industry association played an important role in creating a consensus between government and industry on policy goals and implementation mechanisms. The association frequently submitted its proposals for industrial policies either on demand or on its own initiative, and it also helped the MTI in conducting industrial surveys, devising Korean standards, and enforcing governmental regulations (Kim 1985). Starting with the Second Five-Year Plan, representatives of the KAIA were included in the working group organized to help prepare sectoral plans (Kim 1983, 46-47). Thus, senior executives of private producers got a chance to meet with the middle-level officials of the MTI

---

10. Another center of economic decision-making is the Secretariat of Economic Affairs to the President within the Presidential Office (the Blue House). The locus of real policy-making power has shifted between the chief economic advisers at the Blue House and the EPB depending on the degree of the president's personal involvement.

and experts from the KIET on a regular basis.[11] The coordination between private industry and government agencies is enhanced by informal, crosscutting interpersonal connections between the business elite and high-ranking state officials. The owners of most chaebol involved in automobile production enjoyed direct access to the presidential office, the Blue House. During the Park administration, close and regular contact between chaebol executives and high-ranking economic officials and economic advisers was institutionalized in such well-publicized arrangements as the Monthly Export Promotion Meeting, which the president himself religiously attended.

In the state-business partnership, the state was clearly the senior partner. The reason is simple. As Jones and Sakong put it, "Government control of the banks is the single most important economic factor explaining the directly subordinate position of the private sector" (1980). The long-term sectoral plans were the consensual game plan between the government and the private sector. The sectoral plans for the industry typically contained specific output performance targets, e.g., local content ratio, major investment plans, and estimated requirements for investment resource allocation for the automobile industry (Korean Industrial Development Bank 1985). Sectoral plans are always implemented in a comprehensive fashion. Fiscal incentives, entry permits, trade protection, policy on foreign participation, technological research and development support, allocation of credit and foreign exchange, were organized into a coherent package.

To sum up, the institutional arrangements for formulating and implementing industrial policy for the automobile sector deviated little from the macrolevel characteristics I specified earlier. The only minor exception is that the automobile industry has been characterized by a strong dependence on foreign technology. Korean automakers all signed agreements with one or more auto TNCs as sources of technological license and transfer. The leading American auto TNC, General Motors, has been directly involved in local production via the joint-venture route since the early 1970s. But, as I will show later, this element of foreign presence has had little effect on the way the Korean government organizes and promotes the industry. Furthermore, through various stages of restructuring, the state has, step-by-step, brought the industry in line with other strategic sectors that are typically dominated by a few selected national conglomerates.

In the case of Taiwan the characteristics of macrolevel institutional arrangements permit greater variation of institutional arrangements for the

---

11. Interview in Seoul with a KIET staff researcher, December 1986.

formulation and implementation of industrial policy across sectors. Unlike South Korea, in Taiwan the arena of sectoral policy for the automobile industry is more fluid. Also, the relationship between state officials and private automakers vacillates between collusive at lower levels and bellicose at high levels.

The state agency responsible for promoting industrial growth in the private sector is the Industrial Development Bureau (IDB) under the Ministry of Economic Affairs (MOEA). The IDB was not strategically placed in the overall economic bureaucracy, nor was it empowered with effective policy instruments. For example, the power to set tariff policy for the automobile industry is shared among the IDB, the International Trade Bureau (ITB), and the Ministry of Finance. Within the MOEA, without the backing of the minister the IDB does not always have its way, as the ITB has its own policy priorities. Furthermore, there is no institutionalized mechanism to coordinate the actions of MOEA and MOF except at the cabinet level. The only firm- and product-specific policy instrument under the direct control of the MOEA—the allocation of R&D grants—is administered by the Office of Science and Technology Advisors (OSTA) with very limited IDB input.[12]

The powerful and conservative Central Bank of China (CBC) and Ministry of Finance occupied the commanding heights of the economic bureaucracy. The seclusive CBC is typically put into the trusted hands of the president and beyond the influence even of the head of the Executive Yuan. Originally, this arrangement institutionalized the collective memories among the Mainlander old guard of the politically disastrous hyperinflation on the mainland and the hard-won battle against the triple-digit inflation in Taiwan during the 1949-53 period just as they were consolidating their rule on the island. During the 1960s, bolstered by continued success, the prodevelopment technocrats gradually gained more influence and backing, and institutions such as the planning agencies and the Ministry of Economic Affairs upgraded their responsibilities.[13] But the conservative monetary and financial officials were always in a strategic position to check on the planning technocrats. CBC or MOF officials were appointed to head the supraministerial planning agencies or policy-coordinating task forces that have been created and reorganized from

---

12. Interview with the director of the OSTA.

13. The point agency for private industry, the Bureau of Industrial Development under the MOEA, was upgraded to its current form as late as 1970.

time to time since 1962[14] and they enjoyed the direct control of monetary and fiscal policy tools (*Commonwealth*, November 1984). Under the close scrutiny of the conservative CBC and MOF officials, all domestic banks are risk-averse when it comes to lending and are obsessed with collateral.

There is no mechanism linking sectoral policy with macroeconomic planning, which is more indicative than directive. The government uses its medium- and long-term economic plans primarily to indicate where it thinks the economy is going, to identify potential economic problems, and to project its economic policies. Plans had little binding authority on the actions of the CBC. Plans were often revised, even the investment plans in the public sector.

In Taiwan, intimate institutional links seldom emerge between responsible state agencies and major industrial sectors, with the exception of a few sector-specific policy networks in which state enterprises or parastatals occupy a strategic node.[15] Formally economic planners retained an aloof posture toward the private sector and allowed minimal direct private sector policy input. High-level economic officials approach the task of openly soliciting private policy input with caution because of the prevailing ethos within the state economic bureaucracy that leniency toward private economic actors often constitutes favoritism, and is thus an act of impropriety. Most large firms try to secure personal ties with some high-ranking government or party officials. Most industrial associations are used only by middle-level bureaucrats at the IDB to collect information and convey policy. Thus, domestic auto producers prefer to seek particularistic ties for access to sectoral policies, with the better-connected Mainlander-owned Yue-Loong taking the lead, rather than developing an

---

14. During most of the 1960s and early 1970s, the planning agency, the Council for International Economic Cooperation and Development (CIECD), was headed by C. K. Yen (1964-69), a former finance minister, and later by Chiang Ching-kuo (1969-73), the Generalissimo's oldest son. After Chiang Ching-kuo (CCK) became premier, CIECD was reorganized and downgraded, in 1973, into an advisory agency known as the Economic Planning Council (EPC), and the real economic policy-making power was taken over by a new five-man Finance and Economic Small Group of the Executive Yuan, headed by Central Bank Governor Yu Kuo-hwa. In 1977, when CCK was elected president, the EPC was revitalized to become a supraministerial agency known as the Council for Economic Planning and Development (CEPD) and was again headed by Yu Kuo-hwa. In 1983 Yu was promoted to the premiership and the CEPD was once again downgraded. In recent years, the CEPD performs primarily an advisory role in the policy-making process.

15. One such example is the petrochemical policy network centering around the state-owned China Petroleum.

industrywide network through the medium of an industrial association. It becomes very difficult for the IDB to formulate consensual sectoral development goals, as most domestic automakers, perhaps with the exception of Ford Lio-Ho, have their own private channel to at least some of the high-ranking planning and/or finance officials. Usually, these connections are not effective enough to secure any one of them exclusive privileges, but at times they are sufficiently strong to torpedo policies that infringe upon their vital interests. For the same reason, a rigorous implementation of existing performance requirements would run into difficulty if it threatened the economic viability of existing firms.

Thus, unlike the MTI in Korea, the IDB was incapable of serving as a powerful mainstay and as a guardian for the industry within the overall economic bureaucracy. In Taiwan's less centralized state economic bureaucracy and more fluid state-business relations, to promote an industry with a comprehensive and coherent plan always required the personal commitment of a minister-level policy entrepreneur, typically the head of MOEA, to assert leadership over the private producers, mobilize support and resources within the state economic bureaucracy, win the trust of finance officials, and defuse interagency conflict.[16] But unfortunately, most ambitious ministers have avoided the automobile industry. Three characteristics of Taiwan's automobile industry in the early 1970s complicated the task of coordination and constrained state action, thereby discouraging able economic planning officials from investing their energy, resources, and political entrepreneurship. These were the fact that there was no state agency or enterprise taking part in related R&D or production activities, the dominance of the Japanese TNCs in technical licensing, and a tripartite ownership structure that comprised Mainlander (Yue-Loong), Taiwanese (San-Fu and Sam-Yang), and foreign (Lio-Ho).

The Initial Growth of the Automobile Industry in South Korea and Taiwan

The two East Asian NICs entered the automobile industry under similar sets of structural constraints, and by roughly the same route in terms of governmental promotional schemes, degree of national control, and technological dependence on the Japanese TNCs. In both countries, the automobile industry was initially promoted as an infant industry to be undertaken by indigenous firms under an import-substituting trade regime. Taiwan took the first step to help establish indigenous auto firms,

---

16. The successful cases would include the growth of the petrochemical and semiconductor industries.

but the Korean state has exerted a stronger hand in shaping the formative industry from the beginning. This has, as it turned out, more than compensated for its late start.

The modern production of automobiles in the two East Asian NICs would not have started without promotion by the state. Both South Korea and Taiwan had little experience in automobile-related manufacturing before World War II. During colonial rule their small domestic demand for automobiles and parts was met completely by imports from Japan.[17] The two governments began to promote local manufacture of complete cars at an early stage of postwar development, at a time when their dynamic export-oriented industrialization had barely started and per capita income was still around $100 (at current prices). At that time no auto TNCs paid much attention to the two markets.

Both South Korea and Taiwan entered the modern production of automobiles through the familiar route of SKD kits assembly under foreign licensing. During the formative years, the two governments' policy objectives for the infant auto industry were quite similar. The goal was to gradually increase the value-added portion of domestic production, upgrading the level of local production from SKD and CKD assembly to substantial manufacturing activities with an increasing portion of domestic parts and components.

In Taiwan, the first modern assembly plant was established in 1958 by the Yue-Loong Co., a private firm owned by a well-connected Shanghai industrialist, to produce passenger cars and trucks under a license agreement with Nissan. In 1961, the government in Taiwan promulgated the Measures for the Development of the Automobile Industry, which prohibited new investment in SKD assembly. It also empowered the MOEA to institute import restrictions on parts, components, and finished motor vehicles in any way it saw fit. A three-tier tariff system was enacted, providing a 60% nominal protection rate for finished passenger cars, 40% for commercial vehicles, and 15% for most parts and components (Chen 1980, 141). Also, all imports of motor vehicles for which comparable models were manufactured domestically required special approval. The government also pledged to review the merits of the promotional scheme in four years. In 1964, the government further restricted all new purchases of small passenger cars for commercial use, i.e., taxis, to domestically manufactured vehicles. This was to help the embattled Yue-Loong,

---

17. After the outbreak of the Pacific war, however, Japan began to produce some automobile replacement parts in the two colonies and supplied them to Manchuria, North China, and Southeast Asia. Almost all these parts factories were run by Japanese (Kim and Lee 1980, 279-80).

still the only domestic automaker, then fighting for its survival under the competition of imported motor vehicles. In 1965, at the urging of Yue-Loong, the government decided to extend the existing infant industry protection arrangements for another four years. Also, to enhance the incentives for higher domestic content, the tariff on auto parts and components was raised to 46% while the tariff for finished passenger cars was raised by 5% to 65% (Chen 1981). Under the new tariff system, more new domestic parts and components were produced, some of them under licensing agreements from the Japanese part and component producers through the arrangement between Yue-Loong and Nissan. As soon as the level of protection was raised, the government imposed a 60% local content requirement, which would be applied to all new entrants as well as existing firms. At that time, the 60% requirement was widely regarded as totally unrealistic; however, it was intended to give economic officials broad leeway in deciding how the fulfillment should be defined and implemented. At that time, the MOEA showed much leniency toward Yue-Loong and only a watered-down version of the local content requirement was actually imposed.

The 60% target received wide criticism both from within the economic bureaucracy and from private industry. It was denounced by its critics as a smoke screen for prolonging Yue-Loong's coveted monopoly status in the commercial passenger car market (*Financial News*, June 1986, 154-55). As more local industrialists sought to enter the lucrative auto assembly business, they all found a way to get the ear of one or another high-level official. It became politically difficult for the MOEA not to grant entry to new applicants. As it turned out, the political connection enjoyed by Yue-Loong was not strong enough to defend its monopoly position. To protect its return on the investment in meeting the domestic content requirement, Yue-Loong had tried to persuade the MOEA to adopt a narrow interpretation of "localization" in terms of in-house production, but did not prevail. Between 1967 and 1969, four new firms—San-Fu, Sam-Yang, Lio-Ho, and China Motors (an independent subsidiary of Yue-Loong)—were allowed to enter under a reduced version of the local content requirement. The emerging production structure became increasingly similar to the competition among Japanese auto producers in their home markets. Lio-Ho, with equity participation by Toyota, competed with Nissan's local partner, Yue-Loong, in the small passenger car market, while San-Fu, Sam-Yang, and China Motors, each cooperating with a second-tier Japanese auto firm, went after the small commercial vehicle niche (pickups and vans).

The Korean government launched the modern production of motor vehicles only after the military had come to power. This was four years after Yue-Loong opened its first plant. But the Korean state exerted a

stronger hand in shaping the formative industry from the very beginning. In 1962, as part of the First Five-Year Plan, the state-owned Saenara
Auto Co. established the first modern assembly plant, with an annual capacity of 6,000 cars. This company was set up in technical cooperation
with Nissan. As soon as Saenara went into production, the government
legislated an industry-specific protection bill, the Automobile Industry
Protection Law. This provided tax exemptions for imports of parts and
components, as well as for automobile assemblers, while prohibiting imports of completed automobiles, including both passenger cars and commercial vehicles, except under special circumstances. Also in 1962, the
state sponsored the creation of the Korean Automobile Industry Association to serve as an intermediary between the responsible state agency and
the emerging private producers.

In 1965, the government transferred the state-owned Saenara operation to the privately owned Shinjin Auto Co. and approved its new technical cooperation agreement with Toyota under conditions of about 21%
localization of production. In the following year, the state instituted intensive measures to increase local content. A domestic content schedule
for terminal assemblers was set by the MTI. The target was to increase the
domestic content ratio to more than 50% in five years. The schedule was
rigorously implemented. Domestic producers that failed to meet the localization requirement lost preferential allocation of foreign exchange
(Kim and Lee 1980, 281). In 1969, a detail-oriented domestic content
schedule for domestic parts and components producers was also promulgated. Under the governance of this domestic schedule, the average ratio
of local production increased from 21% in 1966 to more than 60% in 1972
(ibid.).

Under heavy protection and with the expansion of the domestic parts
and components supply, three more private national firms, Asia, Hyundai, and Kia, were allowed to begin production of complete cars during
the 1965 to 1969 period. Kia started producing small cars under a licensing agreement with Mazda and assembled trucks in cooperation with
Nissan. Hyundai initially sought technical cooperation from Ford, while
Asia assembled cars under a licensing agreement with Fiat.

Around the early 1970s, GM and Ford respectively began expressing
interest in entering South Korea and Taiwan, and both preferred establishing a majority-owned subsidiary. On the other hand, the two NICs insisted on their existing policy of a 50 percent ceiling on foreign
ownership. GM eventually complied with the Korean investment guideline and was allowed to form a 50/50 joint venture with Shinjin under a
new corporate identity—GM Korea—in 1972.[18] In the same year, Ford
took advantage of the abrupt pullout of Toyota in the wake of the nor-
malization of relations between Japan and Mainland China and secured a

favorable deal from the MOEA, which was desperate to recoup the loss of a major foreign investor. Ford was allowed to take over Toyota's share in Lio-Ho and made itself the 70 percent majority owner in the reorganized Ford Lio-Ho.

Thus, by the early 1970s, the South Korean automobile industry had an almost identical industrial structure to Taiwan's, and it had achieved a comparable level of local production and exhibited a similar technological dependence on foreign TNCs. Also in both countries the domestic market was still very small. The annual sales in either market in 1970 were fewer than 15,000 units. As a consequence, every local automaker had to produce a range of models at grossly inadequate volumes.

The Critical Decade of the 1970s

In 1973, the Korean government adopted a basic warplan for industrial upgrading—the Heavy and Chemical Plan—that identified automobiles as a priority industry (Kim 1985). The industry was then covered by the various special financing schemes set up for the promotion of the general machinery industry (Chu 1987, ch. 4). The next year, a comprehensive sector-specific promotion plan was promulgated. In the 1974 Long-Term Development Plan of the Automobile Industry, the MTI mapped out the blueprint for developing the industry over the next ten years. In the plan, the Korean government revealed its intention of using the limited domestic market to support the expansion of a few selected automakers. It outlined its ambitious goal of achieving full local production of small passenger cars (more than 90 percent domestic content) by the end of the 1970s and turning the automobile industry into a leading export sector by the early 1980s. The plan called for the production of so-called citizen cars at certain designated manufacturing sites. Those cars should be Korean models with more than 95 percent domestic content and with engines limited to 1.5 liters. The production of citizen cars was supposed to begin in 1975 with a minimum annual capacity of 50,000 units by each producer (Korean Industrial Development Bank 1985). In implementing the new strategy, the MTI restricted manufacturing of small passenger cars to three primary auto firms: Hyundai, Kia, and GM-Korea. Each was required to submit its citizen car development plan for approval. Once approved the producer was not allowed to introduce replacement models within the period set by the MTI (Chen 1981, 19).

Also in 1974, the MTI launched a supplementary long-term plan for the parts and components sector. The plan included a domestic content

---

18. GM Korea was renamed Saehan in 1976.

schedule for parts and component producers. From 1974 onward, the MTI constantly selected new auto part and component items and their designated domestic suppliers for special promotion. These designated producers were to be governed by the domestic content schedule (Yun and Park 1984, 27). Once the local production of a particular component met governmental standards, it was protected under a complete import ban. All three primary producers were also required to cooperate in joint-development of standardized parts and components.

To realize scale economy and prepare domestic automakers for future export expansion, the government gave export the highest priority. Starting in 1977, all three firms were required to set their annual export targets. The initial targeted markets were LDCs such as Southeast Asian and Latin American countries. During the initial export drive, in addition to subsidized export credits and direct export subsidies, the three designated producers were also rewarded with the privilege of being allowed to assemble a limited number of imported CDKs for the domestic upscale market. This lucrative import quota was rationed among the three in proportion to their export performances. Most important, the government encouraged the carmakers to adopt a pricing scheme setting the export price well below cost while selling to domestic consumers at substantial profit margins.[19]

At the same time that the Korean government had imposed market order on the industry and strictly regulated the terms of competition among domestic producers to ensure the industry would grow along the official line, the government in Taiwan continued to rely on structural incentives to induce the desired development. The state did not provide subsidized financial support for private automakers nor did it select the fittest for special promotion. Eschewing more direct forms of policy instruments to influence the existing auto companies, the IDB relied on discretionary administering of tariffs, import restrictions, commercial vehicle licensing, and the power of investment review to influence the development of the industry. Thus, from early 1969, when the earlier infant industry protection measures expired, the IDB began to modify the protection schemes and entry requirements from time to time to apply what they conceived of as a right mix of incentives and discipline to domestic auto producers in order to move the industry forward. Its approach is best summarized by a former IDB director, who compared

---

19. For example, in 1979, the production cost of Hyundai's Pony was around $3,745. The domestic price tag was $4,980 but the export FOB price was set at $2,150 (Chen 1981, 35).

Taiwan's industrial policy to a pressure cooker: "The task is to set the right pressure level for the cooking" (*Financial News*, June 1986, 161).

Even with this limited set of policy instruments, however, the IDB has not been able to employ them in a coherent and consistent fashion because the bureau has not enjoyed much clout in the overall economic bureaucracy. Every time issues in related areas arise, automobile industry policy has been tailored to meet the more immediate policy concerns of other state agencies. As a result, the government never committed itself to a firm and long-standing position on the maximum number of auto producers that it would allow to enter the market,[20] nor did it stick to a consistent policy about restrictions on imports. Instead of imposing a state-sanctioned industry structure, the MOEA has tried to limit new entrants into terminal production by raising the investment requirements stepwise. In 1969, the MOEA instituted a new $25 million minimum equity capital requirement for investment in automobile production. One more car producer went into production under the new guideline. In 1977, Yue-Tian Auto Co., a spinoff of a major motorcycle manufacturer, signed a technical agreement with Peugeot of France to produce passenger cars[21] and became the sixth carmaker on the island.

Also during the second half of 1970, three of the four second-tier producers expanded into the fastest growing small passenger car segment. Right after the approval of Yue-Tian's project, the MOEA decided to admit no more car producers that aimed mainly at the domestic market. The investment guideline was revised to require that all new investment projects must include a plan to export at least 50% of output. The next year, new strings were attached. The minimum local content ratio was raised to 70%. In addition, in meeting local content requirements, a new producer had to select one of six designated major mechanical components for localization (Chen 1980, 72). While it was relatively easy to apply these requirements to new entrants, the IDB did not have effective policy instruments to enforce the new domestic content requirements on the existing producers except for some drastic measures such as cutting off their imports or forcing them out of business. Alternatively, the IDB allowed some loopholes for the existing firms as it was clear that none of the second-tier producers would be able to meet the new standard. Un-

---

20. An executive of Ford Lio-Ho indicated that in the early 1970s, the MOEA was still committed to limiting the number of domestic carmakers to five. But it did not hold firm to this stance.

21. In the same year, China Benz, an import dealer, was also allowed to assemble passenger cars under a technical agreement with Mercedes Benz. But it never went into production.

der the exit clause, existing automakers were allowed to credit their export of parts and components to the fulfillment of the new domestic content requirement up to a certain percentage ceiling.

A direct implication of the state's less restrictive policy on admitting new automakers was that the existing Taiwanese auto producers had to constantly prepare themselves to face intensified competition from new entrants. This, however, was not the only unpredictable economic factor confronting the domestic carmakers. Over the years, the demand for domestically produced cars has been highly sensitive to the state's policy on import restrictions. Between 1969 and 1980, with regard to small passenger cars alone, the government modified its import restriction schemes six times for various reasons—to introduce necessary market discipline, to force domestic carmakers to improve efficiency, or to countervail their collusive pricing strategy (in 1969, 1971, and 1979); to adjust bilateral trade relations with the United States, Western Europe, and Japan (in 1977 and 1980); and to help balance the current account (in 1974) (Chen 1980, 66-68). Some of the changes were demanded by other economic agencies, such as the ITB, the Ministry of Finance, or Council of Economic Development and Planning. They stepped into the auto import policy area and took the podium away from the IDB.

Thus, depending on the restrictiveness of the import policy, foreign motor vehicles accounted for as much as 42% of the total domestic supply or as little as 11.7% during the 1960s and 1970s (Chen 1980). The fluctuation in foreign supply for small passenger cars, which constitute more than half of domestic demand, has been similar although in less drastic terms. These adjustments in import policy rarely involved any advance consultation with the private producers.[22] Throughout the 1970s, the state's policy on restrictions of foreign imports has been a constant source of friction and tension between Taiwan's economic officials and domestic auto producers. By contrast, the state's policy on auto imports never emerged as an issue in South Korea. The complete import ban on finished

---

22. Even well-connected Yue-Loong has been hit with a few surprises. It suffered its first severe blow in 1959, just one year after it went into production. During that year, as soon as Yue-Loong started rolling out chassis for large passenger cars and trucks under the existing double-hurdle protection scheme (tariff and import license quota), the MOEA abruptly abolished the quantity restriction on importing large passenger cars and trucks, on the grounds that as capital goods they were too vital to the economy to be over-protected. Yue-Loong dismantled its stillborn large chassis production and never entered that market segment again.

vehicles contained in the Automobile Industry Promotion Law was in effect for almost a quarter century.[23] The import bans were applied not only to small passenger cars but to small commercial vehicles, trucks, and buses as well. Since the inception of the law in 1965, the import of finished vehicles and chassis under special licenses[24] has never exceeded 5% of total domestic demand, and the import duty for completed motor vehicles was set at 150% (Chen 1981).

The divergent governmental approaches between South Korea and Taiwan set the development of their respective industries on different courses. By the late 1970s, the Korean automakers accomplished most of the policy goals laid down in the 1974 long-term plan. The major Korean producers moved full speed toward the goals of more than 90% domestic content and positioned themselves well for expanding into the foreign market toward the end the 1970s.

With the infusion of subsidized credit and under a state-imposed market order, the Korean car producers have come forward with aggressive investment plans since 1974. The industry's total production capacity increased by 600% from 63,000 units in 1973 to 366,000 in 1980 while small passenger car production capacity increased by an even more astonishing 750%, from 31,000 in 1973 to 238,000 in 1980 (Korean Industrial Development Bank 1985, 775). By 1980, both Hyundai and Kia's citizen car models (Pony and Brisa) were produced with more than 90% domestic content, and Saehan's (formerly GM Korea) Gemini was close (85.5%). Responding to strong government incentives, all three major automakers began working on foreign marketing in 1975, even though they were still at a substantial cost disadvantage compared to their Japanese competitors.[25] Actual export sales started in 1977, with 9,136 units sold, increasing to 31,486 units in 1979 (Korean Industrial Development Bank 1985).

The growth of domestic demand, however, has fallen far behind the expansion of production capacity. During the 1970s, Korea's per capita car ownership was still about half of Taiwan's level. The absolute size of

---

23. At the end of 1985, it was replaced, along with many other sector-specific protection laws, by a more generalized statute—the Industry Development Law.

24. The import clearances were granted primarily to the applications for special vehicles; passenger cars were never allowed except for foreign diplomats and U.S. military personnel.

25. The exact cost advantage enjoyed by the Japanese has been a highly guarded trade secret. One estimate, published by the Korean Ministry of Trade and Industry, suggests that as late as 1979, with the advantages of scale economy and a more efficient production organization, Toyota could produce a comparable model to Hyundai's Pony in Japan at about three-fifths the cost in Korea (Jones and Womack 1985, 401).

Korea's domestic automobile stock, however, was quite comparable to Taiwan's throughout the 1970s. Car ownership in Korea increased from 3.89 units per thousand in 1970 to 12.92 in 1979, and annual domestic sales reached 160,000 units by the end of the 1970s. The investment spree was based on optimistic projections of future growth in the export market,[26] even though initially foreign demand for Korean cars was slow to pick up. As a result, the average capacity utilization rate during the 1975-80 period was only 40.1% (Chen 1981, 42).

During the same period, Taiwan's per capita income was rapidly approaching the threshold for the demand for cars to take off.[27] Automobile ownership increased from 6.7 per thousand to 31.52 during the 1970s, and domestic car sales doubled every four years. Despite this phenomenal growth, Taiwanese domestic producers have been cautious in expanding production capacity. They have kept their investment plan in close step with foreseeable future growth in domestic sales. The average capacity utilization rate between 1976 and 1980 was 68.8 percent. In 1980, total domestic production capacity was about 188,000 vehicles, while total domestic sales were about 150,000. Also, without a secure long-term prospect under an orderly market, none of the domestic producers was willing to adopt a mass production strategy that would enhance their cost competitiveness through the gradual realization of economies of scale. In particular, the automakers and their suppliers refrained from making the up-front lump sum investment required to localize the production of major mechanical components. Instead, each automaker relied on a product differentiation strategy to marginally increase their market share, even in the case of the two leading manufacturers, Yue-Loong and Ford Lio-Ho. To compete on two fronts—with domestic competitors in subcompact models and with foreign producers in the upscale range—both produced a wide range of models and practiced frequent model alteration (*Commonwealth*, August 1984, 110-16). The product differentiation strategy pursued by Taiwan's automakers only intensified domestic producers' technical dependence on their foreign partners and further delayed the possibility of full local production.

---

26. In 1979, the Korean government designated the automobile industry as one of ten strategic export sectors for the 1980s and announced an ultra-ambitious growth target—two million units annual production and one million units exported by 1987.

27. The rule of thumb is that a nation reaches that threshold when the average price of a small car is about five times per capita income. By this estimate, Taiwan reached this point around 1976 and South Korea around 1979 (Chen 1980).

Restructuring Efforts of the 1980s

In the first half of the 1980s, the automobile industry in the two NICs went through a restructuring phase that set the two further apart. In Taiwan, the state elite increasingly felt the need to accelerate the process of industrial upgrading while in South Korea the policy-makers had to address the excesses created by the Heavy and Chemical Plan during the 1970s. Each government dealt with the new challenge within the boundaries of their established patterns of intervention. The Korean government introduced a more restrictive market order on an industry saddled with overcapacity and came to provide more assistance to the troubled private firms. In Taiwan, the state stepped up its direct involvement and increased the economic pressure on the existing automakers.

The second oil crisis caught Korean planners and automakers alike by surprise. The auto industry suffered a major setback and the investment spree came to a standstill under the 1980 stabilization program. Domestic sales dropped from 159,514 in 1979 to fewer than 100,000 in 1980; export sales dropped 16% to 25,253, and the average capacity utilization rate sank to 34.3% (23.5% for passenger cars). The financial structures of all automakers and their parent conglomerates were rapidly deteriorating. With severe overcapacity and projections of future declines, the newly installed Chun government moved swiftly to impose a comprehensive rationalization plan on all of heavy industry in August 1980. As part of the rationalization plan, the MTI implemented a merger plan to create a clear-cut division of labor among domestic automobile makers. Kia, the second largest producer, was ordered to stay out of small passenger car production until 1987, but it was given a monopoly in the light truck business by taking over the truck division of the recently formed Tong-A Auto Co., which was restricted to the production of buses. Trucks over five tons could be built by Hyundai and the Daewoo group, while Asia was given trucks in the eight-to-nine-ton range (*Automotive News*, 7 July 1986, 20).

Originally, the government instructed Hyundai to take over Saehan (formerly GM-Korea), the third largest auto producer, from the Daewoo group and negotiate with its foreign partner, General Motors, to form a new monopoly in the small passenger car market.[28] The negotiations

---

28. In 1978, Daewoo was allowed to buy the Korea Development Bank's 50-percent stake in Saehan Motors. The deal was in part a reward for Daewoo's sacrifices at the Okpo shipyard. In that year, Daewoo, at the government's request, came to the rescue by taking over the huge unfinished shipyard at Okpo from the state-controlled Korea Shipbuilding and Engineering Co. (*Asian Finance*, 15 May 1979, 57).

dragged on for six months as GM refused to accept minor partner status in the new company. After GM reportedly told the government it would leave Korea before going along with the reorganization, the MTI called off the merger plan, and Saehan (which later was renamed Daewoo) remained a 50/50 joint venture between GM and Daewoo (*Asian Wall Street Journal*, 27 April 1981). However, the Korean government has since then persistently pressured GM to transfer management control to Daewoo. It did not take GM very long to learn that without a Korean management team cooperation from the government was hard to get. In late 1982, management control was handed over to Daewoo.

After the reorganization, other supplementary measures soon followed. In 1981, the excise tax for cars was lowered to stimulate domestic demand and the export target was reduced to one-half (Economist Intelligence Unit, 1981, nos. 3-4). Also in 1981, the MTI pumped $120 million in low-interest relief loans into the auto parts and components sector to bail out the troubled suppliers. Under the new and more streamlined market order, the investment spree was resumed as soon as the Korean economy began to recover from its worst recession in the postwar years. Late that year Hyundai launched its plan to build a US$550 million plant with a 300,000 unit annual capacity (*AWSJ*, 9 November 1981). To meet the government's downward adjusted but still ambitious export schedule, Hyundai also invested heavily to improve safety and emission performances and began establishing a marketing infrastructure in the potential foreign markets (*Business Korea*, November 1985, 17-24). Its first attempt to enter the U.S. market was aborted as the Pony model failed to pass safety and emission tests. In 1982, it sold 10 percent of its equity to Mitsubishi in exchange for technical assistance. Daewoo, as soon as it took over the management, also began pushing GM for an export-oriented expansion plan aimed at developed country markets (*AWSJ*, 27 December 1982). In 1984, the stage was finally set for the first Korean plunge into the North American market—Canada. In two years, Hyundai's Pony emerged as Canada's best-selling foreign import.

When Hyundai's Pony knocked on the door of Taiwan's passenger car market in the late 1970s, it probably helped Taiwan's high ranking economic officials make up their minds for a decisive move to turn the local automobile industry around. No prospective auto TNCs responded to the new investment incentives implemented in 1977. They had lost patience with the existing domestic private producers. This left the state officials with only one option. They decided to leave the six automakers behind and come forward with their own investment plan. In January 1978, MOEA submitted to the Executive Yuan a general proposal to establish a large-scale automobile plant with an annual capacity of 200,000 units of compact cars slated primarily for export. In 1979 the automobile industry was classified as strategic and a special task force set up directly under the minister of MOEA to prepare a plan to remedy the prevailing problems afflicting it (Arnold 1989, 188-89). These measures marked the first time the government had tried to formulate a comprehensive sectoral policy for automobile production and the beginning of intensive involvement of minister-level officials in promoting the industry.

In August 1979, the MOEA plan was approved by the Executive Yuan, and later that year it won the personal blessing of the president as he took an occasion to announce the four-point guideline for advancing the industry's development. The main thrust of the new development program was twofold: to promote an export-oriented large-scale auto plant concentrated on the production of small passenger cars, and a new plant producing large vehicles for the domestic truck market and the military.[29] In 1980, two state enterprises, China Steel and Taiwan Machinery, were put in charge of the projects. None of the six private producers was invited or even consulted. The two were each entrusted to recruit prospective foreign partners and negotiate the joint-venture agreements.

Both joint-venture projects ran into serious obstacles. Taiwan Machinery, run by retired army generals and military personnel, went hastily into a joint-venture agreement with General Motors in 1981. A year later, the heavy truck project turned into a financial fiasco.[30] The negotiations between China Steel, the technocrat-controlled state enterprise, and two prospective Japanese firms—Toyota and Nissan—for the proposed small passenger car plant began in 1980. China Steel signed a tentative joint-venture agreement with Toyota in 1981. The agreement contained all three elements that Taiwan's economic officials had hoped for: annual production of 300,000 units, achieving 90% domestic content in five

---

29. The large vehicle plant was pushed by the powerful Defense Ministry, especially by the army, on the ground that the future sale of U.S. military transport equipment was in doubt. Despite the fact that the economic feasibility of this proposal was questionable, the then-minister of MOEA did not have the political clout to resist the pressure and reluctantly went along with the military.

30. The truck operation of the new Hwa-Tung Auto Co. was so uneconomical that it cost 65 percent more than Japanese imports. In 1982 the sudden surge of the Japanese yen vs. the dollar made the cost disparity even worse. One of the partners, the Bank of Communication, was the first to express reservations, finally refusing to extend the credit line. Then the new MOEA minister, Chao Yao-tung, after acknowledging that the plant could survive only under a protracted import ban, decided to break out of the agreement and reimburse GM. Later, the GM share in the joint venture was sold to Hino, a leading Japanese truck producer (*Commonwealth*, September 1982, 28-29).

years, and reaching a 50% export target in eight years. The joint-venture plan looked promising as Chao Yao-tung, formerly the chairman of China Steel, was appointed minister of economic affairs in late 1981. He was not only fully committed to the Big Auto Plant project, as it was popularly referred to, but enjoyed strong support from the premier, Sun Yuan-chuan.

However, by the time Toyota formally submitted its investment plan in 1983 for the MOEA's approval, a dispute emerged. The MOEA was instructed to demand inclusion in the plan of a strictly enforceable year-by-year schedule for reaching domestic content and export ratio targets, while Toyota argued for a more flexible schedule and an exit clause to protect "economic viability" (*Economic Daily*, 28 July 1984). The negotiations dragged on as the MOEA tried to bridge the gap between Toyota and some conservative cabinet members who insisted on these terms. At the same time, the two leading domestic auto producers, which would have the most to lose had the project proceeded, maneuvered to undermine the joint venture, while the four smaller producers were busy preparing for the seemingly inevitable. The territory-bound Yue-Loong was more desperate than Lio-Ho, a multinational subsidiary. It responded with a bold preemptive move by launching a 90,000-unit expansion plan, an aggressive move by Taiwan's standards, and a new auto-design engineering center to develop the island's very first domestically designed model, something it had been urged to do but had resisted for years. The move increased the uncertainty of the economic feasibility of the proposed joint venture by raising the risk of overcapacity (*Financial News*, June 1986, 142-45). Ford, the second largest producer, at first threatened to deinvest if the Taiwan government went ahead with the proposed large-scale plant. After the tentative agreement was signed, it drastically changed its posture and came up with a counterproposal—an export-oriented reinvestment plan. Ford was finally convinced that to protect its grip on Taiwan's market, it had to upgrade and expand its local production facilities to produce certain major components and incorporate Taiwan into its global production network. Ford's proposal was not taken seriously at first.

The joint-venture negotiations also opened up the cleavage between the planning technocrats and conservative financial officials. From the very beginning, the plan got only lukewarm support from the then-powerful CEPD. CEPD Chairman Yu Kuo-hwa, concurrently head of CCB, was known to be skeptical of the Big Auto Plant.[31] In May 1984 Tai-

---

31. The owner of Yue-Loong was reputed to have intimate personal ties with senior finance officials.

wan's cabinet was reshuffled. Chao was "demoted" to chairman of a "downgraded" CEPD and Yu was promoted to premier. It came as a surprise to no one that Yu's hand-picked new minister of economic affairs, Hsu Li-teh, called for a reassessment of the Big Auto Plant project and laid down four principles—general economic viability, local content, export requirements, and technical transfer provision—governing the joint venture. As the negotiations between Toyota and the MOEA turned sour, Ford Lio-Ho found the time propitious to reintroduce its three-stage reinvestment plan, which called for exporting 150,000 units by 1993 on the condition that the production would be exempt from the 70 percent domestic content requirement (*Financial News,* March 1986, 117). Ford's proposal fell short of the MOEA's expectations at that time, but it certainly boosted its confidence at the bargaining table. The MOEA stuck to its negotiating instructions and the talks with Toyota finally collapsed in late 1984.

In retrospect, while Taiwanese economic officials' initial attempt for an export-oriented big auto plant did not come through, their three-year effort did bring about some unexpected improvement on the part of private automakers. Not only did Yue-Loong and Lio-Ho each come up with expansion plans, all the smaller producers made substantial investments to improve efficiency and quality control (*Commonwealth,* August 1984). In hindsight, given the limited direct leverage that Taiwanese state officials had over private producers, this aborted effort turned out to be the more effective way to push private industry forward. While this progress was not enough to turn the industry into an internationally competitive one, it nevertheless paved the way for a further restructuring effort introduced in the second half of the 1980s.

The NICs' divergent strategies, stemming from the varying institutional arrangements of their respective state structures, not only brought about dramatic and differing industrial changes in the automobile industries of South Korea and Taiwan, but increasingly affected the strategies of auto TNCs as well. In the second half of the 1980s, the Korean auto producers rose to become a new factor shaping the dynamics of the global automobile industry. Hyundai's successful invasion of the Canadian market made a strong statement about Korea's competitiveness in world auto sales. It surprised the Big Three. Detroit thus found South Korea an attractive alternative site for offshore sourcing of small cars. At the same time, the voluntary export restriction that held down imports of Japanese cars to the U.S. market also hampered U.S. carmakers' Japanese sourcing strategy because they hadn't been able to get all the small cars they needed from Japan. Both Ford and Chrysler were eager to catch up with General Motors' already established joint-venture with Daewoo.

In 1984, GM signed up Daewoo to produce the Pontiac LeMans subcompact for the U.S. market. GM also signed a separate $40 million joint-venture deal with Daewoo to make starter motors, ignition distributors, alternators, and other complex parts for its worldwide operations (*Fortune*, 10 December 1984). Ford first approached Hyundai but failed to reach an agreement. It then held talks with Kia through its Japanese partner, Mazda, which has an 8 percent equity share in this second-largest Korean producer. In 1985, Kia entered a joint-production agreement with Ford and Mazda. The cooperation started in 1987, the year Kia was officially allowed to resume production of passenger cars. Ford was responsible for marketing the export sales (*Business Korea*, August 1985, 55). Chrysler approached Samsung for a joint-venture in producing small cars in 1984. Samsung initially hoped that an export-oriented joint-production plan might change the minds of the economic planners, but it later dropped the idea after it learned about the government's uncompromising position on enforcing existing market order (*Automotive News*, 7 July 1986, 20).

By mid-1989, all signs indicated that the Korean automakers were closing in on the MTI's target—exporting 210,000 small passenger cars by 1988 and 623,000 by 1992. In 1986, Hyundai entered the U.S. market through its own distribution system and broke the sales record for any new import. The other two Korean producers joined the export drive in 1987 as planned. To consolidate its toehold in the North American market, Hyundai began work on an assembly plant in Canada in 1986, even though a tight trade policy against Korean auto imports loomed on the horizon (*FEER*, 12 September 1986). Hyundai's aggressive strategy and Detroit's new alliance with the South Korean carmakers has prompted the Japanese producers to take defensive moves. After the dramatic appreciation of the yen in 1986 and early 1987, the Japanese no longer enjoyed cost advantages over made-in-Korea subcompacts. It became increasingly imperative for the Japanese TNCs to shift their domestic exports to the upscale segments while relocating the production of subcompacts to the neighboring East Asian NICs. But with the Korean market being virtually locked up, Taiwan at one time appeared to be the prime choice of the Japanese TNCs.

This new wave of foreign interest in Taiwan's automobile industry provided the policy-makers in Taiwan a chance to remedy their two previous failed attempts. In early 1985, the government moved decisively to overhaul the existing investment guidelines and protection regime. The new Automobile Industry Development Program pulled the rug out from under the feet of the local carmakers. The new program was designed to compel the domestic terminal producers to choose between growing along mass production lines or concentrating on key components in cooperation with TNCs. The program envisioned upgrading the parts and components sector to become the world's primary OEM supplier to TNCs (*Economic Daily*, 1 March 1985). The new program also sacrificed the long-standing full domestic production goal for the prospect of exporting finished cars. In essence, the state officials finally came to terms with the TNCs, and decided to accommodate the Japanese automakers' new offshore production strategy.

Under the new program, the tariff for finished cars was scheduled to be lowered to 30% in six years at a rate of 5% annual reductions while the domestic content requirement would be reduced to 50% in three years. Import restrictions would be limited to small Japanese cars, and even that protection scheme might be subject to review in six years, depending on the industry's progress. The new investment guidelines empowered the Foreign Investment Review Board under the MOEA to impose export ratio and technology-transfer requirements on a case-by-case basis. Also, the new investment guidelines for the first time welcomed 100 percent TNC-owned subsidiaries in export-only finished car production or parts and components manufacturing. The new program was expected to bring about a shakeout of the industry, and MOEA officials predicted that probably only two or three producers would remain independent (*Commonwealth*, February 1986, 128). The MOEA encouraged the smaller producers to work out merger plans among themselves or to form joint-ventures with TNCs, but it was not in a position to pick the fittest.

For a while, this vision of the program for the industry appeared realistic. Under the new guidelines, the MOEA swiftly approved Ford's first-stage expansion plan (from 40,000 to 90,000 cars per year); Nissan was allowed to buy up 25% of Yue-Loong's stock; Mitsubishi to own 25% of China Motors; and Toyota was permitted to reenter with few strings. The Japanese began initiating plans for new investments in the part and component sector. Both Nissan and Toyota had plans for transplanting their entire supply system to the fertile soil provided by Taiwan's existing parts and accessory sector. The Japanese auto TNCs were serious about turning Taiwan into their most active offshore production site in the 1990s.

Meeting the Challenge of Economic and Political Liberalization

In both Taiwan and South Korea, the government's plan for the automobile industry had to take up two new challenges in the late 1980s—economic liberalization and political democratization. Both developments would weaken the government's hand in exercising effective influence over the private sector. The automobile industries in the two East

Asian NICs came out of the stormy weather of the late 1980s in rather different shapes.

For both countries, the underlying cause for increased external pressure for opening up domestic markets and upward adjustments of their currency was the huge bilateral trade surplus they enjoyed over their major trading partner—the United States. In the case of Taiwan, this unforeseen development almost halted the 1985 program and further constrained the possible policy actions of the MOEA. Under severe U.S. criticism, the government was forced to abolish the requirement of a mandatory export ratio for new investment in the automobile sector in 1986. The zealots among the foreign auto TNCs looking to select Taiwan as an offshore production site soon had their enthusiasm dampened by a rapidly appreciated NT$ and the looming prospect of future U.S. restrictions on Taiwan-made automobiles. The two new entrants, Subaru and Toyota, substantially scaled down their investment plans and concentrated instead on Taiwan's domestic market. The existing smaller producers turned down the IDB's proposal for joint-development of a single model. Instead, all second-tier producers chose to align themselves with a major Japanese TNC (*Commonwealth*, June 1987). The number of finished carmakers has increased rather than decreased, and none of the existing automakers has a reasonable chance to become a competitive player in the international market. In a nutshell, the six-year program did not precipitate the expected shakeout of the industry.

Failure is an orphan and success has a hundred fathers. The industry now has fewer sympathetic ears within the state economic bureaucracy. No minister-level official is willing to stick his neck out and play the part of a strong advocate for the industry, especially when liberal economic thinking is suddenly in vogue. On the other hand, domestic public opinion has became increasingly impatient about the high price of automobiles. As small passenger cars come increasingly within the reach of more and more of the urban middle class, the tariff policy on imported cars becomes more politicized. In a trend toward a more liberal political environment, many locally elected members in the more assertive Legislative Yuan began questioning the wisdom of the official tariff reduction timetable. They backed the demand of consumer-rights groups, who have been joined by liberal-minded economists, for a deeper cut in the tariff rate. Clearly, the IDB has lost its grip on the timetable of trade liberalization for imported cars. It conceded to the political pressure by adjusting the planned 5 percent annual reduction to a whopping 12.5 percent in 1988. As the IDB reluctantly backed off from the tariff reduction timetable promised by the 1985 program, the alarmed domestic carmakers began to launch their own defense through intensive lobbying.

The reduction of tariffs from 65% to 42.5% between 1985 and 1988 boosted the sale of imported cars, whose competitiveness had already been substantially augmented by rapid appreciation of the NT dollar. Imported car dealers also benefited from the IDB's inability to coordinate supplementary measures administered by other state agencies that might help the domestic carmakers to compete with foreign cars. Car dealerships are not regulated. By providing only minimal after-sale services, some import dealers can keep their overhead down. Also, most import dealers can circumvent the tariff protection wall because of lax enforcement by the Custom Office. One way they do this is to artificially lower their tax base by filing undervalued import price quotes based on forged documents. As a result, the market share of imported cars jumped from 12.7% in 1986, to 17.1% in 1987, to 29.3% in a 340,000-unit market in 1988 (Bank of Communication, 1989). In the first half of 1989, imported cars topped 42%!

Now the IDB is placing its hope for a turnaround of the domestic automobile industry in the next-phase sectoral plan, which will succeed the existing program at the end of 1990. The best hope for the industry is to be part of the TNC offshore sourcing strategy aimed at the prospective Mainland market. At the same time, the policy arena continues to evolve—new actors keep coming in. Consumer rights groups, transportation officials, trade officials, even the association of imported-car dealers all would like to have their say in the new sectoral plan. Most likely, the door for new foreign investment will be open even wider and local content requirements may eventually be dropped altogether. An IDB official indicated that at present, with fewer policy instruments at its disposal, the best thing the government can do, next to pulling itself totally out of the industry, is to provide a reasonably competitive environment and some focused R&D support.[32]

While Taiwan's authorities had to open up its automobile industry for new foreign investment and lower domestic content requirements in order to shore up its international competitiveness, the Korean government and private carmakers have worked together to make national control, full local production, and international competitiveness compatible. Throughout the late 1980s, automobiles continued to be one of the most protected and regulated products of Korean industry. The MTI continued to limit the involvement of other conglomerates in auto manufacturing to ensure an orderly market.

Facing mounting U.S. pressure for trade liberalization and currency

---

32. This will include the creation of a new testing center and government-sponsored joint development of engines. (Interview with Director of IDB, June 1989).

appreciation, the MTI has tried to minimize the trade-off between the need for a reciprocal bilateral trade relationship and the need for an effective protection of the domestic automobile market. The Korean government announced its trade liberalization plan in 1985 to defuse an imminent trade war with the United States. However, the trade regimes for all strategic sectors including automobiles were to be governed by a new Industry Development Law enacted in 1986. This meant that auto trade would be liberalized, at a planned pace. As the first step, the import ban on finished motor vehicles, in effect for almost a quarter century, was lifted at the end of 1986, starting with commercial vehicles. The next year, the liberalization measure was extended to small passenger cars, with the exception of Japanese cars. Also, the MTI slashed the tariff rate for imports from a prohibitive 200% rate for small passenger cars to 100% at the end of 1987 and to 30% in 1988 (*Business Korea*, April 1988, 98). On the surface, the cut in nominal rate was more decisive than Taiwan's. However, in addition to the 30% nominal protection rate, buyers of imported cars have to pay an extra acquisition tax and extra consumption tax for large and medium-sized cars, bringing the total rate to well over 70%.[33] Even at this high protection rate, all imported cars encountered other nontariff hurdles: inspection red-tape and such exotic measures as a government-sponsored antiforeign-luxury campaign that happened to be very effective as large corporation executives are expected to set the example for the rest of the society.[34] Also, the South Korean government has vigorously resisted external pressure for upward adjustment of its currency. From 1986 to 1988, the real exchange rate of the won against the U.S. dollar appreciated only 22%, while during the same period the New Taiwan dollar gained well over 48%. South Korean automakers thus continued to benefit from an undervalued won at home and abroad.

Thus, in 1988, the market share for foreign automobiles was less than 1 percent of the Korean car market, estimated at about 350,000 units. Realizing the crucial role that automotive exports have played for West Germany and Japan, the South Korean government and conglomerates have shown themselves determined to win the uphill battle with the Japanese TNCs in the subcompact car market. Keeping the lucrative domestic car

---

33. According to the current tax system, foreign auto importers have to pay 15% of the car's value as acquisition tax; final buyers must pay another 15%. Consumers buying domestic cars pay only a 2% acquisition tax. Also, under the current two-tier consumption tax scheme, the special consumption tax for over-2,000cc-engine cars is 28% while for cars with engines between 1,500 and 2,000ccs the rate is only 16% (*Business Korea*, April 1988, 99).

34. Interview with one TNC expatriate in Seoul, December 1986. "And who is going to buy an imported luxury before his boss does?" added the interviewee.

market off-limits to foreign competitors, especially the Japanese, has been just one important ingredient of that winning strategy. In 1989, the three Korean passenger car producers expected to increase their productive capacity for small passenger cars to 1.4 million per year. The MTI's declared goal is to build up South Korea to become the world's fifth largest auto-producing country by the mid-1990s.[35]

More important, the concerted planning between state agencies and private automakers was minimally affected by the political liberalization at the end of the 1980s; in particular it was untouched by the 1988 parliamentary elections in which the two main opposition parties won the majority of seats. In South Korea, the past performance of the automobile industry has secured domestic support for the existing sectoral plan at a time when the authoritarian political structure has been substantially weakened. In the more assertive National Assembly, the Trade and Industry Committee is now in the hands of the major opposition component, the Party for Peace and Democracy (PPD). We have seen, however, that such popularly elected legislators, many of whom have received financial support from the chaebol, are often more nationalistic in their economic outlook than technocrats at the EPB or MTI. Economic nationalism is above partisan feud and there have been few disputes over established sectoral goals. PPD members actually wanted to enlarge the role of MTI in banking activities and were against a swift opening of the Korean market (*Business Korea,* August 1988, 33). Officials at MTI have continued to enjoy a firm grip on the timetable of trade liberalization and industry deregulation. They always keep domestic carmakers well-informed as well as prepared. Above all, the Korean carmakers have continued to enjoy a highly predictable business environment despite frequent government shakeups and the recent democratic transition.

V. Conclusion

In this chapter I set out to solve the puzzle of why, although the South Korean and Taiwan governments have pursued very similar sets of industrial objectives and started out from a comparable industrial base in automobile production in the early 1970s, the automobile industry emerged in the 1980s distinctively different in the two countries in every aspect—international competitiveness, production capacity, level of local content, and degree of national control. We concentrated on domestic in-

---

35. ROC embassy in Seoul, 1 April 1989, 45.

stitutional sources for divergent patterns of state intervention and varying degrees of their effectiveness as they bear on the business strategies of
the private sector. To this end, our case study illustrated how the organizational characteristics of the state economic bureaucracy and policy networks linking state agencies and private automakers in each country
have constrained the way the state intervened in the industrial upgrading
process and the way the two interacted. I have also demonstrated the
usefulness of a state-centered model for understanding cross-national differences in policy-induced industrial changes at the sectoral level. In promoting the automobile industry, Korean economic officials always had at
their disposal an extensive array of policy instruments. The application of
these instruments was coordinated into a coherent package that was fi-
nalized into a series of official sectoral plans. Furthermore, the state officials have been able to cut long-term deals with the private sector. The
influence of Taiwan's economic officials over the national private firms
has been hampered by a lack of direct policy instruments and channels of
access into the private sector. In pushing for vertical integration in the industry, the economic officials have consistently failed to overcome the
contradiction between the private sector's short-term business strategy
and the state's long-term industrial development goals.

Our analysis also raised some interesting conceptual questions: We
point to the possibility that, when it comes to state structure, there exist
varying degrees of continuity between the macro and sectoral levels
among the NICs. In Taiwan, the characteristics of the overall state economic bureaucracy and state-society relation at the macrolevel, while
providing a set of powerful constraints, do not by themselves define the
effectiveness of state action and the nature of the state-business relation
at the sectoral level. The sector-specific institutional arrangements for formulating and implementing industrial policy were also shaped by the
global dynamics and existing economic organizations of the sector. On
the other hand, in South Korea, the pattern of state intervention and policy networks in the automobile sector can be viewed as an extension of
what we found at the macrolevel. This varying degree of continuity is
clearly associated with the degree of centralization in both the state economic bureaucracy and the private sector. When the two are both highly
centralized it becomes difficult to separate sectoral or mesolevel institutional arrangements from the macrolevel characteristics, but when this is
not the case, we must allow for significant variation across sectors to the
degree that the state is able and willing to intervene, and consequently, a
disaggregated view of state structure is clearly called for.

Focusing on the policy-induced industrial changes at the sectoral level,
our analysis can offer a few useful lessons to proponents of both developmental state and neoclassical perspectives. The point of contestation be-

tween the two has centered not on the role of East Asian NIC states in macro market-augmenting intervention (R&D support, education investment, export incentives, etc.) but on sector-specific steering (industrial targeting, credit rationing, selection of winner, ordered market arrangements, etc.). The developmental state authors are often criticized for making a leap from the existence of a policy having certain goals to the achievement of the intended effects; the causal connections are not demonstrated (Haggard and Moon 1986, 2). Thus, the developmental state view as a unifying concept for a systematic understanding of the East Asian "miracle" (White 1988) must stand up to the test of sector-specific case studies. So far there is a dramatic paucity of empirical evidence on this question. In our case study, we have demonstrated that the pattern of state intervention and its resultant industrial changes among the East Asian NICs can differ so greatly that it becomes difficult to fold into a neat typology.

The neoclassical view fails to take two things into account: First, it fails to square with the evidence that states differ in their capability for positive intervention (Wade 1987). It is unrealistic to take a position of undifferentiated probability of governmental (nonmarket) failure. Second, it seldom takes into account the oligopolistic nature of many industries at the global level and the strategic trade policies pursued by other major countries. Both conditions may call for direct state intervention (Gereffi and Newfarmer 1985; Stegemann 1989).

Finally, our analysis reveals the complexity and problematic nature of the issue of efficiency. It is difficult to assess the relative strength and weakness of Korea's approach vis-à-vis Taiwan's. Neither neoclassical economists nor developmental state authors possess effective analytical instruments for evaluating the merits or faults of a specific pattern of industrial targeting in terms of dynamic efficiency at the macrolevel. It would require capturing the various distortions associated with industrial targeting on the one hand, and advances in the learning process as well as the development of externalities, e.g., technological diffusion and linkage over time, on the other hand. Most important and more troubling is how to situate this long-term assessment in the context of a dynamic and unforgiving global competitive environment characterized by a myriad of oligopolized markets and various forms of intervention by the governments of almost all major industrialized countries.

Bibliography

Altshuler, A., M. Anderson, D. Jones, D. Roos, and J. Womack. 1984. *The Future of the Automobile: The Report of MIT's International Automobile Programme*. Cambridge: MIT Press.

Amsden, Alice. 1988. *Economic Backwardness in Contemporary Perspective: South Korea's Industrialization Through Learning.* N.p.: Mimeo.

——. 1989. *Asia's Next Giant: South Korea and Late Industrialization.* London: Oxford University Press.

Asian Wall Street Journal (AWSJ). Hong Kong.

Arnold, Walter. 1989. Bureaucratic Politics, State Capacity, and Taiwan's Automobile Industrial Policy. *Modern China* 2 (April): 178-214.

Asian Finance. Hong Kong.

Atkinson, Michael, and William Coleman. 1989. Strong States and Weak States: Sectoral Policy Networks in Advanced Capitalist Economies. *British Journal of Political Science* 19 (January): 47-67.

Automotive News. Detroit.

Balassa, Bela. 1981. *The Newly Industrializing Countries in the World Economy.* New York: Pergamon Press.

Bank of Communication. 1989. *Industrial Survey* 48. In Chinese.

Bennett, Douglas C., and Kenneth E. Sharpe. 1985. *Transnational Corporations versus the State.* Princeton: Princeton University Press.

Bhagwati, J. N. 1978. *Foreign Trade Regimes and Economic Development: The Anatomy and Consequences of Exchange Control Regimes.* Cambridge, Mass: Ballinger.

Business Korea. Seoul.

Caves, R. E., and M. Porter. 1977. From Entry Barriers to Mobility Barriers: Conjectural Decisions and Contrived Deterrence to New Competition. *Quarterly Journal of Economics* 2 (May): 241-61.

Chang-Hwa Commercial Bank. *Quarterly Industrial Survey.* In Chinese.

Chen, Bao-Rei. 1980. *A Study on the Development of the Automobile Industry in the Republic of China.* Council for Economic Planning and Development of the Republic of China, Staff Report no. 230.243. In Chinese.

——. 1981. *A Comparison of the Automobile Industry in China and Korea.* Council for Economic Planning and Development of the Republic of China, Staff Report no. 268.249. In Chinese.

Cheng, Tun-jen, and Stephan Haggard. 1987. *The Politics of Adjustment in the East Asian NICs.* Berkeley: University of California, Institute of International Studies.

Chu, Yun-han. 1987. Authoritarian Regimes Under Stress: The Political Economy of Adjustment in East Asian NICs. Ph.D. dissertation, Department of Political Science, University of Minnesota.

——. 1989a. A Developmental State Under Stress: The Political Economy of Industrial Adjustment in Taiwan, 19731987. *Transformations* 1 (Summer).

——. 1989b. State Structure and Economic Adjustment in the East Asian NICs. *International Organization* 4 (August): 547-672.

Cole, David C., and Park Yong Chul. 1983. *Financial Development in Korea, 19451978*. Cambridge: Harvard University, Council on East Asian Studies.

Commercial Times. Taipei. In Chinese.

Commonwealth. Taipei. In Chinese.

Economic Planning Board. 1982. *The Fifth Five-Year Economic and Social Development Plan, 198286*. Seoul: EPB.

Economic Daily. Taipei. In Chinese.

Economist Intelligence Unit. *Quarterly Economic Review of South Korea*. London.

Evans, David, and Parvin Alizadeh. 1984. Trade, Industrialization, and the Visible Hand. *Journal of Developmental Studies* 20 (December): 22-46.

Evans, Peter. 1979. *Dependent Development: The Alliance of Multinational, State, and Local Capital in Brazil*. Princeton: Princeton University Press.

Far Eastern Economic Review (FEER). Hong Kong.

Financial News. Taipei. In Chinese.

Fortune. 1984.

Gereffi, Gary, and Richard Newfarmer. 1985. International Oligopoly and Uneven Development: Some Lessons from Industrial Case Studies. In *Profits, Progress, and Poverty*, edited by Richard Newfarmer. University of Notre Dame Press.

Gold, Thomas B. 1981. Dependent Development in Taiwan. Ph.D. dissertation, Harvard University.

———. 1986. *State and Society in the Taiwan Miracle*. New York: M. E. Sharpe.

Haggard, Stephan, and Chung-In Moon. 1986. Industrial Change and State Power: The Politics of Stabilization in Korea. Paper presented at the annual meeting of American Political Science Association, August, Washington, D.C.

Ikenberry, John G. 1988. *Reasons of State: Oil Politics and the Capacities of American Government*. Ithaca: Cornell University Press.

Jacobsson, Staffan. 1985. Technical Change and Industrial Policy: The Case of Computer Numerically Controlled Lathes in Argentina, Korea, and Taiwan. *World Development* 3: 353-70.

Johnson, Chalmers. 1982. *MITI and the Japanese Miracle*. Stanford: Stanford University Press.

Jones, P. Leroy, and Il Sakong. 1980. *Government, Business, and Entrepreneurship in Economic Development: The Korean Case*. Cambridge: Harvard University, Council on East Asian Studies.

Jones, Daniel T., and James P. Womack. 1985. Developing Countries and the Future of the Automobile Industry. *World Development* 2: 393-407.

Kim, Chuk-kyo, and Lee Chul-hee. 1980. The Growth of the Automobile Industry. In *Macroeconomic and Industrial Development in Korea*, edited by Chong-Kee Park. Seoul: Korea Development Institute.

Kim, Kwang Suk. 1983. *The Korean Experience in Development Planning, Policy-Making and Budgeting*. World Bank Staff, Working Paper no. 574.

——. 1985. *Industrial Policy and Industrialization in South Korea: 1961-1982*. University of Notre Dame, The Helen Kellogg Institute for International Studies, Working Paper no. 39.

Koo, Bohn-young. 1984. *The Role of the Government in Korea's Industrial Development*. Korea Development Institute, Working Paper no. 8407.

Korean Industrial Development Bank. 1985. *Korean Industry: A Survey*. Seoul. In Korean.

Krugman, Paul R., editor. 1988. *Strategic Trade Policy and the New International Economics*. Boston: MIT Press.

Kwack, Tae-won. 1984. *Industrial Restructuring Experiences and Policies in Korea in the 1970s*. Korea Development Institute, Working Paper no. 8408.

Lake, David A. 1984. The State as Conduit: The International Sources of National Political Action. Paper presented at the annual meeting of the American Political Science Association, Washington, D.C.

Moon, Chung-In. 1987. The Korean Economy in Transition: Political Consequences of Neoconservative Reforms. Paper presented at the Asian/Pacific Studies Institute, Duke University, 5 February.

OECD. 1984. *Long-Term Perspectives of the World Automobile Industry*. Paris: Organization of Economic Cooperation and Development.

Park, Yung chul. 1983. *South Korea's Experience with Industrial Adjustment in the 1970s*. Asian Employment Program Working Papers. Bangkok: ILO, Asian Regional Team for Employment Promotion.

Porter, Michael E. 1980. *Competitive Strategy: Techniques for Analyzing Industries and Competitors*. New York: Free Press.

Republic of China, Embassy in Seoul. *Biweekly Economic Survey of Korea*. Seoul. In Chinese.

Stegemann, Klause. 1989. Policy Rivalry among Industrial States: What Can We Learn from Models of Strategic Trade Policy? *International Organization* 43 (Winter): 73-100.

Wade, Robert. 1985. East Asian Financial Systems as a Challenge to Economics: Lessons from Taiwan. *California Management Review* 4 (Summer): 106-27.

——. 1987. The Role of Government in Overcoming Market Failure: Taiwan, Korea and Japan. In *Explaining the Success of Industrialization in East Asia*, edited by Helen Hughes and Thomas Parry. Sidney: Cambridge University Press.

Westphal, Larry E., Yung W. Rhee, and Garry Pursell. 1981. *Korean Industrial Competency: Where It Came From*. World Bank Staff, Working Papers no. 469.

White, Gordon, editor. 1988. *Developmental States in East Asia*. New York: St. Martin's Press.

Yun, Il Soo, and Byong Mun Park. 1984. *Korean Automobile Part and Component Industry*. Korea Institute of Economics and Technology, Research Report no. 56. In Korean.

7

State Policy and the Development of Taiwan's Semiconductor Industry

Constance Squires Meaney

A considerable body of literature stresses the key role of the state in bringing about rapid economic development in Taiwan. Analysts taking this approach find the state exhibiting a relatively high degree of autonomy from societal demands and pressures inimical to economic growth and a relatively high capacity to intervene effectively in the econ-

I would like to express my thanks to Dr. Yu Tzong-hsien and the Chung Hua Institution for Economic Research, who very kindly provided a research base during my stay in Taiwan in July 1989, and to the Research and Language Fellowship program of the InterUniversity Program for Chinese Language Studies in Taipei (sponsored by Stanford University and the Committee for Scientific and Scholarly Communication, ROC) under whose auspices I conducted some early interviews in the winter of 1988. Special thanks also to Chu Yun-han of National Taiwan University and the Institute for National Policy Research, Taipei, who shared his insights and made possible so many of the interviews conducted in July 1989.

omy to promote national development. They have investigated ways in which a general pattern of state-led growth varies among the NICs.[1]

Studies also have begun to appear that investigate state policy in particular industries in Taiwan. Two recent studies focus on Taiwan's auto industry. Noble examines the collapse of the GM/Hua Tung truck venture in 1982 and argues that one must study domestic political structures and competing development strategies in order to understand NIC policies. Neither liberal economic theory nor state-society focus is sufficient to understand development policies. Arnold contends that the capacity and autonomy of the economic bureaucracy involved in the auto industry has been minimal; the state has been highly constrained by societal and foreign interests, by fundamental policy cleavages, and by bureaucratic politics. In a somewhat different vein, Chu (1987) sees state policy in Taiwan (as of 1985) in both the auto and semiconductor industries as comparatively less effective than that of South Korea.

The present study of state policy in the semiconductor industry presents evidence the preponderance of which supports a case for "the state" in Taiwan as an actor with a relatively high level of autonomy and capacity. The semiconductor and auto industries would appear to represent opposite poles on the spectrum of industrial policy in Taiwan with respect to instruments of state intervention; bureaucratic agencies and individuals involved; the nature of private sector and business-government channels; and successful versus unsuccessful policy outcomes.[2]

Peter Evans's work on the Brazilian computer industry suggests a fruitful approach for investigating the development of Taiwan's semiconductor industry (Evans 1986). Evans makes three points concerning state-centric theories of development. First, he argues that the Brazilian case confirms a view of the state as a relatively autonomous actor shaping development: initiative for the industry's development came from the "en-

---

1. See *inter alia* Gold 1986, Johnson 1987, Haggard and Cheng 1987, Haggard 1986, Chu 1987, and Pang 1988.

2. Analysts of the global electronics industry have asserted recently that Taiwan is poised to become a "world-class player" in semiconductors. The industry will compete aggressively in the Pacific Rim as well as supply Taiwan's own fast-growing computer industry, eliminating dependence on Japan for chips (*Dataquest*, June 1989). Taiwan's exports of computers and related information-industry products are expected to reach US$10 billion by 1992, surpassing South Korea, Singapore, and Hong Kong (*San Francisco Chronicle*, 8 August 1988, C7). More recently the *Far Eastern Economic Review* (2 November 1989) reported some shrinkage in Taiwan's semiconductor industry, linked with slowing down of the computer industry worldwide. All in all, though, the semiconductor industry probably represents a "success story."

trepreneurial state," not capital, and "grew out of a project of national development that required the state as a home not out of local capital's
search for profits" (Evans 1986, 805). Second, simplistic statecentric models that "simply acknowledg[e] that the goals and interests of actors
within the state apparatus may shape the behavior and interests of capital" are insufficient. One requires a "differentiated view of the state apparatus" in which there is relative autonomy within the state for certain
actors who favor a particular view of national development vis-à-vis the
apparatus as a whole (Evans 1986, 805).

Third, the statecentric interpretation "is valid for the crucial moment
of the industry's origins [but] it does not apply in the same way to the industry's subsequent history"—the ability of the state to act autonomously
once industry is established is limited (Evans 1986, 791, 805).

Evans maintains that there are "moments of transition" when it may
be possible for a Third World country to break into an existing industry.
At such moments "the interests of local capital are still undefined and international capital may be caught off balance" (Evans 1986, 805). Taking
advantage of such moments requires a preexisting infrastructure and organizational capacities and regime commitment to development (Evans
1986, 804). The character of dependence, however, is not static and can be
retrogressive; dependence can increase after a period of reduction as a result of technological evolution. This may happen to the Brazilian computer industry due to its dependence on foreign-made chips.

This chapter suggests that the state was indeed the decisive actor in
the development of Taiwan's semiconductor industry: Initiative for development of the industry came from the "entrepreneurial state" and not
local capital's search for profits. Within the state apparatus, there was a
relatively autonomous cluster of actors committed to an idea of national
development that favored building a competitive semiconductor industry
in Taiwan. Regime commitment to development produced and attracted
committed individuals and provided the infrastructure/organizational capacity for Taiwan to take advantage of opportunities presented by the
evolution of the semiconductor industry and the global market.

Unlike its Brazilian counterpart, in Taiwan it appears that avoiding dependence resulting from technological evolution abroad was, or became,
a primary objective: hence the emphasis on semiconductors to begin with
as the critical component of an information industry. Entering the semiconductor field was part of a comprehensive vision that involved the upgrading of Taiwan's industrial structure to make it a center for high-tech
industry (see Gold 1986).

As the semiconductor industry in Taiwan developed, the interests of
the private sector vis-à-vis the state have become more powerful, as
would be expected. Further, more agencies within the state have become

involved in decision-making and budget matters with respect to semi-conductor projects. Processes are more bureaucratized than in earlier days and no single "protector" for semiconductor plans and projects remains on the scene. However, there does remain a core of advisers and sci-tech personnel committed to continued assertion of a leading role for the state in the information industry with respect to the choice of technologies for development and their transfer to private industry (Evans 1987).

A distinctive aspect of the Taiwan pattern is a network of overseas Chinese and foreign advisers that links the state and its R&D organizations with developments in the industry outside of Taiwan and produces recommendations for the long-term development of the information industry. This transnational network of personal and professional ties, which would appear to strengthen Taiwan's competitive position, further differentiates the Taiwan pattern from Latin American ones and may require new concepts with respect to statecentric analysis as well as theories of dependent development.

In the following pages, I outline four stages in the development of Taiwan's semiconductor industry and the role played by the state in each. For each phase I discuss state goals and policy; the key state actors and agencies at the top policy level and the level of interface with industry, noting in particular the overseas Chinese and foreign adviser role; the role of the private sector/local capital (if any); and conflicts regarding the future direction of the semiconductor industry that emerged among state actors or between the state and private sector. These last indicate the degree to which a "group of relatively autonomous actors within the state" shaped the industry according to a particular vision of national development. In general, state intervention took the form of focused R&D (choosing technology, acquiring technology, developing domestic R&D capability; recruitment and training of personnel; resourcing overseas Chinese engineers and foreign advisers to recruit personnel and monitor global trends; providing infrastructural support; and the formation of joint ventures to attract investment and provide vehicles for technology transfer to the private sector.

The four stages are: (1) Phase one (1974-79)—the state, under direction of Y. S. Sun, concludes agreement with RCA for technology transfer and training and recruitment of key personnel; creates the Industrial Technology Research Institute (ITRI) and the Electronics Research Service Organization (ERSO), under the Ministry of Economic Affairs (MOEA), and the Technical Advisory Committee (TAC) in the United States; and builds a pilot facility in ERSO for wafer production. (2) Phase two (1979-83)—state forms joint state-private semiconductor venture United Microelectronics (UMC) and transfers technology and personnel from ERSO to

UMC; creates the Hsinchu Science-Based Industrial Park; creates the high-level Science and Technology Advisory Group (STAG) to provide leadership as Sun becomes premier. (3) Phase three (1984-89)—state initiates VLSI project; forms joint state-MNC-local capital venture, Taiwan Semiconductor (TSMC), which encourages founding of private-sector semiconductor companies and design houses in Hsinchu. And (4) phase four (1989-)—ERSO proposes submicron project, while the leading indigenous computer company, Acer Inc., announces plan to enter semiconductor industry via partnership with Texas Instruments to produce DRAMs.

The First Five-Year Plan for Developing the Semiconductor Industry, 1974-79

Former Premier Y. S. Sun together with a network of overseas Chinese engineers in the United States played the key role in launching the semiconductor industry in Taiwan. Sun, an electrical engineer and native of Shantung province, had been educated on the mainland, trained at the Tennessee Valley Authority in the United States (1943-45), and between 1946 and 1962 served in a series of positions in the Taiwan Power Co., including vice-president and chief engineer and later president. Between 1967 and 1969 Sun served as Minister of Communications and from 1969 to 1978 as Minister of Economic Affairs; in 1978 he became premier, a position he held until his retirement in 1984. Sun was a member of the KMT Central Standing Committee from 1969 onward (Pang 1988). He is described as one of a group of high-level officials with engineering backgrounds who "held a conviction that dynamic economic development could not be based on complete acceptance of current comparative advantage" (Noble 1987, 704).

In the 1970s, the Chinese Institute of Engineers (CIE) held seminars (the Modern Engineering and Technology Symposium, or METS) every two years that brought together Taiwan and overseas Chinese. At that time METS was the main communications channel linking Taiwan and overseas Chinese engineers. The symposiums were initiated by Y. S. Sun. Others active in the organization were Dr. K. T. Li, and Dr. Pan Wenyuan at RCA, who was active in the New York chapter of the CIE.

In August 1974, Sun contacted Dr. Pan in the United States and invited him to Taiwan to produce a study of ways in which the government could upgrade local industry, with the electronics industry playing the leading role. Pan subsequently met with a group of top officials including then-premier Chiang Ching-kuo, then-secretary of the Executive Yuan Walter Fei, Y. S. Sun, and Minister of Communications Yu-shu Kao. Pan recommended that the electronics industry should focus on semiconductor technology and that the technology be acquired from abroad; that a two-part strategic planning team be formed, one part in the United States and one in Taiwan; and that an organizational capability for implementation within the state be set up. A U.S. partner was to be located for an agreement for technology transfer and training (Interviewee #4).

To create an organizational capacity within the state, the Industrial Technology Research Institute (ITRI) was established in 1973-74 by Y. S. Sun.[3] Sun spun off electronics R&D from an existing telecommunications laboratory into ITRI. The telecommunications lab was located in the Telecommunications Directorate in the Ministry of Communications; Sun worked closely in planning the IC project with a leading engineer in the directorate, who served as ITRI's president from 1975 to 1985. Sun's plan for ITRI diverged from an original plan to locate the IC project in the telecommunications lab, and there was opposition from various quarters in the government to creation of the new organization. But Sun wanted a high degree of autonomy for the project and ultimately prevailed. ITRI was placed under the Ministry of Economic Affairs, which Sun at that time headed, thus allowing his direct protection (Interviewee #8). Within ITRI, an organization was set up to develop the IC project—ERIC, which soon became ERSO (Electronics Research Service Organization). Its first head was an engineer from the telecommunications lab, who was succeeded a year later by Dr. Hu Ting-hua from Chiao Tung University. Hu remained a key player in the IC project until leaving for the private sector in the mid-1980s.

ITRI and ERSO originally were entirely funded by the state. By 1988, ERSO received only about 20-25% from the government, with the rest coming from the private sector in the form of fees from companies for developing products. ITRI by 1988 remained 55% government and 45% private sector. At least until the latter part of the 1980s, however, the initiative for long-term projects developed by ITRI had come from within the state and not from the private sector, which has generally brought short-term projects to ITRI's labs. ITRI's budget is screened within the MOEA and approved by the Executive Yuan and the Legislative Yuan.

---

3. Here and elsewhere there is some disparity among interview sources about the role of Y. S. Sun versus that of K. T. Li. One source referred to ITRI as K. T. Li's creation. Dr. Li is generally credited with being the godfather of Taiwan's entire high-tech industry. In the case of semiconductors, however, Y. S. Sun appears to have been the key promoter, while K. T. Li's role is somewhat ambiguous. "K. T. stayed away from ICs," according to one source.

Two other entities, the NSC and the STAG (see below), also approve its budget.

Returning to the early days of the IC project, to create a strategic planning group in the United States, Dr. Pan invited engineers from Bell Labs, IBM, and various universities to form a committee (the Technical Advisory Committee, or TAC) in the United States TAC's tasks were to assist in selecting a particular IC technology on which to concentrate and to recommend a list of U.S. companies to invite to submit bids for a technology-transfer agreement. During this time the TAC group met weekly on Saturday and Sundays to come up with its recommendations. TAC became a permanent organization and remains active in 1989 (Interviewee #4. See also Simon 1980, 573; *Free China Review,* February 1989). Since its early beginnings TAC has on a regular basis provided information on industry trends and on the experience of U.S. laboratories with different approaches to product development (e.g., that have proved to be blind alleys). They submit proposals concerning the next major thrust for the IC program in Taiwan. TAC has three groups within it: a Bell Labs group, an IBM group, and a universities group. They meet four times a year with ITRI and ERSO personnel in Taiwan (as of 1989) (Interviewee #4).

In late 1975, RCA was chosen out of eight companies that submitted bids. The key points of Taiwan's approach were (a) to emphasize training as well as transfer of technology and (b) to solicit private investment and move technology into the private sector (Interviewee #5). It was agreed that RCA over five years would provide technicians, plus technical training in the United States, and design and production (including custom design) capabilities. RCA would transfer all technological advances and design and processing improvements, and ITRI would purchase a certain quantity of wafers. RCA would provide information on product applications (Simon 1980, 502).

Dr. Pan had further recommended the recruitment of forty young engineers in all relevant fields (processing, design, testing, plant engineering, accounting, and reliability studies) to be sent to the U.S. firm for training. They would recruit in Taiwan and among engineering students and graduates from Taiwan living in the United States. Subsequently, Hu Ting-hua personally recruited thirty-five of the trainees in Taiwan, while Dr. Pan recruited the other five in the United States. These included Yang Ting-yuan (later with ERSO and now president of Winbond [Huapang] Electronics, a private semiconductor firm in Taiwan); Shih Chin-tay (later executive vice-president of ERSO and now executive vice-president of ITRI), and C. C. Chang (now director of ERSO); these three key individuals were all graduates of National Taiwan University between 1968 and 1970 (Interviewee #4). The forty individuals went to RCA facilities in the

United States in 1976 to study process technology, testing, and design (Interviewee #8). In the same year, construction began on an IC pilot production facility within ERSO. The forty trainees had completed their program at RCA. In 1977-78, the first trial run of wafers was produced. The trainees returned from RCA to take up positions within ERSO. After the pilot production phase was completed, the objective was to transfer technology to local industry while increasing production capacity and improving quality control (Interviewee #4, and Simon 1980).

Meanwhile, in 1974-75 Taiwan's National Science Council (NSC) began a major drive to establish IC research locally. They launched the "large scale project on microelectronics," which had three parts: IC process technology, personal computer applications, and automation technologies. The labs for IC process technology were at Chiao Tung University; Hu Ting-hua oversaw the program there. When he went to ERSO in 1975 he took many students and faculty with him. Chiao Tung and ERSO have continued to work closely together (Interviewee #2).

Sources involved in the project agree that at the outset there was considerable criticism and skepticism of the IC project from various quarters in the government. It was a very ambitious project in financial terms for that time ($12 million budgeted for 1975-79) (Interviewee #5). The deciding factor appears to have been the fact that ICs were the pet project of Y. S. Sun. He, backed by Pan Wen-yuan and the recommendations of TAC in the United States, were able to overcome all objections at this point and push ahead.

The Second Phase: 1979-83

A central goal of the state's semiconductor project was to move technology out of the lab and into the private sector and create commercial visibility for it (Interviewee #5). The overall goal was to build up Taiwan's self-development capability and infrastructure and improve on technology imported from the United States (for example, to develop silicon gate technology and establish a mask-making capability) (Interviewees #5 and #8). A major development occurring at the outset of the second phase was the formation of the Hsinchu Science-Based Industrial Park. The objectives for the park were to establish an infrastructure needed to create and attract high value-added private enterprises in Taiwan and to establish state-of-the-art R&D capabilities.

Objectives were also to recruit top-level talent and to attract science and technology graduates educated abroad back to Taiwan by providing rewarding employment (*Dataquest* June 1989, pp. 1-2). The government provided a range of assistance for high-tech enterprises locating in the park, including tax holidays; duty-free import of key equipment, raw materials, and semifinished goods; exemption from commodity taxes on exports; and low-interest loans and R&D matching funds (*Dataquest* June 1989, p. 2). Computer manufacturers were the most numerous among the park's enterprises; however, as we shall see, IC companies came to be the second-largest type of business in the park by 1989, ten years after its founding (*Dataquest* June 1989, p. 4). The park's director-general remains Dr. Choh Li, who retired from a position as research director at Honeywell in Minneapolis and went to Hsinchu in 1980 (*San Francisco Chronicle*, 9 March 1988).

To move technology out of the lab, in 1978 Shih Chin-tay, one of the key engineers recruited by Pan and trained at RCA, and his boss at ERSO, Hu Ting-hua, submitted a business proposal for a joint state-private semiconductor venture to the Ministry of Economic Affairs. The MOEA then tried to interest local capital in investing. They approached Datong, Sampo, and Tiko, among others. The private sector proved reluctant, viewing ICs as a highly risky business. Eventually, the government "used its influence" to get contributions from each, which were relatively small. One company (Mitac) refused altogether (Interviewee #5). Meanwhile, to reassure the private companies, ITRI created ITIC, a subsidiary supported by banks and private investors and 40% by ITRI to invest in the IC venture.

The outcome of the state's efforts was the creation of United Microelectronics (UMC), a joint state-private sector venture (state, 44%; private sector, 45%). ERSO spun off plant and equipment and transferred a large contingent of personnel from ERSO to UMC. The president of UMC was Bob Tsao, another one of the original corps of engineers who went to RCA and then to ERSO, and a graduate of Taiwan University at the time of Shih, Yang, and Chang. The new personnel for UMC were recruited locally and trained for about a year in ERSO's facility. ERSO continued to do pilot production of wafers in its facility (Interviewee #5).

After UMC was formed, a conflict emerged between its management, who wanted ERSO's pilot facility closed down, and ITRI, which disagreed. Shih Chin-tay and others argued that ITRI "must remain involved in order to assure continuous R&D" (Interviewee #5). ERSO continued production in its facility, which turned out 15,000 wafers a month; it had the same products as UMC and the same market channels (Interviewee #5). UMC argued that there was no need for the government, via ERSO, to stay in the business of wafer production and sales; ERSO should confine itself to research. The ITRI/ERSO position prevailed.

Meanwhile, under the NSC, the IC process technology program in Taiwan universities was enlarged. Each year, beginning in 1979, one hundred trainees with MS degrees were to be turned out by Chiao Tung as well as Cheng Kung, Tsing Hua, and to a lesser extent NTU. This was done on a project basis organized by the NSC. The NSC asked professors to organize teams and awarded grants for selected proposals. Professors were also invited to work at ERSO to gain industrial experience (Interviewee #2).

With respect to the IC research carried on by ERSO, engineers such as Shih Chin-tay promoted an idea that centered on separating manufacturing and design. In this concept of the appropriate direction for Taiwan's semiconductor industry, Taiwan (via ERSO) would develop a design methodology and train designers who would become small entrepreneurs. Taiwan would stay away from projects with heavy capital requirements, such as DRAM technology, and would concentrate on local-end manufacturing (Interviewee #5). The design orientation within ERSO influenced Taiwan's IC industry for a long time, became a subject of some controversy, and eventually was altered in the direction of a more aggressive strategy (Interviewee #8).

Organizationally, Y. S. Sun was still in charge of the IC project at the outset of the second phase. In 1979 he became premier. After this, according to various accounts, things became more "official," and the semiconductor industry no longer had Sun's direct protection. Two major science and technology meetings were held around this time which approved a plan of Sun's for the future direction of science and technology in Taiwan (the *ke chi fangan*) (Interviewee #8). Sun wanted more formal organizational support for high technology projects in general and semiconductors in particular. He set up eight technical areas under the plan and included ICs within this structure (Interviewee #8).

In a key development, in 1979 Sun set up the Science and Technology Advisory Group (STAG) under the Executive Yuan (cabinet) and asked K. T. Li to be in charge.[4] STAG was the "brainchild" of K. T. and Y. S. The idea behind its creation was to have a group of "independent advisers" because people already involved in the project had "their own ideas" (Interviewee #1). This would mean ERSO. Sun wanted to create an organizational capacity at higher policy level to function as a kind of substitute for his personal influence.

STAG consisted of foreign advisers led by a group of executives formerly from Texas Instruments, including former board chairman Pat Haggerty. Haggerty and Y. S. Sun had known each other for many years

---

4. It appears that K. T. Li was not a particular patron, or protector, of semiconductor projects in the manner of Y. S. Sun.

and the former had played an informal advisory role in the IC program already. K. T. Li, who did the actual recruiting, also knew Haggerty well. Haggerty brought others with him, such as Fred Seitz, also a major figure in the U.S. semiconductor industry. Around 1983, two additional men joined STAG who were to play leading roles: Bob Evans, a former vice-president for development at IBM, and Ken Mackay, formerly of Bell Labs. According to one source, Haggerty had rich experience and product expertise but it was not for this that he was invited in, but for "his vision of how to develop a country" (Interviewee #1).

STAG formulated "action plans" to further the government's goals for rapid development of science and technology (Interviewee #1). The group began functioning in earnest in 1980. From this time on STAG (or individual members of it) was "constantly challenging" some of ERSO's orientations—(people who had "their own ideas"). STAG favored an end to manufacturing in ERSO's pilot facility. They also recommended moving into DRAMs, as a cutting edge technology (Interviewee #5).

Meanwhile, UMC had become highly successful, at the beginning producing "consumer" chips for Taiwan's manufacturers of "toys, telephones, watches, calculators and computers" (AWSJ). In 1983, UMC's wafer production and sales overtook that of ERSO's production facility. It became highly profitable and began to conclude its own R&D and licensing agreements with U.S. companies. In 1985 it went public, with the government remaining as a minority shareholder (23%). Subsequently UMC upgraded and began producing more advanced chips including, by 1989, SRAM memory chips (Interviewee #9).

The Third Phase, 1984-89: Adoption of the VLSI Project and Formation of TSMC

As a prelude to this phase, around 1982, a decision was made within ITRI/ERSO to focus the semiconductor program on VLSI technology. The rationale was that the development of VLSI technology would provide a base for expanding Taiwan's R&D capacity. As was the case with the initiation of the IC project the decision to commit Taiwan to the development of VLSI technology and production was reached and implemented over considerable opposition within the state apparatus. Some said that Japan's MITI had already begun a VLSI project between 1976 and 1980. Taiwan was already two years behind and could never catch up. Moreover, Japan had a support structure that Taiwan lacked—lithography and other capabilities (Interviewee #5). There were objections to

VLSI as too expensive to develop (this position included K. T. Li, according to one source). Almost a year of presentations were made by ERSO in an effort to convince other agencies to go along (Interviewee #8). Some objected that the plan was too ambitious—"Canada and France have tried and failed, how can we succeed?" (Interviewee #4). In addition to the cost of VLSI per se, some felt that semiconductors were drawing too heavy a proportion of resources vis-à-vis other projects such as biotechnology and automation. Academics spoke up for their respective areas (Interviewee #5).

Objections came from another direction as well. According to Dr. Pan, who also made presentations on behalf of the VLSI project to Premier Sun and later Premier Yu, the "fierce" arguments about VLSI were not about whether to do it but whether industry or the government should do it. Industry (which at that time would mean UMC) argued that it should (Interviewee #4). This continued the tension that had emerged between ERSO and UMC. Shih and others at ITRI/ERSO felt that the government should remain involved, "possibly until the year 2000" (Interviewee #5). In this conflict, Evans of STAG supported the VLSI plan favored by ITRI/ERSO. He made the case that UMC alone was still not enough for Taiwan to compete globally. After a year of presentations, there was a special review of the VLSI plan in the Executive Yuan, which finally approved it in 1984. Objections to the VLSI project as overly ambitious for Taiwan were not extinguished, however, and continued to be heard as late as 1986.[5]

After the project's adoption, ERSO began to "plant seeds" in the universities by supporting VLSI design projects. Professors were invited to ITRI during the summers and encouraged to do VLSI design projects with their students at the universities. ITRI would process the wafers they developed (Interviewee #5). However, in the first years of this phase the state's plan for VLSI continued to encounter reluctance of the private sector to invest, on the one hand, and reluctance from other parts of the state to commit large amounts of capital, on the other. A proposal submitted in 1984 by the MOEA for a $250 million joint venture similar to UMC encountered opposition in the cabinet and was abandoned.[6] Meanwhile, Premier Sun had become ill and retired shortly after the adoption of the VLSI plan.

---

5. For example, Chang An-ping (president, China Management Services) argued that VLSI was not a good idea as Taiwan was already too far behind and the required investment was too large (ICRT interview on "high-tech" in Taiwan, broadcast 4 March 1986).

6. See discussion of opposition to VLSI in Chu 1987, 226.

The position of doubters within the government eventually was changed by a series of events involving the fate of some state-of-the-art DRAM technology developed in ERSO labs by Vitelic, a Silicon Valley startup (founded by a Hong Kong Chinese). After the shelving of its joint venture proposal, ERSO had turned to Vitelic and two other small Silicon Valley firms for assistance in bringing in VLSI technology. However, the highly advanced DRAM technology subsequently developed in ERSO's lab by Vitelic was sold by Vitelic to Korea. The Silicon Valley firm maintained that neither the government nor private sector in Taiwan was willing to supply the necessary manufacturing facility for their advanced chip (Chu 1987, 238; Interviewee #5).

Shock waves in the government produced by this untoward event plus the persuasive skills of Evans of STAG on behalf of a new joint-venture plan eventually turned the tide. Evans supported the plan as a means of catching up to the level of state-of-the-art technology. This resulted in a go-ahead for a new joint venture (Interviewee #5). Pursuing its goal of developing VLSI technology and moving it into the private sector, the government formed a second company, Taiwan Semiconductor (TSMC). TSMC was a joint venture formed by the Taiwan government (49%), Phillips (27%), and local private investors (24%). Shih Chin-tay plus C. C. Chang and F. C. Tseng (another member of the original RCA group) assisted in the negotiations with Phillips. The Taiwan side wanted an agreement in which Phillips would not count technology as part of their equity. Thus there was to be no technology transfer from Phillips at the beginning, although Taiwan would have access to future developments.

TSMC was a new concept, a foundry that performs manufacturing for clients; it does no design or marketing. Companies bring masks to TSMC who manufacture the silicon wafers from them. Thus TSMC would not compete with the large companies, only with their manufacturing divisions (Interviewee #3). The concept was to create a large world-class semiconductor facility that could compete with the Koreans and Japanese. TSMC also would service small design houses located in the Hsinchu Science-Based Industrial Park (Interviewee #10). TSMC was to carve out a niche between the large U.S. semiconductor firms and independent chip designers, manufacturing ASICs designed and marketed by others.[7] It was to limit its focus to ASICs and not produce memory chips. This position was later modified as we shall see presently.

The leading character in selling the TSMC package to Phillips was an

7. Taiwan Eyes Asia's Custom-Chip Market, *Asian Wall Street Journal (AWSJ)*, 13 January 1988, p. 1.

overseas Chinese executive, Morris Chang (Chang Tsung-mo), formerly CEO at General Instruments and before that group head for chip production at Texas Instruments. Chang was recruited by K. T. Li in 1985 to head ITRI. Chang also served as chairman of UMC, with Bob Tsao remaining as president.[8]

The local private investors in TSMC were Formosa Plastics (5%) and Sino-American Petroleum (4%) plus a number of smaller investors (1% each). They were all companies that were successful and had dealings with the government already; a certain amount of arm-twisting apparently was involved (Interviewee #10). Morris Chang recruited Jim Dykes, formerly a vice-president of the silicon chip division at General Electric, to head up TSMC.

TSMC by most accounts proved successful in terms of the goals of the state's VLSI plan and the IC development program more generally: Within the year after TSMC's formation, approximately forty chip design houses set up in Hsinchu (*AWSJ*). These were mostly local small entrepreneurs who were already plentiful but had no wafer foundry to serve them before TSMC. Thus they would have had to go to the Japanese or Koreans, who often would demand rights to the design (Interviewee #3; *AWSJ*). In addition, several private semiconductor firms were started up, encouraged by the success of UMC and the existence of the TSMC foundry. As of summer 1989, these included Winbond Electronics, founded by Yang Ting-yuan, who left ERSO taking a large number of personnel with him; Hualon (a subsidiary of the textile manufacturer); and AMPi (*Dataquest*). Vitelic remained in the semiconductor business in Taiwan as well. Other local companies announced intentions to go into semiconductor design and manufacturing, including Acer, Taiwan's leading computer maker (see below), and Formosa Plastics.

Meanwhile, at the high policy level in the state apparatus, STAG had increased its organizational capacity in 1984-85. Two task forces (technical review boards—TRBs) were formed within it: one for electronics and ICs, headed by Bob Evans, and one for telecommunications, headed by Ken Mackay. The TRBs were patterned after the model of the TAC in the United States at the inception of the IC project. The STAG advisers felt that increased organizational capacity was needed, as more actors than just ERSO were becoming involved in semiconductors (Interviewee #1).

The TRBs have both local and overseas Chinese members, but the latter predominate. The membership changes each year, at least partially.

---

8. It was not easy for Chang to sell the joint-venture idea to potential partners, according to one source, because Taiwan was not thought to be "respectable," but he eventually succeeded (Interviewee #5).

About a half dozen local people from ITRI and the MOEA's Industrial Development Bureau (IDB) join the electronics TRB. The overseas Chinese members are selected by Dr. Evans personally, or by his staff. They choose people from appropriate organizations in the United States according to the problem being studied. A team will come to Taiwan for about a week and undergo briefings. Evans attends the final meetings, after which the TRB issues recommendations. These go to the chairman of the NSC and then to ITRI. The TRB recommendations are supposed to be "reference materials," and do not have to be acted upon. However, if a recommendation were not accepted, ITRI would have to explain why (Interviewee #2). Concerned parties have normally been invited to TRB meetings and convinced before STAG makes a recommendation. STAG also has clout because it screens the (high-tech) budget (Interviewee #1). It appears that STAG played a key role both in convincing other agencies within the government to proceed with VLSI and the TSMC venture and in pressuring ITRI/ERSO to modify its design orientation and go into the more costly and risky memory chip business needed to make Taiwan a world-class competitor independent of foreign chip manufacturers.

Phase Four (1989—):
The Submicron Project,
the Decision to Produce DRAMs, and
the Rise of the Private Sector

The fourth phase of the state's program for development and upgrading of the IC industry is focused on the ERSO's submicron project. The submicron project began to be discussed as early as 1985 but was not finally decided upon until 1988; the strategic plan was still being worked out as of summer 1989. Submicron technology is necessary for producing DRAMs. Sources within the state apparatus maintain that the private sector wants cutting-edge (.8 submicron) technology but will not do the research and development itself (Interviewee #1). ERSO, which finally phased out its pilot production facility in 1988, probably will produce some of the chips in-house for industry to take and optimize (Interviewee #2). Some within the government questioned the rationale of having a submicron lab at ERSO when there is already one at Chiao Tung University. This objection appears to have been overcome (Interviewee #4). The submicron plan covers five years and will involve an expenditure of NT$5.5 billion. The six existing IC companies in Taiwan as of mid-1989

(UMC, TSMC, Huapang (Winbond), Vitelic, Hualon, and AMPi) were invited to participate in a consortium. The consortium would involve a fifty-fifty private sector/government contribution for ongoing expenses, with the government paying for 100% of equipment expenses. The project will be ERSO's main focus for the next four years (Interviewee #3). The submicron idea emerged in discussion with the private manufacturers, according to ERSO's Shih. There is more preliminary discussion of proposals and more participation from industry, as opposed to earlier phases where "the vision of a top person became policy." Participation from industry is regular, though informal (Interviewee #5).

The submicron project is related to the question of whether Taiwan should produce DRAMs as well as ASICs. Conflict over this question illustrates the changing character of relations between the state and private sector in the IC industry as the latter has expanded. The original concept behind TSMC was that it would be a foundry for producing ASICs only. This was affirmed strongly by its president, Jim Dykes, in the winter of 1988. Dykes appears to have been an enthusiastic backer of the concept. In 1987-88, a shortage of memory chips hit Taiwan. Local computer makers, in particular Multitech (now Acer), began pressuring the MOEA's IDB to pressure TSMC to begin manufacturing memory chips, according to Dykes. But at that time the IDB turned a deaf ear, which Dykes cited as an illustration of how the government did not interfere with TSMC's operations (Interviewee #10). However, by the summer of 1989, TSMC was going into the business of producing DRAMs. Meanwhile, Dykes had returned to the United States. TSMC's move to make DRAMs as well as ASICs was part of a larger shift in this direction in Taiwan's semiconductor industry.

As mentioned above, the submicron project involves technology necessary for producing the DRAM chip. A STAG recommendation of October 1988 argued that DRAMs are a critical component for the growth of an IC industry; that the world supply of DRAMs at present is unpredictable; that applications (such as VHD-TV) are expanding; that the use of computers is expanding; that there is presently no DRAM technology in Taiwan; and thus the ROC must move into DRAMs (Interviewee #1). The question of whether Taiwan should try to compete in cutting-edge IC technology or have a more modest approach, looking for niches in which Taiwan would have a comparative advantage, appears to have divided STAG and some of the leading engineers and managers in ERSO. In the words of Shih Chin-tay, in the 1979-83 phase STAG was "constantly challenging" ERSO's focus on design, on small entrepreneurs and local-end manufacturing, and on avoiding heavy capital requirements, arguing for a move into DRAMs as the cutting edge of technology (Interviewee #5).

The reversal of the plan to avoid DRAMs appears to have resulted from a combination of change in the world market; successes in Taiwan's IC industry; pressure from Taiwan IC manufacturers, in particular UMC, and Taiwan computermakers, in particular the Acer corporation; and from STAG and the electronics TRB. With the success of TSMC and the burgeoning design houses, former doubters felt that a sufficient industrial base for entry into the DRAM business had emerged in Taiwan (Interviewee #5). The DRAM market appeared less risky because of the antidumping semiconductor agreement between Japan and the United States and the fact that many companies got out of the industry during the chip glut in 1985 (Interviewee #3).

In response to pressure from the private sector, UMC management felt that during the 1979-83 phase, ERSO had lost its leading edge in providing R&D services due to its retention of the wafer manufacturing and sales facility, which absorbed too much of its attention. UMC felt that ERSO should be more aggressive in developing advanced products; it should target well-developed research and acquire it. Taking the initiative, Tsao traveled to Australia in mid-1989 to visit a quasigovernment research organization there that specializes in advanced R&D. The Australian organization has a $50 million grant from its government to develop advanced CAD tools, a 32-bit microprocessor, and other advanced products (Interviewee #9). It was reported that UMC would sign contracts with the Australian firm in September 1989, giving it an 8% share in return for RISC and other advanced chip technologies. A UMC spokesman summed up the company's viewpoint: "Though the local IC industry has made great progress in recent years, many important ICs such as DRAM and RISC (reduced instruction-set computer) among others, still depend on imports from industrialized countries...therefore, we continue to search for foreign partners which will allow us to share their IC technology."[9]

Pressure to go into DRAM and other advanced technologies came from another quarter in the private sector, the rapidly growing Acer Corporation (formerly Multitech). Acer's predecessor, founded with minimal capital by Taiwanese entrepreneur Stan Shih in 1976, became a computer giant after microcomputers took off after 1980-81. Shih came to believe that the local market was large enough to justify a DRAM capacity but, according to an Acer source, TSMC repeatedly refused. The Taipei computer association (a private industry group) brought up the question of DRAMs to the government. Eventually, in 1989, Acer concluded a technology transfer agreement with Texas Instruments that will make Acer the seventh IC manufacturer in Taiwan (Acer had already been an OEM

---

9. *Economic News* (Taiwan) 17-23 July 1989, #755, p. 3.

manufacturer for TI). Acer will acquire a DRAM capacity, raising over $250 million for the project (Interviewee #11).

The emergence of Acer meant for the first time the entry of a player that did not fit the pattern of the overseas Chinese engineers trained by ERSO–ITRI–RCA. Shih was educated in Taiwan, although he has hired many overseas Chinese engineers, technicians, and marketing personnel formerly from IBM in the United States. Shih's world view emphasizes nondependence on outside sources, especially the Japanese; moving out of the low-end computer market, and building of a large, integrated research-oriented company—"I was tired of the small-company mentality here. Small companies never do R&D."[10] It appears that Acer's aggressiveness, success, and high-tech orientation created an environment in which the ERSO/ITRI/TSMC nexus was nudged to move into DRAM technology. An MOEA source indicated that Acer and its agreement with TI was a factor in altering the "conservative" approach of both ERSO and existing companies with respect to "jumping in" to submicron technology (Interviewee #6). An NSC source voiced the opinion that "high, high pressure" from industry, due to its need to ensure supplies as well as a perception of profits to be made, was the initiating factor in going into DRAMs, about which many have doubts (Interviewee #2).

Meanwhile, some pressure for ITRI to work more closely with the privawho did not fit te sector appears to have come from the MOEA's Industrial Development Bureau. In 1989 it sent a regulation to the cabinet requiring ITRI to present projects to industry as soon as they have been approved by the government and ask interested companies to send applications for the technology to the government. Until then ITRI had waited until technology was developed before notifying the private sector (Interviewee #7). This move appears to represent an opposite point of view from a 1986-87 report done within ERSO, which held that the IC project was successful because it was set up as production and manufacturing, not pure R&D, and involved the transfer of a "mature" industrial project, including trained people to the private sector (Interviewee #8). In the past the IDB has pressed ERSO to help small businesses such as the furniture, toy, and umbrella industries use ICs (Interviewee #8).

Another aspect of ITRI's present status concerns a recommendation on the part of Dr. Pan and TAC that ERSO (or, parts of ERSO—components, systems, and communications) be separated from ITRI and combined with the III (the Institute for Information Industry—an institute for computer and software R&D, identified with K. T. Li) to form a new institu-

---

10. *International Herald Tribune*, 30 September 1988, and *Electronic Engineering Times*, 23 January 1989.

tion on a par with ITRI. The rationale is that this would permit better coordination and also overcome a problem with turnover at ERSO. ERSO's
present rate of personnel turnover (35-40% a year) is too great, they argue, to allow it to maintain a two-to-three-year lead over industry. The
turnover results from the fact that ERSO cannot pay competitive wages
with industry, because if its salaries were raised they would have to be
raised for all of ITRI's other divisions as well (biotechnology, robots, materials, energy, and mining). Prominent personnel who have left ITRI include Yang Ting-yuan, who founded Winbond Electronics, taking 60% of
Winbond's 110 employees with him from ERSO. Another is Hu Ting-hua,
the former director of ERSO from the early days who left to join Ham-
brecht & Quist (H&Q) Investment Co. The reorganization plan, which
would allow ERSO to stay ahead of industry, has been proposed for
some time but not accepted as of summer 1989. The minister of communications, among others, apparently would have to be sold on the idea
(Interviewee #4).

Conclusion

The foregoing account makes a strong case that the state played the
leading role in the development of Taiwan's semiconductor industry.
Private industry would not have invested on its own. The state's role was
critical at three points: launching the original IC project, creating UMC,
and creating TSMC. In the first phase (1974-79) the state initiated and
planned the IC project, recruited and trained the key personnel, acquired
IC technology from RCA, and produced and marketed the first wafers.
No initiative came from existing private firms in Taiwan. Led by Y. S.
Sun, the state created a separate organizational capacity for the IC industry in the form of ITRI and ERSO in Taiwan, as well as TAC in the United
States. In the second phase (1979-83), the state transferred technology and
trained personnel into the private sector via the formation and spinoff of
UMC, which it also supplied with plant and equipment. It allowed UMC
to go public and become independent while at the same time maintaining
its own production and marketing facility in ERSO. It also established an
infrastructure for creating, attracting, and assisting high value-added enterprises via the creation of the Hsinchu Science and Technology-Based
Industrial Park. A high-level organizational capacity was created in the
form of STAG, which to a degree replaced the function of Y. S. Sun as
champion of semiconductor plans, after he became premier. The state

also expanded its support of semiconductor R&D projects in selected universities via the NSC.

In the third phase (1984-89) the state initiated a move into VLSI technology and formed TSMC, the existence of which (together with UMC) was critical in attracting private capital into the IC field, in the form of semiconductor companies and design houses. Private capital did not initiate the move to VLSI and showed reluctance to undertake the risky investment. The state further increased its organizational capacity in the form of the TRBs under STAG. It is true that the funds for TSMC were only made available by the state after the Vitelic sale of its new chip to Korea. On the other hand, persuasion from STAG and TAC was a key factor in allowing VLSI proponents to take advantage of the climate created by Vitelic's move and successfully repromote the joint venture idea.

Toward the end of the third period, however, a shift in the balance of the state-private sector relationship began to be visible. The industry had grown to include six companies manufacturing semiconductors: UMC and TSMC, plus Winbond, Hualon, AMPi, and Vitelic. Of these, four were entirely private sector, with one (UMC) a private company with minority government shareholding, taking an independent path. One (TSMC) remained a three-way joint venture. Meanwhile, the computer sector had grown dynamically (with assistance from the state, in the form of creating Hsinchu, but with the initiative basically with the private sector). This created an indigenous group with an interest in the content and direction of the chip industry. Moreover the move of Acer into semiconductors, specifically DRAMs, transferred a considerable amount of initiative into the private sector. It appears that the decision by TSMC to manufacture DRAMs and the entire phase four (the submicron project) were partly a product of "high, high pressure" coming from the private sector to ensure their supply. This would appear to confirm Evans's observation that a statecentric interpretation is less applicable to an industry's history once it has been established. On the other hand, the state's high-level advisory group, STAG, had been urging a more aggressive, cutting-edge orientation for the industry for some time.

Our account does not assume that state policy in the semiconductor case represents an unqualified success story. Critical observers of the program see ITRI-ERSO moving very slowly for a lengthy period (1973-74 to the early 1980s), during which they were working with a rather antiquated technology, committed insufficient funds to investment in R&D, and made little progress in attracting investment and moving technology into the private sector. Only in the 1980s with the emergence of UMC and especially TSMC did a real IC industry materialize in Taiwan. At some critical points the state can be seen as acting only in belated response to actions in the private sector (Vitelic, Acer). But our task here is not to show the state as infallible but only to present a case that supports the notion that states at certain moments can be (a) catalysts and (b) relatively autonomous actors in an industry's development.

Taking a differentiated view of the state apparatus, we see that there was a relatively autonomous organizational locus within (or, attached to) the state apparatus that was committed to promoting the IC program vis-à-vis competitors for funds and to the state's maintaining a leading role in the selection of IC technologies while promoting development of a private sector. ITRI, and within it ERSO, was this locus. ITRI and ERSO assumed an entrepreneurial role but ultimately did not stifle the emergence of a rather vigorous private sector. Meanwhile TAC, the state-initiated network of engineers in Taiwan and the United States, passed on information on technological and market trends to ITRI/ERSO. As the 1980s wore on, ITRI appears to have become somewhat more vulnerable to pressure from other bureaucratic agencies, such as the IDB. The MOEA may have more of an influence in the form of its Office of Science and Technology Advisers, which began to function around 1984-85 (Interviewee #6).

At the level above ITRI, one sees an evolving pattern of leadership that went from a very small core of individuals, led by Y. S. Sun, to a more bureaucratized format with no equally influential single figure. However, Y. S. Sun's creation, STAG, continued to play a key role. Here we see the key role played by foreign advisers and overseas Chinese personnel. The foreign advisers, retirees from major U.S. corporations, appear to have pushed Taiwan further in the direction of striving to become a world-class competitor in semiconductors than would have been the case otherwise. Meanwhile, private companies in Taiwan showed signs of getting ahead of ERSO in pushing into advanced technologies; the submicron project aims at maintaining a leading role for the state in cooperation with the private sector.

We stated at the outset that state policy in the semiconductor case presents a contrast with Taiwan's industrial policy in the automobile industry. In the auto industry, the state's goal of developing an industry competitive in global markets failed to be realized. Taking a differentiated view of the state helps to account for the divergent outcomes. No semiautonomous organizational base (ITRI-ERSO) or cabinet-level advisory group (STAG) devoted to the promotion of policy for the auto industry existed.

A distinctive aspect of the state's approach in the IC case was the tapping of overseas Chinese engineers in the United States, Taiwanese engineers returned from the U.S., and foreign executives. The state placed them in key positions within high-level policy groups and within the quasistate science and technology organizations.[11] This group enjoyed a rather high degree of autonomy vis-à-vis other actors within the state to define goals and implement policies.

While our account has emphasized state autonomy from domestic actors, the role played by foreign advisers and overseas Chinese raises questions about the state's autonomy from external actors. One might ask if we properly speak of "autonomy of the state" (or even of "the state") when speaking of an entity such as STAG, which though attached to the cabinet consists almost entirely of foreign nationals. On balance, I think one can identify STAG as part of "the state" and not an agent of foreign interests. Some of the Americans were drawn to the role of advisers by a desire to support the Nationalist Chinese over the communists. Some saw involvement with high-tech development in Taiwan as part of a strategy for competing with Japan. These interests coincided with the goals of key officials in Taiwan.

This convergence was not simply a matter of a momentary coincidence of interests between actors in the core and semiperiphery as a dependent development model might suggest, but was a product of a complex of personal and professional relationships among Taiwan officials and technical personnel and overseas Chinese and American engineers and executives. To further analyze the emergence of the semiconductor industry (and perhaps other industries) in Taiwan we will need to look more closely at the nature and functions of these kinds of transnational personal and professional links in the formation and pursuit of elite goals. This could lead to some fruitful redefinition of the notions of "the state," its boundaries, and its role in development.

Interviews

Conducted in July 1989 and February-March 1988

1. Executive Secretary, Science and Technology Advisory Group (STAG), Executive Yuan (1989)

2. Vice-Chairman, National Science Council, Executive Yuan (1989)

3. Former President and current Chairman of the Board, ITRI (1988 & 1989)

4. Senior Executive Adviser, ITRI (1989)

5. Executive Vice-President, ITRI (1989)

---

11. Further study of relationships and possible conflicting views regarding national development among these groups (for example, between STAG and TAC) would be valuable.

6. Director, Office of Science and Technology Advisers, Ministry of Economic Affairs (1989)

7. Deputy Director-General, Industrial Development Bureau, Ministry of Economic Affairs (1989)

8. President, Winbond Electronics Corporation (1988 & 1989)

9. President, United Microelectronics Corporation (1989)

10. Former President and Chief Executive Officer, Taiwan Semiconductor (TSMC) (1988)

11. Executive Vice-President, Acer Incorporated (1989)

Bibliography

Arnold, Walter. 1989. Bureaucratic Politics, State Capacity, and Taiwan's Automobile Industrial Policy. *Modern China* 15 (April): 178-214.

Chu, Yun-han. 1987. Authoritarian Regimes Under Stress: The Political Economy of Adjustment in the East Asian Newly Industrializing Countries. Ph.D. thesis, University of Minnesota.

Dataquest newsletter. June 1989. San Jose, California.

Evans, Peter B. 1986. State, Capital, and the Transformation of Dependence: The Brazilian Computer Case. *World Development* 14 (7): 791-808.

———. 1987. Class, State, and Dependence in East Asia. In *The Political Economy of the New Asian Industrialism*, edited by Frederick C. Deyo, 203-26. Cornell University Press.

Gold, Thomas. 1986. *State and Society in the Taiwan Miracle* M. E. Sharpe, Inc.

Haggard, Stephan. 1986. The Newly Industrializing Countries in the International System. *World Politics* 38 (2 - January): 343-70.

———, and Tun-jen Cheng. 1987. State and Foreign Capital in the East Asian NICs. In *The Political Economy of the New Asian Industrialism*, edited by Frederick C. Deyo, 84-135. Cornell University Press.

Johnson, Chalmers. 1987. Political Institutions and Economic Performance: The Government-Business Relationship in Japan, South Korea, and Taiwan. In *The Political Economy of the New Asian Industrialism*, edited by Frederick C. Deyo. Cornell University Press.

Noble, Gregory W. 1987. Contending Forces in Taiwan's Economic Policymaking. *Asian Survey* 27 (June): 683-704.

Pang, Chien-kuo. 1988. The State and Economic Transformation: The Taiwan Case. Ph.D. thesis, Brown University.

Simon, Denis. 1980. Taiwan, Technology Transfer, and Transnationalism: The Political Management of Dependency. Ph.D. thesis, University of California, Berkeley.

8

Taiwan's Financial System and the Allocation of Investment Funds

Jia-Dong Shea
Ya-Hwei Yang

Those who have witnessed the economic development of the Republic of China in Taiwan have generally dubbed it an astounding and unparalleled success. Indeed, the performance of Taiwan's economy in terms of growth, price stability, and distributive equity over the past several decades leaves little doubt that it more than deserves such praise.

Taiwan's impressive economic success has depended largely on the rapid rise of its domestic savings rate and its successful use for domestic capital formation. The expansion of the island's financial system has aided growth by stimulating and mobilizing savings and allocating investment funds. The financial system, however, is often criticized as underdeveloped and inefficient, and is even regarded as an obstacle to further economic growth. Specific instances of inefficiency commonly cited are excessive government intervention in setting interest rates and financial intermediation, or a weak market structure and banking operations.

This chapter reviews the structure and performance of Taiwan's financial system. We are most interested in the system's efficacy in mobilizing savings and its efficiency in allocating investment funds. We will also examine government policies aimed at influencing investment.

Section I outlines the structure of Taiwan's financial system. Section II reviews stimulating and mobilizing savings. Section III examines allocating investment funds, and Section IV takes up government policy, especially selective credit rationing. The conclusion summarizes the findings overall.

I. Taiwan's Financial System

Figure 1 diagrams Taiwan's financial superstructure. This structure is characterized by "financial dualism," that is, it is composed of two subsystems. The first is formal and regulated; it includes financial institutions and markets. The second is informal (unorganized and unregulated) in which lendings and borrowings are channeled through the fragmented curb markets.

A. Financial Institutions[1]

Taiwan's financial institutions can be placed in two categories: monetary institutions, which can create money, and other financial institutions that cannot. Table 1 offers totals in each category.

1. Monetary Institutions

These include six subgroups: the Central Bank, full-service domestic banks, local branches of foreign banks, medium and small business banks, credit cooperatives, and credit departments of farmers' and fishermen's associations.

a. **The Central Bank of China (CBC).** The CBC reopened in Taiwan in 1961, twelve years after the Communists took over mainland China in 1949. In the interim, the Bank of Taiwan performed most functions of a central bank. In 1979, control of the CBC was transferred from the president of the Republic of China to the Executive Yuan.

The CBC and the Ministry of Finance are monetary authorities. The former is responsible for the banking operations of financial institutions, while the latter supervises the administration of the formal financial system.

b. **Full-Service Domestic Banks.** At the end of 1988 there were sixteen domestic banks, with branches covering the entire island. In addition to commercial banking operations, most domestic banks provide savings

---

1. A more detailed description of the financial institutions in Taiwan and their development can be found in Lee and Tsai (1988).

FIGURE 1   The Financial System in Taiwan

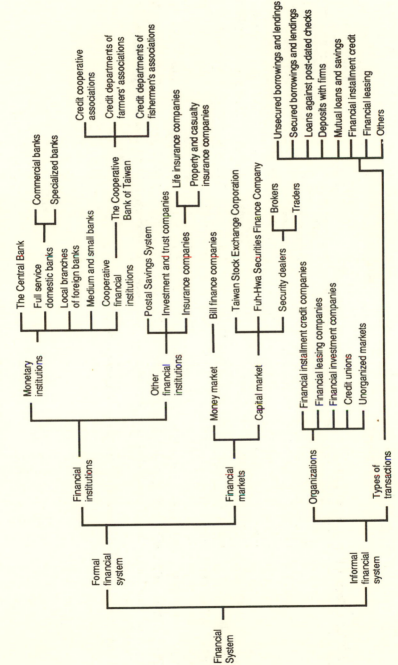

TABLE 1 Units of Financial Institutions

End of year	Total		Domestic banks		Local branches of foreign banks		Medium and small business banks		Credit cooperatives		Credit departments of farmers' and fishermen's associations		Postal savings system		Investment and trust companies		Insurance companies	
	Units	%	Units	%	Units	%	Units	%	Units	%	Units	%	Units	%	Units	%	Units	%
1961	1,359	100	260	19.13	1	0.07	84	6.18	153	11.26	385	28.33	451	33.19	1	0.07	24	1.77
1970	1,827	100	394	21.57	7	0.38	118	6.46	222	12.15	393	21.51	610	33.39	6	0.33	77	4.21
1980	2,830	100	536	18.94	21	0.74	165	5.83	274	9.68	724	25.58	952	33.64	26	0.92	132	4.66
1988	3,645	100	680	18.66	35	0.96	248	6.80	382	10.48	931	25.54	1,173	32.18	42	1.15	154	4.22

Note: The Central Bank of China, Central Reinsurance Corporation, and postal agencies that do not have financial business with the general public are excluded.

Source: Ministry of Finance, *Yearbook of Financial Statistics of the ROC*, 1988.

TABLE 2   Shares of Total Assets and Deposits of Financial Institutions—End of
1988 (%)

	Share of Total Assets	Share of Total Deposits
Domestic banks	55.39	48.84
Local branches of foreign banks	2.88	1.02
Medium and small business banks	6.38	6.15
Cooperatives	14.94	18.48
Postal savings system	13.88	17.85
Investment and trust companies	2.70	3.29
Insurance companies	3.83	4.37
Total	100.00	100.00

Note: The Central Bank of China is excluded. Totals include deposits held by enterprises,
   individuals, and the goverment; trust funds, and life insurance reserves.
Source: Central Bank of China, *Financial Statistics Monthly*, Taiwan District, ROC, June
   1989.

and foreign exchange departments, and some have trust departments.
There are five specialized banks, catering to industrial, agricultural, real-
estate, or export-import financings. Except for the Export-Import Bank of
China, the other four specialized banks in fact perform a variety of functions including commercial and savings banking. Among these, the Cooperative Bank of Taiwan, a specialized bank engaged in industrial and
agricultural financing, is also delegated by the CBC to conduct bank examinations of credit cooperative associations and the credit departments
of farmers' and fishermen's associations.

Although domestic banks have long suffered from severe restrictions
on establishing and operating new units, they remain the backbone of the
financial system in Taiwan. At the end of 1988, they held 55.39% of the
total assets and 48.84% of the total deposits of all financial institutions
(excluding the CBC), as Table 2 illustrates.

c. **Local Branches of Foreign Banks.** Before 1965, monetary authorities
in Taiwan hesitated to open the domestic financial market to foreign
banks. With the end of U.S. economic aid in 1965 and the grave setbacks
to the ROC's official diplomatic relationships in the late 1970s, the
authorities relented and agreed to allow foreign banks to establish
branches in Taipei. This was to encourage foreign investment, strengthen
economic ties with the outside world, and improve domestic banking operations through competition and the transfer of advanced banking management know-how. As a result the number of local branches of foreign

banks increased dramatically from 1 in 1964 to 13 in 1978, and reached 35 by the end of 1988.

Along with relaxing the entry barriers, operational restrictions on foreign banks were also loosened. They were permitted to open branches in Taipei and Kaohsiung city, and were authorized to handle foreign exchange transactions, extend loans to individuals and firms, and engage in trust business. They may also accept local currency deposits—checking accounts, demand deposits, saving deposits, and time deposits, with the total subject to a ceiling of 12.5 times their paid-in capital. Their role in Taiwan is still limited, however, as demonstrated in Table 2.

d. Medium and Small Business Banks. These banks develop from long-standing mutual loan and savings companies. They are specialized banks that extend medium and long-term credit to small- and medium-sized businesses. With the exception of the Medium and Small Business Bank of Taiwan, which operates branches islandwide, other small and medium business banks are restricted to specific districts.

e. Cooperatives. There are three types of credit cooperative in Taiwan: credit cooperative associations and the credit departments of farmers' and fishermen's associations. These may accept deposits from and grant loans to their members, and operate within a certain district only. Therefore, although they accounted for more than 35% of all financial institutions in 1988, their share of total assets and deposits was only 14.94% and 18.48%, respectively.

2. *Other Financial Institutions*

These cannot create money, but they can mobilize idle money to finance investments. These include the postal savings system, investment and trust companies, and insurance companies.

a. The Postal Savings System. Functions of the postal savings system are performed by the Directorate General Remittance and Savings Bank. Besides the remittance services conducted within and outside the country, this bank also accepts savings deposits through its extensive network of post offices. We use the term "postal savings system" to distinguish its financial operations from its other business and services.

Over the past twenty-eight years, the operating units of the postal savings system have accounted for a stable 33% of all financial institutions. Its share of deposits grew from 3.38% in 1961 to 17.85% in 1988, indicating that the postal savings system has done a fine job in mobilizing savings.

The postal savings system is not allowed to extend loans to the public. Until March 1982, all received savings deposits were redeposited with the CBC. The CBC then established long- and medium-term loan funds to extend credit to investment projects through full-service domestic banks at a preferential interest rate. In the period between March 1982 and March 1986, 65% of the savings deposits accepted by the postal saving system were redeposited with four specialized banks to supplement their loanable funds. This ratio, however, was reduced by the Central Bank to 30% in March 1986, and then further reduced to 15% in November 1988 to slow the growth rate of the money supply.

b. **Investment and Trust Companies.** The operations of investment and trust companies include trust-deposit management, direct and syndicated medium- and long-term loans, and investments and securities underwriting. Before 1971, there was only one investment and trust company in Taiwan. By the end of 1988, there were forty-two operating units of investment and trust companies, and their shares of total assets and deposits were 2.70% and 3.29%, respectively.

c. **Insurance Companies.** By 1989, there were eight life insurance and fourteen property and casualty insurance companies in Taiwan. The total number of operating units for all insurance companies jumped from 24 in 1961 to 154 in 1988. Insurance companies' reserve funds are used primarily for lending and equity and securities investments.

B. Financial Markets

Financial markets include all mechanisms for the issuance, trading, and redeeming of claims. Financial markets are classified into the money market and the capital market based on instruments' maturities. The money market deals with instruments with a maturity of less than one year, while the capital market handles instruments with longer maturities.

1. The Money Market

The money market in Taiwan was not well developed until 1976, with the establishment of the first bill finance company. Between 1976 and 1978, three bill finance companies were set up to deal in treasury bills, commercial papers, bankers' acceptances, and negotiable certificates of deposit. The bill finance companies also advise firms on the use of money market instruments and act as underwriters, brokers, and guarantors or endorsers of commercial paper. By the end of 1988, there were three bill finance companies with twelve branches; the outstanding volume of money market bills equaled 14.30% of the total loans and discounts of financial institutions, or 14.02% of the GNP in 1988.

2. The Capital Market

The capital market in Taiwan is composed of the bond market and the stock market, although neither is fully developed. Since firms' bond issuing costs (including yield rates and administrative costs) were usually higher than bank-financing costs, firms preferred bank financing to issuing corporate bonds to raise funds. In addition, the prudent fiscal performance in Taiwan, which prevented a governmental budget deficit problem, worked against the development of an active government bond market. Therefore the bond market has always been very small. By the end of 1988, the outstanding volume of government and corporate bonds equaled only 7.03 percent of the total loans and discounts of financial institutions.

The formal stock market, the Taiwan Stock Exchange Corporation, began operations in February 1962. A securities finance company followed in April 1980 to provide margin and stock loans for securities transactions and to serve as a securities custodian. Although the authorities provided some incentive for listing, the tradition of a low proportion of equity funding, a reliance on bank borrowings, and the desire for close management control and little public disclosure have impeded the growth of the stock market.[2] There were only 130 listed companies by the end of 1986, and the ratio of the market value of listed stocks to GNP was under 20 percent for most of the years before 1986. Even in recent years, when the stock price index had risen from 945 in 1986 to 9,732 in August 1989, the number of listed companies had increased only modestly, from 130 to 167. Data further shows that the turnover rate has been quite high in recent years (162% in 1986, 267% in 1987, and 333% in 1988), indicating that the stock market in Taiwan is not much of a vehicle for investors, but a paradise for speculators.

C. Informal Financial System

The informal financial system comprises all markets where borrowing and lending between and within businesses and households occur without being subject to the supervision and regulation of financial authorities. Except for financial installment credit companies, leasing companies, investment companies, and credit unions, most of these mar-

---

2. The incentives for listing provided by the authorities include that listed companies are offered a 15 percent reduction on corporate income tax for three years, and the shareholders are allowed to receive up to NT$360,000 of dividends plus interest tax free.

kets are fragmented and lack formal organization. These financial transactions include secured and unsecured borrowings and lendings, loans against postdated checks, deposits with firms, mutual loans and savings, financial installment credit, financial leasing, and others. Borrowings from financial institutions and the money market comprise a large segment of the loanable funds of financial leasing and installment credit companies. And the financial investment companies that have prospered in recent years draw deposits illegally from the general public by paying a monthly interest rate as high as 4-9 percent.

To illustrate the relative roles of the formal and informal financial system, we report the composition of the business sector's financing sources in tables 3 and 4. During the period 1964-87, financial institutions provided the business sector 57.50% of the total funds from the financial system, while the informal system (curb market), capital, and money markets accounted for 25.28%, 13.62%, and 3.60%, respectively. If we further decompose the business sector into public and private enterprises, from 1964 to 1987 public enterprise depended primarily on financial institutions as its borrowing source, while private enterprise borrowed only 60.24% from financial institutions, securing 35.23% and 4.52% from the curb market and money market, respectively.

II. The Stimulation and Mobilization of Savings

The role of the financial system in economic development is well understood in the literature. A developed financial system can stimulate and mobilize savings, as well as efficiently allocate investment funds. Stimulating and mobilizing savings can provide more funds for investment, while a more efficient allocation of these funds can lower the marginal capital output ratio.

A. The Stimulation of Savings

Table 5 indicates that the share of gross domestic savings in GNP rose steadily, from 14.91% in 1951-60 to 33.62% in 1981-88, and averaged 24.93% between 1951 and 1988. In recent years, Taiwan has had perhaps the highest savings ratio in the world. Because of this high savings rate, Taiwan's rapid growth has been accompanied by a far lesser rate of foreign borrowing than other developing countries. Table 5 shows that although the saving rate in 1951-71 was slightly less than the investment rate, so that a small proportion of domestic investments would need to be

TABLE 3   Source of Business Financing within the Financial System (NT$ million, %)

Period average	Financial institutions		Money market*		Capital market**		Curb market		Total	
	Amount	%	Amount	%	Amount	%	Amount	%	Amount	%
1964-70	29,892	57.10	0	0.00	8,211	15.68	14,251	27.22	52,354	100.00
1971-75	138,532	67.40	28	0.01	20,071	9.76	46,917	22.83	205,548	100.00
1976-80	372,024	57.16	29,240	4.49	90,730	13.94	158,808	24.40	650,803	100.00
1981-87	874,984	51.09	156,309	9.13	240,941	14.07	440,526	25.72	1,712,761	100.00
1964-87	370,288	57.50	51,688	3.60	95,753	13.62	175,503	25.28	693,231	100.00

Note: * The money market was established in 1975.

      ** The amount of financing from the capital market is defined as the sum of the accumulated net amount of stock issued by listed companies and the outstanding volume of corporate bonds.

Source: Central Bank of China, *Flow of Funds in Taiwan District, ROC*, December 1988; Ministry of Finance, *SEC Statistics*, 1988.

TABLE 4 Composition of Public and Private Enterprise Borrowings from Financial System (NT$ million)

Period average	Financial institutions		Money market		Curb market		Total	
	Amount	%	Amount	%	Amount	%	Amount	%
I. Public enterprises								
1964-70	7,830	97.73	0	0.00	182	2.27	8,012	100.00
1971-75	31,208	99.48	0	0.00	165	0.52	31,372	100.00
1976-80	105,768	96.71	2,343	2.14	1,260	1.15	109,371	100.00
1981-87	219,463	88.70	18,729	7.57	9,237	3.73	247,429	100.00
1964-87	94,831	95.25	5,951	2.65	3,044	2.10	103,825	100.00
II. Private enterprises								
1964-70	22,061	61.06	0	0.00	14,069	38.94	36,131	100.00
1971-75	107,324	69.64	28	0.02	46,753	30.34	154,105	100.00
1976-80	266,256	59.08	26,897	5.97	157,548	34.96	450,701	100.00
1981-87	655,521	53.54	137,580	11.24	431,289	35.22	1,224,391	100.00
1964-87	275,458	60.24	45,737	4.52	172,459	35.23	493,653	100.00

Note: The capital market is excluded.

Source: Central Bank of China, *Flow of Funds in Taiwan District, ROC*, 1988.

TABLE 5 National Savings and Investments (%)

I. Gross Domestic Savings

Period	As % of GNP			Composition			
	Total	Net national savings	Capital consumption allowances	Government	Public enterprises	Private enterprises	Household sector
1951-60	14.91	8.94	5.97	27.85	18.40	33.20	20.55
1961-70	21.07	14.22	6.86	13.12	18.83	27.27	40.79
1971-80	31.85	23.92	7.93	23.23	12.98	22.86	40.93
1981-88	33.62	24.76	8.86	17.83	15.51	20.87	45.78
1951-88	24.93	17.60	7.33	20.65	16.48	26.32	36.55

II. Gross Domestic Investments

Period	As % of GNP	Composition by type of purchaser			Source of finances		
		Government	Public enterprises	Private sector	Net national savings	Capital consumption allowances	Net foreign borrowings
1951-60	16.08	12.53	37.61	49.85	56.33	37.29	6.38
1961-70	21.89	10.74	27.34	61.92	64.70	31.85	3.45
1971-80	30.48	12.56	32.14	55.30	79.58	26.42	-6.00
1981-88	21.78	18.07	27.22	54.71	119.74	42.43	-62.17
1951-88	22.59	13.24	31.28	55.48	78.00	34.08	-12.08

Source: DGBAS, *National Income in Taiwan Area, ROC*, 1988.

TABLE 6   Nominal and Real Interest on Deposits (%)

Period average	Nominal interest rate, 1-year deposits	Change in wholesale price index	Real interest rate on 1-year deposits
1961-70	11.37	1.46	9.91
1971-80	10.93	10.43	0.20
1981-88	8.10	-0.50	8.60
1961-88	10.28	4.21	6.07

Source: Central Bank of China, *Financial Statistics Monthly*, various issues.

financed by foreign borrowing, investments in the later period were financed entirely by domestic savings.

The high savings ratio in Taiwan may be attributed to numerous factors: a high growth rate in real GNP, stable prices, large government savings (20.65% of all savings in 1951-88), the underdeveloped state of the social security system, the tradition of frugality in Chinese culture, a strong desire to establish independent businesses for the family through saving, etc. In addition, the policy of high real rates of interest on deposits, tax exemption on interest on most bank deposits, vigorous savings promotion campaigns by financial intermediaries, and easy access to banking offices surely helped.[3] The real deposit rate is reported in Table 6, which indicates that the real interest rate on one-year deposits averaged 6.07 percent from 1961 to 1988.

Table 7 shows there was one financial institution unit (excluding post offices) for every 9,481 persons in 1980. If we include the postal savings system, the population served by one financial institution unit was further reduced to 6,292 persons. Although this figure is much lower than that of developed countries, the network of financial institutions in Taiwan is still a dense one, considering that Taiwan has the highest population density in the world.[4]

---

3. The factors contributing to the high saving ratio have been discussed by Sun and Liang (1982), Scitovsky (1985), and others.

4. For example, the average population served by one unit of a financial institution was 2,842, 4,249, and 6,292 respectively in the United States, United Kingdom, and Taiwan in 1980. However, in that year, the population densities for these three countries were 24, 229, and 494 persons per square kilometer respectively.

TABLE 7   Population Served by One Unit of a Financial Institution

End of year	Population (1,000s)	Unit of financial institution		Population served by 1 unit	
		Incl. postal savings system	Excl. postal savings system		
	(1)	(2)	(3)	(4)	(5)
1961	11,149	1,359	908	8,204	12,279
1970	14,676	1,827	1,217	8,033	12,059
1980	17,805	2,830	1,878	6,292	9,481
1988	19,904	3,645	2,474	5,461	8,052

Note: Same units as Table 1. Column (4) = (1)/(2); column (5) = (1)/(3).

Source: (1) is from Council for Economic Planning and Development, *Taiwan Statistical Data Book*, 1989. (2) and (3) are from Table 1.

B. The Mobilization of Savings

Household, government, public enterprise, and private enterprise shares of domestic savings and investments were shown in Table 5. The absolute amounts of saving, investment, and financial surplus or deficit for each sector are reported in Table 8, which shows that 64.34% and 58.78% of investments made by private and public enterprises in 1951-87 were financed from internal savings. The remaining 35.66% and 41.22% constituted the financial deficits of private and public enterprises financed by the surplus from households and government. Although the household sector invested 29.15% of its savings in housing, transport equipment, etc. in 1951-87, it remained the most important source of financial surplus. The government invested a major part of its savings (62.26%) in infrastructure, while a large proportion of the remaining surplus was used to finance public enterprises.

We can evaluate the financial system's performance of financial intermediation, or mobilizing savings, by the proportion of household savings or financial surplus that has been channeled into the financial system, and by the proportion of the business sector's investment or financial deficit that has been financed by the system. We report the amount of household savings channeled through the financial system in Table 9, and the proportion of public and private enterprise investment funds secured from the financial system in Table 10.[5]

Table 9 shows that a large and increasing proportion of household

5. The first year for which flow-of-funds statistics were compiled is 1965. Thus

TABLE 8 Sectoral Financial Surpluses and Deficits (NT$ and %)

Period average	Household & nonprofit orgs.				Government				Rest of world	Private enterprises				Public enterprises			
	Saving	Investment		Surplus	Saving	Investment		Surplus	Surplus		Saving		Deficit	Invest-ment	Saving		Deficit
		Amt.	% of saving			Amt.	% of saving			Invest-ment	Amt.	% of invest-ment			Amt.	% of invest-ment	
1951-60	1,125	481	42.73	644	1,357	723	53.28	634	565	2,368	1,662	70.15	707	2,165	1,029	47.53	1,136
1961-70	11,789	2,566	21.77	9,222	4,027	3,175	78.85	852	1,023	15,978	7,682	48.08	8,296	8,245	5,445	66.03	2,801
1971-80	93,286	27,629	29.62	65,657	58,084	30,131	51.88	27,953	-7,402	96,891	53,747	55.47	43,144	74,364	31,300	42.09	43,064
1981-87	370,177	72,553	19.60	297,624	133,084	88,091	66.19	44,993	-311,182	189,195	173,981	91.96	15,213	139,111	122,889	88.34	16,222
1951-87	98,736	22,017	29.15	76,719	42,332	25,863	62.26	16,469	-60,444	66,939	49,967	64.34	16,972	49,230	33,458	58.78	15,772

Source: DGBAS, *National Income in Taiwan Area, ROC,* 1987, 1988.

TABLE 9 Household Sector Saving Through Financial System* (NT$ million, %)

Period average	Total saving (1)	Financial surplus (2)	Saving through financial institutions**			Saving through money and bond markets***			Lending through curb market			Saving through financial system*		
			Amt. (3)	% of total saving (4) =(3)/(1)	% of financial surplus (5) =(3)/(2)	Amt. (6)	% of total saving (7) =(6)/(1)	% of financial surplus (8) =(6)/(2)	Amt. (9)	% of total saving (10) =(9)/(1)	% of financial surplus (11) =(9)/(2)	Amt. (12) =(3)+(6)+ (9)	% of total saving (13) =(12)/(1)	% of financial surplus (14) =(12)/(2)
1965-70	15,358	11,933	7,243	47.16	60.70	604	3.93	5.06	2,410	15.69	20.20	10,257	66.79	85.95
1971-75	56,557	44,027	35,286	62.39	80.15	-457	-0.81	-1.04	6,420	11.35	14.58	41,249	72.93	93.69
1976-80	130,015	87,288	97,297	74.84	111.47	2,816	2.17	3.23	20,556	15.81	23.55	120,669	92.81	138.24
1981-87	370,177	297,624	366,410	98.98	123.11	5,570	1.50	1.87	40,315	10.89	13.55	412,295	111.38	138.53
1965-87	157,228	122,241	142,228	72.26	94.96	2,366	1.78	2.37	18,763	13.31	17.68	163,356	87.35	115.00

Notes: * The stock market is excluded.

** The financial instruments include demand deposits; time, savings, and foreign currency deposits; life insurance reserves, and trust funds.

*** The financial instruments include government securities, commercial paper, domestic bills accepted by banks, corporate bonds, and bank debentures.

Source: Columns (1) and (2): DGBAS, *National Income in Taiwan Area, ROC*, 1987, 1988.

Columns (3), (6), and (9): Central Bank of China, *Flow of Funds in Taiwan District, ROC*, 1988.

TABLE 10 Proportion of Public and Private Enterprise Investment Funds from the Financial System* (NT$ million, %)

Period average	Investment	Financial deficit	Borrowing from financial institutions			Funds from money and bond markets**			Borrowing from curb markets***			Investment funds from financial system*		
			Amt.	% of investment	% of financial deficit	Amt.	% of investment	% of financial deficit	Amt.	% of investment	% of financial deficit	Amt.	% of investment	% of financial deficit
	(1)	(2)	(3)	(4)=(3)/(1)	(5)=(3)/(2)	(6)	(7)=(6)/(1)	(8)=(6)/(2)	(9)	(10)=(9)/(1)	(11)=(9)/(2)	(12)=(3)+(6)+(9)	(13)=(12)/(1)	(14)=(12)/(2)
I. Public enterprises														
1965-70	10,859	3,846	888	8.18	23.10	-17	-0.15	-0.43	61	0.56	1.58	932	8.58	24.24
1971-75	43,509	27,744	9,231	21.22	33.27	501	1.15	1.80	36	0.08	0.13	9,767	22.45	35.20
1976-80	105,218	58,384	24,074	22.88	41.23	4,298	4.09	7.36	229	0.22	0.39	28,601	27.18	48.99
1981-87	139,111	16,222	363	0.26	2.24	4,566	3.28	28.15	444	0.32	2.73	5,372	3.86	33.12
1965-87	77,503	24,664	7,582	11.80	22.90	2,429	2.10	10.45	208	0.31	1.36	10,219	14.20	34.71
II. Private enterprises														
1965-70	21,117	11,162	5,178	24.52	46.39	60	0.28	0.54	2,668	12.63	23.90	7,906	37.44	70.83
1971-75	62,955	34,401	24,920	39.58	72.44	177	0.28	0.51	1,965	3.12	5.71	27,062	42.99	78.67
1976-80	130,827	51,888	41,511	31.73	80.00	13,134	10.04	25.31	22,724	17.37	43.80	77,370	59.14	149.11
1981-87	189,195	15,213	91,872	48.56	603.90	9,516	5.03	62.55	45,659	24.13	300.13	147,047	77.72	966.58
1965-87	105,216	26,300	43,753	36.68	229.04	5,806	3.85	24.79	19,960	15.10	108.34	69,519	55.62	362.17

Notes: * The stock market is excluded.

** Denoting funds raised by issuing commercial paper, domestic bills accepted by banks, and corporate bonds.

*** Includes borrowings from other enterprises and households.

Source: Central Bank of China, *Flow of Funds in Taiwan District, ROC*, 1988.

savings and financial surplus has been held as deposits in financial institutions. In the 1965-87 period, household savings through financial institutions constituted 72.26% of total savings or 94.96% of the household sector's financial surplus. In contrast, money and bond markets attracted only a very minor proportion of household saving, while lending to enterprises through curb markets accounted for only 13.31% of total savings or 17.68% of the financial surplus of the household sector. In sum, 87.35% of the total savings or 115.00% of the financial surplus of the household sector was channeled into the financial system (excluding the stock market) in the period 1965 to 1987.

Savings received by the financial system were used primarily for financing the investments or financial deficits of the business sector. Public enterprises depended on the financial system to provide money for investment or to combat financial deficits much less frequently than did private enterprise (see Table 10). Only 14.20% of the investment funds and 34.71% of the financial deficit of public enterprises were supplied by the financial system (excluding the stock market) over the 1965-87 period. The other major sources of investment funds for public enterprises were internal savings (capital consumption allowance and retained earnings) and government loans and investment.

In the same time period, private enterprises borrowed 36.68% of their investment funds from financial institutions, 3.85% from money and bond markets, and 15.10% from curb markets. For monies to cover debts, private enterprises borrowed 229.04% from financial institutions, 24.79% from money and bond markets, and 108.34% from curb markets. In total, 55.62% of the investment funds or 362.17% of the financial deficit of private enterprises came from the financial system (excluding again the stock market).

The primary function of Taiwan's financial system has thus been to channel household savings to finance investment in private enterprises. This function has been performed quite well. A positive real deposit rate and easy access to financial institutions and their services certainly have benefitted the mobilization of savings, as well as an active informal financial system which the government has never tried vigorously to suppress. As noted in tables 4, 9, and 10, the informal financial system (curb market) has played an important role in attracting household savings and financing the investment needs of private enterprise.

TABLE 11   Relative Shares of Secured and Unsecured Loans of Domestic Banks (%)

Period	Secured loans	Unsecured loans
1961-65	61.12	38.88
1966-70	63.91	36.09
1971-75	55.42	44.58
1976-80	53.99	46.01
1981-85	55.75	44.25
1986-88	60.33	39.67
1961-88	58.28	41.72

Source: Central Bank of China, *Financial Statistics Monthly*, various issues.

III. The Allocation of Investment Funds

For growth to occur, the efficient allocation of investment funds is as significant as the availability of investment funds. Although the financial institutions in Taiwan have a good record in mobilizing domestic savings, their performance in allocating funds has often been criticized. Criticisms include emphasizing collateral over the profitability of the business in granting loans; favoring public enterprises and large firms over private and small- to medium-sized businesses; and giving privileges to exporting industries in lending compared to import-substituting industries and the nontradable sector.

The emphasis on collateral in bank lending is illustrated in Table 11. Secured loans accounted for 58.28% of the loans made by domestic banks over the 1961-88 period. Under such a system it is easy to reject innovative investment plans that promise to be profitable but cannot meet collateral requirements. Preferential treatment for public enterprises and large firms and the prosperity of curb markets are also the natural results of the emphasis on collateral.

The weighting toward public enterprises in obtaining bank loans is evidenced in tables 4, 12, and 13. Table 4 shows that financial institutions financed 95.25% of public enterprises' domestic borrowing (excluding borrowing from the capital market) between 1964 and 1987, while only 60.24% of private enterprises' domestic borrowing was covered by these same institutions. Table 12 indicates that public enterprises were always granted more loans by financial institutions per unit of production value or gross domestic product than private enterprises. In the 1965-87 period, public enterprises were given loans of NT$0.2211 for each dollar of final output while private firms received only NT$0.1154. Similarly, the ratio

TABLE 12   Ratio of Financial Institution Loans Relative to Total Production
and GNP, Public vs. Private Enterprises (%)

Period average	Loans/Total value of production		Loans/GNP	
	Public	Private	Public	Private
1965-70	14.91	8.31	27.86	17.90
1971-75	19.38	11.86	38.04	29.18
1976-80	24.38	12.07	56.69	31.38
1981-87	28.60	13.70	63.29	35.03
1965-87	22.11	11.54	47.12	28.50

Note: Loans from financial institutions for each year are given as the average of year-end
loans for the current and previous years.

Source: Central Bank of China, *Flow of Funds in Taiwan District, ROC,* 1988; DGBAS,
National Income in Taiwan Area, ROC, 1988.

of loans from financial institutions relative to a firm's contribution to
gross domestic product averaged 47.12% for public enterprises but only
28.50% for private firms. Narrowing this comparison to manufacturing
alone, Table 13 reveals that public manufacturing enjoyed a share of
loans (20.20% on average in 1980-87) from financial institutions that was
much larger than its share (10.29%) of net value added (domestic factor
income).

To compare the availability of loans from financial institutions for
large versus medium and small businesses, in Table 14 we report the
composition of domestic borrowings of private enterprises with different

TABLE 13   Relative Share, Net Value Added, and Loans from Financial
Institutions, Public and Private Manufacturing (%)

Year	Share of net value added		Share of loans	
	Public	Private	Public	Private
1980	9.36	90.64	21.67	78.33
1981	9.49	90.51	23.85	76.15
1982	11.04	88.96	25.29	74.71
1983	11.77	88.23	25.16	74.84
1984	10.92	89.08	21.64	78.36
1985	9.12	90.88	18.31	81.69
1986	10.09	89.91	15.26	84.74
1987	10.54	89.46	10.45	89.55
Average	10.29	89.71	20.20	79.80

Note: Loans from financial institutions for each year are measured as the average of year-
end loans for the current and previous year.

Source: DGBAS, unpublished data on GDP and factor income by kind of econommic
activity; Central Bank of China, *Report on the Survey of Financial Conditions of the
Public and Private Enterprises in Taiwan Area, ROC, various issues.*

TABLE 14 Source of Domestic Borrowing by Private Enterprises in 1983 by Scale of Assets (%)

Source of domestic borrowing	Scale of assets (NT$ million)							
	Under 1	1-5	5-10	10-40	40-100	100-500	500-1,000	Above 1,000
Financial institutions	10.50	31.05	44.09	50.90	59.27	66.41	65.80	70.10
Money and bond markets	0.00	0.00	0.00	0.26	1.04	4.42	15.94	19.61
Curb markets	89.50	68.95	55.91	48.84	39.69	29.17	18.26	10.29
Total	100.00	100.00	100.00	100.00	100.00	100.00	100.00	100.00

Source: Derived from Table 4 in Liu (1988), which is compiled from the CBC's 1983 *Survey on the Financial Condition of Private Enterprise in the Taiwan Area.*

assets in 1983. This table shows very clearly that the larger the firm, the easier it was to get financing from both financial institutions and the money and bond markets. The smaller the scale of assets, the greater the dependence on curb market financing.

To test the assertion that collateral was emphasized over profitability and that exporting industries were given advantages in applying for bank loans, we need to demonstrate which manufacturing industries were favored. We attempt to do so by dividing the manufacturing sector into twelve industries and estimate the following "bank-financing equation" by applying the pooling data of twelve private manufacturing industries over the period 1974-87:

$$(\frac{BL}{DL})_{i\,t} = a_1 + \sum_{j=2}^{12} a_j D_j + b_1(\frac{TBL}{TDL})_t + b_2(\frac{FA}{DL})_{it} + b_3(\frac{KI}{TA})_{it} \tag{1}$$

$$+ b_4 ER_{it} + b_5(\frac{BL}{DL})_{i,t-1}$$

where subscript i denotes private manufacturing industry and subscript t denotes year, and

BL_i = loans from financial institutions of industry i

DL_i = total domestic borrowings of industry i

$TBL_t = \sum_i BL_{i\,t}$: total loans from financial institutions of the whole private manufacturing sector in year t

$TDL_t = \sum_i DL_{i\,t}$: total domestic borrowings of the whole private manufacturing sector in year t

FA = fixed assets

KI = capital income

TA = total assets

ER = export ratio

D_j = dummy variable for industry j

In this equation, $(BL/DL)_i$ measures the proportion of financing demand of industry i met by loans from financial institutions, $(TBL/TDL)_t$ denotes the general market condition of the availability of bank loans in year t, and FA/DL and KI/TA represent the collateral factor and profitability respectively.

$(BL/DL)_{t-1}$ is included as an explanatory variable to capture the impact of the closeness of a previous relationship with the bank. We expect the estimated values of b_1 and b_5 to be positive. If the above criticisms are true, the regression result should also show significantly positive values for b_2 and b_4, and an insignificantly positive or even negative value for b_3. As for the coefficients of industrial dummies, a larger a_j indicates that industry j received preferential treatment when applying for loans.

The private manufacturing sector is divided into twelve industries. The data covers 1974 to 1987. The data on loans from financial institutions, total domestic borrowings, fixed assets, and total assets of each industry were obtained from the *Report on the Survey of Financial Conditions of Public and Private Enterprise in the Taiwan Area* published by the CBC.[6] The data on capital income, defined as the sum of rent, interest, and profit of each private manufacturing industry, was adopted from the unpublished data of DGBAS. The export ratio is measured by the ratio of export value relative to production value. The export value of each industry was compiled from Monthly Statistics of Exports and Imports published by the Ministry of Finance, and the production value comes from DGBAS's national income statistics. The first industry, used as the reference in defining industrial dummies D_i ($i=2,...,12$) for the other eleven industries in the bank-financing equation, is the food and beverage industry.

The ordinary least squares method is applied to estimate the bank-financing equation, and the regression result is reported as Equation (1) in Table 15. According to this equation, the general availability condition (*TBL/TDL*), export ratio (*ER*), and the previous bank-financing ratio ((BL/DL)t-1) have significantly positive impacts on the current bank-financing ratio. Although the collateral factor (*FA/DL*) and profitability (*KI/TA*) also have positive effects, their regression coefficients are insignificant.

To further test the robustness of the above result, we drop the 1974 data, a year of high inflation (the wholesale price index rose 40.58 percent in that year), and omit the miscellaneous products industry (the twelfth industry) from the data set since the contents of that industry may have varied significantly with time. The regression results, based on the data set covering the period 1975-87 for eleven industries, are reported as equations (2), (3), and (4) in Table 15. These three equations all show significantly positive coefficients for *TBL/TDL*, *FA/DL*, *ER*, and (BL/DL)t-1,

---

6. Since the survey made by the Central Bank usually covers the financial conditions of the current and the previous year, we have two sets of data for most of the years. In regression, the averages of the two sets of BL/DL, TBL/TDL, FA/DL, and TA are applied.

TABLE 15 Regression Results of Bank-Financing Equation

	Equation #							
	(1)		(2)		(3)		(4)	
	(12 industries, 1974-87)		(12 industries, 1975-87)		(11 industries, 1974-87)		(11 industries, 1975-87)	
Explanatory variable	Coeff.	t-value	Coeff.	t-value	Coeff.	t-value	Coeff.	t-value
Constant	0.05027	0.992	0.06940	1.280	0.01371	0.276	0.03721	0.700
D2 (Textiles and clothing)	-0.04288	-1.383*	-0.05111	-1.573*	-0.04961	-1.621*	-0.05585	-1.732**
D3 (Wood and bamboo products, nonmetallic furniture)	-0.08366	-2.197**	-0.08813	-2.172**	-0.08129	-2.158**	-0.07984	-1.984**
D4 (Paper, printing, and publishing)	-0.01587	-0.756	-0.02365	-1.090	-0.02530	-1.230	-0.03457	-1.625*
D5 (Chemicals)	-0.01325	-0.663	-0.01744	-0.845	-0.02090	-1.084	-0.02567	-1.264
D6 (Nonmetallic mineral products)	-0.07158	-2.511**	-0.08634	-2.929**	-0.08157	-2.837**	-0.09809	-3.267**
D7 (Basic metal industries)	0.00635	0.382	0.00895	0.525	0.00375	0.235	0.00709	0.432
D8 (Fabricated metal products)	-0.13178	-5.186**	-0.14113	-5.328**	-0.12965	-5.182**	-0.13640	-5.218**
D9 (Machinery and equipment)	-0.07892	-2.798**	-0.08648	-2.935**	-0.07526	-2.663**	-0.08145	-2.723**
D10 (Electrical and electronic machinery and equipment)	-0.08196	-2.454**	-0.08686	-2.473**	-0.08866	-2.700**	-0.18859	-2.566*
D11 (Transport instruments)	-0.00636	-0.365	-0.00381	-0.209	-0.01046	-0.632	-0.00812	-0.466
D12 (Miscellaneous)	-0.17896	-2.936**	-0.18452	-2.915**	—	—	—	—
TBL/TDL	0.41598	4.960**	0.43738	4.753**	0.37994	4.720**	0.38925	4.438*
FA/DL	0.03186	1.124	0.04228	1.572*	0.04931	1.833**	0.06215	2.240*
KI/TA	0.06425	0.736	0.02640	0.285	0.14805	1.478*	0.09604	0.866
ER	0.11158	1.422*	0.11504	1.402*	0.12214	1.564*	0.11471	1.403*
$(BL/DL)_{t-1}$	0.44029	7.254**	0.38254	5.718**	0.48987	8.351**	0.43986	6.749*
R^2	0.8318		0.8171		0.8484		0.8344	

* Significant at the 10% level; **significant at the 5% level.

while the profitability factor *KI/TA* has an insignificantly positive impact in two of the three equations. These results provide support for the charge that financial institutions in Taiwan have emphasized collateral rather than the borrowers' profitability when rationing loans, and that exporting industries are favored over others.[7]

The privileged status given to exporting industries in obtaining bank loans has been regarded generally as a successful policy measure for stimulating exports and economic growth. However, it has also distorted the fund allocations among exporting, import-substituting, and nontrading sectors, and contributed to the dilemma of a huge trade surplus in recent years.

The regression coefficients of the industrial dummies reported in Table 15 are then ranked as the first four columns in Table 16. These indicate that food and beverages (Industry 1); paper, printing, and publishing (Industry 4); chemicals (Industry 5); basic metal (Industry 7); and transport instruments (Industry 11) have been favored consistently when applying for loans, while wood and bamboo products (Industry 3); nonmetallic mineral products (Industry 6); fabricated metal products (Industry 8); electrical machinery and equipment (Industry 10); and miscellaneous products (Industry 12) have suffered discrimination. Although the factors affecting financial institutions' preferences among industries still require further investigation, Table 16 does show that the preference order of bank financing has an insignificantly positive, or even negative, rank correlation coefficient with the order of production growth rates of private manufacturing industries. This result indicates that the financial institutions have not allocated loans according to industries' growth potential.

Financial institutions' preference for lending to public enterprises and large businesses may have also distored the allocation of investment funds. Public enterprises in Taiwan have often been criticized for their inefficiency in operations and investment. The prosperity and important role of medium and small businesses indicate that large businesses may not necessarily be superior in operational or investment efficiency. Table 17 reports the relative factor-proportion and productivities of public versus private manufacturing and of large versus medium and small manufacturing businesses. The easier access to bank loans for public enterprises and large firms inevitably allowed these companies to adopt more capital-intensive technologies, which results in higher productivity

---

7. In a similar study, which did not include *TBL/TDL* and *ER* as explanatory variables, Shea and Kuo (1984) came to the same conclusion, that collateral rather than profitability was the key factor considered by financial institutions in granting loans, based on the pooling data of nineteen industries over the period 1975-82.

TABLE 16   Rank Correlation between Preference Order of Bank Financing and
Order of Production Growth Rate

Private manufac-turing industry	Preference order of bank financing				Production growth rate, 1974-86* (%)	Order of production growth rate**
	(1)	(2)	(3)	(4)	(5)	(6)
1	2	2	2	2	7.36	11 (10)
2	6	6	6	6	9.49	10 (9)
3	10	10	8	7	9.70	9 (8)
4	5	5	5	5	10.80	6 (5)
5	4	4	4	4	14.45	3 (2)
6	7	7	9	10	7.17	12 (11)
7	1	1	1	1	12.98	5 (4)
8	11	11	11	11	10.13	7 (6)
9	8	8	7	8	9.99	8 (7)
10	9	9	10	9	16.75	2 (1)
11	3	3	3	3	13.80	4 (3)
12	12	12	—	—	16.80	1 (—)
Spearman rank correlation	-0.1169	-0.1169	0.1091	0.1909	——	——

Note: * Industrial production statistics for 1987 did not separate private and public
enterprise production by industry.
** The number in parenthesis is the order of production growth rate when
industry 12 is excluded.

Source: (1)-(4): Table 15. (5): Ministry of Economic Affairs, *Industrial Production Statistics
Monthly.*

for labor and a lower productivity for capital in public and large enterprises relative to private and medium and small enterprises, as shown in
Table 17.[8] If we could reallocate resources in such a way as to shift some
capital from public and large enterprises to private and medium and
small enterprises in exchange for some labor, the total productivity of the
entire economy might potentially increase.

In short, the allocation of investment funds may not have been completely satisfactory in terms of efficiency. The efficiency loss can be attrib-

---

8. Strictly speaking, a correct comparison on factor productivities should be
based on marginal productivities rather than average productivities. What is
reported in Table 17 is simply comparisons of average factor productivities.

TABLE 17   Comparison of Factor Proportion and Productivity

Year	(1) Public vs. private manufacturing					(2) Large vs. medium and small business manufacturing		
	Assets in operation /Labor	Total value of production /Labor	Net value added /Labor	Total value of production /Assets	Net value added /Assets	Assets in operation /Labor	Operating revenues /Labor	Operating revenues /Assets
1966	3.56	2.42	4.37	0.68	1.21	—	—	—
1971	3.67	2.21	3.17	0.60	0.83	—	—	—
1976	5.51	2.27	1.42	0.41	0.26	—	—	0.48
1981	6.21	3.93	2.16	0.63	0.36	3.42	1.75	0.51
1986	7.03	3.01	3.80	0.43	0.54	3.48	1.87	0.55
Average	5.19	2.77	2.99	0.55	0.64	3.45	1.81	0.51

Source: (1) is derived from DGBAS, *Report on Industrial and Commercial Census, Taiwan-Fukien Area, ROC*, various issues. (2) is from Bank of Taiwan, *Report on the Survey of Financial Conditions of Industries, Taiwan Area, ROC*.

uted to four main factors: government ownership of the major banks, strict entry regulations, interest rate control, and selective credit rationing policies.

The government in Taiwan owns and manages most domestic banks. Among the sixteen domestic banks, only four are private (defined as banks in which the government owns less than 50% of the capital). These four accounted for only 8.66% of the total assets and 7.90% of the total loans of domestic banks at the end of 1988. The banks administer many regulations affecting the personnel, accounting, budgeting, and auditing of public enterprises. These have turned government-owned banks into bureaucracies that operate inefficiently and are sluggish in implementing financial innovations. Under this system, the clerks of the government-owned banks are blamed if there is a default on loans. This makes them unwilling to take financial risks, resulting in an overemphasis on collateral when determining loan eligibility.

To prevent financial instability due to competition among financial institutions, the authorities have maintained strict regulations on the establishment of new domestic financial institutions and branches. Also, bank deposit rates and lending rates before 1980 were set or controlled by the CBC at levels lower than the market-clearing rates. The combined factors of entry restrictions and interest rate control weakened the market competition, which in turn vitiated the capacity of the price mechanism in efficiently allocating investment funds.

Furthermore, setting interest rates lower than the market equilibrium rate resulted in excess demands for the banks' loanable funds. Credit rationing became necessary, which inevitably invited governmental intervention. The selective credit rationing policies adopted by the authorities and their impact are examined next.

IV. The Impact of Financial Policies

Faced with the problem of excess demands for loanable funds, the government adopted financial policies to accommodate the financing needs of specific industries, economic activities, and borrower groups in order to promote economic growth or to equalize to some extent the availability of bank loans among borrower groups. These included financing policies for exports, industry, machine imports, and strategic industries, as well as setting up specialized banks and other selective credit-control policies. Of these, the export financing and strategic industry financing policies will receive further discussion.

A. Review of Selective Credit Rationing Policies[9]

The CBC has often adopted a special loans policy to direct the allocation of funds. These have been several times extended through government-owned commercial banks and specialized banks. After extending the special loans, banks may rediscount the loans to the CBC. The volume of special loan rediscounts and their share in the CBC's total claims on monetary institutions are reported in columns (1) and (3) of Table 18. Column (3) indicates that special loan rediscounts constitute a major part of the borrowing by monetary institutions from the CBC for most years.

The special loans have been designed to finance the particular needs of agricultural and industrial sectors and promote the growth of exporting activities and strategic industries. To promote machine imports, the government promulgated regulations in 1973, 1975, and 1978 that allowed firms to borrow indirectly from the CBC through designated banks while buying machines from abroad. The approved amounts are shown in column (4) of Table 18.

The CBC provided US$600 million in 1978, with US$300 million planned for financing major export industries and the other US$300 million for technology-intensive industries. As shown in column (5) of Table 18, 86.17 percent of the total available amount had been extended in 1988.

Other selective credit rationing policies exist, such as the so-called medium-and-long-term credit special fund of the Central Bank, set up in 1973 to finance basic construction and long-term investment, with funding coming primarily from redeposits of the postal savings system. In addition, six government-owned banks were set up or designated to specialize in industrial, agricultural, real-estate, medium and small business, and export-import financings, as well as special loan programs for agriculture, medium and small business, venture capital, etc. The Ministry of Finance and the CBC have often ordered financial institutions to strengthen or limit their loans to certain economic activities, industries, or borrower groups.

B. Export Financing Policy

Taiwan is a small, open economy with a high degree of trade dependency. Export financing policy has been a key element of the economy since export promotion was proposed as the main economic develop-

---

9. A more detailed description of selective credit rationing policies before 1982 can be found in Lee and Chen (1984).

TABLE 18   Special Loans

Year	(1) Special loan rediscounts* (NT$ million)	(2) Total claims of CBC on monetary institutions (NT$ million)	(3) (1)/(2) (%)	(4) Cumulative machine import loans by CBC (US$ million)	(5) Extended amount and % of US$600 million in CBC special loans (US$ million)	(5) (%)
1962	1,354	1,925	70.34			
1963	1,085	3,888	27.91			
1964	1,647	5,837	28.22			
1965	3,242	9,131	35.51			
1966	4,458	10,118	44.06			
1967	5,267	11,641	45.25			
1968	6,866	13,915	49.34			
1969	6,651	14,421	46.12			
1970	7,173	14,423	49.73			
1971	8,195	16,410	49.94			
1972	7,298	16,983	42.97			
1973	24,552	42,467	57.81	231		
1974	40,258	66,116	60.89	258		
1975	44,814	78,302	57.23	400		
1976	35,605	100,726	35.35	419		
1977	34,740	160,941	21.59	437		
1978	37,218	239,479	15.54	464		
1979	59,494	282,615	21.05	481	35	5.83
1980	82,252	287,685	28.59	521	118	19.67
1981	106,400	191,000	55.71	563	196	32.67
1982	166,683	226,319	73.65	592	307	51.17
1983	120,561	181,381	66.47	624	358	59.67
1984	89,330	122,113	73.15	657	453	75.50
1985	53,733	57,329	93.73	677	469	78.17
1986	39,895	53,842	74.10	679	477	79.50
1987	48,800	57,703	84.57	680	497	82.83
1988	8,500	9,240	91.99	694	517	86.17

Note: *Data from the Bank of Taiwan is excluded for 1962-76.

Source: Central Bank of China, *Annual Report of the Central Bank, ROC,* and CBC, *Financial Statistics Monthly,* Taiwan District, ROC.

ment strategy in the 1960s.[10] In addition to their high priority in credit rationing, export activities have been granted special low-interest rates to provide preshipment production financing and funds for importing raw materials. The difference between the export loan rate and the minimum interest rate for secured loans is illustrated in Table 19 and Figure 2. After the 1970s, as continual trade surpluses began to pile up foreign exchange reserves, the authorities gradually reduced the interest rate difference.

When we multiply the interest rate difference by the amount of export loans granted to manufacturing industries financed by domestic banks, and then divide this volume by exports, we arrive at the ratio of the export-loan subsidy, shown in the last column of Table 19. This measures the savings on export costs due to the interest rate subsidy. This ratio decreased from 0.2522% in 1971 to 0.0113% in 1987.[11] Savings on costs certainly stimulated exports to some degree.

Next, we would like to see whether the distribution of export loans is consistent with the distribution of exports among manufacturing industries. In principle, an industry with more exports is supposed to get more export loans from banks. We report the ranked order of export loans and exports of seven manufacturing industries over the period 1975-87 in Table 20. The Spearman rank correlation coefficient is then calculated, and we find that the orders of export loans and exports do have a positive relationship each year.

C. Financial Policies for Strategic Industries

In the 1980s, improving the industrial structure became an important policy issue. Therefore, in 1982 the government promulgated policy measures to promote the growth of strategic industries. These were selected based on six criteria: a large linkage effect, high market potential, high technology intensity, a large value-added, a low energy coefficient, and low pollution. The selected fields at that time included mechanical, information, and electronics industries. Later, the criteria were broadened to include biochemical and material industries. The government provided firms belonging to the strategic industries with special medium

---

10. Other export incentives include rebates of custom duties and commodity taxes on imported raw materials, tax exemptions, retention of foreign exchange earnings for the import of raw materials and machinery, etc.

11. Schive et al. (1978) estimates that export loan subsidies and tax rebates totaled NT$2.88, $4.39, $5.71, and $3.11 per US dollar export in 1961, 1966, 1971, and 1976 respectively, while the exchange rate was NT$40 per US$ between 1960 and 1972 and NT$38 per US$ in 1976.

TABLE 19   Export Loan Subsidy

	(1)	(2)	(3)	(4)	(5)	(6)
				Export loans to manufac- turing industries by domestic banks		[(3)*(4)]/(5)
			(2)-(1)			
		Minimum interest rate for secured loans*			Exports of manufac- turing industries	Ratio of export loans subsidy
	Export loan rate					
Year	(%)	(%)	(%)	(NT$ million)	(NT$ million)	(%)
1963	7.50	14.94	7.44	—	—	—
1964	7.50	14.04	6.54	—	—	—
1965	7.50	14.04	6.54	—	—	—
1966	7.50	14.04	6.54	—	—	—
1967	7.50	13.63	6.13	—	—	—
1968	7.50	13.32	5.82	—	28,460	—
1969	7.50	13.32	5.82	—	38,252	—
1970	7.50	13.30	5.80	—	53,429	—
1971	7.50	12.25	4.75	3,983.14	75,019	0.2522
1972	7.50	11.63	4.13	6,200.25	113,869	0.2249
1973	8.17	11.81	3.64	8,304.08	162,744	0.1857
1974	10.99	15.89	4.90	8,094.75	207,104	0.1915
1975	7.80	13.48	5.68	6,761.58	190,804	0.2013
1976	7.00	12.83	5.83	8,934.83	296,727	0.1755
1977	6.62	10.91	4.29	9,924.00	339,278	0.1255
1978	6.50	10.50	4.00	10,750.58	453,043	0.0949
1979	8.75	11.98	3.23	12,609.42	563,724	0.0722
1980	10.53	13.50	2.97	12,597.08	693,953	0.0539
1981	11.55	14.19	2.64	15,345.67	807,134	0.0502
1982	9.79	11.18	1.39	19,151.67	843,147	0.0316
1983	8.05	8.60	0.55	20,981.75	979,856	0.0118
1984	7.86	8.31	0.45	20,593.25	1,178,811	0.0079
1985	7.41	8.08	0.67	20,422.08	1,197,951	0.0114
1986	5.79	7.20	1.41	17,427.67	1,475,760	0.0167
1987	5.50	6.75	1.25	15,162.33	1,674,866	0.0113
1988	5.50	6.87	1.37	16,374.00	—	—

Note: *The prime rate is used after March 1985 when that system was established in Taiwan. Monthly interest rate data are averaged to get yearly data.

Source: Central Bank of China, *Financial Statistics Monthly*, Taiwan District, ROC. Depart-
ment of Statistics, Ministry of Finance, *Monthly Statistics of Exports and Imports*,
Taiwan Area, ROC, 1988. Department of Statistics, Ministry of Finance, *Monthly
Statistics of Exports and Imports*, Taiwan Area, ROC, 1988.

TABLE 20   Order and Rank Correlation of Export Loans and Exports

		Food	Textiles, wearing apparel, dyeing and trimming yarn and fabrics	Lumber, bamboo, cane, and cork products	Chemicals & chemical products	Non-metallic mineral products	Basic metal industries products	Metal products	Rank correlation
1975	A	2	1	5	3	7	6	4	0.8929*
	B	3	1	5	4	7	6	2	
1976	A	2	1	6	3	7	5	4	0.8241*
	B	4	1	5	3	7	6	2	
1977	A	2	1	6	3	7	5	4	0.6429
	B	4	2	5	3	6	7	1	
1978	A	6	2	4	1	5	7	3	0.6786*
	B	4	2	5	3	7	6	1	
1979	A	2	1	6	3	7	4	5	0.3929
	B	5	2	4	3	7	6	1	
1980	A	2	1	6	3	7	5	4	0.7143*
	B	4	2	5	3	7	6	1	
1981	A	2	1	6	3	7	5	4	0.5714
	B	5	2	4	3	7	6	1	
1982	A	2	1	6	3	7	4	5	0.5357
	B	4	2	5	3	7	6	1	
1983	A	4	1	6	2	7	3	5	0.4286
	B	5	2	4	3	7	6	1	
1984	A	4	1	6	3	7	2	5	0.3214
	B	5	2	4	3	7	6	1	
1985	A	4	1	6	2	7	3	5	0.5000
	B	4	2	5	3	7	6	1	
1986	A	2	1	6	3	7	5	4	0.6429
	B	4	2	5	3	6	7	1	
1987	A	4	1	6	3	7	5	2	0.8571*
	B	4	2	5	3	6	7	1	
Avg.	A	2	1			6			0.5357
	B	4	2			5			

Note: A=Export loans, B= Exports for individual industry. * = significant at 5% level.

and longterm low-interest loans. These loans were extended by the Bank of Communications and the Medium-and-Small Business Bank of Taiwan, with 20-25% of the funds provided by the Executive Yuan's Development Fund and the remaining 75-80% provided by the two

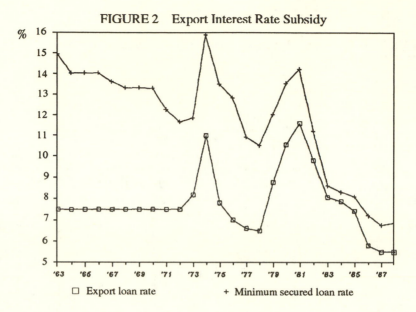

FIGURE 2   Export Interest Rate Subsidy

□ Export loan rate   + Minimum secured loan rate

participating banks. The interest rate difference between the strategic loans and the prime rate has been around 1.75-2.75%. In addition to financing strategic industries, the preferential loans were expanded to fund the purchase of automation equipment and domestic machines, and firms' investment projects for environmental protection. The actual extended amounts are listed in Table 21.

This preferential loan policy was from the beginning subject to severe criticism by scholars. It was felt that the policy produced economic distortions, while some of the selection criteria for strategic industries were criticized as improper or inconsistent with one another. Recently, Yang, Jen, and Chou (1989) reviewed the impacts of preferential loans on strategic industries. They distributed questionnaires, and then performed a path analysis on the survey data to test whether the preferential loans significantly influenced capital costs, investments, and operational efficiencies of firms. They found that the effects of preferential loans in reducing capital costs and stimulating investment were not significant, nor were preferential loans an important factor affecting firms' operational efficiency.

The government in Taiwan has tried in earnest to affect the allocation of investment funds through selective credit rationing policies. In the early stages of economic development, in the 1950s and early 1960s, Taiwan's economy lacked investment funds, the private sector needed entre-

TABLE 21   Preferential Medium- and Long-Term Loans, December 31, 1988
(NT$ thousands)

	Medium Business Bank of Taiwan		Bank of Communications		Total	
	Amt.	%	Amt.	%	Amt.	%
1. Investment project for strategic industries	4,866,252	20.28	29,238,576	35.609	34,104,828	32.142
2. Investment project for automation equipment	7,045,254	29.36	26,575,925	32.366	33,621,179	31.686
3. Investment project for domestic-produced machines	8,700,725	36.26	21,584,814	26.288	30,285,539	28.542
4. Investment projects for environment protection and pollution prevention	— —	— —	4,146,611	5.050	4,146,611	3.908
5. GMP projects*	— —	— —	41,930	0.052	41,930	0.040
6. Cooperative export and new product development	3,385,215	14.10	— —	— —	3,385,215	3.190
7. CEPD-supported projects**	— —	— —	521,764	0.635	521,764	0.492
Total	23,997,446	100.00	82,109,620	100.00	106,107,066	100.00

* GMP stands for Good Manufacturing Product.
**CEPD is the Council for Economic Planning and Development.

preneurs, and the industries that had comparative advantages could be easily identified. Under such circumstances, the strategy of depending on selective credit rationing rather than price mechanisms to allocate investment funds to public enterprises, exporting activities, and industries that were supposed to have a comparative advantage might have been appropriate. In the 1970s and 1980s, however, when the Taiwanese economy had a greater supply of investment funds and private entrepreneurs, and industries with comparative advantages were no longer easily identifiable, the government's continued dependence on selective credit rationing policies naturally produced distortions and invited criticism. And given the total supply of investment funds, the government's intent to allocate more funds to preferred borrowers in order to stimulate economic growth became contradictory to the objective of equalizing the availability of bank loans among borrower groups based on the consideration of equity. Various selective credit rationing policies adopted by the government in Taiwan to fulfill these two objectives, therefore, served only to complicate the allocation system.

Conclusion

The financial system in Taiwan has performed the functions of stimulating and mobilizing savings very satisfactorily. Its performance in allocating investment funds, however, and the government's use of selective credit rationing to influence this process, still requires improvement.

We have learned, on the positive side, that the widespread system of postal savings and the credit departments of farmers' associations, combined with the policy of a positive real-interest rate on deposits, have helped stimulate and mobilize savings. Further, where interest rates are controlled, funds are in short supply, and the formal financial system is underdeveloped, an active informal financial system is helpful in mobilizing savings and meeting the financing needs of those discriminated against by the formal system.

On the negative side, strict entry regulations and government ownership of financial institutions adversely affect financial development and the allocative efficiency of investment funds. Interest rate control, when it sets rates lower than the market-clearing rate, also has a negative effect on allocative efficiency, even when the rates set are above the inflation rate. And selective credit rationing policies, although not severely distortive of resource allocation at the beginning stages of economic development, are not recommended at later stages.

Since 1980, the financial system in Taiwan has been widely regarded as a major bottleneck for economic growth. The authorities have recognized these problems and adopted several measures to improve them. Interest rate control has been gradually phased out; the restrictions on the operation of foreign banks have been relaxed to a large extent; new private banks will be allowed to open in the near future; and some of the government-owned banks are scheduled for privatization. Although it would be premature to evaluate the effects of these policy changes now, they will almost certainly be of great benefit to the financial development and allocative efficiency of investment funds in Taiwan.

Bibliography

Asian Development Bank. 1985. *Improving Domestic Resource Mobilization Through Financial Development*. Manila, September.

Chiu, P. C. H. 1981. Performance of Financial Institutions. In *Experiences and Lessons of Economic Development in Taiwan*, edited by K. T. Li and T. S. Yu. Taipei: Institute of Economics, Academia Sinica.

Galenson, W. 1979. *Economic Growth and Structural Change in Taiwan*. Ithaca: Cornell University Press.

Kuo, S. W. Y. 1983. *The Taiwan Economy in Transition*. Boulder, Colorado: Westview.

Lee, Y. S., and S. C. Chen. 1984. Financial Development in Taiwan: Review and Prospective. In *Proceedings of the Conference on Financial Development in Taiwan*. Taipei: Institute of Economics, Academia Sinica, December. In Chinese.

Lee, Y. S., and T. R. Tsai. 1988. Development of the Financial System and Monetary Policies in Taiwan. In *Proceedings of the Conference on the Economic Development Experiences of Taiwan and Its New Role in an Emerging Asian-Pacific Area*. Taipei: Institute of Economics, Academia Sinica..

Liu, S. H. 1988. The Development and Prospect of Financial Institutions in Taiwan. In *Proceedings of the Conference on the Modernization of Service Industries in ROC*. Taipei: Chinese Economic Association. In Chinese.

Lundberg, E. 1979. Fiscal and Monetary Policies. In *Economic Growth and Structural Change in Taiwan*, edited by W. Galenson. Ithaca: Cornell University Press.

Schive, C., et al. 1978. *A Study on the Effective Protection Level of Major Industrial Products in Taiwan*. Taipei, May. In Chinese.

Scitovsky, T. 1985. Economic Development in Taiwan and South Korea. In *Food Research Institute Studies*. Stanford: Stanford University Press.

Shea, J. D. 1983. Financial Dualism and Industrial Development in Taiwan. In *Proceedings of the Conference on Industrial Development in Taiwan*. Taipei: Institute of Economics, Academia Sinica, March. In Chinese.

Shea, J. D., and P. S. Kuo. 1984. The Allocative Efficiency of Banks' Loanable Funds in Taiwan. In *Proceedings of the Conference on Financial Development in Taiwan*. Taipei: Institute of Economics, Academia Sinica, December. In Chinese.

Shea, J. D., M. Y. Liang, Y. H. Yang, S. H. Liu, and K. M. Chen. 1985. A Study on the Financial System in Taiwan. *Economic Papers* 65. Taipei: Chung-Hua Institution for Economic Research, June. In Chinese.

Sun, C., and M. Y. Liang. 1982. Savings in Taiwan, 1953-1980. In *Experiences and Lessons of Economic Development in Taiwan*, edited by K. T. Li and T. S. Yu. Taipei: Institute of Economics, Academia Sinica.

Tsiang, S. C. 1982. Monetary Policy of Taiwan. In *Experiences and Lessons of Eco-*

nomic Development in Taiwan, edited by K. T. Li and T. S. Yu. Taipei: Institute of Economics, Academia Sinica.

Yang, Y. H. 1982. An Economic Analysis of the Exports Financing System in Taiwan. *Economic Papers* 13. Taipei: Chung-Hua Institution for Economic Research. In Chinese.

Yang, Y. H., L. C. Jen, and R. C. Chou. 1989. *An Evaluation of the Effects of Preferential Policies for Strategic Industries.* Chung-Hua Institution for Economic Research. In Chinese.

9

Monetary Policy in Taiwan: Third Quarter 1961 to Fourth Quarter 1988

Fa-Chin Liang

Introduction

During the past four decades, Taiwan's economy has performed remarkably. As is shown in Table 1, the economy's average real GNP growth rates were 7.33%, 10.23%, 9.11%, and 9.02%; its average inflation rates in terms of GNP deflator were 9.58%, 3.21%, 11.11%, and 2.18%; and its average unemployment rates were 3.93%, 3.08%, 1.61%, and 2.31%, respectively, for the periods 1953-60, 1961-70, 1971-80, and 1981-87. From 1952 to 1987 M1B as a percentage of nominal GNP rose from 7.78% to 50.74% and M2 as a percentage of nominal GNP rose from 11.46% to 135.08%. Thus the income velocity of M1B declined steadily from 12.85 in 1952 to 1.97 in 1987 and that of M2 declined from 8.97 in 1952 to 0.74 in 1987.

An interesting question is how the monetary authorities in Taiwan employ policy instruments to realize these achievements. The main pur-

Thanks are due to professors Mei-Ying Huang, Weng-Tzong Hsiao, and To-Far Wang for their valuable comments. The errors that remain are the author's alone.

TABLE 1   Selected Indicators for the Taiwan Economy (percent)

	1953-60	1961-70	1971-80	1981-87
Average rate for:				
Real GNP growth	7.33	10.23	9.11	9.022
Unemployment	3.93	3.08	1.61	2.31
GNP deflator	9.58	3.21	11.11	2.18
CPI	9.84	3.40	11.08	3.10
WPI	8.87	2.00	10.73	-0.35
M1B/nominal GNP (%)	9.26	13.94	23.65	33.75
M2/nominal GNP (%)	14.91	33.23	58.00	97.88
Income velocities				
M1B	11.01	7.33	4.36	3.11
M2	7.03	3.10	1.77	1.08

Source: Calculated from data in *Taiwan Statistical Data Book*, 1988.

pose of this study, therefore, is to investigate how the monetary authorities react to changes in the policy goals they are mandated to achieve.

In Section I, we will survey the major goals of monetary policy in Taiwan and the instruments that the Central Bank of China (henceforth, the CBC) has used to achieve them. In Section II we will propose a reaction-function model to study the behavior of the monetary authorities and to describe the available data. In Section III we will estimate reaction functions for each of the monetary instruments. The purpose of these estimates is to quantify how the monetary authorities react to changes in goals with the instruments under their control. A brief conclusion will sum up the empirical results of the study.

I. Major Goals and Instruments of Monetary Policy in Taiwan

A. Major Goals of Monetary Policy

Generally speaking, monetary policy has several major goals, namely, full employment, price stability, economic growth, and balance of payments equilibrium. Specifically, however, according to the Central Bank Act, the primary goals of the CBC are: to promote financial stability, to guide sound banking operations, to maintain the stability of the internal and external value of the currency, and to promote economic growth within the scope of the above goals.

Except for guiding sound banking operations, which belongs to the field of banking administration and inspection, the other aims can be fitted squarely into the general major goals of monetary policy. As was shown, the average unemployment rates in Taiwan have been very low; therefore efforts to achieve full employment are not as important to the CBC as to other economies' monetary authorities. Hence the major goals for monetary policy in Taiwan can be summarized as follows:

1. economic growth
2. price stability
3. balance of payments equilibrium
4. exchange rate stability

B. Major Monetary Instruments Employed

In order to achieve these goals, the CBC has employed the following instruments extensively:

1. interest rate policy
2. rediscount rate policy
3. required reserve ratio policy
4. sterilization policy
5. open-market operations

There follows a brief review of each of these policies.

1. Interest Rate Policy. The monetary authorities successfully employed a high interest rate policy to curb hyperinflation in the late 1940s (Irving and Emery 1966). Since then the CBC has raised interest rates whenever the economy was threatened by inflationary pressure. This can be seen in Figure 1 from the relationship between the rate of change for one-year's savings and time deposits and inflation rates in terms of GNP deflator. The high interest rate policy not only helped to curb inflation by means of attracting time and savings deposits into the banking system, but also helped to mobilize savings to finance economic growth.

2. Rediscount Rate Policy. The CBC used rediscount rate policy and the management of rediscount and refinancing facilities quite often as one of its major monetary policy instruments. As is evident from Figure 2, during the past decades the rediscount rate was adjusted whenever there was inflation.

234

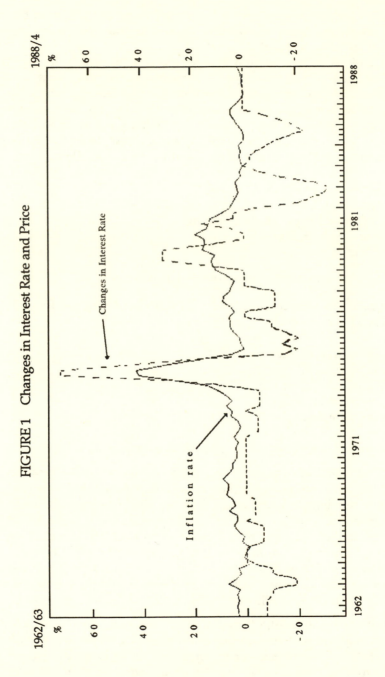

FIGURE 1 Changes in Interest Rate and Price

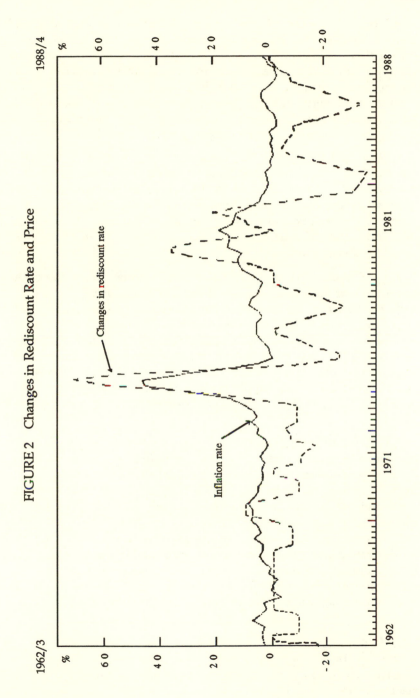

FIGURE 2   Changes in Rediscount Rate and Price

Changes in rediscount rate

Inflation rate

1962/3

1988/4

As for the rediscount and refinancing facilities, they consist of (1) NT$ accommodations for the reserve deficiencies of commercial banks; (2) NT$ rediscount of export and other trade bills; (3) US$ refinancing for importing essential raw materials and livelihood stocks; (4) NT$ refinancing for medium- and long-term financing; and (5) US$ refinancing for importing machinery and equipment. The purposes of these measures range from the role of lender of last resort to that of providing special encouragement for exports and economic growth (Chiu 1981).

3. Required Reserve Ratio Policy. From 1 July 1948 to 1 April 1989, the required reserve ratios of deposit banks in Taiwan were changed twenty times.[1] Thus this policy has been used extensively to achieve the goals set by the CBC. Among them, one of the most important was price stability. The relationship between the rate of change of the required reserve ratio and the inflation rate shown in Figure 3 can offer some evidence for this account.

4. Sterilization Policy. Within the period under study, the exchange rate system of the economy was either a fixed or a heavily managed float system. Therefore, the balance of payments strongly affected the net foreign asset component of the monetary base. In order to offset these foreign sector influences on the monetary base and therefore on the money supply, the CBC actively adjusts its net domestic credits. The aim of this sterilization policy is to partially offset influences from the foreign sector and to bring the money supply under control. The behaviors of changes in the CBC's net foreign assets and net domestic credits are shown in Figure 4.

5. Open-market Operations. Although open-market operations are the best weapon of the central banks both for defensive and for dynamic operations in developed countries, these operations were not available to the CBC in the early years because the financial market was underdeveloped and the market for government bonds was thin. The first open-market operations were taken as late as 4 January 1979.[2]

Furthermore, unlike the open-market operations conducted by the central banks in developed economies through buying or selling government bonds, the open-market operations implemented by the CBC are primarily through issuing or redeeming the CBC's treasury bills, certificates of time deposit, or savings bonds. In other words, while the central

---

1. See Table 12A, Required Reserve Ratios of Deposit Banks, in *Financial Statistics Monthly* (Taipei: CBC, August 1989): 64.

2. For a description of the open-market operations in Taiwan and its development, see, for example, Hsu 1989 and Khatkhate 1977.

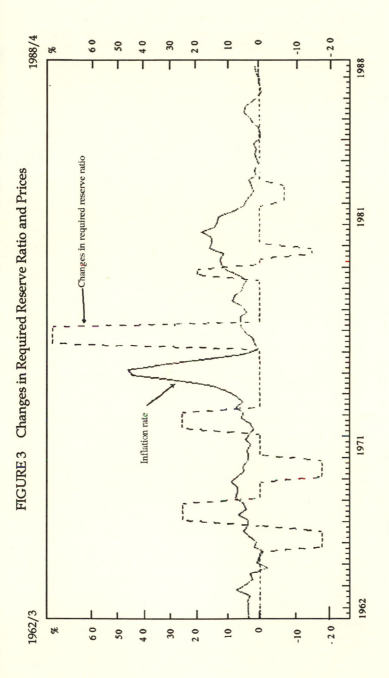

FIGURE 3 Changes in Required Reserve Ratio and Prices

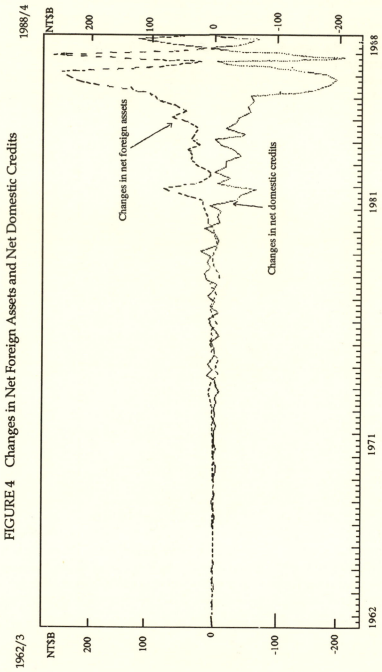

FIGURE 4   Changes in Net Foreign Assets and Net Domestic Credits

banks in developed economies conduct open-market operations by changing their specific assets, the CBC carried out the operations by adjusting its specific liabilities. For example, the CBC first issued its certificates of time deposit to commercial banks in August 1972 to reduce the high reserve position and to cope with inflationary pressure.

Since the data for open-market operations are not available to the public, we have to approximate the data loosely with the following equation:[3]

$$OMO = \Delta(GS + PES + PRES + FIS - CBTB$$
$$- CBCD - CBSB) \tag{1}$$

where

OMO = open-market purchase if positive, open-market sale if negative

GS = CBC holdings of government securities

PES = CBC holdings of public enterprise securities

PRES = CBC holdings of private enterprise securities

FIS = CBC holdings of financial institution securities

CBTB = CBC issue of treasury bill-B

CBCD = CBC issue of certificate of time deposit

CBSB = CBC issue of savings bond

All of the above items are in billions of NT$. The behavior of the open-market operations is shown in Figure 5.

II. The Model and the Data

The previous section shows that the major goals of monetary policy in Taiwan are economic growth, price stability, balance of payments equilibrium, and exchange rate stability. In order to achieve these goals, the CBC actively employs the monetary policy instruments under its con-

---

3. This concept of open-market operations overlaps in part the changes in the CBC's net domestic credits.

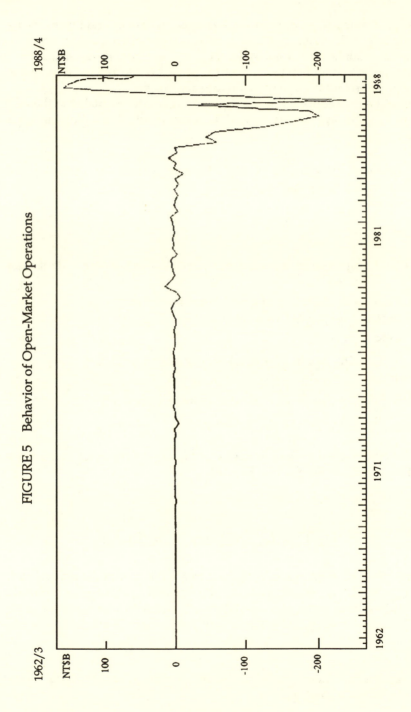

FIGURE 5   Behavior of Open-Market Operations

trol. These policy measures focus on interest rates, rediscount rates, required reserve ratio, sterilization, and open-market operations.

In order to learn how the CBC responds to changes in major policy goals, we are going to estimate the behavior of these policy instruments with respect to the policy goals. The technique we will apply is the reaction-function model.[4]

The reaction-function model assumes that the monetary authorities are trying to maximize a utility function that contains two types of arguments: namely, a policy instrument variable, e.g., interest rate, at time t, $X(t)$, and a policy goal variable, e.g., economic growth, at time t, $Y(t)$. Under these assumptions, a general form of the utility function can be expressed as:

$$U(t) = -aX(t) - bX(t)^2 - c\,[X(t) - X(t-1)]^2$$
$$-f\,[Y(t) - Y(t)^*]^2 \tag{2}$$

where all the coefficients are positive and $Y(t)^*$ is the target value of $Y(t)$. Under this specification, the utility function expresses that the authorities would like the level of the policy instrument to be low, and its change to be small; and they would also like the difference between Y and its target value Y^* to be as small as possible.

If the authorities view the goal variable as being influenced not only by the policy instrument but also by exogenous variable Z, then their maximization behavior will be constrained by what they see as a reduced form of a model representing the economy:

$$Y(t) = Y\,[X(t), Z(t)] \tag{3}$$

The authorities will maximize their utility as represented by utility function (2) subject to the constraint (3), by changing the level of the policy instrument according to (see Aftalion 1987):

$$X(t) = \frac{-a}{2(b+c)} - \left(\frac{f}{b+c}\right)\left(\frac{\partial Y}{\partial X}\right)[Y(t) - Y(t)^*]$$

$$+ \left(\frac{c}{b+c}\right)X(t-1) \tag{4}$$

---

4. For general discussions and empirical estimates of reaction functions, see papers cited in references.

Therefore, a general form of the reaction function to be estimated can be specified as:

$$x_t^i = a_0 + a_1 y_t^1 + a_2 y_t^2 + a_3 y_t^3 + a_4 y_t^4 + a_5 x_{t-1}^i + \varepsilon_t \tag{5}$$

where

x_t^i = the ith monetary policy instrument under consideration, where $i = 1,...,5$

y_t^i = the ith policy goal variable, here, $i = 1,...,4$, they are respectively economic growth, price stability, exchange rate stability, and balance of payments equilibrium

x_{t-1}^i = the lagged value of the ith monetary policy instrument under consideration

and ε_t = stochastic error term

The sign of a_i ($i=1,...,4$) depends on the relationship between instrument variables and goal variables.

The reaction functions in this essay are estimated with the quarterly data from third quarter 1961 to fourth quarter 1988 (1961.III to 1988.IV).[5] There are several reasons for studying this period rather than the period since the late 1940s. First of all, the CBC was formally reactivated on 1 July 1961. Second, the topics on monetary policy and development in the earlier period of Taiwan economic development have been well documented (Liu 1970, Lundberg 1979, Tsiang 1981). Last, but not least, is the data availability.[6]

III. The Reaction Functions Estimated

Based on the previous descriptions, the reaction functions for the CBC concerning its implementation of policies on interest rates, required reserve ratios, rediscount rates, sterilization, and open-market operations

---

5. All of the data used here are taken from EPS Taiwan Financial Statistics Data Bank and EPS National Income Statistics Data Bank, the Computer Center of the Ministry of Education.

6. Consistent series for money supply are only available since 1961.III.

are estimated with the data available in Taiwan. Their results are as follows.[7]

A. The Reaction Function for Interest Rate Policy

Although there are several kinds of interest rates in Taiwan, their behaviors are very similar. Therefore, we choose the interest rate on one-year savings deposits as representative of the CBC's interest rate policy instrument.

As was stated in equation (5), the explained variable in this reaction function is the interest rate at time t, and the explanatory variables are the annual growth rate of real income $\dot{y}_t$ and that of the GNP deflator $\dot{p}_t$, as well as the levels of exchange rate e_t and the changes in the net foreign assets of the CBC in billions of NT$, ΔNFA_t, and the lagged dependent variable, the interest rate at time $t\text{-}1$, r_{t-1}. The changes in the foreign assets of the CBC are used to represent the goal of the balance of payments equilibrium. The purposes of other variables are self-explanatory.

The estimated results of this reaction function are:

$$r_t = 0.9525 \quad + \quad 0.0360\dot{y}_t \quad + 0.0619\dot{p}_t \quad - \quad 0.0043e_t \quad - \quad 0.0021\Delta NFA_t$$
$$\quad\quad (1.1730) \quad\quad (2.4626) \quad\quad (7.5453) \quad\quad (-0.2044) \quad\quad (-1.8531)$$
$$\quad\quad (0.2408) \quad\quad (0.0138) \quad\quad (0.0000) \quad\quad (0.8381) \quad\quad (0.0639)$$

$$\quad\quad + \quad 0.8458r_{t-1}$$
$$\quad\quad\quad (23.5361)$$
$$\quad\quad\quad (0.0000) \quad\quad\quad\quad\quad\quad\quad\quad\quad\quad\quad (6)$$

$$SEE = 0.5059 \quad F=259.9935 \quad DW=1.8054 \quad \bar{R}^2=0.9412$$

where

r_t = annual nominal interest rate on one-year time deposits and savings deposits at time t

---

7. The parameter estimates from reaction functions do not provide information about the actual policymakers' preference. The parameter estimates combine information on policymakers' preferences along with the reduced-form parameters of the macro-economy. The process can be visualized as a constrained optimization; the reaction functions emerge from the maximization of the policymakers' preference, subject to the reduced-form equation that describes the economy (Demopoulos, Katsimbris, and Miller 1987: 1029).

$$\dot{y}_t = \left(\frac{y_t}{y_{t-4}} - 1 \right) * 100 = \text{annual economic growth rate in terms of}$$

real GNP

$$\dot{p}_t = \left(\frac{p_t}{p_{t-4}} - 1 \right) * 100 = \text{annual inflation rate in terms of GNP defla-}$$

tor

e_t = exchange rate in terms of NT\$ per US\$ at time t

$\Delta NFA_t = NFA_t - NFA_{t-1}$ = changes in the net foreign assets of the CBC in billions of NT\$ at time t

r_{t-1} = annual nominal interest rate on one-year time and savings deposits at time $t-1$

t = a subscript to represent time in quarter

The figures in the first set of parentheses below the estimated coefficients are the t-value and those in the second set are the probabilities showing levels of significance.

Theoretically, we expect that the sign for the coefficients of explanatory variables in equation (6) will be positive for $\dot{y}$, $\dot{p}$, and e, but negative for ΔNFA. The reasons are as follows. The higher the growth or inflation rate, the more restrictive monetary policy is expected, therefore the higher the interest rate will be. As for the exchange rate, a higher e means a devaluation of NT\$ with respect to US\$, so a higher interest rate is required to attract capital inflows to restore the NT\$'s exchange value. Therefore, the relationship between interest rate and the exchange rate should be positive. Since a higher positive change in net foreign assets indicates a favorable balance of payments, a lower interest rate is required to bring it to equilibrium.

In order to see whether the instrument reacts differently to internal and external phenomena, we divide the targets into internal goals, consisting of economic growth and price stability, and external goals, consisting of exchange rate stability and balance of payments equilibrium. We then perform a general hypothesis test[8] for each of the policy instruments discussed in this chapter as follows.

Suppose the general linear regression model for the reaction function in this chapter is:

---

8. The author would like to thank Professor Mei-Ying Huang for suggesting this test. For a discussion and examples of general hypothesis testing using an F-value, see Wallace and Silver 1988, 224-42.

$$x_t^i = a_0 + a_1 \dot{y}_t + a_2 \dot{p}_t + a_3 e_t + a_4 \Delta NFA_t + a_5 x_{t-1}^i \tag{7}$$

where $\dot{y}$ and $\dot{p}$ are internal goals, e and ΔNFA are external goals; x_t^i's are policy instrument variables such as interest rate, rediscount rate, required reserve ratio, changes in net domestic credit of the CBC, and open-market operations at time t, and x_{t-1}^i is x^i at time $t-1$.

To test the joint significance of internal goals versus external goals, we are interested in testing the following composite null hypothesis for the internal goals:

$$H_0^i: a_1 = 0, a_2 = 0 \tag{8}$$

$$H_a^i: a_1 \neq 0, a_2 \neq 0 \tag{9}$$

where the superscript i denotes internal goals, while for the external goals we are testing the composite null hypothesis:

$$H_0^e: a_3 = 0, a_4 = 0 \tag{10}$$

$$H_a^e: a_3 \neq 0, a_4 \neq 0 \tag{11}$$

where the superscript e denotes external goals.

In order to carry out this general hypothesis testing, we run separately the restricted regression:

$$x_t^i = a_0 + a_3 e_t + a_4 \Delta NFA_t + a_5 x_{t-1}^i \tag{12}$$

for the case of internal goals, and the restricted regression:

$$x_t^i = a_0 + a_1 \dot{y}_t + a_2 \dot{p}_t + a_5 x_{t-1}^i \tag{13}$$

for the case of external goals.

After running the unrestricted regression of equation (7) and restricted regression of either equation (12) or equation (13), we compute an F-statistic defined in equation (14):

$$F = \frac{(SSE_r - SSE_u)/m}{SSE_u /(n - k - 1)} \tag{14}$$

where

SSE_r = the sum of squared errors of the restricted regression

SSE_u = the sum of squared errors of the unrestricted regression

m = the number of restrictions implied by the null hypothesis

n = number of observations

k = the number of independent variables in the general model

Using the information we got from equation (6) as an unrestricted regression and that from equation (12) as a restricted regression for testing the null hypothesis in equation (8), the F-value we calculated according to equation (14) is 30.37623, which is well above the critical value of 3.08. Thus we have to reject the null hypothesis of equation (8) that assumes the coefficients for internal goals variables are zero.

On the other hand, when we use the same information from equation (6) and that from equation (13) in testing the composite null hypothesis of equation (10), the calculated value of F we have is 1.7172 which is below the critical value.

The general hypothesis testing carried out in the previous paragraphs shows that the CBC used its interest rate policy primarily to achieve the internal goals of economic growth and price stability.

B. The Reaction Function for the Rediscount
   Rate Policy

As was stated, the rediscount rate policy is also one of the major policy instruments used by the CBC. In order to see how it was used to achieve major monetary policy goals, we estimate the reaction function of the rediscount rate with respect to economic growth, price stability, exchange rate stability, and the balance of payment equilibrium.

The reaction function we get for the rediscount rate policy looks like equation (15).[9]

$$rd_t = \quad -0.0524 \quad + \quad 0.0338\dot{y}_t + \quad 0.0515\dot{p}_t + \quad 0.0065e_t$$
$$(-0.0576) \qquad\qquad (2.1405) \qquad (5.8153) \qquad (0.2263)$$
$$(0.9541) \qquad\qquad (0.0323) \qquad (0.0000) \qquad (0.8210)$$

$$-0.0013\Delta NFA_t \qquad + 0.9076 rd_{t-1}$$

---

9. The serial correlation in equations with *rho* are corrected with the Cochrane-Orcutt method.

$$(-1.1784) \qquad (21.5807)$$
$$(0.2387) \qquad (0.0000) \qquad\qquad (15)$$

$$SEE = 0.4103 \quad F=494.4899 \qquad DW=2.0767 \qquad R^2=0.9724$$
$$rho = 0.3697$$
$$(3.3536)$$
$$(0.0008)$$

where

rd_t = the rediscount rate at time t

rho = coefficient of first-order autocorrelation

rd_{t-1} = the rediscount rate at time t-1

Other variables are as previously defined.

All of the signs of the coefficients in equation (15) are as expected. While the coefficients for economic growth and inflation rate are significant at 5% and 1% levels respectively, those for exchange rate and the balance of payments are insignificant.

In order to see whether the rediscount rate policy also reacts differently to internal and external goals, the same general hypothesis testing of equations (7) to (14) was performed for the rediscount rate policy. The calculated F-value for testing the internal goals, i.e., the null hypothesis of equation (8), is 19.0946, while that for the external goals, or the null hypothesis of equation (10), is 0.7017. The results show again that we have to reject the hypothesis assuming that the coefficients for internal goals in the reaction function of rediscount rate policy are zero, while we are unable to reject a similar hypothesis for the coefficients of external goals. Based on this hypothesis testing, we may also conclude that the rediscount rate policy was primarily aimed at internal goals.

C. The Reaction Function for Required Reserve Ratio Policy

The required reserve ratios of deposit money banks in Taiwan are classified according to the nature of the banks and that of the deposits. The banks are classified into commercial banks, industrial banks, and savings banks, while the deposits are classified as demand deposits (or passbook deposits for saving banks) and time deposits.[10] As a result, there are six categories of required reserve ratios. However, since all of the ratios follow the same pattern of changes, we choose the required reserve ratio for demand deposits at commercial banks as a representative instrument. Furthermore, due to the fact that the ratio structure was changed on 21 July 1975, we employ a dummy variable, D, which is 1 after 1975.III and 0 elsewhere, to capture the structural change. The estimated results for the required reserve ratio policy are as follows.

$$
rr_t = \quad 7.7225 \quad + \quad 0.0476\dot{y}_t \quad + \quad 0.0354\dot{p}_t \quad - \quad 0.0153e_t
$$

$$
\quad\quad (3.6127) \quad\quad\quad (1.5442) \quad\quad\quad (2.0457) \quad\quad\quad (-0.3281)
$$

$$
\quad\quad (0.0003) \quad\quad\quad (0.1225) \quad\quad\quad (0.0408) \quad\quad\quad (0.7422)
$$

$$
\quad -0.0047\Delta NFA_t \quad +6.0134D \quad + \quad 0.4422rr_{t\text{-}1}
$$

$$
\quad\quad (-1.9729) \quad\quad\quad (7.4463) \quad\quad\quad (6.0866)
$$

$$
\quad\quad (0.0485) \quad\quad\quad (0.0000) \quad\quad\quad (0.0000) \quad\quad\quad\quad\quad (16)
$$

$$
SEE = 1.1260 \quad F = 293.2675 \quad DW = 1.3696 \quad \bar{R}^2 = 0.9543
$$

where

rr_t = the required reserve ratio for demand deposits at commercial banks at time t

$rr_{t\text{-}1}$ = rr at time $t\text{-}1$

D = a dummy variable which is 1 from 1975.III and 0 elsewhere

and other variables are as previously defined.

Most of the signs of the coefficients in equation (16) are right except that for exchange rate. It has a wrong sign and insignificant coefficient. In order to test the joint significance for internal and external goals for the case of the required reserve ratio policy, we did the same general hypothesis testing as before.

The resulting F-value for the hypothesis of equation (8), or for the internal goals, is 3.09, which just meets the critical value, but that for the hypothesis of equation (10), that is, for the external goals, is only 1.9525. These results indicate that the required reserve ratio was used to achieve the goals of economic growth and price stability, but not for the balance of payments equilibrium or exchange stability.

---

10. See the table cited in footnote 1.

D. The Reaction Function for the Sterilization Policy

As was shown in the introduction, the CBC employed the sterilization policy actively to offset changes in its net foreign assets by changing its net domestic credits. In order to see how the changes in the CBC's net domestic credits react to the major monetary policy goals, we estimate the following reaction functions for the sterilization policy.

$$\Delta NDC_t = \begin{array}{cccc} 92.9669 & - & 0.0282\dot{y}_t & - & 0.2077\dot{p}_t & - & 2.2624e_t \\ (7.5693) & & (-0.1238) & & (-1.7467) & & (-7.2269) \\ (0.0000) & & (0.9015) & & (0.0807) & & (0.0000) \end{array}$$

$$\begin{array}{cc} -0.8356\Delta NFA_t & + 0.0783\Delta NDC_{t-1} \\ (-29.7419) & (2.3694) \\ (0.0000) & (0.0178) \end{array} \tag{17}$$

$$SEE = 10.6506 \quad F = 255.7038 \quad DW = 2.0661 \quad R^2 = 0.9444$$
$$rho = -0.2994$$
$$(-2.9524)$$
$$(0.0032)$$

where

ΔNDC_t = $NDC_t - NDC_{t-1}$ = the quarterly changes in the CBC's net domestic credits in billions of NT$ at time t

ΔNDC_{t-1} = ΔNDC at time $t-1$

All of the coefficients in equation (17) have the right sign, and those for $\dot{p}$, e, and ΔNFA are significant at the 10%, 1%, and 1% levels respectively. The results indicate that the CBC utilized its sterilization policy extensively to cope with the problems stemming from changes in price level, exchange rates, and the balance of payments. The estimated coefficient of ΔNFA in equation (17) shows that the CBC changes its net domestic credits to sterilize about 84% of changes in its net foreign assets.

To see if the coefficients for internal or external goal variables are jointly significant, the above hypothesis test was taken. The calculated F-value for the hypothesis of equation (8) is 1.5636, which is lower than the critical value, but that for the hypothesis of equation (10) is 477.9644, which is well above the critical value. This indicates that the sterilization policy is aimed at external goals rather than the internal goals.

E. Reaction Function for Open-Market Operations

$\mathbf{A}$s was stated in Section I, since no data for open-market operations are available to the public, we use a proxy defined by equation (1), and estimate the reaction function for open-market operations to get:

$$OMO_t = \quad 136.4584 \quad - \quad 1.4775\dot{y}_t \quad - \quad 0.7689\dot{p}_t \quad - \quad 2.8281e_t$$

$$\quad\quad\quad (4.3475) \quad\quad (-2.5032) \quad\quad (-2.5446) \quad\quad (-3.4976)$$

$$\quad\quad\quad (0.0000) \quad\quad (0.01231) \quad\quad (0.0109) \quad\quad (0.0005)$$

$$\quad\quad -0.6934\Delta NFA_t \quad + 0.2634 OMO_{t-1}$$

$$\quad\quad (-14.4130) \quad\quad (4.8493)$$

$$\quad\quad (0.0000) \quad\quad (0.0000) \quad\quad\quad\quad\quad\quad\quad\quad (18)$$

$$SEE = 21.3677 \quad F = 65.1228 \quad DW = 1.7031 \quad R^2 = 0.7970$$

A priori, the signs for all of the coefficients for policy goal variables in equation (18) should be negative. The estimated results in the equation meet this requirement. Furthermore, the coefficients for $\dot{y}$, $\dot{p}$, e, and ΔNFA are all significant at a 1% level. The result seems to show that the CBC reacts to these policy goals with the open-market operations under its control.

A similar general hypothesis testing has been carried out for the open-market operations. The calculated F-value for testing the null hypothesis of equation (8) is 4.9053 and that for testing the null hypothesis of equation (10) is 104.6851. Both are higher than the critical value. Therefore, the test shows that the open-market operations are significant for both internal and external goals.

Conclusion

The CBC adopted policies toward interest rates, rediscount rates, required reserve ratios, sterilization, and open-market operations to achieve its major goals, such as economic growth, price stability, balance of payments equilibrium, and exchange rate stability.

This study used a reaction-function model to fit the data for Taiwan for the period 1961.III to 1988.IV. The results show that interest rate policy, rediscount rate policy, and required reserve ratio policy were mostly aimed at internal goals, such as economic growth and price stability; sterilization policy was applied to achieve external goals, namely, balance of payments equilibrium and exchange rate stability; while open-market operations were used toward both internal and external goals.

Bibliography

Aftalion, F. 1983. The Political Economy of French Monetary Policy. In *The Political Economy of Monetary Policy: National and International Aspects*, edited by D. R. Hodgman, 7-25. Boston: Federal Reserve Bank of Boston, Conference Series #26.

———. 1987. Factors Affecting French Monetary Policy. In *Monetary and Exchange Rate Policy*, edited by D. R. Hodgman and G. E. Wood, 49-68. London: Macmillan.

Basevi, G., M. Calzolari, and C. Colombo. 1983. Monetary Authorities' Reaction Functions and the European Monetary System. In *The Political Economy of Monetary Policy: National and International Aspects*, edited by D. R. Hodgman, 228-44. Boston: Federal Reserve Bank of Boston, Conference Series #26.

Chiu, Paul C. H. 1981. Performance of Financial Institutions in Taiwan. In *Conference on Experiences and Lessons of Economic Development in Taiwan*, 427-48. Taipei: Academia Sinica.

Christian, J. W. 1968. A Further Analysis of the Objective of American Monetary Policy. *Journal of Finance* (June): 456-77.

Computer Center, Ministry of Education; and Institute of Economics, National Taiwan University. 1988. *Manual for EPS Taiwan Financial Statistics Data Bank*. Taipei. In Chinese.

———. 1989. *Manual for EPS Taiwan National Income Statistics Data Bank*, 2nd ed. Taipei. In Chinese.

Demopoulos, G. D., G. M. Katsimbris, and S. M. Miller. 1987. Monetary Policy and Central-Bank Financing of Government Budget Deficits: A Cross-Country Comparison. *European Economic Review* 31: 1023-50.

Dewald, W. G., and H. G. Johnson. 1963. An Objective Analysis of the Objectives of American Monetary Policy, 1952-1961. In *Banking and Monetary Studies*, edited by D. Carson, 171-89. Illinois: Irwin.

Fisher, D. 1970. The Instruments of Monetary Policy and the Generalized Trade-off Function for Britain, 1955-1968. *The Manchester School* (September): 209-22.

Goodrich, R. L., and E. A. Stellwagen. 1986. *Forecast Master: Multivariate Time Series Forecasting*. Massachusetts: Scientific Systems.

Hsu, Y. S. 1989. Open-Market Operations (in Taiwan). A Lecture Note. Taipei: The Center for Training of Financial Institution Employees (May). In Chinese.

Irving, R. J., and R. F. Emery. 1966. Interest Rates as an Anti-Inflationary Instrument in Taiwan. *National Banking Review* (September): 1-11

Johnston, J. 1984. *Econometric Methods*, 3rd ed. New York: McGraw-Hill.

Khatkhate, D. R. 1977. Evolving Open Market Operations in a Developing Economy: The Taiwan Experience. In *Finance in Developing Countries*, edited by P. C. I. Ayre, 92-101. London: Frank Cass & Co.

Li, K. T. 1988. *The Evolution of Policy Behind Taiwan's Development Success*. New Haven: Yale University Press.

Liang, F. C. 1983. An Estimation of Macroeconomic Policy Reaction Functions, Policy Instruments Elasticities, and Trade-off Coefficients in Taiwan. *Taipei City Bank Review* (March): 1-22. In Chinese.

———. 1985A. Money Supply and Inflation in Taiwan. In *Taiwan Financial Development*, edited by C. S. Yu and K. C. Liu, 411-51. Taipei: Academia Sinica. In Chinese.

———. 1985B. Money Supply, Inflation and the Balance of Payments in Taiwan. In *Essays on Money and Finance*, edited by K. S. Liang and T. H. Lin, 383-408. Taipei: Institute of Economics, National Taiwan University. In Chinese.

Liu, F. C. 1970. *Essays on Monetary Development in Taiwan*. Taipei: Academia Sinica.

Lundberg, E. 1979. Fiscal and Monetary Policies. In *Economic Growth and Structural Change in Taiwan*, edited by Walter Galenson, 263-307. New York: Cornell University Press.

Mosley, P. 1984. *The Making of Economic Policy*. Sussex: Wheatsheaf Books.

Shea, J. D., J. T. Lee, and W. L. Mao. 1987. *Monetary and Fiscal Policies for Economic Development*, Conference Series #7. Chung-Hua Institution for Economic Research.

Skully, M. T., and G. J. Viksnins. 1987. *Financing East Asia's Success: Comparative Financial Development in Eight Asian Countries*. London: Macmillan.

Tsiang, S. C. 1981. Monetary Policy of Taiwan. In *Conference on Experiences and Lessons of Economic Development in Taiwan*, 249-69. Taipei: Academia Sinica.

Wallace, T. D., and J. L. Silver. 1988. Econometrics: An Introduction. New York: Addison-Wesley.

Wood, J. H. 1967. A Model of Federal Reserve Behavior. In *Monetary Process and Policy*, edited by G. Howich, 135-66. Illinois: Irwin.

10

Fiscal Policy and Economic Development in Taiwan: A Digression on the Effects of Taxation on Income Distribution

Chu-Wei Tseng
Wei-Lin Mao

Introduction

The task of evaluating the contributions of fiscal policies to economic development in Taiwan is somewhat exploratory. Because the channels through which the policies may affect the economy, and the impacts, whether transitory or permanent, on economic development are extremely difficult to assess, countercyclical fiscal policies may not be a preoccupation during a period of rapid transition. Thus, comparing steady states will not yield much in understanding the economic development process.

As the government dominates the economy, it would seem to be more important to investigate the way fiscal policies were played; whether they were steering the growth or were just usual reactions to the routine influences.

Some previous empirical studies using Taiwan data did show quite significant relationships between fiscal policies and growth. Tsui, Wang,

Pong, and Wang (1989) regressed the GDP growth rate on that of investment and labor productivities, in which the latter are connected with taxation and exports (see Appendix I). Chou and Sun (1986) employed a macroeconomic model and input-output analysis to explore the impact of public investments on private investment and economic growth. They found that in the short run public investment did have a significant crowding-out effect on private investment. There is no doubt that fiscal variables will contribute to economic growth, at least in the short run, under the neoclassical paradigm. But looking at a further horizon, under a mixed economic system where planning and market mechanisms play comparably key roles, will this conclusion still hold? Our essay aims to provide some evidence and justifications.

Our approach differs from previous empirical works on Taiwan's development in three respects: (1) we employ a new methodology; (2) we emphasize examining the planning characteristics of public enterprises and government; and (3) we explore the effects of fiscal policy on economic development in a framework of rational expectations.

In addition, Taiwan's "deviant" performance, experiencing rapid growth with equity, has been of interest to academics and policymakers. It is generally understood that taxation has been used as a means to improve income distribution. Thus, whether the government has significantly contributed to reducing inequality should be examined in a study of fiscal policy and economic development. We, therefore, will take some space to digress on the impact of taxation on income distribution.

Features and Implications of
Past Fiscal Policies

There have been three distinct features of Taiwan's fiscal policies during the past four decades. First, a persistent tight budget policy has been adopted, which usually yields a surplus. Second, the conservation of government expenditures made the fiscal instruments less likely to be the variables propelling the economy onto the highway of expansion. But they may have contributed to steering a middle course called rational planning. Third, Taiwan has one of the lowest outstanding public debt ratios relative to GDP among any of the developed or developing economies. All these traits point to the potential for huge government budget surpluses. And that has indeed been the case.

Now, the times have changed. In fiscal year 1989, the projected budget deficit will reach as high as NT$100 billion, the largest since 1950. It seems that the decisionmakers are confident that there will be little problem with fiscal illusions, and Ricardian neutrality is assumed. Although this dramatic change was inevitable, the conditions under which the fiscal variables will operate are still ambiguous. If the current fiscal measures were taken simply as a stabilizing tool, as before, this policy change may prove practical in promoting economic health. However, because of the recent drastic change toward more democracy in the political system, a more careful examination is now needed of the risk of raising a potential Leviathan. Proper management of fiscal policies will then become critical.

Public investments in Taiwan constitute an increment in the fixed capital formation of the public sector, which can be further decomposed into two categories: government investment and public enterprise investment. The role of public investment in contributing to growth has been controversial. In ex post analysis public investment does contribute to growth in Taiwan. The question is, did public investment actually crowd out the private sector's intention to invest, which usually is considered to be one of the major sources of economic growth? A well-designed public investment program is supposed to be planned over a long time frame and should not be affected by "noise." But, paradoxically, the government has treated its investments as a stabilization tool in order to offset the economic gap caused by insufficient private investment. In the 1950s and early 1960s, most of the capital needed in Taiwan was externally financed. After U.S. foreign aid terminated in 1975, public investment filled the slack; it has been the major source ever since. During the 1970s and 1980s, the share of public investment (including government and public enterprise) in total investment has persistently remained above 40 percent on the average. The emphasis on planning using the concept of permanent income implies that public investment should respond to the permanent level of GDP rather than to the transitory variations. Rather than pursue further theoretical argument, it might be more practical to perform some empirical study.

A popular method is to decompose GDP into permanent and cyclical components using Beveridge and Nelson's (1981) methodology. We have attempted the same approach and found very unsatisfactory results for Taiwan's data in decomposition of GDP.[1] We therefore adopt another method to resolve the problem.

---

1. The model that best fit using 1951-88 data was

$$GDP(t)\text{-}GDP(t\text{-}1) = 0.152 + (1+0.399L)\mu(t)$$
$$\quad\quad\quad\quad\quad (10.95) \quad\quad (2.51)$$

L = Lag operator

The Relationship Between Fiscal Expenditures and Economic Growth

$\mathbf{A}$n alternative method using a similar concept is to develop a "permanent income rational expections" hypothesis (hereafter, PIRE hypothesis) which asserts that government expenditures are determined by its view of permanent national income. Borooah (1988) has used OECD country data to examine whether their experiences provide evidence. The same approach has been employed here. We will briefly describe the model-setting first, which is mainly based on Flavin (1981), then empirically test the PIRE hypothesis, as it applies to Taiwan.

The model is drawn from Borooah (1988) as in the following: Based on rational expectation hypothesis, we may express permanent income (Y^*) as

$$Y^* = \left(\frac{r}{1+r}\right)_i \sum_{i=0}^{\infty} (E_t - E_{t-1}) \, Y_{t+i} \, (1+r)^{-i} \tag{1}$$

where

$Y =$ real GDP

$r =$ real interest rate

$E =$ expectation operator

And by the permanent income hypothesis (Alt and Crystal 1983), we have

$$G_t = kY^*_t + \mu_t \tag{2}$$

where

---

which has the property that its gain function has a coefficient much larger than one: (1 + 0.399). It implies that an innovation of 10 units raises its permanent level by 14 units, thus a positive shock will "keep" actual income below its new permanent level for two and a half years. It is a strange cycle and cannot be confirmed by facts. Hence, we use another method introduced by Flavin (1981) which synthesizes the work of Hall (1978).

G = real government expenditure

μ_t = error term

k = some constant

Combining (1) and (2) yield

$$G_t = [1 + r(1-k)] + \left[\frac{rk}{(1+r)}\right]_{i=0}^{\infty} \sum (E_t - E_{t-1}) Y_{t+1} (1+r)^{-i}$$

$$-(1+r)\mu_{t-1} + \mu_t \tag{3}$$

Suppose GDP is generated by an ARMA (p, q) process, we have

$$Y_t = \sum_{i=0}^{p} a_i Y_{t-i} + e_t + \sum_{i=1}^{q} b_i e_{t-1} = \sum_{i=0}^{\infty} \theta_i e_{t-1}, (\theta_0 = 1) \tag{4}$$

Given error e_t in forecasting Y_t

$$\sum_{s=0}^{\infty} (E_t - E_{t-1}) Y_{t+s} (1+r)^{-s} = \sum_{s=0}^{\infty} [(1+r)^{-s}\theta_s] e_t \tag{5}$$

By substituting (5) into (3), we have

$$G_t = [1 + r(1-k)] G_{t-1} + r\Phi e_t - (1+r)\mu_{t-1} + \mu_t \tag{6}$$

where

$$\Phi = [\sum_{s=0}^{\infty} (1+r)^{-(s+1)} \theta_s]$$

Then the unrestricted version of (6) will be

$$G_t = [1 + r(1-k)] G_{t-1} + r\Phi k e_t + \beta_0 Y_t + \dots$$

$$+ \beta_{p-1} Y_{t-(p-1)} + \mu_t \tag{7}$$

Since the objective of this study is to seek explanations of the fluctuations in government expenditures, the hypothesis is to see whether government expenditures were targeted at the expected growth of national income in Taiwan. In the context of PIRE, a two-step procedure is adopted:

First, we must determine the order of autoregressive process for GDP which is generated by

$$Y_t = a_0 + a_1 Y_{t-1} + \dots + a_p Y_{t-p} + e_t \tag{8}$$

Second, using residuals of the above as explanatory variables, we then run a regression of (7) as

$$G_t = \alpha + \delta_1 G_{t-1} + \delta_2 e_t + \delta_3 T + \beta_0 Y_t + \dots + \beta_{p-1} Y_{t-(p-1)} + \mu_t \tag{9}$$

in which β_i's measure the excess sensitivity of government expenditures with respect to GDP. If β_i's are nonzero, it implies that the government may use expenditure as a stabilization policy instrument. If PIRE sustains, such sensitivity should be zero in the sense that the government won't overrespond to the new information contained in the current GDP. δ_2 stands for the "surprise" factor affecting G, and T is a time trend to capture the demographic effects on G.

Empirical Results

Using annual data from 1951 to 1988 (see Appendix II), we intended to see how Taiwan's fiscal policies respond to the new information contained in the current GDP. Three different ways of treating the fiscal variables are attempted (government expenditures, government investment, and public enterprise investment). The order of autoregression for GDP, after appropriately correcting for autocorrelation, and the estimation results of the regression are presented in Table 1. From the outcome, AR(1) is selected as the GDP generating process.

All three fiscal variables mentioned above are shown to be policy tools for stabilization. Thus, the "unexpected" or "surprise" elements in the evolution of GDP did play a significant role in explaining changes in fiscal policy operations. The only difference is that government expenditure responded without delay, while government and public enterprise investments present some lags in implementation. This seems reasonable, since public investments are mostly predetermined in the planning process with only partial flexibility to cope with GDP "surprises." The results of the PIRE model for a mixed economy do implicitly suggest that a role

TABLE 1   Estimation Results for Regressions

1. Order determination of AR(P) for GDP

AR(1): GDP = 9536.9 - 0.89 GDP(-1)   AIC = 677
              (7.112)   (-12.19)
AR(2): GDP = 9536.9 - 0.93 GDP(-1) + 0.04 GDP(-2)   AIC = 794
              (7.112)   (-5.55)   (0.27)
AIC = Akaike Information Index

2. PIRE model results

Dependent variables	Explanatory variables					
	Intercept	Lag (dependent)	e	T	Y	$Y_{(-1)}$
EXPN	117.0	0.384	-0.043	17.04	0.094	-0.024
	(1.16)	(2.45)	(-1.606)	(1.75)	(3.609)	(-0.494)
GFIX	1515	3.892	0.072	-344.6	-0.184	0.517
	(4.78)	(5.14)	(0.944)	(-4.44)	(-2.83)	(4.44)
PUFIX	102.3	-11.88	0.072	278	0.004	0.133
	(1.27)	(-4.92)	(1.77)	(5.095)	(0.147)	(2.73)

EXPN = government expenditures
GFIX = government investment
PUFIX = public enterprise investment

Estimates from SAS AUTOREG procedures. Numbers in parentheses are *t*-values.

for economic planning existed in Taiwan. The fiscal policy variables are targeted to the "planned" GDP. They displayed an "excess sensitivity" to GDP changes, while ignoring to some degree the shock factors to themselves. In other words, fiscal policies in Taiwan reacted well to GDP "surprises," but not to other "surprises" such as tax rate changes. The fiscal policies are, therefore, not rational in the sense that the government responds properly all the time.

A Digression on Taiwan's Income Distribution

It is widely held that successful economic development should be identified not only with rapid growth but also with improved income distribution. If economic growth leads to greater inequality in income distribution and widens the increasing gap between the rich and the poor, not only is the general public prevented from sharing the fruits of economic development, but social unrest and urban crisis can ensue. A more equally distributed income has been, therefore, an ultimate objective of Taiwan's efforts, and compared to various countries' development experiences, Taiwan is identified as an exception that has been able to make considerable progress toward narrowing the income gap while undergoing rapid economic growth (Chenery, et al., 1974; Kuo, Ranis, and Fei, 1981).

Government policies are considered to have been essential in Taiwan's successful development. Among various measures, taxes are the most explicit instruments used to eliminate poverty and improve income distribution. However, not all taxes are progressive. The favorable impact of progressive taxes upon income distribution may well be offset, at least in part, by the adverse impact of regressive taxes. What we are interested in is the use of the taxation system by Taiwan's government vis-à-vis the goal of achieving equality.

For many reasons, however, assessing the progress against poverty is not straightforward (Reynolds and Smolensky 1977). In recent years, much has been written about the technical difficulties inherent in measuring the effects of all levels of government upon the size distribution of income. In addition to the versatile definitions of income redistribution, study of this question involves a number of alternative assumptions about the incidence of various taxes (Browning and Johnson 1979; Pechman and Okner 1974; Pechman 1985). Under the constraints of these inherent difficulties, several comparisons will be made in order to elucidate the redistributive effects of the taxation system in Taiwan, with the emphasis upon the special characteristics of land value tax.

A. Tax Burden Distributions of Two Different Incidence Assumptions

R ecently, Tsui, Wang, and Wang (1989) have attempted to estimate the tax burdens distributed among households in Taiwan for various taxes. By employing P-O (Pechman and Okner) and B-J (Browning and Johnson) approaches, respectively, with minor reasonable modifications of the latter, they concluded that the overall tax burden distributions in Taiwan have been shown as slightly U-shaped. The burden distributions trace a roughly similar pattern across the income classes for the period from 1976 to 1986.[2]

Tables 2 and 3 indicate that, in 1986, the effective tax rate for all taxes was 21.59 percent in the lowest income class and 22.12 percent in the highest income class under incidence assumptions I (Table 2, the B-J hypothesis). In contrast, the ratio was 26.69 percent in the lowest income class and 21.75 percent in the highest under incidence assumptions II (Table 3, the P-O hypothesis). Among the various taxes, the effective tax rate for income taxes (e.g., business income tax, personal income tax) was 2.96 percent in the lowest income class and 9.24 percent in the highest, or about three times the rate of the poorest bracket, under B-J assumptions. However, the difference in effective tax rates for income taxes between the richest and the poorest income groups was broadened under P-O assumptions. Sales taxes in both incidence assumptions were all shown to be pro-rich, with higher regressivity under incidence assumption II than assumption I. As for property taxes, in 1986, though the tax burden was lower on the average, the effective tax rate in the lowest income class was smaller than in the uppermost income class under incidence assumption I, and vice versa under incidence assumption II.

During the period 1976 to 1986, the effective tax rate of all taxes on average decreased from 23.22 percent to 19.19 percent under incidence assumption I and from 25.62 percent to 20.78 percent under incidence assumption II. The total tax burdens throughout the middle income classes were rather proportional to the income increases. However, under the P-O hypothesis, the effective tax rate in each year was largest in the lowest income percentile; and even under the more progressive B-J assumptions, there were five years of the period from 1976 to 1986 in which the largest tax burden was levied on the poorest income group. Since the pattern of tax distribution has not been changed during the period we have examined, the rather heavy tax burden on the lowest income class, relative to the richest income group, would be regarded as one of the essential problems that the current tax system faces. Furthermore, in the past ten years, the decreases in the effective rate of sales tax was the major factor in overall tax-burden reduction. In contrast to the slightly increasing effective income tax rate over the period, it implies that the share

---

2. Taxes in Taiwan are classified into three groups: (1) income taxes, including personal income tax, business income tax, and land value increment tax; (2) property taxes, including estate and gift tax, house tax, land value tax, agricultural land tax, deeds tax, security transaction tax, and mining lot tax; (3) sales taxes, including the commodity tax, value-added tax, stamp tax, customs duties, harbor construction dues, amusement tax, slaughter tax (abolished since 1987), license tax, monopoly revenues, feast tax (abolished since 1980), and salt tax (abolished since 1977). For the detailed tax incidence assumptions, see Tsui, Wang, and Wang (1989).

TABLE 2   Effective Tax Rates under Incidence Assumption I, 1976-86

Year	Income taxes			Sales taxes			Property taxes			Total taxes		
	Lowest income quintile	Highest income quintile	All families	Lowest income quintile	Highest income quintile	All families	Lowest income quintile	Highest income quintile	All families	Lowest income quintile	Highest income quintile	All families
1976	2.65	7.4	3.26	22.72	15.45	18.49	1.43	2.10	1.47	26.80	24.95	23.22
1977	2.97	8.87	3.43	20.15	15.68	18.64	1.30	2.20	1.24	24.41	26.74	23.31
1978	3.08	7.71	3.88	21.00	14.68	17.09	1.09	1.70	0.99	27.21	24.09	21.96
1979	2.03	8.72	3.85	20.94	15.07	18.05	0.79	1.81	0.99	23.76	25.60	22.89
1980	2.80	7.85	3.85	18.22	14.38	16.79	0.87	1.44	0.93	21.90	23.67	21.57
1981	3.15	7.69	4.15	22.37	13.13	15.67	0.99	1.40	0.94	26.51	22.21	20.76
1982	1.83	7.48	3.77	17.08	11.91	14.49	0.95	1.58	1.04	19.86	20.98	19.30
1983	2.73	8.02	3.80	16.79	11.51	14.07	0.91	1.55	0.96	20.42	21.08	18.83
1984	4.50	7.78	3.98	19.47	12.16	14.42	1.27	1.33	0.91	25.24	21.27	19.30
1985	2.85	7.72	3.93	17.17	11.44	13.74	1.02	1.16	0.92	21.04	20.31	18.59
1986	2.96	9.24	4.33	17.47	11.64	13.95	1.17	1.24	0.92	21.59	22.12	19.19

Source: Tsui, Wang, and Wang 1989.

TABLE 3 Effective Tax Rates under Incidence Assumption II, 1976-86

Year	Income taxes			Sales taxes			Property taxes			Total taxes		
	Lowest income quintile	Highest income quintile	All families	Lowest income quintile	Highest income quintile	All families	Lowest income quintile	Highest income quintile	All families	Lowest income quintile	Highest income quintile	All families
1976	2.56	6.77	3.85	26.60	15.56	18.97	2.68	3.17	2.44	31.84	25.50	25.62
1977	2.31	7.71	4.10	22.16	15.83	19.18	4.87	3.41	2.33	29.34	26.95	25.61
1978	3.44	7.34	4.52	23.00	14.50	17.95	2.81	2.84	2.12	28.11	24.68	24.58
1979	2.27	7.85	4.49	25.35	14.81	18.59	2.88	3.34	2.34	30.50	26.01	25.42
1980	2.72	7.30	4.40	22.64	13.98	17.39	2.70	2.68	1.99	28.06	23.96	23.78
1981	2.50	7.42	4.59	27.54	12.61	16.21	2.98	2.61	2.09	33.01	22.64	22.89
1982	1.87	7.22	4.10	20.83	11.30	15.03	2.53	2.78	2.17	25.22	21.29	21.29
1983	2.41	7.76	4.19	21.72	10.79	14.66	2.47	2.71	2.02	26.59	21.26	20.86
1984	2.61	7.50	4.26	24.25	11.57	15.02	2.82	2.38	1.86	29.67	21.45	21.14
1985	2.31	7.55	4.22	21.94	10.81	14.32	2.70	2.38	2.02	26.94	20.75	20.56
1986	2.63	8.65	4.68	22.27	11.15	14.60	1.79	1.95	1.50	26.69	21.75	20.78

Source: Tsui, Wang, and Wang 1989.

of income tax in total taxes has been regularly increased along with economic development.

B. The Special Design of Land Value Tax

Differing from most countries, whether developed or underdeveloped, Taiwan's land value tax (LVT) follows a uniform graduated (progressive) rate schedule, the tax rate rising with multiples of the "progressive starting value" (PSV).[3] The tax rates of the LVT have been set high and steep enough to serve as a possible potent revenue generator and, most important, an effective income redistributor (King 1988; Riew 1986; Tseng and Chen 1989). However, as indicated in tables 2 and 3, property taxes were not very progressive in terms of income redistribution for both incidence assumptions. Under the P-O hypothesis, the effective property tax rate in the lowest income class for some years were even higher than those of the uppermost income class. What is more, Table 4, by assuming the tax burden fully remained with the taxpayers, demonstrates that below the seventh income class, the effective land value tax rate was decreasing while above that level the ratios, which were all below 0.7 percent, appear in a zigzag pattern. In addition, with an average effective tax rate of about 0.9 percent, the LVT was in fact not an important revenue producer and hence cannot claim to serve as an effective instrument of redistribution.

This failure may be attributed to factors such as underestimation of assessed land value, wide value ranges (brackets) in tax schedules, or lenient tax preferences as Riew (1986) critically suggested. However, more important is the need to reevaluate the basic feature of the land value tax regarded as an income redistribution means, i.e., the appropriateness of a local tax intentionally used to reach a nationally demanded objective of income equality in a world of diverse property varieties.

C. The Impact of Taxation on Income Distribution

One convenient way to examine the impact of taxes on income distribution is to compare the Gini coefficients before taxes with those after taxes. If all taxes were allocated by the initial distribution of income, i.e., the taxes were proportional to income increases, Gini coefficients would be identical for the before- and after-tax distributions. According to tables 2 and 3, we know that although income taxes of Taiwan were

---

3. For details, see King (1988) and Riew (1986).

TABLE 4   Effective Rate of Land Value Tax by Income Groups, 1987

Taxable Income Classes (NT$)	Effective Tax Rate (%)
1-75,000	3.14
75,000-150,000	1.83
150,000-240,000	1.01
240,000-330,000	1.04
330,000-500,000	0.77
500,000-670,000	0.53
670,000-920,000	0.57
920,000-1,220,000	0.45
1,220,000-1,520,000	0.50
1,520,000-1,820,000	0.57
1,820,000-2,250,000	0.52
2,250,000-2,800,000	0.66
2,800,000-3,400,000	0.64
3,400,000-4,000,000	0.68
over 4,000,000	0.39
Average	0.89

Source: Data Processing Center, Ministry of Finance, Republic of China.

progressive across the income classes, the overall tax burdens were only slightly progressive (under B-J assumptions), or even regressive (under P-O assumptions), due to the highly pro-rich characteristics of sales taxes. Therefore, the taxes actually levied on families contributed to no significant reduction of income inequality in Taiwan.

On the other hand, by employing Kakwani's (1977) formula, the factors of changes in after-tax income distribution could be ingeniously decomposed into three categories: i.e., changes in tax progressivity, changes in average tax rate, and changes in before-tax income distribution. In Table 5, we find that the higher the tax progressivity and average tax rate and the more equal the before-tax income distributions are (as shown in the table by negative signs), the more equal the after-tax income would appear; and vice versa. Furthermore, in both incidence assumptions, the effects of individual factors on the after-tax income distribution were not uniform over the period we examined. However, we conclude that, relative to the tax progressivity and average tax rate, the status change in the before-tax income distribution was the most important element in explaining the improvement of after-tax income distributions. This implies that there have been other factors, which must have contributed more to the improvement of income distribution in Taiwan.

From Table 6, the pattern of overall distribution of personal income in

TABLE 5 Decomposition of Changes in After-Tax Income Distribution

Rates of Change	Percent Change by Year									
	1976-77	1977-78	1978-79	1979-80	1980-81	1981-82	1982-83	1983-84	1984-85	1985-86
	Incidence Assumption I									
Tax progressivity	0.29	-0.31	0.05	0.18	0.42	0.0	-1.18	0.47	0.05	-0.37
	(14.33)	(27.11)	(3.65)	(-6.26)	(46.68)	(0.68)	(-124.6)	(-183.45)	(3.16)	(-25.62)
Average tax rate	-0.01	0.21	-0.16	0.18	0.09	0.14	0.07	-0.06	0.07	-0.08
	(-0.67)	(-18.03)	(-10.55)	(-6.27)	(9.54)	(24.82)	(8.55)	(21.53)	(4.88)	(-5.48)
Before-tax distribution	1.73	-1.04	1.57	-3.29	0.39	0.43	1.93	-0.67	1.39	1.90
	(86.34)	(90.91)	(106.9)	(112.53)	(43.79)	(74.5)	(234.05)	(261.92)	(91.97)	(131.1)
After-tax distribution	2.0	-1.14	1.47	-2.93	0.9	0.57	0.83	-0.26	1.51	1.45
	(100)	(100)	(100)	(100)	(100)	(100)	(100)	(100)	(100)	(100)
	Incidence Assumption II									
Tax progressivity	-0.62	0.06	0.13	0.42	0.92	-0.15	-0.17	0.91	-0.04	-0.06
	(63.73)	(-10.11)	(9.25)	(-18.12)	(53.16)	(-39.01)	(-9.96)	(273.03)	(-2.55)	(-3.92)
Average tax rate	0.01	-0.02	0.02	-0.05	-0.05	-0.07	-0.01	0.01	-0.02	0.01
	(1.24)	(3.02)	(1.42)	(2.36)	(-3.12)	(-19.21)	(-0.36)	(3.09)	(-1.35)	(0.38)
Before-tax distribution	1.57	-0.59	1.21	-2.68	0.86	0.6	1.84	-0.59	1.43	1.7
	(162.49)	(107.09)	(89.33)	(115.76)	(49.96)	(158.22)	(110.32)	(-176.12)	(103.9)	(103.54)
After-tax distribution	0.97	-0.55	1.35	-2.32	1.73	0.38	1.67	0.33	1.38	1.64
	(100)	(100)	(100)	(100)	(100)	(100)	(100)	(100)	(100)	(100)

NOTE: The figure in parenthesis is the total share in the change of after-tax distribution.
Source: Tsui, Wang, and Wang 1989, 40.

TABLE 6   Distribution of Personal Income in Taiwan, Various Years

Year	Ratio of Highest Fifth to Lowest Fifth	Gini Coefficient
1964	5.33	0.321
1966	5.25	0.323
1968	5.28	0.326
1970	4.58	0.294
1974	4.37	0.287
1976	4.18	0.28
1977	4.21	0.284
1978	4.18	0.287
1979	4.34	0.285
1980	4.17	0.277
1981	4.21	0.281
1982	4.29	0.283
1983	4.36	0.287
1984	4.4	0.287
1985	4.5	0.29
1986	4.6	0.296
1987	4.69	0.299

Source: *Report on the Survey of Personal Income Distribution in Taiwan Area* (1988), Directorate-General of Budget, Accounting, and Statistics, Executive Yuan, Republic of China.

Taiwan shows a striking improvement prior to 1980. In 1964 the Gini co-efficient was about 0.321. By 1980 the Gini coefficient dropped to 0.277. This substantial improvement in overall income distribution during the 1960s and 1970s can be traced primarily to the rapid development of la-bor-intensive industries, which created job opportunities, particularly for unskilled labor, and the competitive market structure, in which most pri-vate enterprises were small- and medium-sized in scale with rather thin profits. The share of wages (compensation) in total income—which con-sists of compensation, entrepreneurial income, property income, and transfer income—increased over time prior to 1980 (Table 7). Due to the fact that wage income was usually more equally distributed than other incomes, particularly property income, this consequently conforms to the drastic reduction of inequality in overall income distribution over the whole period (Kuo, Ranis, and Fei 1981; Kuo 1983).

Since 1980 Taiwan has been experiencing dramatic political and eco-nomic changes. These have been totally different from before and can be characterized as facing the challenges of increasing protectionism and keen competition in world markets, of rapid and huge accumulation of

TABLE 7 Sources of Personal Income, Various Years

Year	Compensation of Employees	Entrepreneurial Income	Property Income	Transfer Income
1964	42.36	44.19	8.23	5.22
1966	46.93	38.84	8.57	5.66
1968	48.71	33.91	11.04	6.34
1970	53.7	29.36	10.13	6.81
1972	58.18	26.38	10.44	5.0
1974	60.31	25.16	10.49	4.04
1976	60.42	24.8	9.27	5.51
1977	58.87	24.01	12.0	5.12
1978	60.85	22.43	12.05	4.67
1979	60.11	23.92	11.4	4.57
1980	61.33	21.88	12.45	4.34
1981	62.13	21.26	12.0	4.61
1982	60.56	22.02	12.38	5.04
1983	60.34	22.15	12.02	5.49
1984	60.17	22.12	11.89	5.82
1985	59.95	22.2	12.0	5.85
1986	59.55	22.27	12.1	6.08
1987	59.44	22.59	11.89	6.08

Source: *Report on the Survey of Personal Income Distribution in Taiwan Area* (1988), Directorate-General of Budget, Accounting, and Statistics, Executive Yuan, Republic of China.

foreign reserves, of pervasive environmental and labor movements, and of a severe labor shortage. All these difficulties point to the possibility of malfunctioning of the equalization engine, which used to effectively reduce income inequality, and of causing an equality deterioration problem. The Gini coefficient increased from 0.277 to 0.299 over the period from 1980 to 1987, and the ratio of the highest 20 percent income group to the lowest 20 percent rose from 4.17 to 4.69. Relative to the share of compensation in total income—around 60 percent over this period—the share of property income registers at a slightly higher level than before. Therefore, it is evident that taxation was not a major cause of reduction in income inequality during this period. Consequently, unless a tax reform aimed at enhancing the redistributional function is conducted, other public policies, which would have influences upon income distribution before taxes, might be the effective instruments in improving final income distribution in contrast to government taxes.

Conclusion

One of the major concerns of this essay is the way that fiscal policies operate in a mixed economy such as Taiwan. It is evident that the fiscal variables, such as government expenditures, government investment, and public enterprise investment, are all sensitive to GDP changes in Taiwan. This assures us that fiscal policies were being used as stabilization instruments. Although the fiscal variables did react well to the GDP "surprises," the fiscal policies in Taiwan are still far from being rational, in the sense that they did not respond to all shocks in the economy.

In addition, taxes are usually used as the most important measure to eliminate poverty and improve income distribution. Because of its exceptional production of growth with equality, it is important to elaborate on the role that the government played in Taiwan in achieving this equality. The evidence we have shows that taxation was not a major cause of reduction in income inequality. This implies that to improve income distribution, policies other than taxation carry a larger share of the accountability.

Bibliography

Alt, James E., and Alec Crystal. 1983. *Political Economics.* Brighton, Sussex: Wheatsheaf Books.

Auerbach, Alan J., and Laurence J. Kotlikoff. 1987. *Dynamic Fiscal Policy.* New York: Cambridge University Press.

Barro, Robert. 1981. Output Effects of Government Purchases. *Journal of Political Economy* 89: 1086-1121.

———. 1984. The Behavior of U.S. Deficits. In *American Business Cycle,* edited by R. Gorden, 361-94. Chicago: University of Chicago Press.

Bernheim, Douglas. 1989. A Neoclassical Perspective on Budget Deficits. *Journal of Economic Perspective* 3: 55-72

Beveridge, S., and C. Nelson. 1981. A New Approach to Decomposition of Economic Time Series into Permanent and Transitory Components. *Journal of Monetary Economics* 7: 151-74.

Borooah, V. 1988. Permanent Income, Rational Expectations, and Government Consumption. In *Explaining the Growth of Government,* edited by J. Lybeck and M. Henrekson. North-Holland: Elsevier Science Publishers.

Boskin, Flemming Govini. 1987. *Private Saving and Public Debt.* New York: Basil Blackwell.

Browning, E. K., and W. R. Johnson. 1979. *The Distribution of the Tax Burden.* Washington, D.C.: American Enterprise Institute for Policy.

Chenery, H., U. S. Ahluwalia, C. L. G. Bell, J. H. Duloy, and R. Jolly. 1974. *Redistribution with Growth.* London: Oxford University Press.

Chou, J., and K. L. Sun. 1986. Government Spending, Public Investment, and Crowding-out Effects. Paper presented to the Chinese Economic Association, Annual Meeting. In Chinese.

Directorate-General of Budget, Accounting, and Statistics, Taiwan. 1988. *Report on the Survey of Personal Income Distribution in Taiwan Area.* Executive Yuan, Republic of China.

——. 1989. *Statistical Yearbook.* Executive Yuan, Republic of China.

Flavin, Matt. 1981. *Fundamental Concepts of Information Modeling.* New York: Yourdon Press.

Hall, R. 1978. Stochastic Implications of the Life Cycle–Permanent Income Hypothesis. *Journal of Political Economy* 86: 971-87.

Kakwani, N. C. 1977. Measurement of Tax Progressivity: An International Comparison. *The Economic Journal* 84: 254-67.

King, W. S. 1988. *Land Value Taxation in Taiwan: Present Status.* Mimeograph, National Chengchi University.

Kuo, Shirley W. Y. 1983. *The Taiwan Economy in Transition.* Boulder, Colorado: Westview Press.

Kuo, Shirley W. Y., Gustav Ranis, and John C. H. Fei. 1981. *The Taiwan Success Story: Rapid Growth with Improved Distribution in the Republic of China, 1952-1979.* Boulder, Colorado: Westview Press.

Kydland F., and E. Prescott. 1980. A Competitive Theory of Fluctuations and Feasibility and Desirability of Stabilization Policy. In *Rational Expection and Economic Policy,* edited by S. Fischer, 169-98. Chicago: University of Chicago Press.

Pechman, J. A. 1985. *Who Paid the Taxes, 1966-1985?* Washington, D.C.: The Brookings Institution.

Pechman, J. A., and B. A. Okner. 1974. *Who Bears the Tax Burden?* Washington, D.C.: The Brookings Institution.

Reynolds, Morgan, and Eugene Smolensky. 1977. *Public Expenditures, Taxes, and the Distribution of Income: United States, 1950, 1961, 1970.* New York: Academic Press.

Riew, John. 1986. *Property Question in Taiwan: Merits, Issues and Options.* Mimeograph. Pennsylvania State University.

Romer, David. 1988. What Are the Costs of Excessive Deficits? In *NBER Macroeconomics Annual,* edited by S. Fischer, 63-96. Boston: MIT Press.

Tobin, J., and W. Buiter. 1980. Fiscal and Monetary Policies, Capital Formation and Economic Activities. In *The Government and Capital Formation*, edited by George Von Furstenberg. Cambridge, Massachusetts: Ballinger Publishing.

Tseng, Chu-Wei, and J. M. Chen. 1989. *A Study on Land Value Tax in Taiwan*. Report of the Tax Reform Commission, Republic of China, vol. 45. In Chinese.

Tsui, Wai-Cho. 1985. The International Expenditure Comparison Index—The Case of Taiwan. *The National Chengchi University Journal* 52: 59-74. In Chinese.

Tsui, Wai-Cho, C. Wang, and W. H. Wang. 1989. *A Study on Tax Burden Distribution Among Households*. Report of the Tax Reform Commission, Republic of China, vol. 4. In Chinese.

Tsui, Wai-Cho, C. Wang, H. S. Pong, and W. H. Wang. 1989. Evaluation of the Current Taxation System in Taiwan. *Report of the Tax Reform Commission*, vol. 8. Taipei: Republic of China. In Chinese.

Von Furstenberg, George. 1980. Public vs. Private Spending: The Longterm Consequence of Direct Crowding Out. In his, ed., *The Government and Capital Formation*. Cambridge, Massachusetts: Ballinger Publishing.

Appendix I

Tsui's (1989) Results for Comparison

Dependent Variables	Intercept	T	DT	IT	t	S	G	EX	R^2
I	0.287	-4.23				0.705	1.27	0.608	0.33
	(0.737)	(-1.24)				(0.928)	(2.195)	(2.26)	
I	-0.18		-10.4	1.967			0.744	0.30	0.41
	(-0.39)		(-2.14)	(0.407)			(1.168)	(2.2)	
L	0.028	-0.135		0.0009				0.25	
	(0.83)	(-0.55)			(1.69)			(2.22)	
L	0.009		-1.36	0.305	0.002			0.029	0.40
	(0.3)		(-2.4)	(1.05)	(2.97)			(1.57)	
G	0.092		0.267I			0.72L			0.75
	(6.0)		(7.75)			(1.5)			

G, I, L, and EX are growth rates for GDP, investment, labor, and exports. T, DT, and IT are ratios of total, direct, and indirect tax to GDP; t and s are the time trend and savings rate respectively. Figures in parentheses are t-values.

Source: Tsui, Wang, Pong, and Wang (1989, 556).

Appendix II

Data for PIRE Model

Year	GDP	EXPN	GFIX	PUFIX
1951	1,308.70	353.31	219.46	185.80
1952	1,465.68	405.95	263.59	227.82
1953	1,601.88	410.95	341.55	205.87
1594	1,755.15	485.52	198.72	203.01
1955	1,897.53	516.70	236.83	176.35
1956	2,001.75	591.87	241.60	132.25
1957	2,149.44	633.79	206.82	142.67
1958	2,296.53	680.62	273.74	138.21
1959	2,472.95	733.82	293.41	161.03
1960	2,625.24	747.69	320.70	178.66
1961	2,806.21	780.78	334.82	191.64
1962	3,028.22	850.50	357.63	212.64
1963	3,311.27	892.52	411.26	234.02
1964	3,713.26	953.68	333.21	261.89
1965	4,130.07	989.73	320.06	266.15
1966	4,495.97	1,073.77	465.84	301.86
1967	4,980.09	1,182.09	658.64	340.92
1968	5,436.93	1,287.23	836.77	386.63
1969	5,921.93	1,425.03	948.65	444.14
1970	6,595.09	1,544.18	1,052.73	565.91
1971	7,444.27	1,620.07	1,397.24	586.33
1972	8,433.50	1,703.81	1,608.42	611.03
1973	9,515.53	1,810.56	1,271.63	812.80
1974	9,626.50	1,647.14	1,199.56	473.01
1975	10,105.42	1,863.51	1,908.97	727.51
1976	11,505.61	2,068.20	1,755.28	884.46
1977	12,673.83	2,295.03	1,378.06	1,050.89
1978	14,396.08	2,437.89	1,551.46	854.57
1979	15,572.84	2,640.50	1,546.95	747.19
1980	16,708.42	2,845.29	1,689.44	741.64
1981	17,739.31	3,105.58	1,614.70	754.86
1982	18,246.93	3,271.47	1,664.91	858.76
1983	19,666.07	3,395.41	1,497.14	797.19
1984	21,558.50	3,580.01	1,262.58	828.43
1985	22,499.29	3,786.03	1,136.54	877.54
1986	24,913.80	3,942.33	1,213.23	1,002.67
1987	27,988.29	4,216.14	1,333.92	1,102.90
1988	29,816.66	4,603.10	1,380.78	1,308.88

GDP = real Gross Domestic Product (in million NT$); *EXPN* = government expenditure consumption (deflated); *GFIX* = fixed capital formations by government (deflated); *PUFIX* = fixed capital formations by public enterprises (deflated).

Source: *Statistical Yearbook* (1989). Directorate-General of Budget, Accounting, and Statistics, Executive Yuan, Republic of China.

11

Income Levels and Occupations of
Public vs. Private University
Graduates and the Efficiency of
Government Investment
in Higher Education

Chia-Lin Cheng
Yu-Hsia Chen

Introduction

The importance of the accumulation of human capital to economic growth, especially its significance in the growth of developing nations, has been widely recognized in the literature (Strumilin 1929; Walsh 1935; Meir 1984; Psacharopoulos 1988; Otani and Villanueva 1989). If history is to be an example, we can see that India's large-scale investment in its steel and iron industries did not result in rapid economic growth for the country. Japan, on the other hand, ever since the Meiji Restoration period has placed a great emphasis on building its educational system, and may have thus laid down a strong foundation from which the country has created a series of economic miracles. Schultz (1961) has stressed that the growth of a nation's GNP cannot be wholly explained by its increase in physical capital, labor, and land; he included human capital as one of the factors making up the aggregate production function. Similarly, scholars have regarded human capital as an important contributing factor in Taiwan's rapid economic growth in the past thirty years (Kai 1989; Li 1989; Hou and Chang 1981).

Undeniably, the so-called creation of human capital in Taiwan is in large part the result of its universal and constantly expanding system of formal education.[1] In the past thirty to forty years, the planning and development of formal education in Taiwan has been primarily directed by the government. The government, through the Ministry of Education, controls nearly every aspect and stage in the development of the educational system. This control extends to regulating the total number of schools, as well as their types and levels; the number of students permitted to enroll in any particular school; the maximum number of students per classroom and per grade level; credential requirements and methods of teacher evaluation for all instructors; and levels of tuition. This extends even to regulating school curricula—content and number of required courses, the minimum and maximum credit requirements for every major—regulatory measures that apply to both public *and* private institutions. However, this government policy-dictated formal educational system has not been able to provide enough educational opportunities to satisfy the extraordinarily strong demand, especially for higher education in Taiwan, where acceptance rates for universities have averaged around 30% every year. According to Table 1, each year on average some 43% of students taking the entrance examinations are *retaking* them. In 1986, most notably, nearly 50% of the students who were taking the college entrance exams were taking them for the second or third time, or more. There is no clearer evidence than this for the excess demand in Taiwan for higher education, and it is a demand that has persisted for many years.

On the other hand, the students generated by this higher-education system have faced employment difficulties upon graduation, or have been made aware of the "nonapplicability" of their fields of study to available jobs. Tables 2 and 3 show that college-educated unemployed persons made up 16.04% of the total unemployed population in 1978, which then increased to 20.86% in 1988, and this figure has shown a tendency to continue increasing with each passing year. Among the college educated who were employed during the period 1984 to 1988, around

---

1. Beyond formal education, both on-the-job training and research and development are also means by which human resources may be accumulated and improved. In Taiwan, however, the importance of these other factors have only been recognized in recent years, and data for them are lacking and incomplete. Therefore, they will not be discussed in this study.

TABLE 1   Ratio of Current-Year High School Graduates to Noncurrent
Graduates Taking College Entrance Examinations, 1972-86

		Took test			Admitted	
Year	Total	Current year (%)	Noncurrent year (%)	Total	Current year (%)	Noncurrent year (%)
1972	83,971	n.a.	n.a.	22,633	n.a.	n.a.
1973	98,073	58.75	41.25	24,235	n.a.	n.a.
1974	93,204	n.a.	n.a.	25,010	66.42	33.58
1975	97,859	n.a.	n.a.	25,742	n.a.	n.a.
1976	94,807	53.81	46.19	26,166	57.27	42.73
1977	91,907	65.91	34.09	26,603	68.38	31.62
1978	94,850	66.62	33.38	26,799	67.92	32.08
1979	94,696	(94.03)	(5.97)	27,687	(93.09)	(6.91)
1980	97,183	50.00	50.00	28,416	54.36	45.64
1981	97,964	54.27	45.73	29,243	58.41	41.59
1982	95,906	n.a.	n.a.	29,945	n.a.	n.a.
1983	96,421	n.a.	n.a.	30,803	n.a.	n.a.
1984	98,236	n.a.	n.a.	31,503	n.a.	n.a.
1985	102,004	53.61	46.29	32,473	55.05	44.95
1986	110,384	50.92	49.08	33,848	55.07	44.93

Note: Obviously there is an error in the data for 1979, but the reason for this is unclear. In
the reported data from 1972 to 1975 and from 1982 to 1984 there is no data for the
ratio of current-year high school graduates to all test takers.

Source: Wu, Ts'ung-min, 1988, 2, Table 1.

25% were employed in fields unrelated to their previous fields of study.
The most obvious indicator of the "nonapplicability" problem is the high
number of college graduates who participate each year in the postal service civil examinations, competing for jobs that require only a high school
diploma. This underutilization of valuable human resources is a great
waste for both the individuals in question as well as for the nation. It is
apparent that the government's present policies for higher education and
education investment leave much to be desired, and it is imperative that
criticism and suggestions for improvement be made to address this long-
existing imbalance in Taiwan's educational system.

Among the most striking features of the government's education in-

TABLE 2   Percent of College Educated among the Unemployed

Year	1978	1979	1980	1981	1982	1983	1984	1985	1986	1987	1988
%	16.04	16.87	19.51	18.48	16.11	17.26	19.13	18.47	18.40	19.25	20.86

Source: Kai 1989, 16, Table 4.

TABLE 3   College-and-Above Educated Workers Employed in Jobs Not
Related to Their Fields of Study

Year	1984	1985	1986	1987	1988
%	25.0	25.8	24.1	24.7	26.0

Source: Kai 1989, 18, Table 5.

vestment policy is the large differential in funds distributed to public institutions versus private institutions. In 1989, for example, the total government budget for universities and colleges was NT$42.2 billion, whereas subsidies for private universities and colleges amounted to only 2.1 billion, not even 5% of the total annual budget. If we include only universities in our calculation, then the total budget for public institutions in 1989 was NT$18 billion, whereas total subsidies for private universities amounted to NT$1 billion, or, slightly higher than 5% of the total budget. There are about 70,000 students enrolled at public universities and 103,000 students at private universities. Therefore if we calculate government investment per student, the gap in funding for public vs. private institutions seems even more incommensurate.

Furthermore, the government has set strict standards for tuition rates at both public and private institutions. Table 4 shows that in 1989 the tuition set by the Ministry of Education for science colleges was NT$9,080 per semester at public universities, and NT$26,290 at private universities [NT$26,290 = US$1,052 at mid-1992 exchange rates, up from US$657 in 1985—ED.]. Regulated tuition rates for arts, law, and business colleges were even lower. Therefore, private institutions are unable to rely on higher tuition rates to offset the enormous difference in subsidies received from the government. According to an estimate by the Ministry of Education, the annual total educational investment (both government and private) for each public university student amounted to NT$31,000 in 1975, and 134,000 in 1981; in the same period, per capita private university education investment was estimated to be 10,000 and 49,000 respectively (Ministry of Education 1975). In other words, the per capita educational investment in 1975 for a public university student was 3.1

TABLE 4   1989 Tuition Ceilings for Public and Private Institutions (NT$)

College type	Private	Public
Sciences, engineering	26,290	9,080
Arts, law	22,260	6,980
Business	22,280	7,390

NOTE: Per semester, set by the Ministry of Education.

times that of a private university student; in 1981, 2.73 times. The absolute difference in 1975 was NT$21,000, and in 1981 it was as high as 85,000. Whether such a disparity in per capita educational investment is reflected in the income level and occupation distribution of college graduates entering the work force is undoubtedly an important question worth investigating. In addition, further explorations of this issue may enable us to make a more solid assessment of the comparative efficiency of government educational investment in public vs. private institutions.

Though the investigation into the efficiency of government educational investment in public and private universities is a project that promises to have potentially significant implications for policy, it is an issue that has rarely been explored by scholars in Taiwan. Wu Hui-lin (1988) utilized the factor "Whether individual is a public university graduate" in a study determining returns on human labor of college-educated workers, while using a dummy variable method to do a regression analysis, finding that public university graduates earn higher incomes than private university graduates. We believe, however, that Wu's study is flawed. It does not take into consideration the fact that there is a difference in the students admitted to public and private universities. An examination of the distribution of the minimum test score standards for admission at various institutions clearly indicates that, almost without exception, the highest scorers choose to enroll in public universities. If we are to accurately compare the education at public and private universities and its effects on the income levels of their graduates, we must control for this basic difference, so as to prevent a selectivity bias in our study.

The occupation and income level data on which Wu Hui-lin's 1988 study was based was for recent graduates, eight months or a year and eight months after graduation. We contend that most college graduates are not able to find jobs that are best suited for them immediately following graduation. There is a considerable period of adjustment before most graduates settle into permanent jobs or careers. Therefore, the income level of a recent graduate may not be the most accurate reflection of his or her labor-market productivity. In our opinion the most meaningful measure would be of income levels both shortly after graduation and also after the graduate has spent some time in the labor market.

Most of the literature on this subject abroad has compared public vs. private schools, or students from schools of different "quality."[2] Studies of the former utilize standardized tests scores, such as asking whether there are significant differences in students' math scores (Coleman et al.

---

2. The "quality" of a school refers to the average faculty salaries, the ratio of faculty members to students, the average length of a semester, etc.

1966; Coleman, Hoffer, and Kilgore 1981; Noell 1981, 1982; Hanushek 1986; Jimenez, Lockheed, and Wattanawaha 1988); comparisons of schools presumed to be of different quality usually look for significant differences in graduates' income levels (Morgan and Sirgeldin 1968; Johnson and Stafford 1973; Wachtel 1976; Card and Krueger 1990). Both methods have limits. Standardized test scores do not necessarily correlate with labor-market productivity after graduation. Nor is the use of graduates' income levels to assess schools reliable, because factors affecting income include not only school quality but also family background, local job market demand, personal ability, etc. Some studies, such as Card and Krueger (1990), have included family background and varying local job market demand as factors in determining income, but still attempt no measure of personal ability or potential, either at graduation or on entrance into their respective schools.

In truth, income is only one measure of career success. Sociology recognizes also a definite social ranking of various occupations; the concept of "occupational prestige" functions as an index for the social status of a given job. The degree of occupational prestige of one's job thus can also be an indicator for the degree to which one is "respected by others" (Kao Shu-kui 1986). For example, while the average income of college professors may be lower than that of upper-level employees in business and industry, the "occupational prestige" of college professors is usually higher. Therefore, besides simply comparing the income levels of public and private university graduates, we believe that a further investigation of the degree of occupational prestige of graduates' jobs would yield a more accurate comparison of differences in employment opportunities and the efficiency of educational investment in public vs. private university graduates. As far as we know, no one has yet attempted to explore this facet of the subject.

For this study we have constructed a micromodel, then collected the data to test the model through a random sample survey of public and private university graduates from the class of 1979. We attempt to compare public vs. private university graduates' first occupations immediately after graduation with those held ten years later, evaluating them in terms of income and occupational prestige. The empirical results then enable us to analyze the relative performance of public and private universities in view of the large cost differentials, and to evaluate the efficiency of previous government educational policy. We hope to use these results to assist in future policy formulation so that the most efficient utilization of limited resources may be achieved. In Part I of this chapter we establish the empirical model; in Part II we discuss the survey process, sample, and data; in Part III we present the results of our empirical study and proceed to analyze the data. Findings are summarized in the conclusion.

I. Research Methods

This study uses a survey to investigate the income level and occupation distribution of one group of public and private university graduates. Since the factors influencing income and occupation level consist not only of the schools themselves, but also of individual ability, family background, and various other factors, we will therefore first attempt to determine, from the viewpoint of economic theory, the factors affecting income levels and occupation. Then we will use a statistical multiregression method to determine the significant effects of these various factors, so that we may use our results comparatively to discuss their policy implications. The explanations for the models are as follows:

A. Income model

In this study we will use the micro econometric model

$$Y = a_1 + a_2 D + Z\beta + \varepsilon \ldots \ldots \ldots \ldots \ldots \ldots \ldots \tag{1}$$

Y represents monthly income, D represents the dummy variable (private university graduate = 1, public university graduate = 0), and ε represents the error term. Z represents vectors of other factors of variables that may affect income. These include family factors—number of years of education received by parents, the number of siblings[3]; personal factors—including respondent's intelligence as estimated by the minimum admission test score of respondent's college major[4]; the respondent's hu-

---

3. We were originally going to include the income levels of the respondents' parents, but among the 191 respondents only 78 supplied data on their fathers' earnings in the past (when respondents were in college), and only 42 had information on their fathers' present earnings; data on respondents' mothers' earnings were even more scarce. Since the addition of parental income would decrease the sample size by 60 percent we decided not to include it in equation (1).

4. In Taiwan, the entrance examination scores of public university students are usually higher than those of private university students, and thus there is a basic difference in student quality. We had considered using respondents' IQs, entrance examination test scores, or entrance ranking averages as the variable representing respondents' intelligence and ability; however, since most had already forgotten this data, we elected to use the minimum admission test score required of respondents' majors at the time of test-taking, and whether the respondents had taken the entrance exams more than once, as the indicators.

man capital factors as represented by years of education attained, seniority in the workplace, and length of workweek. The dummy variables are listed below:

$D1$ = 1 repeat test taker of entrance examinations

   0 onetime test taker

$D2$ = 1 male

   0 female

$D3$ = 1 ancestry belonging to other Chinese provinces

   0 Taiwanese ancestry

$D4$ = 1 employed in Taipei area

   0 employed elsewhere

$D5$ = 1 employed in Taichung area

   0 employed elsewhere

$D6$ = 1 private sector job

   0 public sector job

$D7$ = 1 obtained job through examination

   0 obtained job through other means

$D8$ = 1 obtained job through personal connections

   0 obtained job through other means

$D9$ = 1 received on-the-job training

   0 did not receive on-the-job training

$D10$ = 1 graduate of a college of arts

   0 graduate of other college

$D11$ = 1 graduate of a science college

   0 graduate of other college

$D12$ = 1 graduate of a college of law

   0 graduate of other college

Theoretically, the higher the minimum required test score for admission into the respondent's particular major, the higher the intelligence or ability of the respondent; thus we have predicted a positive effect. However, those students who have taken the entrance examinations more than once may not have as high an intelligence or ability, and therefore the expected sign is negative. Normally speaking, the greater the accumulation of human resources, the greater the productivity, and thus the higher the income level; therefore the coefficients representing number of years of education received and seniority should be positive values, and the relation of length of workweek to income level should be positive as well. Among the factors concerning the respondent's family, a greater number of siblings means that each child receives a proportionally smaller share of parental resources (including both time and money), and therefore would imply a slighter degree of personal development prior to formal education, and would therefore have a negative effect on level of income after graduation; thus we have assigned this coefficient a negative sign.

According to the results of Wu Hui-lin's (1988) study, college-and-above educated males earn more than college-and-above educated females, and this difference is statistically significant. Also, graduates of colleges of science on the average earn more than graduates of colleges of business; and graduates of colleges of arts and of law on the average earn less than graduates of colleges of business. Thus we predict that $D2$ and $D11$ will have positive signs, while $D10$ and $D12$ will have negative signs.[5]

As for the dummy variables $D6$, representing private sector employment, $D4$ and $D5$, representing job location, and $D7$ and $D8$, representing means by which employment was obtained—the signs for these variables, as well as for the coefficient representing the level of education obtained by the respondent's parents, are impossible to determine theoretically. Finally, the sign of the coefficient a_2 of the dummy variable (D), which represents having graduated from a private university, is also impossible to determine beforehand. If a_2 turns out to be a positive value and significant, then it would imply that, after controlling for other factors affecting income, private universities make a significantly greater contribution to income level than public universities; if a_2 has a negative value and is significant, then it would show that public universities make a greater significant contribution to income than private ones. Regarding efficiency, when a_2 has a positive value and is significant or when a_2 is in-

---

5. The reason the sample does not include graduates from engineering, medicine, and agriculture is that as recently as ten to fifteen years ago very few of the private universities had these colleges, and a comparison between public and private university graduates of similar majors would be difficult. Also, in this study we at first planned to perform separate regression analyses on the four colleges of arts, sciences, law, and business, but since the samples from each of these were too small, the degree of freedom would be low and the regression analysis would not yield very meaningful results. Therefore, we have combined the data from graduates of all four colleges, and have used three dummy variables to eliminate the gap between the colleges caused by different levels of market demand for different majors.

significant, we can say roughly that there is a higher level of efficiency at private universities, since we know from the discussion in the introduction that private institutions have far smaller budgets than public institutions. It may even be true that a_2 can be negative (and significant) and still represent greater efficiency than at public universities because, on average, the total per capita educational investment at public universities is more than twice that of private universities.

B. The Occupational Prestige Distribution Model

Besides comparing levels of income we will also compare the relative levels of "occupational prestige" of graduates' first jobs and jobs held ten years after graduation. We will then determine whether a significant difference does exist for graduates of public universities as opposed to private universities, which we will use to evaluate the efficiency of educational investment in public vs. private institutions.

We must first quantify occupational prestige. In their 1989 study, Ts'ai Shu-ling and Ch'ü Hai-yuan obtained data for subjective ratings of occupational prestige, for the average number of years of education attained, and for average monthly income (in thousands of NT dollars) to perform a regression analysis. They came up with the following estimation equation:

$$\text{Subjective occupational prestige rating} = 20.59 + 2.62 \cdot (\text{average number of years of education}) + 0.418 \cdot (\text{average income, in thousands of NT dollars}) \quad (2)$$

The coefficient for the average number of years of education (2.62) and the coefficient for income level (0.418) are both statistically significant, and the degree to which the combination of the two explanatory variables can account for subjective occupational prestige variance is as high as 70% ($R^2 = 0.7$). Therefore in this study we will use their regression estimation equation to determine the average occupational prestige ratings for, respectively, respondents' first jobs after graduation and jobs held ten years after graduation, as well as to estimate the standard deviation. We will then look to see whether there is a significant difference in average occupational prestige ratings of jobs held immediately after graduation, and jobs held ten years after graduation by public university and private university graduates. A more detailed enumeration of our method of comparison is as follows:

If we take

Zp = occupational prestige mean rating for public university graduates

Sp = standard deviation of occupational prestige for public university graduates

Zr = occupational prestige mean rating for private university graduates

Sr = standard deviation of occupational prestige for private university graduates

Np = sample size of public university graduates

Nr = sample size of private university graduates

According to the central limit theorem, the distributions of Zp and Zr approach normal distribution and their standard deviations are respectively

$$\sqrt{\frac{Sp^2}{Np}}$$

and

$$\sqrt{\frac{Sr^2}{Nr}}$$

If the two distributions of Zp and Zr are mutually independent, then

$$Z = (Zp - Zr) \Big/ \sqrt{\frac{Sp^2}{Np} + \frac{Sr^2}{Nr}} \tag{3}$$

approaches standard normal distribution. Therefore, under the set significance level of α, we need only compare the Z value with the critical value $Z\alpha$, and we would be able to determine whether there is a significant difference between Zp and Zr.

If the occupational prestige mean rating of private university graduates is significantly greater than that of public university graduates, then it demonstrates that the positive effect of private universities on graduates' occupational prestige is greater than that of public universities, showing that instruction at private universities is more efficient. If there is no significant difference between occupational prestige averages of public vs. private university graduates, it may still imply that private university instruction is more efficient than public university instruction. The reasoning behind this last conclusion is the fact that the percentage of public university graduates who go on to attend graduate school is higher (public 22%, private 13%), and therefore the average number of years of education obtained by these graduates is greater. Since the number of years of education attained functions as an explanatory variable determining occupational prestige, therefore it is possible that the occupational prestige of public university graduates will prove to be higher than that of graduates of private universities.[6] Consequently, with the premise of such large differentials between the per capita education investment at public universities and at private universities, we may conclude that private university instruction is very possibly more efficient than instruction at public universities. Even in the case of the occupational prestige average of public university graduates being significantly higher than that of private university graduates, due to the extremely large differential in per capita education investment, we would still not be able to positively conclude that public university instruction is more efficient than private university instruction before conducting further analyses and comparisons.

II. Sample and Data

In the survey conducted for this study we used as our population those who graduated from universities in June 1979. First, we took random samples of departments from each of the colleges of arts, science, law, and business, resulting in the following four departmental majors: Chinese language and literature, chemistry, political science, and business management. We then surveyed the public and private university students who graduated in June 1979 from these four departments. The public universities that were included in the survey were National Taiwan

---

6. In equation (2), the first explanatory variable, "average number of years of education of a particular job," represents the average number of years required for various occupations; however, we do not have data on this particular factor, so we have used the actual number of years of education attained by the respondent to substitute for the average number of years of education required for the respondent's occupation.

University (243 students), National Chengchi University (254 students), National Tsing Hua University (47 students), National Taiwan Normal University (183 students), National Chungyang University (40 students), National Cheng Kung University (146 students), and National Chung Hsing University (156 students). A total of 1,069 students were surveyed from the seven public institutions. Included among the survey of private universities were Tunghai University (157 students), Fu Jen University (312 students), Soochow University (359 students), Chungyuan University (100 Students), Tanchiang University (331 students), Feng Chia University (176 students), and Wenhua University (187 students), totaling 1,622 students from seven private institutions.[7]

Among the 2,691 surveys handed out to students, 306 were completed and collected, constituting a return rate of 12 percent. Of those who responded, 106 were living abroad at the time of the survey; therefore, the number of respondents on whom we had enough detailed data to do a regression analysis was at the most 200. Characteristics of the variables presented in Part I's empirical model are listed in tables 5 and 6 .[8]

III. Empirical Results of the Study

A. Income Model

In order to compare first job and job held ten years after graduation, we performed separate regression analyses of equation (1), reporting the results in tables 7 and 8.

Although the coefficient of determination (R^2) in Table 7 is 0.33, its adjusted R2 ($\overline{R}^2$) is only 0.10, showing that all the explanatory variables can account for only 10% of the variance in first-job income level. Fur-

---

7. The universities which in 1975 did not offer a Chinese language and literature major included Tsing Hua University, Chungyuan University, and Feng Chia University. Only National Taiwan University, National Chengchi University, and Soochow University offered a political science major. Tsing Hua University did not have a business management major, and only National Chengchi University did not offer a chemistry major.

8. Among the 200 surveys returned, not all respondents answered every question. Two of those surveyed were housewives; since it is difficult to estimate income earned on domestic work and caretaking, we discounted these two respondents from our sample. Therefore, the sample size on which we could perform a regression analysis was fewer than 200 students.

TABLE 5   First Job Following Graduation — Variables from Equation (1)

Variable	Sample size	Mean	Standard deviation
Monthly income (NT$ thousands)	109	16.43	10.83
Type of university (private=1, public=0)	191	0.66	0.48
Minimum exam score for admission	190	411.75	35.28
Repeat test taker (yes=1, no=0)	153	0.42	0.49
Sex (male=1, female=0)	190	0.66	0.47
Ancestry (other privinces=1, Taiwanese=0)	189	0.35	0.48
Occupation sector (private=1, public=0)	123	0.68	0.49
Job location (Taipei area=1, elsewhere=0)	106	0.70	0.46
Job location (Taichung area=1, elsewhere=0)	106	0.13	0.34
How obtained job (exam=1, other=0)	104	0.36	0.48
How obtained job (connections=1, other=0)	104	0.21	0.41
Length of workweek (hours)	111	34.06	18.09
Number of years of education	191	16.53	1.34
College of arts graduate (yes=1, no=0)	191	0.35	0.48
College of science graduate (yes=1, no=0)	191	0.22	0.42
College of law graduate (yes=1, no=0)	191	0.05	0.22
Number of siblings	189	3.48	1.67
Years of education of father	183	9.84	4.39
Years of education of mother	185	6.98	4.09

Note: Sample size = number of respondents for whom relevant data is available. The dummy variables for colleges of arts, sciences, and law use the yes responses to "College of business graduate" on the questionnaire as the standard group. The dummy variables for How obtained job, examination or connections, use as the standard job the response "attained job on one's own."

thermore, its statistic is not significant at the 10% level, showing that the explanatory power of all variables is not strong, and we cannot reject the null hypothesis that all coefficients of the explanatory variables are equal to zero. This is likely for the reason suggested in the introduction, that income levels of first jobs are not the best indicators of labor capability, and that starting salaries have little to do with the various explanatory variables, and thus the combined power of all variables is limited.

In terms of the explanatory power of the individual variables listed in Table 7, with the exceptions of the estimated coefficients "minimum required exam score for admission," "whether respondent is a repeat test-taker," "length of workweek," and "whether respondent is a college of science graduate" that had signs opposite from those previously predicted, signs of all other estimated coefficients are as expected. However, even at the 10% significance level, the above four coefficients are still not

TABLE 6 Occupation Ten Years after Graduation — Variables from Equation (1)

Variable	Sample size	Mean	Standard deviation
Monthly income (NT$ thousands)	191	40.45	23.38
Type of university (private=1, public=0)	191	0.66	0.48
Minimum exam score for admission	190	411.75	35.28
Repeat test taker (yes=1, no=0)	153	0.42	0.49
Sex (male=1, female=0)	190	0.66	0.47
Ancestry (other privinces=1, Taiwanese=0)	189	0.35	0.48
Occupation sector (private=1, public=0)	189	0.58	0.49
Job location (Taipei area=1, elsewhere=0)	188	0.72	0.45
Job location (Taichung area=1, elsewhere=0)	188	0.11	0.31
How obtained job (exam=1, other=0)	176	0.40	0.49
How obtained job (connections=1, other=0)	176	0.19	0.40
Length of workweek (hours)	182	40.65	12.53
On-the-job training (yes=1, no=0)	191	0.46	0.50
Seniority (years on job)	178	5.97	3.36
Number of years of education	191	16.53	1.34
College of arts graduate (yes=1, no=0)	191	0.35	0.48
College of science graduate (yes=1, no=0)	191	0.22	0.42
College of law graduate (yes=1, no=0)	191	0.05	0.22
Number of siblings	189	3.48	1.67
Years of education of father	183	9.84	4.39
Years of education of mother	185	6.98	4.09

significantly different from zero. Except for the dummy variable "private sector employment" and the variable "number of siblings," in fact, only the coefficients of private sector employment and the number of siblings are significantly different from zero at the 10% level. The reason that income levels at private sector jobs are higher than income levels for jobs in the public sector may be due to the fact that jobs in the private sector are usually more unstable than those in the public sector. Private sector jobs usually have less comprehensive and less secure retirement benefits, so they must entice prospective employees by offering them higher salaries. The risk of business failure, which deters prospective employees, is another factor that compels the private sector to pay higher salaries than the public sector.

An individual's number of siblings has a significantly negative effect on his or her income level after graduation. As discussed in the last section, graduates who have larger numbers of siblings tend to receive a proportionally smaller share of parental resources (including time, money,

TABLE 7   First Job Following Graduation — Results of Regression Analysis of
Equation (1)

Variable	Coefficient	t value
Constant	4.82	0.090
Type of university (private=1, public=0)	-9.22	-1.41
Minimum exam score for admission	-0.01	-0.07
Repeat test taker (yes=1, no=0)	5.37	1.46
Sex (male=1, female=0)	4.06	0.90
Ancestry (other privinces=1, Taiwanese=0)	3.58	0.94
Occupation sector (private=1, public=0)	7.84*	1.78
Job location (Taipei area=1, elsewhere=0)	-2.19	-0.48
Job location (Taichung area=1, elsewhere=0)	0.89	0.15
How obtained job (exam=1, other=0)	4.44	1.08
How obtained job (connections=1, other=0)	6.72	1.63
Length of workweek (hours)	-0.02	-0.20
Number of years of education	1.19	0.97
College of arts graduate (yes=1, no=0)	-5.26	-1.19
College of science graduate (yes=1, no=0)	-4.22	-0.41
College of law graduate (yes=1, no=0)	-8.75	-1.34
Number of siblings	-1.83*	-1.85
Years of education of father	-0.41	-0.78
Years of education of mother	0.36	0.61

Note: Sample size = 70, R^2 = 0.33, $\overline{R}^2$ = 0.10, F = 1.43.
    * The coefficient is significantly different from 0 at the 10% level; the same holds for
      the F statistic.

etc.). However, the negative effect on graduates' income levels could be
also due to the fact that these individuals, in order to lighten their parents' financial loads, tend to be more anxious to find jobs quickly than
those graduates who have fewer or no siblings, and so the first group of
graduates are content to quickly settle into first jobs, even if lower or less
competitive wages are offered. In this study we are of course most concerned with the effects of public and private universities on the income
levels of their graduates' first jobs, and whether there is a significant disparity in their effect. As we know from Table 7, the coefficient of the
dummy variable "private university graduate" is -9.22 with a t value of -
1.41, meaning that the effect of public universities on the income levels of
their graduates' first jobs is greater than that of private universities; however, this effect is not significant. It is probable that employers, without
any previous work record or experience by which to evaluate job candidates, must hold to the general belief that public universities are better
than private ones, and thus private sector employers offering high sala-

ries tend to offer their jobs to recently graduated public university graduates. On the other hand, since starting salaries for jobs in the public sector are not affected by whether the employee graduated from a public or a private university, the difference between the two is not significant.[9]

We would expect our graduates to have more established careers ten years out from the university. Table 8 reports these results. Here the adjusted R^2 ($\bar{R}^2$) is 0.30, showing that our variables account for 30% of the variance in job income. Not only is this result a great improvement upon the result obtained in Table 7, it is also satisfactory in terms of the cross-section data. Furthermore, the F statistic is still significant at the 1% level, indicating that the null hypothesis that the coefficients of all explanatory variables are equal to zero has been rejected. Correspondingly, the regression results of graduates' first jobs (Table 7) prove that the previously proposed hypothesis that jobs held after a longer period of time following graduation are a better reflection of a worker's productivity is correct; and also, that all related theoretical explanatory variables can effectively explain the difference in income levels.

Now let us look more closely at the estimated coefficients of individual explanatory variables. As Table 8 shows, the coefficient of the dummy variable representing private university graduates is 13.33, and its t value (2.32) is significant at the 5% level. This indicates that private universities exert a greater influence than public universities on their graduates' income levels at jobs held ten years after graduation; besides, the approximately NT$13,000 monthly difference is quite substantial. Since the effect was achieved with a much lower per capita educational investment, the long-term career benefit of private university education appears to validate a greater efficiency at private institutions, or at the least, a closer correspondence with the actual demands of the job market and of society.

The surveys returned by respondents indicated that the percentage of

---

9. Another reason for the fact that all explanatory variables in Table 7 are not significantly different from zero at the 5% level may be the problem of multicollinearity. After examination we ascertained the condition number to be 176.40—which is not a low number—and this shows that a multicollinear relationship does exist between the explanatory variables. But as long as the sample size is large enough (here it is 70), multicollinearity only makes the standard deviation of estimated coefficients larger, but does not affect the unbiasedness and consistency of the coefficients. Therefore, even if the problem of multicollinearity changes the dummy variable "private university graduate" from significant to insignificant, it still does not affect the conclusions drawn from this study—that employers offering higher salaries tend to hire public university graduates when there are no previous work records by which to evaluate job candidates.

TABLE 8   Occupation Ten Years after Graduation — Results of Regression
Analysis of Equation (1)

Variable	Coefficient	t value
Constant	-115.88**	-2.30
Type of university (private=1, public=0)	13.33**	2.32
Minimum exam score for admission	0.28***	2.66
Repeat test taker (yes=1, no=0)	-5.22	-1.53
Sex (male=1, female=0)	3.74	0.96
Ancestry (other privinces=1, Taiwanese=0)	4.56	1.37
Occupation sector (private=1, public=0)	11.44***	2.48
Job location (Taipei area=1, elsewhere=0)	-5.64	-1.39
Job location (Taichung area=1, elsewhere=0)	-14.93***	-2.42
How obtained job (exam=1, other=0)	-4.48	-0.92
How obtained job (connections=1, other=0)	-7.53*	-1.78
Length of workweek (hours)	0.20	1.62
On-the-job training (yes=1, no=0)	4.59	1.54
Seniority (number of years on job)	0.18	0.38
Number of years of education	1.41	1.01
College of arts graduate (yes=1, no=0)	-6.64*	-1.81
College of science graduate (yes=1, no=0)	14.09	1.56
College of law graduate (yes=1, no=0)	-3.87	-0.62
Number of siblings	-0.63	-0.68
Years of education of father	-0.16	-0.37
Years of education of mother	-0.15	-0.35

Note: Sample size = 118, R^2 = 0.42, $\bar{R}^2$ = 0.30, F = 3.55***.

* The coefficient is significantly different from 0 at the 10% level; the same holds for
the F statistic.

** The coefficient is significantly different from 0 at the 5% level; the same holds for
the F statistic.

*** The coefficient is significantly different from 0 at the 1% level; the same holds
for the F statistic.

public university graduates who were at the time residing abroad was as
high as 53%, as opposed to 21% of private university graduates. We were
only able to analyze the group that remained in the country, as we could
not get detailed information from those who had gone abroad. It is possible that those overseas had successful careers that could have changed
the overall picture of public university efficiency. But the departure from
the country of such a large part of the publicly funded graduates will not
have aided Taiwanese economic growth even if these graduates as individuals should prove to have been successful in their new homelands.
Therefore it is reasonable from a public policy standpoint to look, as we

have done, only at the graudates who remained in Taiwan. It is reasonable also from this standpoint to conclude that in terms of development of the domestic economy the government's allocation of the great majority (about 95%) of higher education investment to public universities may not be the most effective means of distribution.

Also worth mentioning is the fact that among the 2,691 surveys handed out, including those to graduates abroad, the rate of return was not even 12%. Since all the respondents who participated in the survey knew that this was a study of comparative income and distribution levels of public vs. private university graduates, there is the possibility that private university alumni earning relatively high salaries would have had a greater tendency to respond to the survey, to demonstrate that, in fact, private university graduates were not inferior to their public university counterparts. Under these circumstances, the sample that we are using in this study would not be a random sample, and selectivity bias may exist. However, in analyzing our sample we discovered that out of 1,622 private university graduates surveyed, 178 responded—about 11%, which does not differ greatly from the 12% response rate of public university graduates (128 responded, out of 1,069 surveyed), and thus the selectivity bias should not be too great. Of course, any further studies concerning this subject should address these uncertainties for greater in-depth examination. At present, the empirical results of this study can only hope to offer some tentative conclusions.

The signs of the estimated coefficients of all other variables were mostly as expected, but the estimated coefficient of the dummy variable "male" was 3.74, with a t value of 0.96, showing that if we take into account other factors affecting income level such as personal ability, family background, etc., there is not a significant difference between income levels of male and female graduates. This is different from the conclusions of Wu Hui-lin's 1988 study. The explanation for the discrepancy may be that Wu Hui-lin did not account for other factors affecting income level such as personal ability, family background, etc.

The coefficient for the variable representing minimum exam score required for admission is 0.28, which reaches statistical significance—thus demonstrating that the minimum score required for admission, used to represent the respondent's intelligence, does indeed have a positive effect on a graduate's income level at jobs held ten years after graduation. The coefficient for the variable "repeat test-taker" is negative (-5.22); it is close to being significantly different from zero, and therefore corresponds to the anticipated theoretical effect. Also, the coefficient of the variable representing private sector employment is positive (11.44) and significantly different from zero, showing that most private sector salaries are higher than public sector salaries by an average of NT$11,440 monthly. The coef-

ficients of the dummy variables representing Taipei or Taichung area job
locations are negative, but only the coefficient for the Taichung area is
significant. This demonstrates that Taipei and Taichung area salaries are
on the whole lower than the salaries for jobs located in the south of Taiwan. However, only between Taichung and southern Taiwan salaries is
the salary differential significant. As predicted, the length of the workweek has a positive effect on income level, but its effect is not significant.

The salaries of graduates of colleges of arts is on the average lower
than those of graduates of colleges of business, and salaries of graduates
in science are higher than business graduates. The income levels of colleges of law graduates, however, are not significantly different from
those of graduates of colleges of business. As for the other variables predicted to affect income level, "on-the-job training" and "the number of
years of education attained" both have positive effects on income levels,
thereby suggesting that the human capital theory is still meaningful. The
educational level attained by parents, the level of seniority, and the
number of siblings all seem to have no significant effect on a graduate's
income level.[10]

In comparing tables 7 and 8, we discover that except for the two variables representing private or public sector employment and the number
of siblings, all other factors have no significant effect on the income levels
of graduates' first jobs. On the other hand, those factors that significantly
affect the graduates' income levels at jobs held ten years after graduation
include "public or private university graduate," "private sector employment," the "minimum required entrance score of respondent's major,"
and the "obtaining job through connection"; in addition, the factors
"whether respondent is a repeat test-taker," "whether respondent has received on-the-job training," and the "number of years of education attained" all have a close-to-significant effect.

Whereas the number of siblings has a significantly negative effect on
the income level of a graduate's first job, this is not the case ten years
later. There are several possible explanations for the shift here. We discussed above why a large number of siblings might dispose a first-time
job seeker to settle quickly for any available opening. Later in life brothers and sisters are likely to be on their own and thus reduce the pressure
to make job decisions to reduce burdens on parents. The respondent himself may also by this time have gained a greater understanding of the labor market, and be free to find a more suitable job.

---

10. The condition number of the regression in Table 8 is 174.92, showing that
multicollinearity does exist; however, it does not affect the results of this study.
For a more detailed explanation, please see note 9.

We now come to the central question of this part of the study: the contribution of public and private university education to career incomes. As we know from Table 7, a private university education is not a significant factor in producing income advantages over public education for first-time job seekers.

Later in life, as Table 8 indicates, the reverse is true. Here the coefficient of the dummy variable representing private university graduate has changed from -9.22 in Table 7 to 13.33, at statistical significance. What this indicates is that the positive effect private universities have on its graduates' income levels at jobs held ten years after graduation is greater than the effect public universities have on their graduates. Furthermore, since per capita educational investment in private university students is significantly less than in students at public universities, the results found above clearly imply that private university instruction is more efficient than public university instruction, and that it corresponds more closely to societal and job market demands.

With the qualification discussed above, that our study does not include incomes of graduates living abroad, which may favor public university graduates, we believe that from a policy perspective for domestic economic growth the government should consider readjusting its distribution of higher education resources. The government should reallocate a reasonable amount of the educational investment it has placed in public universities to private universities, so that resources for education could be utilized to the maximum efficiency and effectiveness. In addition, the strict regulation of tuition levels at private universities should be abandoned in order to allow private institutions to raise the funds needed to perform their social function. This could help minimize the gap between public and private university per capita educational investment, and at the same time could decrease the excess demand for higher education in Taiwan.

B. Occupational Prestige Distribution Model

The empirical results of the comparison between the occupational prestige levels of public and private university graduates in their first jobs and in jobs held ten years later, and of whether there are significant differences, are listed in tables 9 and 10 respectively.

As shown in Table 9, the mean for occupational prestige ratings of public university graduates' first jobs is 73.16, which is greater than the private university occupational prestige mean of 70.23. Although the standard deviation of public university graduates' occupational prestige ratings is 7.97, which is also higher than the private university standard deviation of 5.48, the highest (98.02) and lowest values (65.83) for public

TABLE 9   Occupational Prestige Ratings for First Jobs Held by Public vs. Private University Students Graduating in 1979

	Sample size	Mean	Standard deviation	Minimum	Maximum
Public	32	73.16	7.97	65.83	98.02
Private	77	70.23	5.48	63.66	92.00

TABLE 10   Occupational Prestige Ratings for Jobs Held Ten Years after Graduation (1979) by Public vs. Private University Students

	Sample size	Mean	Standard deviation	Minimum value	Maximum value
Public	65	81.12	14.28	68.76	166.99
Private	126	80.63	8.20	66.67	109.53

university graduates' occupational prestige ratings are both higher than the highest (92.00) and lowest (63.66) values for private university graduates' occupational prestige ratings. Our occupational prestige distribution model presented in Part I anticipated such higher standing for public university graduates' first jobs. A possible explanation for this phenomenon could be that a higher percentage of public university graduates go on to pursue graduate studies (public 22%, private 13%), and since the number of years of education attained figures as one of the two explanatory variables affecting occupational prestige, the mean occupational prestige ratings of public university graduates is clearly going to be higher than the mean occupational prestige ratings of private university graduates.

In addition, students with extremely high entrance examination scores almost always enrolled at public universities (especially at National Taiwan University), and these students may have also gone on to attain a high level of education and to earn high incomes; therefore, they may have contributed to the fact that the greatest value and standard deviation of the occupational prestige ratings of public university graduates are higher than for private university graduates. In order to ascertain whether there is a statistically significant difference in occupational prestige ratings of public and private university graduates' first jobs and jobs held ten years after graduation, we employed the central limit theorem, and the hypothesis that the two means are mutually independent, in order to determine whether the means of occupational prestige ratings for public and private university graduates are equal.

From the mean and standard deviation data given in Table 9, using equation (3) we were able to determine that

$$Z = \frac{(73.16 - 70.23)}{\sqrt{(7.97)^2/32 + (5.48)^2/77}} = 1.24$$

At the 10% significance level, the Z value is less than the Z critical value of 1.645, and therefore the null hypothesis that the two means are equal cannot be rejected. In other words, there is no significant difference between the occupational prestige means of public and private university graduates' first jobs.

In examining tables 9 and 10, we clearly see that both sets of statistics tell an identical story—an inspection of the statistical results reveals that there is no difference between the occupational prestige level of public and private university graduates in jobs held ten years after graduation. In truth, its Z value of 0.255, is even less than the Z value of graduates' first jobs. We have said that jobs held after a longer period of working usually provide a better reflection of an individual's productivity; therefore, we reach the same conclusion for the occupational prestige model as we did for the previously presented income model. We know that per capita educational investment at private universities is far lower than per capita educational investment at public universities; yet, there is no significant difference between the occupational prestige levels of public and private university graduates. There is especially a lack of significant difference between occupational prestige of public and private university graduates in jobs held ten years after graduation, and this clearly shows that public university instruction is not more efficient than private university instruction. We can even say that private universities are able to more effectively use their educational resources than public universities.

However, we must once again emphasize here that, as with the income model analysis, we are using as our sample group those graduates who remained in Taiwan for employment. Since the average education and income level of graduates who reside abroad are usually higher than those who remain in Taiwan, the above occupational prestige analysis results may have underestimated the positive effect that public universities have had on the occupational prestige of their graduates.[11]

---

11. The comparison of occupational prestige is highly problematic; since, as one critic has pointed out, the reliability of the occupational prestige level determined solely from the two variables "number of years of education attained" and "income level" is questionable. But under the limitations of our present data and of previous studies, we have no choice but to tentatively use these two var-

Conclusion

The primary objective of this study was to compare the distribution of income and occupational prestige levels of public and private university graduates, in the hopes of using the empirical results of our study to determine future directions for government investment in higher education. The data that we have used in this study comes from a survey of university students who had graduated in 1979. First we determined, from an economic theory viewpoint, the factors affecting individual income levels; then we used a statistical multiple regression method to estimate whether a significant difference existed between the effects public and private universities have on the income levels of their graduates. Since income level is not the sole indicator of an individual's job performance or of his societal contribution, we therefore also attempted to determine the average subjective occupational prestige ratings of public and private university graduates.

The empirical results of this study reveal that although public universities have a greater effect on the income levels of the first jobs held by their graduates than private universities, the difference in effect is not significant. This difference could be due to the existing general belief that public universities are better than private universities. On the other hand, there are also many work units (especially public sector work units) where starting salaries are not affected by employees' public or private university affiliation. Therefore, on the average, the starting salaries of public university graduates are not significantly higher than the starting salaries of private university graduates. Worth mentioning is the fact that in regards to income levels of first jobs, the explanatory power of our model is not strong (R^2 is 10%), which is further proof for our theory that first jobs held immediately after graduation are usually not the best indicators of an individual's labor market productivity. Conversely, the model used in this study to explain income levels of graduates at jobs held ten years after graduation has achieved very satisfactory results, with an R^2 approaching 30%. As for income levels of graduates' later jobs, the most important discovery is that public universities have a smaller effect on their graduates' incomes than private universities, and that the difference between the two is statistically significant. Since the per capita educational investment in students at public universities is far higher than

---

iables—both of which have been considered important theoretically—in taking first steps toward a discussion of this issue. A more detailed comparison of the difference of public and private university graduates' occupational prestige could be the direction for future studies on this subject.

that at private universities, this result provides convincing support for the theory that private university instruction is more effective and efficient than public university instruction.

As for determining occupational prestige, our analysis of the empirical results shows that whether for first jobs or for jobs held ten years after graduation, the mean occupational prestige rating of public university graduates is higher than that of private university graduates. The difference between the two, however, is not significant, especially for jobs held ten years after graduation. Therefore, the conclusion that we have reached for the occupational prestige distribution model is identical to our conclusion for the income model, which is that the private university instruction is more efficient than public university instruction.

The empirical data taken for this study did not include university graduates residing abroad. Therefore, the empirical results of our study may have underestimated the effect that public universities have had on their graduates' income levels . However, even if the efficiency of public university instruction is not lower than private university instruction, the fact that a far higher percentage of public university graduates choose to stay abroad, and the fact that private universities still have a greater positive effect on their graduates' income levels ten years after graduation shows that, at least from the viewpoint of domestic economic development, the government may not be achieving the most effective and efficient distribution of resources.

The most important policy implication of this study, therefore, is that the government should redirect a reasonable amount of the subsidies presently allotted to public universities to private institutions. In addition, the government should eliminate its strict regulation of private university tuition levels so that the gap between public and private university per capita educational investment may be minimized. Although at present the government is beginning to gradually relax its tuition restrictions for private universities, and has begun to give private universities small subsidies, most private universities find that the tuition they receive from students is barely enough to maintain staff and daily expenses. For some private institutions, the tuition received is not even enough to cover these costs. In addition, private universities are now faced with the prospect of increased competition stemming from new policies which are allowing for new schools to be founded. If we wish to see the establishment of a first-rate private university system in Taiwan, the government must eliminate its existing bias in favor of public institutions, so that in the future public and private universities will be able to compete on an equal footing—a competition which would prove to be constructive, and which would fundamentally elevate the quality of higher education in Taiwan.

Bibliography

Card, David, and Alan Krueger. 1990. Does School Quality Matter? Returns to Education and the Characteristics of Public Schools in the United States. NBER working paper #3358.

Chang, Jui-meng. 1970. Education and Economic Development in Taiwan. Master's thesis. Institute of Economics, National Taiwan University, June.

Chen, Ch'iung-tzu. 1975. A Study of the Educational Budget of Taiwan. Master's thesis. Graduate School of Public Finance, National Chengchi University, June.

Chiang, Feng-fu. 1988. Education Achievement and Economic Development in Taiwan. Paper presented at the Conference on Successful Economic Development Strategies of Pacific Rim Nations, Chung Hua Institute for Economic Research (ROC) and the Global Economic Action Institute (U.S.).

Coleman, James, et al. 1966. *Equality of Educational Opportunity.* Washington, D.C.: GPO.

Coleman, James S., Thomas Hoffer, and Sally Kilgore. 1981. *Public and Private Schools.* Report to the National Statistics Center by the National Opinion Center.

——. 1981. *High School Achievement: Public, Catholic, and Private Schools Compared.* New York: Basic Books.

Denison, Edward F. 1964. Measuring the Contribution of Education to Economic Growth. In *The Residual Factor and Economic Growth.* Paris: OECD.

——. 1987. *Why Do Growth Rates Differ?* Washington, D.C.: Brookings Institution.

Dore, Ronald Philip. 1976. *The Diploma Disease.* New York: Allen and Unwin.

Fang, Jeffrey M. 1971. Education and Economic Growth in Taiwan, 1952-1965. *Industry of Free China* 36:6.

Freeman, Richard. 1976. *The Overeducated American.* New York: Academic Press.

Gannicot, K. 1972. *Rates of Return to Education in Taiwan, ROC.* Planning Unit of the MOE.

Hanushek, Eric. 1986. The Economics of Schooling: Production and Efficiency in Public Schools. *Journal of Economic Literature* 3: 1141-77.

Haveman, Robert H., and Barbara L. Wolfe. 1984. Schooling and Economic Well-Being: The Role of Nonmarket Effects. *Journal of Human Resources* 3: 377-407.

Hsieh, Min-jui. 1979. Evaluation of the Contribution of Economic Growth to Education Investment in Taiwan. *Journal of China Statistics* (June).

Hsieh, Shen-lung. 1990. A Discussion of Taiwan's Higher Education Tuition Policy. Master's thesis. Institute of Economics, Tsing Hua University, June.

Hou, Chi-ming. 1979. Education, Human Resources, and "Fair" Economic Development: The Case in Taiwan. Paper presented at the Conference on Taiwan Human Resources, December.

——, and Ching-hsi Chang. 1981. Education and Economic Growth in Taiwan:

The Mechanism of Adjustment. Paper presented at the Conference on Experiences and Lessons of Economic Development in Taiwan, Institute of Economics, Academia Sinica.

Jimenez, Emmanuel, Marlaine Lockheed, and Nongnuch Wattanawaha. 1988. The Relative Efficiency of Private and Public Schools: The Case of Thailand. *World Bank Research Observer* 2: 139-64.

Johnson, G., and F. Stafford. 1973. Social Returns to Quantity and Quality of Schooling. *Journal of Human Resources* 8 (Spring): 139-55.

Kai, Che-sheng. 1989. Higher Education and Its Relation to the Use of Human Resources in Taiwan. Tan Chiang University Institute of Education Studies, and the Foundation for 21st Century Studies, November.

Kao, Shu-kui. 1986. Personal Factors Affecting Occupational Prestige—Gender, Age, Educational Level—and a Discussion of Their Relationships to Occupational Prestige. *Journal of Population Studies*, Taipei: Taiwan Institute of Population Studies, June.

Li, Chin-t'ung. 1989. Higher Education and Economic Development. Tan Chiang University Institute of Education Studies and Foundation for the 21st Century Studies, November.

Lockheed, Marlaine, S. Vail, and B. Fuller. 1987. *Why Textbooks Affect Achievement in Developing Countries: Evidence from Thailand.* EDT Series 53, World Bank Education and Training Department.

Marin, Alan, and George Psacharopoulos. 1978. Schooling and Income Distribution. *Review of Economics and Statistics* 58, no.3: 332-38.

McCuster, H. F., and H. J. Robinson. 1962. *Education and Development: The Role of Education Planning in the Economic Development of the Republic of China.* Stanford Research Institute.

Meier, Gerald M. 1984. *Leading Issues in Economic Development.* New York: Oxford University Press.

Mingat, Alain, and J. P. Tan. 1986. Financing Public Higher Education in Developing Countries: The Potential Role of Loan Schemes. *Higher Education* 15, no. 3: 283-97.

Ministry of Education. 1975. *Educational Cost and Analysis of Budget.* Taipei: Ministry of Education Planning Department Publication, no. 7, August.

Morgan, J., and I. Sirgeldin. 1968. A Note on the Quality Dimension in Education. *Journal of Political Economy* 76 (September): 1069-77.

Noell, J. 1981. The Impact of Private Schools When Self-Selection Is Controlled: A Critique of Coleman's "Public and Private Schools." Unpublished paper, Office of Planning, Budget, and Evaluation, U.S. Department of Education.

———. 1982. Public and Catholic Schools: A Reanalysis of "Public and Private Schools." *Sociology of Education* 55: 123-32.

Otani, I., and D. Villanueva. 1989. *Theoretical Aspects of Growth in Developing Countries: External Debt Dynamics and the Role of Human Capital.* International Monetary Fund.

Psacharopoulos, George. 1983. Education and Private versus Public Sector Pay. *Labor and Society* 8, no. 2: 123-34.

———. 1984a. Assessing Training Priorities in Developing Countries: Current Practice and Possible Alternatives. *International Labor Review* 123, no.5: 569-83.

———. 1984b. The Contribution of Education to Economic Growth: International Comparisons. In *International Comparisons of Productivity and Causes of the Slowdown*, edited by John W. Kendrick. Cambridge, Mass.: Ballinger.

———. 1985. Returns to Education: A Further Internal Update and Implications. *Journal of Human Resources* 20, no. 4: 584-604.

———. 1988. Education and Development: A Review. *World Bank Research Observer* 3, no. 1.

Ram, Rati. 1984. Population Increase, Economic Growth, Educational Inequality, and Income Distribution—Some Recent Evidence. *Journal of Development Economics* 14: 419-28.

Schultz, T. W. 1961. Education and Economic Growth. In *Social Forces Influencing American Education*, edited by N. B. Henry. Chicago: University of Chicago Press, for the National Society for the Study of Education.

Shih, Chien-sheng. 1976. The Contribution of Education to Economic Development in Taiwan. Paper presented at the Conference on Population and Economic Growth in Taiwan, Institute of Economics, Academia Sinica.

Strumilin, S. G. 1968 (1929). The Economic Significance of National Education, the Planned Economy. Reprinted in *Readings in the Economics of Education*. Paris: UNESCO.

T'sai, Shu-ling, and Hai-yuan Ch'ü. 1989. *First Steps toward a Structure of a Table for Objective and Subjective Occupation Ratings*. Institute of Studies of Three Principles of the People (June).

Tseng, Feng-i. 1978. The Yield Rate of University Education Investment: The Case of Taiwan. *Taiwan Bank Quarterly* 29, no. 1, (April).

Tu, Fu-chen. 1977. Education Investment and Economic Growth in Taiwan. *Economic Research* 20 (June).

Wachtel, Paul. 1976. The Effects on Earnings of School and College Investment Expenditures. *Review of Economics and Statistics* 58 (August).

Walsh, J. R. 1935. Capital Concept Applied to Man. *Quarterly Journal of Economics* 49, no. 1: 255-85.

World Bank. 1986. *The Financing of Education in Developing Countries: An Exploration of Policy Options*. Washington, D.C.

Wu, Chung-chi. 1976. The Estimated Contribution of Education to Economic Development in Taiwan. *Taiwan Bank Monthly* (September and October).

Wu, Hui-lin. 1988. Deciding Factors in Labor Returns for College-and-Above Educated Workers in Taiwan—An Empirical Analysis. Paper presented at the Conference on the Taiwan Labor Market (January).

———, and K'un-ling Miao. 1990. Differences in Earnings of College-and-Above

Educated Workers Upon First Entering the Job Market. Paper presented at the Conference on Labor Resources, Taiwan Institute of Economics, and the Labor Committee of the Legislative Yuan (August).

Wu, Ts'ung-min. 1988. The Phenomenom of Repeat Test-Taking and the Demand for College Education in Taiwan. Paper presented at the Conference on the Taiwan Labor Market (January).

Part II:
Social and Political Aspects of Economic Development

12

Ideological Reflections and the Inception of Economic Development in Taiwan

Chen-Kuo Hsu

What has been the political basis of Taiwan's successful economic development? How and why was this basis laid? These questions are still puzzles to many students of Taiwan's politicoeconomic development. Simon Kuznets has suggested that

> A fuller analysis would have to include a view of the guiding social and party philosophy, the experience and training of the decision makers and workers involved, the mechanism by which the interests of various groups were satisfied and their responsiveness maintained, and not the least, the characteristics of the native islander population that favored the positive response and outcome. (1979, 27)

Edwin Winckler adds: "The basic nature of the political system remains undefined.... We need to know the relative weights of setting, personality, security, economics, and ideology, and how these elements fit together" (1981, 13-17). While giving high marks to state intervention, Alice Amsden expresses some curiosity about how the same Kuomintang (KMT) government with its record of miserable failure in the past could learn "new tricks" in managing economic policies in Taiwan (1979, 342; 1985, 83).

This inquiry focuses on the KMT's economic ideology and its impact on the adoption and institutionalization of a capitalist development strategy in Taiwan. Economic ideology here refers to high-ranking political and economic officials' perception of and preferences for the economic system and government economic functions. Through the analysis of the KMT's ideological transitions, we will attempt to show how the party's leaders extricated themselves from deep egalitarian concerns and a strong commitment to statism and reached a new conceptual consensus centered on private ownership.

The most convenient way to examine the KMT's economic ideology is to start from its official doctrine, the Principle of the People's Livelihood (or Doctrine of Livelihood). Here let us cite one article of the 1947 ROC Constitution:

> The national economy shall be based on the Principle of the People's Livelihood and shall seek to effect equalization of land ownership and restriction of private capital in order to attain a well-balanced sufficiency in national wealth and the people's livelihood.

The Principle of People's Livelihood is an economic ideology developed by Sun Yat-sen, founding father of the KMT. Today, the government leaders still insist that Sunist ideology is the cornerstone of Taiwan's successful economy. What is the real relationship of this doctrine and Taiwan's economic development strategy? How did Nationalist leaders and economic officials interpret Sun's ideology and apply it to their economic policies? There are a series of stages in the KMT's ideological evolution. We will take these up beginning with the period of doctrinal confusion after the "Party Purification" in 1927, the advocacy of "planned economy" from 1935 to 1945, and the new conceptual reflections in terms of the "planned free economy" since around 1945. Finally, we will see the adoption of this new conceptual thinking in Taiwan since 1949.

The Syncretic Nature of
the Doctrine of Livelihood

Sun's doctrine is eclectically composed of three parts: socialism, a planned industrialization, and statism based on traditional legalistic Confucianism. In the first decade of the Republic, Sun professed a moderate socialism. Influenced by the main currents of thought of his time, he considered the widening disparity between the rich and poor as a serious defect in Western industrialization. To avoid the same mistake in China, he borrowed from the American socialist Henry George the idea of levying a single tax on land. Through "regulating land rights," he hoped to stem the overweening growth of the Chinese capitalist class. "Regulating land rights" and "restricting private capital" (or "restricting private capital and developing national capital") eventually became two defining ideas for Sun's followers.

Sun also was deeply committed to the industrialization of China. To achieve this goal, he consistently and firmly urged the introduction of foreign investment. In 1912, while withdrawing from the presidency, he even asked his successor to entrust him, in a civilian status, with the task of building a Chinese railroad network. He advocated a system of "government ownership and private management." He is recorded as saying that privately managed businesses were more efficient than public ones. This part of Sunist ideology included some liberal elements.

In line with the Confucian literati's view, however, Sun also strongly favored a paternalistic statism. He believed that "ruling, educating, rearing, protecting" (*kuan, chiao, yang, wei*) were four basic governmental functions. The state thus should be responsible for the population's "food, clothing, housing, and transportation." In food administration, for example, Sun regarded the Bureau of Food Control as the most important agency to be established at the local government level. Such a bureau would take on the responsibility of purchasing and selling all food products. Sun also held that at the community level a Local Self-Management Act should require each person to contribute six hours a day for one or two months each year to help the local government. People who did not participate should pay to the government an equivalent value in money. Such service could mobilize enough labor for road construction, developing waste land, and constructing houses and buildings for civic use. Sun, however, seemed totally unaware of the awesome power and wealth that the government would have to command in order to do all these things. He also had little to say about whether government efforts to provide these four functions might intrude so strongly upon private economic activities and property rights as to stifle private enterprise.

KMT Ideological Conflicts and the Adoption of "Planned Economy"

Due to the syncretic nature of Sunist doctrine, people could give it different interpretations in accordance with their own preferences. In fact, each of the three parts was emphasized in different periods of Nationalist economic policy development. From 1924 on, in adopting the strategy of creating alliances with the Soviet Union and the Chinese Communists, as well as endorsing an anticapitalist peasant-worker coalition, Sun's socialism turned radical. Strong anticapitalist and anti-imperialist slogans consequently became rampant within the KMT. Under this frame, economic policy (such as "land to the tiller") became a means by which to mobilize social support. Economic policy came to have essentially political purposes.

The radical strategy caused a sharp left-right cleavage within the KMT. Chiang Kai-shek then initiated a surprise purge of the Communists under the rubric of Party Purification in 1927. This action wiped out Communist members but not their ideology. The strategy and ideology of class struggle, developed during the movement of the Northern Expeditions, still retained considerable force. Serious left-right ideological and factional conflicts thus still remained in the party. In Shanghai, the General Chamber of Commerce, representing the large local merchants, bankers, and industrialists, made an effort to acquire legitimate status in the new government and attempted to influence the formulation of economic policy. On the other head, the merchant associations, representing the middle and small merchants and supported by militant party members, still sought to pursue class struggle and attempted to eliminate the Chamber of Commerce, accusing its members of being compradors of foreign imperialism. As a result of the failure to reconcile these divergent group interests and ideological orientations, the party was incapable of creating a consistent and positive policy toward private business (Coble 1980, 1-12, 269; Fewsmith 1980, 222-69; Hsu 1987, 3-10).

Ideological conflicts were displayed also in intellectual debates among prominent figures. A leading left-wing party ideologue, Ch'en Kung-po, claimed that much of Sunist doctrine was based on socialist postulates and these should be retained even after the split with the Communist Party. A leading right-wing proponent, Tai Chi-t'ao, advocated, on the contrary, that all socialist elements be carefully scrutinized and clarified. He proposed that concepts such as "the harmony of social class" and other traditional meliorist ideas in Sunist doctrine be strengthened and used as the basic principles for organizing Chinese society.

By 1932, however, these intellectual debates ended when the KMT Central Committee came under the domination of Chiang Kai-shek and his faction (Wang 1985, 175-76, 228, 231-35).

Chiang, Tai, and other associates then launched the Movement of National Economic Construction in 1935. In the name of "planned economy" this new development strategy emphasized statism based on traditional statecraft. As Chiang analyzed it in 1935, "the exhaustion of China's national economy" was due to breakdowns "between men and things," or "between men and events," and to the "lack of adjustment and lack of integration among the various parts or units that made up production." These breakdowns were caused by "social unawareness" and "social ignorance of the significance of production." The state thus had to call up and conduct a political and social mass movement to wake up or educate people and "make all kinds of human resources and physical resources fit into place in a complete and proper setting." To push the movement, a new administrative hierarchy was to be created with the highest echelons located in the central government and the lowest units in county administration. Party cadres, government officials, and military officers were to be responsible for putting this new movement for national reconstruction in place. For achieving direct government control of economic resource allocation, the state established measures such as "commodity-to-commodity exchange," "total purchase and total sale," "tax in kind," and rational distribution. As to policy goals, it emphasized "self-sufficiency and self-support," "equal distribution," and even "the union of farmers and soldiers."

Excepting its appeal to Confucian values in its moral incentives, the mass movement and military-economic-complex style of organization of this "planned economy" was not much different from that of the Chinese Communists. The emphasis on the state's role and the preference for egalitarianism still were the main themes in economic ideology. These collectivist ideas and behaviors also seemed to be compatible with the very underdeveloped environment in the Chinese interior during the war period.

Emergence of the "Planned Free Economy"

Near the end of the Anti-Japanese War, the Nationalist government began to consider a new strategy for the postwar period. The basic guideline for this new strategy first appeared in December 1944 in the "Principle Guiding the First Economic Construction Program" issued by the 148th Regular Meeting of the National Defense Supreme Study Commission. This document was then endorsed by Chiang Kai-shek himself in a national broadcast on 10 October 1945. Chiang stated that "the First Economic Construction Program should combine economic freedom for the population with a national economic plan" (Ching 1951, 78-79). The essence of the new strategy was then summed up in a more detailed proposal called "The Establishment of Postwar Economic Institutions," drafted by the Executive Yuan in November 1945, and in another document titled "The Five-Year Draft Plan for Material Construction," presented by the Central Planning Bureau in December. The latter document especially underscored the importance of promoting domestic capital formation. The authors estimated the required amount of such capital according to private, public, and foreign sources and allocated one-third of the total amount to each source. In the first stage, however, only government and foreign sources were available, but the document called for a gradual expansion of private capital as recovery improved (Ching 1951, 79-82). The 1945 documents also stressed the application of state power in economic planning, selecting strategic industries, and improving investment environments. In addition, they called for contributions from highly educated people with managerial and other skills, rather than party cadres, administrative officials, or military officers.

It is significant that the 1945 documents recognized the need and importance of "enterprise freedom" and decided to assign major responsibilities to technocrats in the enlargement of economic policies. It is possible, however, to view the 1945 documents as effect rather than cause, that is, as a measure of the already growing strength of new technocrats in China. The rise of new technocrats, in this view, is principally a consequence of the expansion of higher education. In 1912, the first year of the Republic, China had only four universities, with 446 registered students and a total of 3,084 past graduates. In 1945, the number of universities and colleges increased to 89 with 11,669 registered students and 139,955 cumulative graduates (Hsu 1987, 265-66). Many of these highly educated people entered the government and took advanced managerial and technical positions. This led to a fundamental change in the state's elite structure and improved the state's capability in dealing with economic policy management. Specifically, two economists trained at Columbia University worked in the Ministry of Economy and the Central Planning Bureau, and joined in drafting parts of the 1945 documents. They certainly were key figures in contributing liberal elements to the KMT's ideology.

The 1945 policy statements, however, presented only a glimmer of a new vision. This new impulse would not be sufficiently strong to shape postwar economic policies. In the takeover policy after the Japanese surrender, for example, the government immediately placed most of Japanese public and privately owned enterprises under state control. This action alone reduced the proportion of private economic control from 33 to 22 percent.

In Taiwan, evidently, we find sharp conflicts over economic ideology and policy between the first Nationalist governor-general, Ch'en Yi, and local elites. With a large number of confiscated properties, Ch'en Yi made an effort to create a state-dominated economic system based on "four public pillars" (production, transportation, foreign trade, and the monetary system) and a large monopolistic business sector. Japanese private enterprises that had significant Taiwanese investment were converted by the new administration into government-merchant joint-managed businesses. In addition, Ch'en Yi planned to promote cooperativization in small private businesses and farms.

Ch'en Yi frequently stressed his faith in Sun Yat-sen's Doctrine of Livelihood and aspired to realize this idea in Taiwan. Yet what he saw in Sunist ideology was egalitarianism and statism. He also frequently used the principle of "restriction of private capital and development of national capital" to justify his policy.

Ch'en's desire for government control was even reflected in his demands for conformity in dress. In a public address, he proclaimed:

> We need a careful study of what color, what material, and what style of clothes are good looking, convenient, and economical. In accordance with such a study, the clothes should be manufactured on a large scale and then distributed to governmental officials and civilians. The problem of dress uniforms can be reasonably solved. (Ch'en Yi 1946, 117-18)

Extraordinarily, Ch'en Yi always admired the Soviet Union for its success in planned economy and regarded its State Planning Commission as a model for economic planning and control. He contended that the Central Planning Bureau under the Chinese central government should be comparable to the State Planning Commission in the Soviet Union (Ch'en Yi 1946, 25-26). In fact, the Chinese Central Planning Bureau was one of the major organizations involved in drafting the 1945 documents of the "planned free economy." Ch'en, we assume, did not like this new ideological change.

Ch'en Yi's economic policy and ideas sparked strong opposition (Hsu 1987, 101-13). In terms of ideological confrontation, for example, a leading local columnist, Ch'en Fung-yuan, delivered a direct attack on Ch'en Yi's basic policy guidelines:

> This approach has the appearance of conforming to the economic strategy of the Livelihood of the People doctrine, and tries to achieve the goal of increasing national capital and restricting private capital. But this theory is designed for a utopia made up by muddleheaded thinkers, and it can not be realized in the real world. (1946, 16-18)

Moreover, appealing to liberal currents on the mainland, Ch'en Fengyuan urged:

> This is the time for the government to change its wartime control policies and adopt policies of the planned free economy. The government

should help private enterprises develop while repressing speculative tendencies. At the present stage, we should orient the Chinese economy to the road of industrialization. (Ibid.)

On the mainland, Shanghai business circles presented the same type of demands. Placing a large number of industries under state control, they contended, not only wasted resources in poor management but also lost an important source of revenue. They charged that the takeover policy added to the government's financial troubles in dealing with the very difficult situation after the Anti-Japanese War.

In fact, the financial situation was more serious than even most of the government's critics imagined. During the Anti-Japanese War, the government had relied on the printing press as a principal measure to cover its financial deficit. The government further expanded note issues to support military expenditures in the Civil War and administrative expenses in the newly recovered area. These notes circulated at an ever higher velocity throughout the economy. After the collapse of peace talks and the erruption of total civil war, the long-term hidden monetary crisis burst out on 10 February 1947.

To cope with skyrocketing inflation and the dearth of consumer goods in the urban centers, the government on 17 February initiated the Emergency Economic Performance Act. This was an attempt to reestablish the "total control" measures that had been in effect during the Anti-Japanese War. But the government did not have sufficient power or facilities in Shanghai and the newly recovered metropolitan area to implement these draconian regulations. Needless to say, the effort failed and inflation rekindled anew. A series of much more severe economic disasters followed in connection with the military failures and political disorder (Pepper 1980, 95-131; Eastman 1984, 172-203).

But what interests us in the emergency act was the continued recognition that officials "should help the private sector to become a major force for supplying commodities demanded by the market, for the government will sell goods only to adjust market forces" (Ching 1951, 131-32). Still more significant, the act proposed selling public enterprises to private bidders to reduce the government's deficit.

The Shanghai business association regarded the sale of public enterprises as the most productive section of the whole emergency act. But they warned that the government should not keep profitable industries and just give up the nonprofitable ones. The evidence shows that the government did produce a short list of public-managed enterprises it had decided to sell to the private sector (Hsu 1987, 60-62).

On 24 March 1947 the government issued the Economic Reform Act. This measure confronted in a serious way some basic defects in the government's economic policy management. We find for example the following statements:

> Our past problems relate to the absence of any linkage between monetary policy and economic policy as well as the failure to coordinate financial-monetary policies and matters related to production. (Ching 1951, 135)

By emphasizing the importance of production, they appeared to be relaxing their pressure for the "restriction of private capital," a sine qua non for KMT policymakers. For example, we find this statement:

> We have long known about the "restriction of capital" as outlined in the Doctrine of Livelihood, but we should first achieve some minimal level of productive construction before doing anything else. We should first make the people wealthy, and then increase the national wealth. We should first make it possible for the masses to support themselves, and then we will have enough funds to finance our policies. (Ching 1951, 136)

The authors of the reform document also called on the government to make an explicit statement endorsing "the profit-oriented motivation of private entrepreneurs." They presented a new interpretation of Sunist doctrine:

> An economy depends on successful organization. In a society based on a free market economy, its organizational capacities are promoted by the profit motive of private entrepreneurs. The government should take major responsibility for structuring organization so that it can induce the combination of land, labor, and capital in appropriate ways for enhancing production and fulfilling national reconstruction. The economic purpose of the Three Principles doctrine is to search for the best way to achieve happiness and the benefits of livelihood. Our doctrine takes the best features of a free market economy and a planned economy and tries to integrate them. Under such an integrated plan, the government and the people can coordinate their activities and cooperate to find the best division of labor by which to achieve success in a given time frame. (Ching 1951, 148)

In the postwar period, despite these appeals, the KMT government came close to repeating the mistakes it had made in the 1920s. It placed military and political goals ahead of economic and financial ones. A preference for big government and a continued leaning toward egalitarianism also interfered with incorporating social elites and business groups. At least at the level of concept, however, ROC officials began to realize that increased productivity should preceed equal distribution or raising government revenue. And that increased productivity could be more effectively achieved by the use of liberal principles such as entrepreneurship and the market than by a mass movement stimulated by spiritual and moral incentives. Egalitarian goals could be more effectively reached by levying taxes than by restricting private capital.

The Adoption of
"Planned Free Economy" in Taiwan

After the central government moved to Taiwan in 1949, the KMT leaders displayed a strong anticommunist posture that effectively minimized socialist elements and enhanced liberal elements in the party's economic ideology. This switch clearly appeared in an important article entitled "To Conduct the Revolution from a New Beginning," published by Chang Kai-shek's major ideological theorist, T'ao Hsi-sheng, on the eve of the KMT's Party Reform. T'ao seriously charged that the Nationalists had never freed themselves of Communist ideological influence and that the KMT was "infected by the Communist poisons":

> It...has created two propensities within our party: "control" [fung chih] on the one hand and "national management" [kuo ying] on the other. Moreover, it has produced two maneuvers: using the ideas of socialism to strike capitalists, and standing on the position of capitalism to deal with labor. The result is that both capitalists and labor have suffered while only bureaucrats have achieved some quick profits. The confusion in thought leads to confusion in policies; the policy debacle then allows bureaucrats to make manipulations for their own profit. To effect radical reform, we should realize the real value of liberty. We should not unreasonably hate liberalism. (T'ao 1949)

Chiang Kai-shek, too, delivered speeches to expound some new anticommunist ideas. For example, the KMT in the pre-1927 period had often said that "the Doctrine of Livelihood is Communism," thereby stressing similar ultimate aims between Marxian communism and Sun's collectivist doctrines. Now Chiang took pains to distinguish the Doctrine of Livelihood from any similarity to communist goals. He reinterpreted as well some ambiguous ideas, such as the national ownership of land in Sunist ideology. As a top political leader, Chiang also made a serious effort to define and integrate the basic national goals. In the political realm, Chiang defined ultimate national policy goals in terms of "the counterattack against the Mainland and the construction of Taiwan." In fact, once the Nationalist government moved to Taiwan the hundred-mile Taiwan Strait not only protected the island from Communist "liberation," but also prohibited the Nationalists from making any "counterattack." It effectively turned the hot war into the cold war. Because a military offensive was impossible but the reconstruction of Taiwan was achievable under Nationalist rule, Chiang himself came to define the construction of Taiwan as the fundamental work of "anticommunism and resistance to the Soviets." This was a shift away from political unification by means of military force, which had always held the place of pride since the beginning of the Republic. The economy now for the first time was given the first priority.

In defining the aim of economic development, Chiang now upheld "equality and wealth" (*chun fu*) as the ultimate goals for achieving the ideal of Sun's Doctrine of Livelihood. He disallowed "equalization of land right and restriction of capital." Putting "equality and wealth" in the first place marked the ideological transition implied in the Economic Reform Act of 1947. This new policy slogan symbolized that the Nationalists had overcome the dilemma of egalitarianism, which had been a problem from the very beginning of the Republic. Surprisingly, we find that the Chinese Communists used exactly the same slogan in 1984 to present their new economic ideology.

Chiang also offered some evaluations of the performance of economic policy programs. He tended to trust premiers and major economic policy officials to initiate and carry out policies. In the 1950s, President Chiang, Premier Ch'en Ch'eng, economic official Yin Chung-jung, and a few others constituted the core of the power structure in economic policy. "Separation between reigning and ruling," as Chalmers Johnson phrased it, was then firmly established (Hsiung 1981).

After the Party Reform, the KMT government immediately proposed its famous land reform program. This plan called for government purchase of land and its subsequent sale to tenant farmers. Landlords were compensated with shares of stock from four large public enterprises. In the Legislative Yuan, some legislators accused the government of violating Sun's guidelines for restricting private capital. Other legislators and government officials countered by using Sun's ideology to defend the new strategy of endorsing the private sector. Government officials, furthermore, tended to say that they still respected the restriction policy but would rather let people make money and then use tax measures to promote income distribution. "Restriction of private capital" thus was no longer an obstacle to the new economic development strategy (Hsu 1987, 196-203).

The major architect of Taiwan's industrial policy, Yin Chung-jung, made efforts to restore the private cotton textile business withdrawn from Shanghai. He encouraged the growth of local private manufacturing industries. Yin himself exemplified the best of the technocrats since the founding of the Republic. He finished his higher education in 1925. Then he had pursued a varied career in public and private fields, including domestic and foreign trade. In 1945, Yin was premier T. V. Soong's secretary in charge of confidential affairs in economic administration. In this position, Yin probably joined in drafting the part of the 1945 documents issued by the Executive Yuan. After moving to Taiwan, Yin became a promoter of the new "planned free economy."

He maintained that people should "not fear the enlargement of enterprises" and "not fear enterprises making profits" (Yin 1954a). On the other hand, he also advocated the need for government guidance and planning along with free enterprise. The following statement represents his central ideas:

> Under the existing circumstance, Taiwan's industrial development must be carried out as quickly as possible and there should be no waste of resources. These two aims, however, cannot be achieved under a laissez faire economy; their achievement must depend upon the active participation of the government in the economic activities of the island through deliberate plans and its supervision of their execution. In other words, the development of Taiwan's industry should proceed according to plans. But what is meant by plans here is quite different from the planned economy of the Communist totalitarian states, which implies control over all means of production and all economic activities. What I mean is merely that the government, in its position as formulator of an overall plan, decides upon the types and limits of industrial development in a certain period from the standpoint of [which will be] developed first, while the development of certain other industries, which are of less importance, may be temporarily delayed; and the government can also decide to what extent certain industries should be developed within a certain period. Within this broad scheme, the various industries and any unit among them have the fullest freedom of operation. This, therefore, is still a free economic system. (Yin 1954b, 4-11)

Yin was not a KMT member. He had usually avoided official ideology and talked about economic policy in a very practical way. From 1954 onward, however, he became virtually a spokesman for the KMT's economic ideology. At the Revolutionary Practice Academy, the highest KMT cadre training agency, Yin gave lectures to interpret the strategy of Taiwan's economic development in line with the 1945 policy statements and Sun's Doctrine of Livelihood (Yin 1955). This illustrates the convergence of conceptual policy thinking between party and technocrats.

Bibliography

Amsden, Alice H. 1979. Taiwan Economic History: A Case of Etatisme and a Challenge to Dependency Theory. *Modern China* 3 (July).

———. 1985. The State and Taiwan's Economic Development. In *Bringing the State Back In*, edited by Peter B. Evans, Dietrich Rueschemeyer, and Theda Skocpol. Cambridge: Cambridge University Press.

Coble, Parks M. 1980. *The Shanghai Capitalists and the Nationalist Government, 1927-1937.* Cambridge: Harvard University Press.

Ch'en, Feng-yuan. 1946. The Fundamental Problem of Restoring Taiwan Industry (in Chinese). *Taiwan Ping Lun* (Taiwan Commentary), 1 September.

Ch'en, Yi. 1946. Progress and Research. In *Ch'en chan-kuan chih-t'an yen-lun-chi* (Governor-General Ch'en Yi's collected speeches, first year in office). Taipei: Taiwan Provincial High Commissioner's Office.

Ching, Chi Pu, editor. 1951. *Ching-chi wen-t'i tsu-liao hui-pien* (Compilation of documents on economic problems). Taipei.

Eastman, Lloyd E. 1984. *Seeds of Destruction.* Stanford: Stanford University Press.

Fewsmith, Joseph. 1980. The Emergence of Authoritarian Corporatist Rule in the Republic of China: The Changing Pattern of the Business Association in Shanghai. Ph.D. dissertation, University of Chicago.

Hsiung, James C. 1981. *The Taiwan Experience, 1950-1980.* The American Association for Chinese Studies.

Hsu, Chen-Kuo. 1987. The Political Base of Changing Strategy toward Private Enterprise in Taiwan, 1945-1955. Ph.D. dissertation, Ohio State University.

Kuznets, Simon. 1979. Growth and Structural Shifts. In *Economic Growth and Structural Change in Taiwan*, edited by Walter Galenson. Ithaca and London: Cornell University Press.

Pepper, Suzanne. 1980. *Civil War in China.* Berkeley: University of California Press.

T'ao, Hsi-sheng. 1949. To Conduct the Revolution from a New Beginning (in Chinese). *Chung Yang Jih Pao* (Central Daily News), 13-19 December.

Wang, K'e-wen. 1985. The Kuomintang in Transition: Ideology and Factionalism in the "National Revolution," 1927-1932. Ph.D. dissertation, Stanford University.

Winckler, Edwin A. 1981. National, Regional, and Local Politics. In *The Anthropology of Taiwan Society*, edited by Emily A. Ahern and Hill Gates. Stanford: Stanford University Press.

Yin, Chung-jung. 1954a. An Adverse Current in Taiwan Industrialization (in Chinese). *Chung Yang Jih Pao* (Central Daily News), 18 April.

———. 1954b. A Discussion on Industrial Policy for Taiwan. *Industry of Free China* 5 (May).

——. 1955. Problems of Taiwan's Economic Construction (6 April 1955, in Chinese). In *Yin Chung-jung hsien-sheng nien-p'u ch'u-kao* (The primary draft of Yin Chung-jung's biography in chronological order), edited by Shen Yun-lung, 286-318. Taipei: Chuan Chi Wen Hsueh Ts'ung Agency, 1972.

13

Women, Export-Oriented Growth, and the State: The Case of Taiwan

Lucie Cheng
Ping-Chun Hsiung

During the last decade, three areas of scholarship have developed independently of each other: development studies, feminist studies, and studies of the role of the state. Not until recently has there been some cross-fertilization among the three areas (Charlton, Everett, and Staudt 1989). This chapter, drawing on the insights of these fields, is an effort to contribute to the ongoing discussion of the relationship between economic development and the system of male domination. We argue that as patriarchy and capitalism have penetrated the family, enterprises, and the state they have promoted the exploitation of women as low-waged and nonwaged income-generating workers, and as nonwaged domestic workers responsible for the reproduction of labor and for care of the elderly. The twin ideologies that dominate state and society actively promote "the double burden" as an acceptable and even aspired-to woman's role in the service of national development. This role, in turn, is a necessary, although not a sufficient, contributor to the nation's economic advancement in a competitive world system. We will ground our discussion on the period of rapid economic growth in Taiwan from the mid-1960s to the late-1970s and will include more recent data when relevant.

Among the many factors that have been identified as responsible for Taiwan's economic "miracle," perhaps the least controversial is the availability of an elastic and cheap labor supply. Several scholars have pointed out that women are an especially important component of this labor

(Bian 1985; Chou 1989; Diamond 1979; Gallin 1984a, 1984b; Koo 1987; Kung 1983; P. K.-C. Liu 1984; Y.-L. Liu 1985; Tsay 1985). Despite their contributions to the economic growth of Taiwan, women as a group have not benefitted equally in comparison to men. Women are still under-represented in the upper echelons of occupations (Y.-L. Liu 1985, 40), and their average wage continues to be a fraction of their male counterparts' (Bian 1985, 270-71; P. K.-C. Liu 1984, 96). How is this gender difference maintained and reproduced? Research has focused on gender-specific so-cialization patterns, the influence of cultural traditions, and discrimina-tory practices of employers. We attempt to integrate these discussions by examining the role of the state vis-à-vis women and development. We will show how, under the "economy in command" orientation and with the support of a male-dominated civil society, the state manages to en-sure the availability of an elastic and cheap female labor force by per-petuating and institutionalizing a patriarchal, capitalist ideology. The advancement of Taiwan's position in the world system is dependent on the specific use of women's labor as cheap wage workers, unwaged fam-ily workers, and unpaid service-providers.

Women's Labor and Economic Development in Taiwan

Discussions of women's labor and economic development have largely concentrated on female labor force participation and em-ployment. Taiwan is justifiably proud of its record on the quantity and quality of its female work force. In 1951, shortly after the Guomindang (GMD, the Nationalist Party) government relocated to the islands, the male labor force participation rate was 90.0% and the rate for females was 42.1%. Both rates decreased until 1966 when male participation dropped to 81.4% and female to a low of 32.6%. The reasons for these decreases are not entirely clear. Based on age-specific data by sex, P. K.-C. Liu and Hwang (1987) attribute them to rising levels of education, a low eco-nomic growth rate, compulsory military service, high fertility rate, and statistical artifacts due to a change in reporting definition. In any case, the early trend of decline for female labor force participation is generally seen as benign or even to some extent "positive," a result related more to improvement of the quality of labor and intensified childbearing and not so much to traditional gender discrimination. This conclusion masks the fact that negative effects of demographic factors on women's labor force participation are not natural, but are socially produced.

There is no doubt that the expansion of educational opportunities for women has had many beneficial results. Among these has been an improvement in the quality of the female labor force. Unfortunately, more education for women may not mean more gender equality. As Greenhalgh (1985) observes, up to a point the relationship between women's education and the decrease in their labor force participation reflects increased gender inequality. Young women were given the opportunity to finish junior high and high schools before entering the labor force to help their brothers gain more education. The increase in education for women in Taiwan has not increased women's status vis-à-vis men. Instead, it has resulted in higher returns to their families from their exploitation. Parents tended to increase investment in their daughters' education just enough to enable the child to gain a well-paid job.

The negative relationship between fertility and labor force participation observed by P. K.-C. Liu and Hwang (1987) is more a social construct than a physical inevitability. For example, the requirement that women leave the labor force for an extended period to assume responsibility for child care is a "social" rather than a "biological" one. By tying rewards exclusively to individual productivity while ignoring societal needs, what appear to be gender-neutral capitalist employment practices actually punish women.

Elasticity in Women's Labor Force Participation

Most discussions of gender and labor force participation in Taiwan begin with 1966, when the impact of economic restructuring was first reflected in the labor market. From that year on, women's labor force participation rate, despite its zigzag pattern, has shown an upward trend. By 1987, 3.1 million, or 38.1% of the total labor force, were women (Directorate-General of Budget 1989, 5). In comparison to 1966, when 32.6% of all females 15 years and older were in the labor force, the percentage for 1987 was 46.5. Three characteristics of women's labor force participation support the argument that women are especially important to Taiwan's economic growth: the timing of the increase, its long-term growth pattern, and women's low wage level.

The sharpest rise in women's labor force participation occurred between 1966 and 1973, the period marked by labor-intensive, export-

TABLE 1   Labor Force Participation and Unemployment by Gender, Taiwan, 1965-1987

Year	LFP rate[a]		Growth rate[b]		Unemployment rate	
	Male	Female	Male	Female	Male	Female
1965	82.6	33.1	2.1	0.8	2.3	5.9
1966	81.4	32.6	2.1	2.0	2.3	4.9
1967	80.9	33.7	3.0	7.5	1.8	3.5
1968	80.2	34.4	2.8	5.9	1.6	2.0
1969	79.2	35.4	2.9	7.0	1.6	2.6
1970	78.9	35.5	3.9	4.2	1.5	2.2
1971	78.4	35.4	3.5	3.7	1.5	2.1
1972	77.0	37.1	2.2	8.9	1.2	2.1
1973	77.1	41.5	3.4	16.0	1.1	1.7
1974	78.2	40.2	4.9	0.3	1.3	2.0
1975	77.6	38.6	2.7	-0.8	2.1	3.1
1976	77.1	37.6	2.7	0.8	1.6	2.1
1977	77.8	39.3	4.2	8.1	1.7	2.0
1978	78.0	39.2	4.5	3.2	1.6	1.9
1979	77.9	39.2	2.5	3.4	1.2	1.5
1980	77.1	39.3	1.3	3.0	1.1	1.5
1981	76.8	38.8	2.2	1.7	1.2	1.6
1982	76.5	39.3	2.3	4.1	2.3	2.3
1983	76.4	42.1	1.8	9.6	2.7	2.7
1984	76.1	43.3	2.0	5.2	2.4	2.5
1985	75.5	43.5	1.7	2.8	2.9	2.9
1986	75.2	45.5	2.0	7.1	2.8	2.5
1987	75.2	46.5	2.2	4.4	2.0	2.0

Notes: a. Percentage of LFP.
             b. Increases in number of workers in labor market.
Source: Directorate-General (1988), 52-53.

oriented industrialization. During that period, as Table 1 shows, the female labor force participation rate rose from 32.6% to 41.5%, while male rates remained relatively stable with some decline. This trend reflects a change in the economic policy of Taiwan which in turn is conditioned by the transformation of the international division of labor.

Massive restructuring of capitalism in the mid-1960s created an opportunity for peripheral and semiperipheral countries to seek advancement in the world system. Taiwan was able to mobilize its resources to take advantage of this opportunity. Adequate foreign investment and domestic accumulation, enough state autonomy from both the constraints of world economy and powerful domestic interest groups, political stability, and access to markets provided the conditions for Taiwan to develop a viable economic policy based on export (Crane 1982, Evans and Pang 1989, Winckler and Greenhalgh 1988). The pursuit of labor-intensive, export-oriented development required a particular kind of labor force, one that was relatively large in number, flexible in flow, and inexpensive. Female labor, for reasons that we will discuss later, fits these requirements especially well. The ready supply of female labor has reduced labor costs and increased Taiwan's competitiveness in the world market (Bian 1985, Gallin 1990). In addition, the use of female labor helps to ease the impact of inflation in core countries such as the United States (Mies 1986). The elasticity of female labor relative to male labor is indicated by the greater fluctuation in women's participation rates over time. In contrast with male rates, female rates are more sensitive to changes in the world economy (Chiang and Ku 1985, 89). The rise and decline of female rates corresponds to business cycles in Taiwan (Chou 1989, 437-38).

Table 1 shows the difference in annual growth rates of male and female labor force participation. While male rates hover between 1.3 in 1980 and 4.9 in 1974, female rates not only have a much wider range, but also show a much wider zigzag pattern. The growth of women in the labor force peaked in 1973, when the rate reached 16%. This increase was due to labor-intensive industrialization. The growth rate, however, dropped to 0.3% in 1974 and reached a negative of -0.8% in 1975 when Taiwan's economy was severely affected by the oil crisis. Afterward, it took almost a decade for women's participation rate to reach the same average level of growth as before the economic recession. A comparison of the unemployment rates between women and men shows similarly greater elasticity for women (Table 1). There are more frequent fluctuations in women's rates and the difference between each change is generally larger.

Women's employment is not only more susceptible to the business cycle, it is also more affected by individual and family life-cycle events. Age, marital status, and number of children play a more significant role in determining women's than men's labor force participation. Women tend to withdraw from the marketplace between age 25 to 34; that is, after the worker's marriage and the birth of her first child. They reenter the labor market after 35 as their family responsibilities lighten. A great majority leave the labor market entirely after 55 years of age, perhaps to care for the elderly members of the family. Males, on the other hand, stay in the job market until they reach retirement age (Table 2).

The differential impact of marital status is more obvious when we compare female and male rates in Table 3. While gender makes a difference in labor force participation, the difference is the smallest for single

TABLE 2   Labor Force Participation Rate by Age and Gender, Selected Years

Age	1966		1974		1983	
	Male	Female	Male	Female	Male	Female
15-19	54.6	54.7	49.9	52.4	76.4	39.2
20-24	84.0	46.6	78.7	54.3	36.2	60.9
25-29	97.3	28.9	96.6	36.7	75.9	46.5
30-34	98.1	28.7	98.8	37.8	95.3	46.9
35-39	98.3	33.2	98.8	53.5	98.1	48.9
40-44	96.9	30.6	98.5	47.9	98.1	48.0
45-49	95.1	27.4	96.1	41.4	96.1	52.9
50-54	89.1	20.0	89.0	32.6	89.8	35.0
55-59	71.4	11.7	82.8	19.4	79.7	26.8
60-64	46.2	6.0	52.7	7.0	60.2	15.6
65+	17.2	1.5	11.8	1.0	15.4	2.7

Source: Tsay (1985), 303.

persons. For those who are married, male rates are more than double those of females for all age groups. The presence of children under six years of age greatly reduces the likelihood of married women's labor force participation (Y.-L. Liu 1985, 76-77). When employment and promotion rules are developed with male workers in mind, women are disadvantaged because of interruptions caused by domestic responsibilities. Women's more frequent and early exits from the labor market for reproductive and caring purposes perpetuate their exploitation as cheap labor.

TABLE 3   Percentage of LFP for Male and Female by Marital Status and Age, Taiwan, 1984

Age	Male			Female		
	Single	Married	Divorced/ widowed	Single	Married	Divorced/ widowed
15-19	30.2	90.8	--	33.4	30.7	100.0
20-24	70.5	97.3	100.0	76.8	34.1	91.3
25-34	91.2	98.9	94.7	86.1	41.8	71.5
35-44	89.0	98.4	96.2	76.0	50.0	63.2
45-54	83.3	94.6	90.3	61.5	39.5	43.3
55-64	50.3	75.4	56.7	42.6	21.8	20.5
65+	10.4	18.0	8.5	32.4	4.3	1.7

Source: Liu (1985), 25.

TABLE 4 Gender Distribution by Industry, Taiwan, Selected Years

	1966		1970		1980		1988	
	M	F	M	F	M	F	M	F
Agriculture, etc.	42.6	46.0	35.1	40.6	20.2	18.1	15.2	10.6
Mining	2.0	0.4	2.7	0.8	0.9	0.3	0.5	0.2
Manufacturing	17.2	17.5	19.7	21.9	29.3	39.9	31.7	39.0
Utilities	1.0	0.2	1.0	0.3	0.6	0.1	0.6	0.1
Construction	4.8	0.6	7.0	0.7	11.7	2.0	10.6	1.9
Commerce	11.4	13.7	14.0	16.1	15.0	17.9	17.7	22.5
Transportation, etc.	5.9	1.7	7.0	1.9	7.7	2.3	7.3	2.1
Finance	15.2	19.9	13.6	17.8	2.0	2.5	2.9	3.8
Services	--	--	--	--	12.8	16.8	13.7	19.9
N	2,702	945	3,121	1,425	4,357	2,191	4,946	2,986

Note: Numbers (N) are in thousands, for age 15 and older.

Source: 1966, 1970, 1980: P. K.-C. Liu and Hwang (1987), p. 100; 1988: Directorate-General (1988), pp. 8-9.

Women's Labor as Cheap Labor

Just how cheap has women's labor been in Taiwan? We will examine both the difference between male and female wages, and women's wages alone. The Taiwan government has publicized the cheap wages and docility of its labor force to attract foreign investment. A number of scholars have emphasized low wage and lack of benefits as characteristic of female labor (Cumings 1987, Deyo 1989, Kung 1983). In fact, many would argue that these features are the raison d'être of female employment in capitalism. As tables 4 and 5 show, after two decades of development, women workers are still concentrated in the most labor-intensive industries, where wages are typically low (see Table 4), as well as at the lower end of the occupational ladder of all industries (see Table 5).

As in other countries, women's wages in Taiwan are only a fraction of their male counterparts'. In fact, the gap between male and female earnings not only has persisted but, in some occupations and industries, has widened over the past two decades (P. K.-C. Liu 1984, 95-98; P. K.-C. Liu and Hwang 1987; Y.-L. Liu 1985, 56-66). Table 6 shows that in five out of nine industries there has been a deterioration of women's wages relative to men's during the past decade. The gains in wage equality observed in the 1970s had mostly eroded by the 1980s. Using 1980 data, P. K.-C. Liu

TABLE 5   Occupational Distribution by Gender, Taiwan, Selected Years

		1970		1980		1984		1988[e]	
		M	F	M	F	M	F	M	F
Professional &	(a)	0.3	—	0.3	—	0.3	—		
technical	(b)	2.6	0.6	2.4	0.6	2.8	0.8		
workers	(c)	9.4	12.0	11.0	14.5	10.9	14.3		
	(d)	22.8	23.8	26.9	33.1	26.2	32.6	6.2	7.8
Administrative	(a)	0.1	—	—	—	—	—		
& managerial	(b)	9.3	1.0	2.6	0.1	2.5	0.2		
workers	(c)	5.3	1.6	1.1	0.2	1.1	0.2		
	(d)	6.8	2.0	1.8	0.3	1.6	0.2	1.3	0.2
Clerical	(a)	0.5	0.3	0.6	0.5	0.5	0.8		
workers	(b)	6.3	8.3	14.6	13.6	14.4	14.5		
	(c)	13.0	12.8	15.6	26.9	15.3	26.4		
	(d)	19.7	14.7	21.4	21.4	20.1	22.4	11.5	20.3
Traders	(a)	0.1	—	—	—	—	—		
	(b)	4.7	4.5	3.1	0.9	3.0	0.8		
	(c)	32.8	38.5	30.7	30.2	31.7	30.3		
	(d)	0.9	1.2	0.7	1.1	1.0	14.1	14.4	15.1
Service	(a)	—	—	0.1	0.3	—	0.2		
workers	(b)	1.6	1.6	2.4	1.1	2.1	1.1		
	(c)	11.8	21.8	14.6	20.3	15.3	22.3		
	(d)	22.3	39.7	22.6	27.6	23.4	30.5	7.3	11.8
Agricultural &	(a)	98.0	99.5	98.4	99.0	98.4	98.7		
related	(b)	1.0	0.6	—	—	—	—		
workers	(c)	0.6	—	0.1	—	0.1	—		
	(d)	0.7	—	0.2	—	0.3	—	15.1	10.6
Production,	(a)	1.1	0.2	0.6	0.3	0.6	0.2		
transportation,	(b)	74.5	83.3	74.9	93.6	75.2	82.6		
& related	(c)	27.2	13.2	26.9	7.8	25.6	6.4		
workers	(d)	26.8	18.6	26.4	16.5	27.4	13.2	44.1	34.2

Notes: a. Agriculture
b. Manufacturing
c. Service
d. Commerce
e. All industries
Source: P. K.-C. Liu and Hwang (1987), 140-41; Directorate-General (1988).

TABLE 6   Proportion of Average Monthly Female Wage to Male Wage by
Industry, Taiwan

	1973	1978	1984	1988
Agriculture	—	56.8	51.9	55.0
Mining	37.2	65.8	53.6	55.2
Manufacture	54.4[a]	61.0	61.1	57.6
Utilities	68.5[a]	75.1	74.0	81.6
Construction	65.4	75.8	68.0	71.9
Commerce	—	72.6	68.0	68.4
Transport	71.7	71.2	75.0	76.7
Financial services	—	59.2	68.0	65.1
Social and personal	71.3	72.7	75.7	72.8

Note: a. For manufacturing and utilities, the percentages are calculated from data for 1972.
Source: 1973: Directorate-General (1974), 682; 1978 and 1984: Y.-L. Liu (1985), 61-62; 1988:
Directorate-General (1988), 90-91.

(1984) found that the wage differentials cannot be explained by human capital variables.

Gender discrimination is widely recognized in Taiwan, although not widely condemned. A study of employment advertisements in newspapers reveal that males are preferred for higher paying jobs, while for lower paying jobs ads often stipulate that "only females may apply" (*Funu Xinzhi* 59, 1987, p. 8). The state on the one hand proclaims that men and women are equal, but on the other condones gender discrimination in its own employment practice (Zheng and Bo 1987). Women are excluded from participating in civil service examinations for certain prestigious government jobs, such as high-level jobs in the customs department, the diplomatic services, international journalism, and the labor department. For some civil service jobs, the number of women cannot exceed a certain quota. For example, in 1985, the civil service examination for consular personnel was slated to admit fifty persons, but the public was informed that no more than seven would be women (Zheng and Bo 1987, 8). When confronted with these and other discriminatory practices, government officials often respond by saying that it is better for women and for society if women concentrate on what they do best. For example, the Minister of Interior proclaimed publicly that women should take pride in freeing their husband from family worries and not be so concerned about whether or not they themselves can become department heads (*Funu Xinzhi* 5, 1982, pp. 13-14). The labor force participation and employment rates overestimate the progress women have made in remunerative work since both include a large number of unpaid family workers, most of whom are female. As Table 7 indicates, although unpaid work done by

TABLE 7 Percentage Distribution of Women and Men as Unpaid Family
Workers, Selected Industries, 1966-1986

		Agriculture		Manufacturing		Commerce		Services	
		M	F	M	F	M	F	M	F
1966	(a)	28.7	74.9	4.4	12.1	8.3	41.6	2.0	7.2
	(b)	48.8	51.2	48.6	51.4	31.9	68.1	34.9	65.1
1971	(a)	23.0	78.9	2.8	9.7	8.2	43.2	2.0	5.7
	(b)	38.4	61.6	32.3	67.7	27.0	73.0	36.5	63.5
1976	(a)	20.9	71.4	2.5	4.7	6.6	36.3	1.3	4.6
	(b)	38.0	62.0	44.6	55.4	26.5	73.5	34.2	65.8
1981	(a)	16.1	65.8	2.4	4.6	6.2	36.3	1.4	5.2
	(b)	37.1	62.9	43.1	56.9	22.0	78.0	28.6	71.4
1986	(a)	16.5	67.3	1.9	5.3	6.6	36.3	1.4	5.8
	(b)	34.7	65.3	30.7	69.3	19.9	80.1	22.5	77.5

Notes: a. Proportion of total male/female employed who are unpaid.
         b. Proportion of total unpaid workers who are male/female.
Source: Chou (1989), 450-57.

males and females has declined, there has been an increase in the proportion of unpaid work done by females since 1966. In every industry, the
proportion of unpaid female workers exceeds that of their male counterpart. Among unpaid family workers, women exceed men by a large margin. What labor can be cheaper than unpaid labor?

The expansion of women's paid and unpaid income-generating labor
is directly tied to the state's export-oriented growth strategy. Fiscal and
tax policies favoring firms willing to export (*Directory of Taiwan* 1963, 164-
74; Yu 1981) provided incentives for families to send their women to
work or to respond to the state-sponsored "living-room factories" program to take advantage of family and neighborhood female labor. By
linking domestic and paid work in the same space, women's labor was
intensified and their work days lengthened. The increase in women's labor force participation and employment does not necessarily indicate an
improvement in women's lives, nor does it indicate a rise in women's
status. On the contrary, it may simply reflect an intensification of
women's exploitation resulting from the addition of nondomestic employment with meager reward to the burden of domestic work. Women's

increased employment is a requirement for the survival of capitalism; it is not to be confused with a victory in gender equality.

Women, the Sex Industry, and the State

A n often ignored area of women's labor that has contributed signifi-cantly to capital accumulation in Taiwan is their sexual labor. Dis-cussions on this topic are quite numerous, but most have focused on its morality and the physical exploitation of women, not on its economic role. Since the 1950s, Taiwan has been considered a haven for male tour-ists. In addition to registered brothels, commercial sexual services under various guises are widely available. These include barber shops, bath houses, massage parlors, bars, coffee houses, and restaurants, some of which are conveniently labeled by the government as *teding* or *tezhong yingye* or specialized businesses. Table 8 shows that while the number of brothels declined after peaking in 1967, the number of *Jiujia* or "restau-rants with waitresses" more than doubled during the same period. Un-fortunately, data on these specialized businesses are no longer published, although it is widely known where one can buy sexual services (*Funu Xinzhi 66*, 1987, p. 10). Most recently, a new type of sex business has come into being that is graphically referred to as the "beef market."

Two conditions greatly facilitated the growth of the sex industry in Taiwan and other developing countries: American military presence and the United States' initiative to tie tourism to Third World development. One of the well-known but relatively unexplored consequences of the Korean War and the Vietnam War is the increase of the sex trade in Asia. Used as favorite R&R sites for American soldiers, cities in Taiwan, South Korea, Thailand, and other Southeast Asian countries became lucrative markets for the exploitation of women's sexual labor (Kim 1987, Truong 1990). The infrastructures developed for the sex industry continued to serve a burgeoning tourist trade after the wars ended.

The development of Third World tourism is closely related to the global political economy (Truong 1990). Truong argues that in order to save the heavy investment banks had made in aircraft industries in the 1950s, the U.S. government began to promote tourism as a development strategy for the Third World, especially for Asian countries. Tourism was hailed as a peace-maintaining, harmony-producing industry. But the po-litical and cultural functions of tourism were not enough to induce devel-oping countries to spend millions of dollars to buy passenger airplanes, construct luxurious hotels, and build other tourism infrastructure. After a

TABLE 8   Number of Sexually Oriented Businesses in Taiwan, 1946-1973

	Hotel	Tea & coffee room	Restaurant w/waitress	Cabaret	Brothel
1946	866	—	—	11	216
1947	969	—	—	—	—
1948	932	—	—	—	—
1949	902	—	—	—	—
1950	801	—	31	—	—
1951	842	346	56	—	—
1952	892	546	88	—	—
1953	961	786	86	—	—
1954	1,093	930	54	—	—
1955	1,137	930	52	—	—
1956	1,251	1,001	—	—	—
1957	1,326	984	—	—	249
1958	1,479	1,043	—	—	349
1959	1,576	1,030	—	3	424
1960	1,671	963	—	8	463
1961	1,782	1,002	—	11	476
1962	1,897	793	—	15	453
1963	2,014	825	—	17	412
1964	2,143	801	—	27	529
1965	2,272	859	—	32	509
1966	2,403	756	—	31	489
1967	2,949	765	76	46	636
1968	2,662	629	163	33	452
1969	2,802	596	449	25	384
1970	2,864	568	429	25	355
1971	2,916	511	372	25	337
1972	2,974	485	342	25	319
1973	2,997	451	407	25	311

Source: Directorate-General (1974), 188-89.

concerted effort of the United States, tourist projects became eligible for financial and technical assistance from the international development programs of the World Bank, the United Nations, and other international agencies. It was the attraction of tourism as a way to gain foreign currency that prompted many Asian countries to use tourism as a development strategy.

The Taiwan government began to promote tourism in the mid-1950s, immediately following the conclusion of the Korean War. Since then, heated debates over its efficacy have periodically taken place in the Provincial Assembly and among the populace. Supporters of tourism combine economic, political, and cultural arguments. They point to its potential in earning foreign exchange, attracting foreign investment, and expanding foreign trade (Deng 1975, 402). Politically, tourists are described as valuable messengers who can tell the world about the progress in Taiwan and therefore raise its international status. In addition, tourism can promote Chinese traditional culture (Zhou 1966). Opponents, however, argue that the net economic advantage of tourism has not been demonstrated, and the negative social effects overshadow all the other advantages (Y. Li 1987, Qu 1984). Women's organizations and human rights activists have accused the government of colluding with sex traders by not enforcing existing laws or passing new legislation that would legalize prostitution rather than making invidious and useless distinctions between "public" or registered sexual laborers and "private" or underground ones (*Funu Xinzhi* 1986-87). Even supporters admit that due to the profit-seeking motives of some businesses, tourism has led to the burgeoning of the sex trade and has "affected the moral fiber of Taiwan" (Zhan 1966, 59). In fact, the government keeps the price of sexual labor low by prohibiting women in the "specialized businesses" from forming unions on the grounds that their occupations "violate the good mores of society" (*Funu Xinzhi* 69, 1988, p. 14).

Tourism is an "experience commodity" that necessitates the commoditization of personal services (Truong 1990). Tourists are to be made to feel welcome and "at home." Promotional campaigns endorsed by government agencies and tourist industries attempted to build a market by focusing on aspects of hospitality, such as female submissiveness, caring, and nurturing, as well as sexual temptation (*Directory of Taiwan* 1963, 178-80). Tourist booklets distributed at government handicraft stores and offices contain advertisements that magnify the sexual appeals of Taiwan women. Operators of sex package tours give detailed descriptions in words and pictures of the kinds of sexual services available and their costs to show that foreign visitors can enjoy uninhibited sex. A government publication, praising the achievements of Taiwan since its recovery from Japanese occupation, highlighted the "inexhaustible sources of pleasure" available (Deng 1975, 403-04).

To combat sexually transmitted diseases, which would threaten the tourist business as well as embarrass the government, a number of laws were promulgated to control prostitution and other sex trades. These laws take two general approaches: to make sexual contacts safe by requiring prostitutes to obtain and display health certificates, and to limit the number of specialized businesses by increasing the licensing fees and tax. Although neither approach has been successful, these laws did provide an official guide to relatively safe sex, and increased the revenue of the state. The link between women's sexual labor and foreign trade is a popular theme among well-known local writers (Huang 1981). While we have no way to determine the specific dollar contribution of the sex industry to the economy, it is certain that it forms an important part of the tourist revenue. Tourism is included in economic discussions as an export; its revenue ranks fourth to sixth of all exports during the last two decades (Deng 1975, 402). Table 9 shows the increase in tourist revenues from 1956 to 1973, the period of export-led growth.

As Table 9 also shows, the number of tourists has jumped from fifteen thousand to more than 824 thousand during the same period. The increase is largely due to the influx of Japanese tourists. In 1957, Americans outnumbered all tourists, with 70%; by 1973, American tourists comprised less than 20% while Japanese made up 72% of all tourists (Directorate General 1974, 516-17). Japanese males are notorious as consumers of sexual tours, and their behavior has been the target of continuing demonstrations by Japanese women as well as women in other Asian countries (*Funu Xinzhi* 1987, Kim 1987, Truong 1990). When the International Lions Club met in Taipei, newspapers splashed pages of materials on where visitors can go to "buy spring." Taiwan women demonstrated with banners in Chinese, English, and Japanese: "Welcome to Taiwan for Friendship, But Not for Sex Tours" (*Funu Xinzhi* 62, 1987, p. 6).

Traditional ideology of self-sacrifice and submissiveness plays an important role in the sex trade, as girls "volunteer" or are forced by their real or adoptive parents to trade sexual labor for family survival or for the education of their male siblings (*Funu Xinzhi* 47, 1986, pp. 2-3; X. Lu 1986). While no official figures are available, women workers in the sex industry were popularly estimated at more than 300,000 in 1989, including those brought from Southeast Asia and girls as young as 11 from local ethnic groups. Their customers include a large number of overseas Chinese and foreign visitors looking to satisfy their sexual appetites at an affordable price, and more importantly, with state protection. Women's sexual labor, like women's labor in other areas, is consciously exploited in Taiwan's strategy for national development. It functions as an exotic commodity for "tourist attraction and helps to fill airplane seats and hotel rooms. National accounts benefit from taxes on accommodation, food, drinks and services. Unlike their flesh, the contribution of prostitutes' labor to the process of accumulation remains invisible" (Truong 1990, 128). The state condemns the women who are engaged in this trade and periodically arrests those who lack official certification, yet the state also encourages the continuation of exploitation by treating sexual labor as a tourist attraction.

TABLE 9   Tourist Industry in Taiwan

	Total number of tourists	Growth rate (%)	Total revenue from tourism (US$)	Growth rate (%)
1956	14,974	—	935,876	—
1957	18,159	21.3	1,134,938	21.3
1958	16,709	8.0	1,044,313	-8.0
1959	19,328	15.7	1,208,000	15.7
1960	23,636	22.3	1,477,251	22.3
1961	42,205	78.7	2,637,914	78.7
1962	52,304	23.9	3,269,000	23.9
1963	72,024	37.7	7,202,000	120.3
1964	95,481	32.6	10,345,000	43.6
1965	133,666	40.0	18,245,000	76.4
1966	182,948	36.9	30,353,000	66.4
1967	253,248	38.4	42,016,000	38.4
1968	301,770	19.2	53,271,000	26.8
1969	371,473	23.1	56,055,000	5.2
1970	472,452	26.9	81,720,000	45.8
1971	539,755	12.2	110,000,000	34.6
1972	580,033	7.5	128,707,000	17.0
1973	824,393	42.1	245,882,000	91.0
1974	819,821	-0.6	278,402,000	13.2
1975	853,140	4.1	359,358,000	29.1
1976	1,008,126	18.2	466,077,000	29.7
1977	1,110,182	10.0	527,492,000	13.2
1978	1,270,977	14.5	608,000,000	15.3
1979	1,340,382	5.5	919,000,000	51.2
1980	1,393,254	3.9	988,000,000	7.5
1981	1,409,465	1.2	1,080,000,000	9.3
1982	1,419,178	0.7	953,000,000	-11.7
1983	1,457,404	2.7	990,000,000	3.9
1984	1,516,138	4.0	1,066,000,000	7.7
1985	1,451,659	-4.3	963,000,000	-9.7
1986	1,610,385	10.9	1,333,000,000	38.4

Source: Directorate-General (1987), p. 397. Revenue income for 1956-61 from Taiwan
Shengzhengfu Xinwenchu (1965), 18-32.

Women's Unwaged Domestic Labor

National statistics do not reveal the necessary but monotonous, fragmented, and time-consuming domestic work that most women do without wage. Studies continue to show that men do not participate in household labor to any appreciable degree in most societies, including Taiwan (Y.-H. Lu 1984, Miller and Garrison 1982). Those who share this work with women do so selectively and reluctantly. Taiwan women, socialized to believe that domestic work is part and parcel of womanhood, may complain, but they do not generally expect help from their menfolks.

What is the relationship between women's unwaged domestic labor and economic development? At the most basic level, women, as housewives and mothers, reproduce the labor force that creates growth. But women's unwaged domestic work is more than the physical reproduction of labor. Surveys indicate that housewives are the principal agents of domestic consumption. In Taipei, household expenditures in 59.4% of all families are managed by the wife, and another 14.7% by other women in the family (*Funu Xinzhi* 16, 1983, pp. 6-7). The model of the middle-class housewife in Taiwan involves a highly developed consumption style, which provides a market for ever-increasing commodities and services. It is no wonder that consumer education is almost exclusively directed toward females, and that women are beginning to realize their potential to influence the behavior of large corporations.

Through the maintenance of the family, women provide stability and emotional support to its members. Chinese tradition views women's role in maintaining harmony at home and in the neighborhood as critical to national development (Diamond 1973, P. K.-C. Liu and Hwang 1987). Both Taiwan and the People's Republic of China continue to promote this image through mass campaigns, education, and media indoctrination.

The heated debates in the 1970s in Europe and in the United States among scholars and politicians regarding "wages for housework" point to the economic value of this unpaid work (Kaluzynska 1980). Unpaid domestic work became a public issue in Taiwan when *Funu Xinzhi*, the leading feminist magazine, reported in 1983 that the economic value of a housewife in middle-income families was about NT$35,500 a month, more than the salary of an associate professor in a university (vol. 16, 1983:17). This estimate only includes cooking, laundering, cleaning, caring for the elderly, and tutoring children twice a week. Excluded are the economic value of household management and consumption-related labor typical of housewives such as shopping for food, clothing, and daily necessities. More recently, the magazine *Money* (*Qian*) calculates that, depending on the number and ages of children, a middle-class wife has to earn a minimum of NT$18,620 to $36,620 per month to make her employment outside worthwhile (*Qian* 1990, 162). The cost to the family of having the housewife employed outside for wages is staggering when we consider that the median monthly income of college-educated women is NT$17,146.

Various types of caring, such as child care, care for the elderly, and care for the infirm performed by women without pay reduce the cost of social welfare for the state. These savings have been especially significant for Taiwan since it has allocated a large percentage of its resources to security and defense. Women's unpaid domestic labor frees capital to be directed toward more productive investment as defined by the state.

It has been argued that the benefits of economic development will trickle down to women. However, the experience of advanced countries gives us little confidence in this prediction. Economic development has not reduced the burden of women's household labor as expected. A male-dominated state apparatus does not treat women's interest as a high priority. Machines and services considered by women to be most useful to alleviate their workload are not easily accessible in developing countries. When household mechanization occurs, it changes the way some housework is done, but does not greatly reduce the time spent in doing housework. The time that is reduced in an area of work often is taken up by other housework, or by a rise in housework standards.

Mechanization and commercialization of housework create opportunities for waged work for all women but produce different consequences for women of different classes. Working-class women will make the machines and provide the household services to allow middle-class women to seek better employment. Both classes of women are increasingly required to earn a wage to prevent the family from slipping from its standard of living. While middle-class women will gain some alleviation from their domestic responsibilities, working-class women who cannot afford to buy the machines or hire others to perform the services will continue to be burdened. Data from Taiwan indicate that among married female professional and managerial workers, more than 15 percent rely on servants for child care (Y.-H. Lu 1984, 367).

Economic growth has created more leisure, but this leisure has not led men to share domestic work with women. In fact, it is women's unpaid domestic labor that creates leisure time for men. Studies have shown that employed men have more leisure time than both employed women and full-time housewives (Waring 1988, 163). Men prefer to spend their leisure with other men. In the United States they drink, play cards, attend sports events, go camping or fishing, or watch TV. In Taiwan, men may engage in other activities, but it is doubtful that they will do housework.

The flexible nature of domestic labor is especially conducive to exploitation. Much housework does not have to be done in a specific amount of time because the standards are variable: high or low standards of cleanliness, ironed or unironed clothes, and so forth. Therefore, it does not prohibit women from taking on either unpaid family income-producing work, or waged labor. In other words, it allows women to be doubly burdened without appearing so. The blind acceptance of a patriarchal concept of labor defined by men and based on the characteristics of male labor prevents the recognition of a large portion of women's labor as labor.

Waged Work and Unwaged Work: The Continuity of Women's Work

Mies (1986) argues that we are accustomed to viewing women's work with concepts developed on the basis of men's work under capitalism. Most men work for a certain number of hours a day, away from home, and uninterrupted by household concerns. Men are paid regularly and their jobs are to a varying extent protected by the state. Women's work does not have the same characteristics. Women are primarily household workers, although an increasing number are engaged in income-generating activities. Many work in the informal economy, insecure and unprotected. Their work is continuous and with frequent interruptions, but the interruptions are an integral part of women's work. It is misleading to think of women's work with categories developed for the accounting of men's work. Thus feminist scholars have argued the need for a new concept of labor built upon the concrete labor of women (Beneria 1982, Mies 1986, Waring 1988). Some case studies of the working lives of women in Taiwan's export economy may be helpful in this construction.

Women's daily work schedules are arranged around their familial responsibilities as wife, mother, and daughter-in-law.

1. May-cheng comes to paint glasses at the small factory around 8 in the morning after her husband leaves for work. Around 11, she goes back to her apartment, which is five doors down the alley, to prepare lunch for him. After her husband leaves for work around 1 o'clock, she comes back to work until 5:30 or 6 when she goes home to prepare for dinner. She continues to paint the glasses at home after dinner while she waits for water to do the family's laundry or other chores. She doesn't go to sleep until after midnight.

2. A-hsia and her sister-in-law share the responsibility of caring for their father-in-law. They each take care of him for 15 days per month. During the half month of A-hsia's turn, she gets up around 6 and prepares both breakfast and lunch for him before she comes to work because he insists on eating his noon meal at 11:45. A-hsia goes home at 12 o'clock to eat the leftovers. She comes back to the factory at 12:50 and goes home to cook around 5:10. After dinner, she comes back to work in the factory until 9.

3. This week is A-chou's turn to stay at home and look after her father-in-law who has been confined to bed for the last 10 years. She can only work in the factory from 1 to 3 when he takes his nap. She rushes into the factory, squats on the floor, and removes as many rubber bands from the drawers as she possibly can. During the whole time, the only word she utters is "good-bye" when she leaves.

Women often have to compromise their waged labor outside the family with their unwaged labor in the family business. When a man is thinking of getting married, he calculates how much he has to spend for the engagement party, bride price, and wedding, and how much of his investment will be recovered when his wife joins the labor force.

When I congratulated Lin, an owner of a factory who just got engaged, he talked about his bride-to-be: "I don't intend to get a decorative vase. I also don't need sex; if I want sex, I can get cheap sex on the street. I heard that she is very good at bookkeeping. People say that she is really thrifty and hardworking too. The other day, I ran into her in the market, she was riding a 125 cc motorcycle. You know, she is really physically very strong." When I asked him how much he had to spend in total, he said it will be about NT$400,000. "It is worth it. People think I have a pretty good deal, you know," Lin said.

It is quite understandable why many women quit their jobs in the factory after their marriage; the totality of their labor, for income and for reproduction, is required by the family as unwaged labor.

Lu finished elementary school and didn't want to continue because she didn't think she could pass the unified entrance examination for junior high. She went to work in a garment factory in the Tan-zi Export Processing Zone for more than 10 years. Her marriage was arranged by her parents. She had to quit her job because the factory run by her husband's family needed her labor. She didn't get paid working in the family's factory. It was only last year when the family business slowed down that Lu start looking for jobs outside. Even after Lu found a job in the neighborhood, she still had to compensate for her missed unwaged labor in the family factory by coming up with a special work arrangement:

> Lu's schedule starts around 7 in the morning. She has to get ready for work by 7:15. Before leaving home for waged work, she first works in the family factory for 30 minutes. She and her two sisters-in-law take weekly turns to cook for workers in the family factory. Lu works for wages in Xin-liang, a hardware store, from 8 to 12 during the weeks when it is not her turn to cook lunch, and returns at 1 p.m. In other weeks she leaves Xin-liang at 11 and gets back at 12:30 instead of at 1 p.m. when other workers come back from their lunch. After she finishes work at the hardware store, she resumes work in the family factory again from 4:30 to 5:30. Lu is paid hourly by the hardware store because she does not work 40 hours every week.

The complex and overlapping work schedule reflects the integration of women's productive and reproductive roles and their waged and un-waged labor.

How is the continuing exploitation of women's labor in all its com-plexity maintained, and the resulting gender inequality perpetuated? What role does the state play?

The Capitalist Patriarchal State of Taiwan

Several scholars have argued that the GMD state of Taiwan has been and continues to be a patriarchal state (Diamond 1975; Gallin 1984a, 1984b). This is best seen through the activities of its Women's De-partment and a semiofficial organization, the Chinese Women's Anti-Aggression League. Both of these institutions advocate patriarchal values and sponsor programs and projects that are mere extensions of women's familial roles. Women are encouraged to participate in

> voluntary sewing of clothing for military personnel, collection and do-nation of cash, clothes, and foodstuffs for needy military dependents, the operation of 35 milkbars for needy children, the maintenance of schools and orphanages for war orphans and the children of civil ser-vants and military personnel, assistance to retired servicemen, collec-tions of clothing for Vietnamese refugees, and aid for KMT [GMD] soldiers returned from Burma and Vietnam, and relief services to needy women and overseas Chinese girl students in Taiwan. (Diamond 1975, 15)

Women's subordination in Taiwan is not simply a continuity of tradi-tional values and culture. It is a product of patriarchal capitalism in which the interests of the capitalist, the state, and the international mar-ket are served (Gallin 1984b, Gates 1979). As Gates puts it, "the KMT has fostered patterns that are more than conservative, for it has not simply maintained or returned to tradition. Instead, it has encouraged certain tendencies through new political means and a changing economy to a higher level than they could possibly have reached in the past."

Through the mass media and educational system, the state plays an active role in encouraging "an ideological environment that relegates women to menial labor and household tasks." The result is a patriarchal capitalist system whereby women's unpaid domestic and underpaid public labor are appropriated "without altering cultural definitions of male and female roles or transforming the structure of male status and authority within the family" (Gallin 1984a, 398). A study of elementary and middle school textbooks used in Taiwan shows that scientists, positive political leaders, and scholars are invariably males; and those caring for households are all females. Furthermore, the personal qualities associated with male characters are ambition, courage, persistence, wisdom, adventurousness, and so forth, whereas those associated with female characters are filial obedience, courtesy, and warmheartedness (*Funu Xinzhi* 1988).

Fostering Women's Double Burden: The Community Development Program

As pointed out earlier, the adoption of an export-oriented development strategy necessitates the availability of a flexible and cheap labor supply, and women have met that need extremely well. But women's employment is also feared as potentially threatening to men and to family stability. These two concerns are reflected in the state's Community Development Program, which promotes the perpetuation of women's double burden. In 1968, the government designed a ten-year community development program that was later extended several times. The goal of this program is to "improve the people's material as well as spiritual lives" (Taiwan Shengzhengfu Shehuichu 1987, 19). The program not only deals with problems in food, clothing, living, transportation, and leisure, but also proposes to enhance Chinese traditional moral values and social norms in the local community. Women are important in the Community Development Program both as a target group for special training and as essential implementers of the program. Their participation has been crucial to the success of the program.

Organizational Structure

There are Community Development Committees at the provincial, district/county, and town/village levels. The governor, mayor, chief, and other officials serve as the chair of the committee at each respective level to monitor and evaluate the program. In addition, each community has a community council with 9 to 17 members, one of whom is designated as the director. Members are theoretically elected by the heads of households in the community, and the director is either elected by council members or handpicked by the district/county official. Until 1983, more than one-fourth (26%) of the council members and another one-fourth (24.4%) of the directors were designated by the state (Taiwan Shengzhengfu Yanjiu Kaohe Weiyuanhui 1983, 67-68).

The incorporation of the newly established Community Development Program into the preexisting bureaucratic system means that women have been excluded from the decision-making process at the governmental level. Furthermore, since council members are elected by the heads of households rather than by individual residents in the community, women have almost no chance of becoming members of the council in their own communities. The exclusion of women in decision-making at the local level is all the more serious when the state increasingly penetrates into the life of the community.

The result of this organizational pattern is seen in a survey conducted in 1983 to evaluate the achievement of the Community Development Program. Of the total 1,810 council members from 127 communities, less than seven percent (6.7%) were women (Taiwan Shengzhengfu Yanjiu Kaohe Weiyuanhui 1983, 54). When residents who hold decision-making positions in community affairs were asked who they thought best suited to be the director of the Council Committee, less than one percent (0.9%) mentioned women in the neighborhood (Taiwan Shengzhengfu Yanjiu Kaohe Weiyuanhui 1983, 131).

Program Contents

There are three substantive areas of the Community Development Program: basic engineering/construction projects, production and social welfare, and ethics and morale. Within each of these three major areas, programs or activities are designed and carried out in local communities. The *Keting gongchang* or "living-room factory," and the *Mama jiaoshi* or "Mother's Workshop" programs are directly related to women. These two programs illustrate that the state ideology on women's role remains patriarchal in essence though its emphasis shifts as Taiwan's economy develops.

Living-Room Factories

The "living-room factory" program is also referred to as the family subsidiary employment program. It is designed to solve the labor shortage problem by mobilizing surplus labor in the community/family to engage in production. State officials reasoned that by introducing homework and similar forms of production into the local area, people's living standard will be improved while national productivity is increased, thus "community development and economic development will enhance each other" (Economic Construction Commission [EEC] 1978, 1).

After surveys conducted under state sponsorship found that there were many "idle women" in local communities, a proposal to establish "living-room factories" was developed (EEC 1978, 2). The government provided special loans for families intending to purchase machines to do homework. Workshops were conducted to train housewives to apply themselves to productive work. Many "living-rooms" were converted into "factories," housewives became workers, and work became "housewifized."

One of the consequences, of course, has been that those families whose female members do homework in their living-rooms experienced an improvement in their living standards. However, a greater benefit can be claimed by others. Capitalists were relieved of a labor shortage because a new segment of the population was incorporated into the production line. This helped to ease the pressure for potential wage increase. Since many living-rooms were converted into "factories" and the workers worked at home, capitalists were able to avoid expenditures on factory facilities, energy, dormitories, and management. The incorporation of women into living-room factory work is capitalist patriarchal because those homeworkers were treated more as homemakers who were willing to work, rather than workers who worked at home. They were not provided with health insurance to which most factory workers were entitled. Nor were they protected by the minimum wage regulations, since they were paid on a piece-rate basis. The society as a whole was able to benefit from productivity increases, consumer price stabilization, and economic growth. The state boasts that the informal/subsidiary employment arrangement typical of living-room factories reduces potential conflict between capitalists and workers (EEC 1978, 3).

The consequences of homework in industrial Europe and America are well known (Daniels 1989). What distinguishes the Taiwan case is the active promotion of homework by the state, and the institution of national programs such as the Mother's Workshops to ensure that women will not lose sight of their responsibilities as "good wives and fine mothers."

Mother's Workshops

Mama *jiaoshi*, or the Mother's Workshop Program, a companion of the "living-room factories," is a subarea within the project of ethics and morality enhancement. Many state officials have underlined the importance of the program in itself and for the success of the Community Development Program as a whole. In 1984 Zhao Shoubo, director of the Department of Social Affairs of the province, stated:

> Mama Jiaoshi is a sound idea and a wonderful institution. To educate a woman into a good mother is equal to educate the whole family well. If every family lives in comfort and happiness, the society will be peaceful and prosperous, united and harmonious. Ultimately, the whole country will be strong and well-off. Therefore, the Mother's Workshop Program has a great responsibility. (Zhao 1984, 27)

An editorial in the official journal *Shequ Fazhan Jikan* (Community Development Quarterly) points out that, among the seventy-seven programs and activities proposed by the government to achieve the goals of the Community Development Program, at least thirty-nine cannot be accomplished without the Mother's Workshop Program.

> Programs on community beautification, environmental improvement, community safety, vocational and skills training, sanitation and health instruction, nutrition improvement, cultural and leisure activities, interior decoration, neighborhood harmony, adult education and public service, and so forth, are within the scope of the Mama Jiaoshi.... Unless these are taught, learned, discussed, and absorbed by women through the Workshops, these programs forever remain only as slogans. (*Shequ Fazhan Jikan* 28, 1984, p. 4)

The Mother's Workshop Program, according to its initiator Governor Xie Dongmin, who later became the vice-president of the Republic of China (1989), is also designed to "alleviate societal uneasiness and disorder created by economic development...such as increases in divorce rate and adolescent crimes, negligence of the elderly, and widespread hedonism and prodigality." As a government document (Taiwan Shengzhengfu *Gonggao*, 8027, 1973) states,

> Chinese society is built upon the family and sustained by traditional virtue. And, the mother is the center of a family. Only competent and virtuous mothers can raise stable families. The prosperity of the society and the strength and growth of the country all depend upon people's morality, which is contingent upon stable families. Therefore, we conclude that promoting virtuous and responsible motherhood is the most crucial issue today.

The state claims that the most important aim of the Mother's Workshop Program is to "propagate government orders, promote developmental and educational programs in the local community, and celebrate national festivals. Taking care of mother's interest and need is only secondary" (Zhao 1984, 24). In other words, various courses held in the local community in the name of Mother's Workshop are simply means through which the main objectives set by the state can be accomplished.

Numerous Mother's Workshops were conducted in local communities. Beginning in 1977, the state has sponsored regular training courses for supervisors and instructors of local Mother's Workshops. The state has also published a ten-volume set called *Mother's Readers* to guide these workshops. Written in simple Chinese language and heavily illustrated, these volumes are no more than thirty pages each. Their subjects include family planning, child care, prenatal care, infant care, food and nutrition, housecleaning, family finance management, family life management, and clothing selection, construction, and care (Taiwan Shengzhengfu Shehuichu 1977a). Additional materials, such as "Supplementary Readings for the Mother's Workshop," were published periodically (Sili 1985). By 1989, a total of 8,130 supervisors had been trained by the government and more than 160,000 copies of the readers have been distributed.

The influence of the program can also be shown by the number of workshops held. By 1984, a total of 4,063 communities had implemented the Community Development Program in Taiwan. About 90% of them held Mother's Workshops in their communities in 1984 alone. One-third of the counties/cities in the province (7 out of a total of 21) have a community sponsor rate of 90%. Among them, three counties/cities have a Mother's Workshop in every local community (Zhao 1984, 26).

In 1987, local officials and representatives from twenty-one counties/cities responsible for the Mother's Workshop Program gathered at a conference called by the Department of Social Affairs. Every county/city gave a summary report on what has been accomplished. Ten reported statistics on how many Mother's Workshop classes were organized in the local community of their counties/cities. The number of classes sponsored by each local community varied widely, and ranged from once a year to twice per month (see Table 10).

In urban areas most participants are middle-class housewives (Zhao 1986), although women from various class backgrounds have attended the program as well (Taiwansheng 74-75, 1987). Especially in rural areas, the Mother's Workshop Program has played important educational roles, such as distributing information on family planning, infant care, and nutrition.

Workshops are usually held at community centers over the weekend, and are centered around four areas: ethics and morality, sanitation and

TABLE 10   Number of Mother's Workshops Sponsored by County/City, 1987

Number of workshop classes per community per year	Number of county/city
1+	1
3	1
6	4
8	1
12+	2
24	1
Nonspecified	11
Total communities	21

Source: Taiwansheng (1987), 20-40.

public health, homework and productive skills, and leisure activity and social services. The ultimate goals of ethics and morality education are to get women in the community to "practice proper etiquettes, respect womanhood virtues, pay attention to motherhood, and increase harmony in the family" (Zhao 1984, 25). Women are taught, for example, how to prepare nutritious food for the family, what the proper makeup is when attending social gatherings with their husbands, and how to take care of the elderly with chronic diseases. Training on productive skills is connected with the "living-room factory" program. Courses on leisure activity planning and social services encourage women to organize themselves "to visit the aged, orphans, the handicapped, the mentally retarded, and military and poor families [in the local community]" (Zhao 1984, 26). A person in charge of the training courses for supervisors of the Mother's Workshops Program once said, "In a modern society, women have to play at least four different roles: they have to be pretty women, lovely wives, responsible mothers, and successful professionals" (M.-X. Xie 1985). An example of the content and attendance of these workshops is provided in Table 11 for Tainan County between 1985 and 1986.

As Table 11 shows, more than one thousand classes were conducted with more than ten thousand participants in Tainan County in 1985 and 1986. The figures do not distinguish frequent participants from one-time attendants. However, the table does show that the most frequently sponsored courses are recreationally oriented. Women have also actively participated in courses on makeup, family relationships, homemaking, and public health.

State officials have lamented that some Mother's Workshop Programs have focused too much on recreation. Vice-President Xie claimed that "mothers in the community become indulged in such activities [folk dancing]. They neglect their husband and overlook their children. As a

TABLE 11   Activities and Attendancy of Mother's Workshops, Tainan County, 1985-1986

Courses & activities	Total classes		Attendance		Average attendance per class	
	1985	1986	1985	1986	1985	1986
Family relations (mother & son, spouses, mother-in-law & daughter-in-law)	100	35	1,342	976	13.4	27.6
Public health (sanitation, family planning, emergency care)	90	57	1,402	1,004	15.6	17.6
Homemaking (cooking, flower arrangement, interior decoration)	308	170	2,735	1,725	8.9	10.1
New knowledge (crime prevention, makeup, social skills)	84	79	1,628	1,234	19.4	15.6
Productive skills (bamboo handcrafts, embroidery, knitting, and toy, ornament, and pin making)	66	61	851	612	12.9	10.0
Recreational activities (camping, BBQ, folk dancing)	707	659	3,522	4,126	5.0	6.3
Social services (visit elderly, poor, and community services)	68	79	536	350	7.9	4.4
Total	1,423	1,150	12,016	10,018		

Source: Taiwansheng (1987), 32-33.

result, more problems have been created in the family" (J. Li 1985, 59). Another government official points out:

The purposes of the Mother's Workshop is to bring forth sweet and happy family, thereby a stable and harmonious society eventually. Courses on parenting and occupation skills are means to achieve these goals. The Mother's Workshop is not limited to skill training, such as cooking, flower arranging, or folk dancing. Some local communities have focussed on such trivial activities and lost sight of the main objectives of the program. (Zhao 1984, 24-27)

Several points can be made regarding the "living-room factory" and the Mother's Workshop programs. First, the ways women were incorporated in the programs reinforced their submissive and dependent status in the family and society. Women's waged work was based on its subsidiary and supplementary character, even though their income was essential to the family. Women were not treated as workers but as housewives in need of some pocket money. Female workers at a living-room factory were told by local officials to lie about their wages to visitors to hide the fact that they were paid below the minimum (personal communication). They were also subjected to all the hazards of chemical pollution, unstable income, and other problems faced by workers in the informal economy. Second, women's roles as mother and caretaker were reinforced by programs emphasizing their "moral obligation" to the family, and to other people in need. Women were asked to take up the "double burden" for the good of the whole society. Third, the Community Development Program was a top-down program. It is based on the male-dominated bureaucratic structure and ignores preexisting social networks in the community, which are often centered around women. The failure to take into account these local personal networks has excluded women's participation in the decision-making process, and by that exclusion has created many unnecessary difficulties for the success of the state-sponsored programs.

Conclusion

The demand for flexible labor in the contemporary world system means that women are especially courted. They are often said to prefer flexible work because of their own desire to care for their families. Stable families, harmonious neighborhoods, and orderly society can be achieved through the fulfillment of motherhood. Working for wages is encouraged by the state as long as it does not interfere with women's role as wives, mothers, and daughters-in-law. And the best way for society to induce women to do both is to provide opportunities for flexible work. It is not flexible work that we object to, but its evaluation. Flexible work is cheap, insecure, unprotected, and taken for granted. Here a socially produced condition is taken as natural, and perpetuated by the state, the society, and the family. The success of the export-oriented growth strategy of Taiwan is related to a system of male domination that provides incentives for firms and families that exploit women's labor. Beyond economic strategies, the state controls and disciplines female workers by perpetuating the "double burden" ideology through educational institutions and state-sponsored community programs such as the "living-room factory."

Bibliography

Beneria, Lourdes, ed. 1982. *Women and Development: The Sexual Division of Labor in Rural Societies.* Westport, CT: Praeger.

Bian, Yu-yuan. 1985. Funu laodong dui jingji fazhang zhi gongxian [The contribution of female labor to economic development—A case study of Taiwan]. In *Funu zai Guojia Fazhan guochengzhong de Jiaose Yantaohui Lunwenji* [Proceedings of conference on the role of women in the national development process in Taiwan], 261-74. Taipei: National Taiwan University, Population Studies Center.

Charlton, Sue Ellen, Jana Everett, and Kathleen Staudt. 1989. *Women, the State and Development.* Albany, NY: State University of New York.

Chiang, Lan-hung Nora, and Yenlin Ku. 1985. *Past and Current Status of Women in Taiwan.* Taipei: National Taiwan University, Population Studies Center.

Chou, Bi-ar. 1989. Industrialization and Change in Women's Status: A Reevaluation of Some Data from Taiwan. In *Taiwan: A Newly Industrialized State,* edited by Hsin-huang Michael Hsiao, Wei-yuan Cheng, and Hou-sheng Chan, 423-61. Taipei: National Taiwan University, Department of Sociology.

Crane, George T. 1982. The Taiwanese Ascent: System, State and Movement in the World Economy. In *Ascent and Decline in the World-System,* edited by Edward Friedman, 93-113. Beverly Hills: Sage.

Cumings, Bruce. 1987. The Origins and Development of the Northeast Asian Political Economy: Industrial Sectors, Product Cycles, and Political Consequences. In *The Political Economy of the New Asian Industrialization,* edited by Frederic Deyo, 44-83. Ithaca, NY: Cornell University Press.

Daniels, Cynthia R. 1989. Between Home and Factory: Homeworkers and the State. In *Homework,* edited by Eileen Boris and Cynthia R. Daniels. Urbana and Chicago: University of Illinois Press.

Deng, Wenyi. 1975. Sanshinianlai de Taiwan Guanguang Luyu Shiye [Tourist industries in the last thirty years in Taiwan]. In *Taiwan Guangfu Sanshinian*

[Thirty years after Taiwan's recovery from Japanese occupation], 337-409. Taizhong: Taiwan Shengzhengfu Xinwenchu.

Deyo, Frederic C., ed. 1987. *The Political Economy of the New Asian Industrialization*. Ithaca, NY: Cornell University Press.

Deyo, Frederic C. 1989. *Beneath the Miracle: Labor Subordination in the New Asian Industrialism*. Berkeley: University of California Press.

Diamond, Norma. 1973. The Middle Class Family Model in Taiwan: Woman's Place Is in the Home. *Asian Survey* 13 (September): 853-72.

———. 1975. Women under Kuomintang Rule: Variations of the Feminine Mystique. *Modern China* 1 (1): 345.

———. 1979. Women and Industry in Taiwan. *Modern China* 5 (3): 317-40.

Directorate-General of Budget, Accounting and Statistics, Republic of China. [Various years]. *Zhonghuaminguo Tongji Nianjian* [Statistical yearbook of the Republic of China]. Taipei.

———. 1974. *Zhonghuaminguo Tongji Tiyao* [Statistical abstract of the Republic of China]. Taipei.

———, and Council for Economic Planning and Development. 1989. *Taiwan Diqu Renli Yunyung Diaocha Baogao* [Report on the manpower utilization survey in Taiwan area]. Taipei.

Directory of Taiwan. 1963. Taipei: *The China News*.

Economic Construction Commission. 1978. *Ruhe yi Shequ Fazhan Fangshi Tuixing Jiating Fuye zhi Yanjiu* [How to promote family subsidiary work through community development]. Taipei.

Evans, Peter, and Chien-kuo Pang. 1989. State Structure and State Policy: Implications of the Taiwanese Case for Newly Industrializing Countries. In *Taiwan: A Newly Industrialized State*, edited by Hsin-huang Michael Hsiao, Wei-yuan Cheng, and Hou-sheng Chan, 3-30. Taipei: National Taiwan University, Department of Sociology.

Funu Xinzhi [Awakening]. 1982-89. [Various Issues.] Taipei.

Funu Xinzhi. 1988. *Liangxing Pingdeng Jiaoyu Shouce* [Handbook on gender equal education]. Taipei.

Gallin, Rita S. 1984a. The Entry of Chinese Women into the Rural Labor Force: A Case Study from Taiwan. *Signs* 9 (3): 383-98.

———. 1984b. Women, Family and the Political Economy of Taiwan. *Journal of Peasant Studies* 12 (1): 76-92.

———. 1990. Women and the Export Industry in Taiwan: The Muting of Class Consciousness. In *Women Workers and Global Restructuring*, edited by Kathryn Ward, 179-92. Ithaca, NY: Cornell University Press.

Gates, Hill. 1979. Dependency and the Part-time Proletariat in Taiwan. *Modern China* 5 (3): 381-407.

Greenhalgh, Susan. 1985. Sexual Stratification: The Other Side of "Growth with Equity" in East Asia. *Population and Development Review* 11 (June): 265-314.

Hsiao, Hsin-huang Michael, Wei-yuan Cheng, and Hou-sheng Chan, eds. 1989. *Taiwan: A Newly Industrialized State.* Taipei: National Taiwan University, Department of Sociology.

Huang, Chunming. 1981. *Shayunala Zaijian* [Sayonara goodbye]. Taipei: Yuanjing.

Jones, Gavin, ed. 1984. *Women in the Urban and Industrial Workforce, Southeast and East Asia.* Canberra: Australian National University.

Kaluzynska, Eva. 1980. Wiping the Floor with Theory: A Survey of Writings on Housework. *Feminist Review* 6.

Kim, Elaine. 1987. Sex Tourism in Asia: A Reflection of Political and Economic Inequality. In *Korean Women in Transition,* edited by Eui-young Yu and Earl H. Phillips, 127-44. Los Angeles: California State University, Center for Korean-American and Korean Studies.

Koo, Hagen. 1987. The Interplay of State, Social Class, and World System in East Asian Development: The Cases of South Korea and Taiwan. In *The Political Economy of the New Asian Industrialization,* edited by Frederic Deyo, 165-81. Ithaca, NY: Cornell University Press.

Kung, Lydia. 1983. *Factory Women in Taiwan.* Ann Arbor: University of Michigan Press.

Li, Jianxing. 1985. Shequ Mamajiaoshi yu Shequ Jiaoyu [Community Mother's Workshops and community education]. *Shequ Fazhan Jikan* 29 (December): 58-59.

Li, Yuanzhen. 1987. Chuji Wenti, Bubu Jiannan [Difficulties in facing the problems of young prostitutes]. *Funu Xinzhi* 57 (February): 1.

Liu, Paul K.-C. 1984. Trends in Female Labour Force Participation in Taiwan: The Transition toward Higher Technology Activities. In *Women in the Urban and Industrial Workforce, Southeast and East Asia,* edited by Gavin Jones, 75-99. Canberra: Australian National University.

Liu, Paul Ke-chih, and Kuo-shu Hwang. 1987. *Relationships between Changes in Population, Employment and Economic Structure in Taiwan.* Taipei: Academia Sinica.

Liu, Yu-lan. 1985. *Taiwan diqu funu renli yunyung huigu yu zhanwang* [Utilization of women's labor in Taiwan: Past and future]. Taipei: Meizhi Tushu Gongsi.

Lu, Xiulian. 1986. *Qing* [Affection]. Taipei: Dunli.

Lu, Yu-hsia. 1984. Women, Work and the Family in a Developing Society: Taiwan. In *Women in the Urban and Industrial Workforce, Southeast and East Asia,* edited by Gavin Jones, 339-67. Canberra: Australian National University.

Mies, Maria. 1986. *Patriarchy, Accumulation on a World Scale.* London: Zed Books.

Miller, Joanne, and Howard H. Garrison. 1982. Sex Roles: The Division of Labor at Home and in the Workplace. *Annual Review of Sociology* 8: 237-62.

Population Studies Center. 1965. *Funu zai Guojia Fazhan guochengzhong de Jiaose Yantaohui Lunwenji* [Proceedings of conference on the role of women in the national development process in Taiwan]. Taipei: National Taiwan University, Population Studies Center.

Qian [Money]. 1990. 5, pp. 156-86. Taipei.

Qu, Haiyuan. 1984. Seqing yu Changji Wanti [Sex and the prostitution problem]. In *Taiwan Shehui Wenti* [Social problems in Taiwan], edited by Guoshu Yang and Qizheng Ye, 543-71. Taipei: Juliu.

Shequ Fazhan Jikan [Community Development Quarterly]. Various issues. Taipei: Zhonghuaminguo Shequ Fazhan Yanjiu Sunlian Zhongxin.

Sili Shijian Jiazheng Jingji Zhuanke Xuexiao. 1985. *Mama Jiaoshi Buchong Jiaocai* [Supplementary instructional materials for Mother's Workshops]. Taizhong: Taiwan Shengzhengfu.

Taiwan Shengzhengfu. 1973. *Gonggao* [Public document] No. 8027. Taizhong.

Taiwan Shengzhengfu Shehuichu. 1977a. *Mama Duben* [Mother's readers]. 10 vols. Taizhong.

——. 1987. *Taiwansheng Shequ Fazhan Houxu Dierqi Wunian Jihua Gongzuo Shouce* [Handbook of the second five-year community development program of the provincial government]. Taipei.

Taiwan Shengzhengfu Xinwenchu. 1965. *Taiwan Guangfu Ershinian* [Twenty years after Taiwan's recovery]. Taipei.

Taiwan Shengzhengfu Yanjiu Kaohe Weiywanhui. 1983. *Taiwansheng Shinianlai Shequ Fazhan Chengxiao zhi Pingjian ji Weilai Fazhan zhi Yanjiu* [Evaluation of the ten-year community development program in Taiwan and its future direction]. Taipei: Taiwan Shengzhengfu Yanjiu Fazhan Kaohe Weiyuanhui.

Taiwansheng Seventy-four/Seventy-five Niandu Shequ Mamajiaoshi Fudao Renyuan Zuotanhui Zonghe Jishi [Proceedings of the 1985-86 community Mother's Workshop supervisors seminar]. 1987. Taipei.

Truong, Thanh-Dam. 1990. *Sex, Money and Morality: Prostitution and Tourism in Southeast Asia*. London: Zed Books.

Tsay, Ching-lung. 1985. Xingbie chayi [Sex differentials in educational attainment and labor force development in Taiwan]. In *Funu zai Guojia Fazhan guochengzhong de Jiaose Yantaohui Lunwenji* [Proceedings of Conference on the Role of Women in the National Development Process in Taiwan], 277-308. Taipei: National Taiwan University, Population Studies Center.

Waring, Marilyn. 1988. *If Women Counted: A New Feminist Economics*. San Francisco: Harper & Row.

Winckler, Edwin A., and Susan Greenhalgh, eds. 1988. *Contending Approaches to the Political Economy of Taiwan*. Armonk, NY: M. E. Sharpe.

Xie, Meng-xiong. 1985. Shequ Mamjiaoshi yu Jiazheng jiaoyu [The community Mother's Workshop and homemaking education]. *Shequ Fazhan Jikan* 29 (December): 60-61.

Yu, Zongxian. 1981. Duiwai Maoyi [Foreign trade]. In *Woguo Jingji de Fazhan* [Economic development of our country], edited by Chia-lin Cheng, 301-84. Taipei: Shijie Shuju.

Zhan, Chunjian. 1966. Dangqian Fazhan Guanguang Shiye de Tujing [Directions of tourism development]. In *Guanguang Shiye Lunji* [Essays on tourism], edited by Huiyan Zhou, vol. 1, pp. 4-16. Taipei: Zhongguo Wenhua Xueyuan.

Zhao, Shoubo. 1984. The Current Status and Future Prospective of Mother's Workshops in Taiwan. *Shequ Fazhan Jikan* 28 (December): 24-27.

———. 1986. Qianghua Mamajiaoshi de Gongneng [Strenthening the function of Mother's Workshops]. In *Taiwansheng Mamajiaoshi Fudao Renyuan Yanxihui Shouce* [Handbook for supervisors of the Mother's Workshops], pp. 1-2. 1986. Taipei.

Zheng, Zhihui, and Qingrong Bo. 1987. Zhengshi Zhiye Funu soshou de Jiuye Qishi [Looking seriously at the discrimination faced by working women]. *Funu Xinzhi* 58 (March): 19.

Zhou, Huiyan, ed. 1966. *Guanguang Shiye Lunji* [Essays on tourism], vol. 1. Taipei: Zhongguo Wenhua Xueyuan.

14

Attitudinal Changes
of Farmers in Taiwan

Cheng-hung Liao
Chun-chieh Huang

One of the most striking developments that postwar Taiwan shares with other countries lies in the changes of value systems among farmers, especially their attitudes toward agriculture. In his studies on innovation and change in French agriculture, Henri Mendras observed the vanishing of peasants in France and concluded, "if economic structures are changed within a region, they will within a few years change the mentality of the inhabitants" (Mendras 1970, 246). Changes in value orientation such as Mendras observed in rural France can also be found in postwar Japan. Fukutake indicates that after the Meiji Restoration, and particularly since World War II, Japan experienced the collapse of physiocratic ideology and the emergence of farmers regarding agriculture as a business (Fukutake 1967). As agriculture experienced "modernization" in France and Japan, farmers in these countries became uprooted. They were no longer the earthbound peasants. They became calculating farmers equipped with modern knowledge of production. Such drastic changes in the ways of farming resulted in the reorientation of value systems among French and Japanese farmers.

A similar course of development may be observed in postwar rural Taiwan. We have indicated in another essay that agricultural modernization in postwar Taiwan caused or accelerated changes of value orientation among Taiwan's farmers (Huang and Liao 1987).

Since the implementation of land reform in Taiwan, there have been significant changes in farmers' attitudes toward land, toward farming, and toward social groups, etc. However, few of these changes have been systematically analyzed. This essay is intended to explore the nature of these changes, with the hope of revealing their relationship to social and economic development.

Our data are derived from two systematic sampling surveys. One was conducted in April-May 1984, with 440 farmers interviewed; the other was conducted between December 1985 and January 1986, with 455 farmers and 169 nonfarmers interviewed.[1]

I. Agricultural Developments
since World War II

One of the most important factors contributing to agricultural developments in Taiwan was the successful implementation of land reform programs. A series of land reform policies were designed in the late 1940s and early 1950s to create a surplus from the agricultural sector for use in the takeoff of local industries (Hsiao 1981). Agricultural policies before 1972 may best be characterized as aiming at "developmental squeeze." The implementation of land reform policies changed not only the structure of land ownership but also the sociopolitical structure in rural Taiwan. In terms of land ownership, the share of owner-cultivated land in total cultivated land increased from 55.88% in 1948 to 82.78% in 1953 (Liao, Huang, and Hsiao 1986, 21), and to 85.01% in 1985 (Directorate-General of Budget, Accounting, and Statistics 1987). The proportion of tenant farmers dropped from 38.71% in 1948 to 21.00% in 1953 and 4.49% in 1988 (Department of Agriculture and Forestry 1988).

The agriculture growth rate increased rapidly after the implementation of the Land-to-the-Tiller Program in 1951-53. This was described at the time as a stage where agriculture supported industry. During the 1953-64 period, about ten years later, the emphasis was shifted to labor-intensive farming. The advancement of agricultural technology was remarkable in this period. New and improved techniques were continually being developed and put into practice. New crops, chemicals, fertilizers,

---

1. For details of the sampling procedures and characteristics of the samples, see Liao, Huang, and Hsiao 1986, 309-12, and Liao and Huang 1988, 10-11, 45-46.

and other production inputs became increasingly available, and farmers made effective use of them.

Land reform was one of the major contributions to rural development. The sale of public lands to tenants (1951-60) and the Land-to-the-Tiller Program gave farmers the incentives to adopt multiple-crop farming and resulted in a rapid increase in productivity. At this stage, agriculture played a multiple role. It supplied nonagricultural sectors with food and industrial raw materials. It earned the necessary foreign exchange for importing industrial machinery and equipment. The transfer of capital from the agricultural to the industrial sector laid the foundation for further development. Agricultural development in turn induced industrial development and caused further socioeconomic changes. The living standards of farmers improved, and their value system and behavioral patterns underwent tremendous changes. As Yang pointed out, farmers were not as conservative as before. They put more effort into farming and expected their children to be better educated. They were more actively involved in public affairs (Yang 1970, 132-67). Taiwan farmers during this period demonstrated a strong commitment to the land and general satisfaction with life.

During the mid-1960s, however, the economic structure of Taiwan reached a turning point. Industry had developed, and the agricultural sector witnessed several crises. The vast outflow of rural people to urban areas led to a labor shortage in the agricultural sector. But an increase in the number of farm households also resulted in a decrease in farm size and fragmentation of holdings. To attack this problem, the land consolidation project was undertaken in conjunction with an irrigation program.

Economically, the annual growth rate of agricultural production dropped from 5.7% in 1965-68 to 1.5% in 1969-72. The total share of agricultural production in NDP dropped from 24.9% in 1965-68 to 16.4% in 1969-72. Farm family income as a percentage of nonfarm family income declined from 69.8% in 1965 to 66.5% in 1972.

The 1964-72 period might be called the transitional stage from agriculture to industry, i.e., the decline of agriculture amidst industrial boom. Before 1964 the agricultural sector always contributed a larger share than industry to total national production, but after 1964 this order was reversed.

In previous stages the social aspect of development was relatively neglected and the human factor had not been adopted as an intellectual or a practical focus in approaches to rural development. Economic growth, on the whole, had been tackled more in technological terms. Toward the end of the 1960s, however, technological factors were no longer deemed the only factors in rural development. Human resource development became one of the major concerns among various developmental strategies.

Since 1972, protection and subsidy have been the major characteristics of agricultural policy. The long-term imbalance between the agricultural and industrial sectors had resulted in serious agricultural crises. Many farms lay idle and rural youths were trying to escape from farming. In order to cope with the problems arising from this crisis, and to bring about a balance between the industrial and agricultural sectors, the government announced the Accelerated Rural Development Program on 27 September 1972. This included measures ranging from repealing the compulsory purchase program and the fertilizer-rice bartering system, to encouraging village industry. Measures under the slogan "Raise Farmers' Income and Enhance Rural Development" were implemented in 1978, and the Programs for Basic Construction and Raising Farmers' Income have been carried out since 1982. Various programs adopted integrated measures such as strengthening farmers' organizations, improving farmers' education, improving agricultural management, improving the marketing system of agricultural products, assisting rural youths in career development, and improving medical and sanitary service.

Among the various measures to improve efficiencies in cultivation and to increase farm income, the enlargement of farm size is seen as fundamental. However, land reform in Taiwan has resulted in overprotection of tenants at the expense of landlords (Yang 1970). The land system has become so rigid that there is little possibility of enhancing farm size by renting farmland. Most farmers who have obtained nonfarm jobs would still like to own their farmland for economic and social security, and will not lease their land to others because of the rigid land reform regulations. The problem of farm size has become a bottleneck for agricultural development in Taiwan.

To attack this problem, the second phase of land reform was taken toward the end of the 1970s. The emphasis of the second phase was not on the distribution of land ownership, but on improving land use. The basic guidelines for the second-phase farmland reform were: (1) to promote land use efficiency; (2) to enlarge farm size; (3) to modernize Taiwan's agriculture; and (4) to encourage farmers' interest in farming. Based on these guidelines, a number of measures were proposed, such as providing credit, vocational training, land consolidation, regional planning, joint farming, and revision of laws or regulations. All these measures were designed to raise farmers' income and to improve their living standards.

In the past four decades or so, rural Taiwan has experienced changes from homogeneity to heterogeneity that have become especially apparent since the 1970s. Agricultural production has become more and more pluralistic. The number of part-time farming families has increased rapidly. For example, the percentage of the adult population that belongs to a farm family has declined from 41.6% in 1960 to 23.8% in 1980 and 21.8% in 1986. In the same period the proportion of full-time farmers among all working farmers has decreased from 47.6% to 9.0%, while the proportion of part-time farmers has increased from 52.4% to 91.0%. In the meantime, the island has experienced rapid economic growth, educational development, growth of mass media, and improved transportation.

All these new developments have undermined the very foundation of the agrarian mentality established before the 1960s. Agriculture is no longer the fundamental sector of national economy. Farming has become a means, rather than the purpose, of life. Land has become a transferrable commodity rather than a sacred family property. In the accelerating modernization process, farmers in rural Taiwan are changing from their previously fixed, static way of life. As a corollary of this change, the value systems of Taiwan farmers have experienced restructuring and reorientation.

II. Farmers' Changing Attitudes toward Agriculture

The farmers' attitudes toward agriculture can be understood in terms of their attitudes toward adopting innovations, toward farming and toward farmland.

In early research on farmers' adopting innovations, various findings suggest that fewer than 16% of farmers belonged to the category of "early adopters" (Rogers 1958, Wu 1964). The survey we conducted in December 1985-January 1986, however, showed that Taiwan's farmers were quite open-minded in adopting agricultural innovations and in farm management. Among the 455 farmers interviewed, 47.5% were willing to be the first to adopt new species and techniques. In regard to obtaining new knowledge and techniques for farming, 76.9% agreed that this was very important and necessary; only 6.4% responded "not necessary." As for the comparison of "new" and "old" methods of farming, 59.6% thought that the new methods were much better than the old; only 3.3% believed that the old methods were better than the new. This data indicates that in the adoption of innovations, Taiwan's farmers show a modern attitude rather than a traditional one.

Farmers attitudes toward innovation vary with the profitability of agricultural production. In the several years right after the implementation of land reform farmers' morale was high, due to the large increase in income from farming. They were eager to innovate in order to increase productivity. However, during the period of agricultural crisis in the mid-1960s and 1970s, most farmers were greatly disappointed because farming became unprofitable compared with other industries. Therefore they had little desire to improve or invest in their farmland. After 1972, the various official campaigns, such as the Accelerating Rural Development and the Second-Phase Land Reform programs, gradually resulted in improved agricultural profitability. Farmers' attitudes toward farming became positive again. This attitudinal change was reflected in the fact that 53.6% of them switched to high-value crops when the price of traditional crops dropped. It also showed in the way farmers financed improvements of farm facilities: 68.1% wanted to borrow from banks or farmers' associations, but only 10.5% would seek help from their relatives and friends. This indicates the market-oriented character of farming and the disintegration of primary groups as a cohesive force in present-day rural Taiwan.

Not all these attitudinal changes are heading in the direction of modern agriculture. Farmers still possess traditional values that may be detrimental to modernization. For example, 65.9% preferred a farm operated by their own family members, while 26.8% preferred joint or cooperative farming. Only 2.2% believed that entrusting others to take care of their farms would be better. Regarding the inheritance of farmland, 50.0% wanted to distribute their land equally among their children, 35.6% favored joint farming by their children, and only 9.0% intended to leave the land to the eldest son.

Such attitudes have adversely affected the implementation of the "Enlarging Farming Scale" policy. Farmers must give up the traditional attitude that immediate family members should operate their own farms and must develop new attitudes favoring joint farming or entrust-farming. It is also important to maintain the integrity of the farmland, so that the land will not be subdivided into smaller pieces when inherited.

Farmers' attitudes toward land were greatly affected by the land reform and subsequent social changes. Since the 1950s, rural Taiwan witnessed the passing away of the landlord stratum and the rise of the petty farmers as a class. As a side effect of the land reform program, the traditional attitude toward land ownership as a source of status distinctions changed. The possibility of economic upward mobility through accumulation of land has been reduced (Gallin 1964, 322). Encouraged by the success of land reform, Taiwan farmers in the early 1950s were thrown into a ferment by their repossessing the land. During that period, farmers' attitude toward agriculture was full of confidence and optimism. As indicated by an islandwide survey, 85% of the farmers believed that the tenants' livelihood would be tremendously improved as soon as they received the land. Moreover, 69% of the tenants believed that they would eventually have the land they were farming (Rapper 1953, 156). It is not an exaggeration to say that land reform created the Taiwanese farmers' strong commitment to the land, which was the foremost outstanding aspect of farmers' attitudes toward agriculture in the 1950s and 1960s. Land, in the minds of farmers, was the ultimate source for their emerging sense of security. And most farmers thought that selling land inherited from the family was shameful (Yang 1970). However, our recent survey shows that 75.0% of farmers did not have such feelings, while 57.6% did not even agree that land was an indicator of one's social status.

The agricultural crisis and the expansion of industry since the mid-1960s could explain why farmers treated land as a commodity in the 1970s. The decline of agriculture caused farming income to shrink sharply. The share of farming income in the total farm family income dropped from 66.0% in 1966 to 45.2% in 1971, 28.8% in 1981, 31.7% in 1984, and 36.7% in 1985 (Liao, Huang, and Hsiao 1986, 27; Department of Agriculture and Forestry 1987, 347). As a result of this economic situation, an increasing number of farmers since the mid-1960s have lost confidence in agriculture. The survey we conducted in 1984 on 450 farming households revealed that 59.3% believed farming was a profession with no hope. Among this group, those who lived in the specialized agricultural production areas were the most pessimistic (Liao, Huang, and Hsiao 1986, 282). Thus, it is not surprising that a high percentage of farmers surveyed were dissatisfied (48.6%) or very dissatisfied (16.6%) with farming as a way of life (ibid., 327). A fact worth noting, however, is that the majority of farmers were reluctant to leave agriculture (53% reluctant; 7% very reluctant). Such hesitation was especially apparent among those farmers who lived in the low agricultural area (76.2%) (ibid., 328).

The concomitance of farmers' pessimistic view of agriculture and their reluctance to leave agriculture can be explained not only in terms of the lack of education and training necessary for changing jobs, but also in their new attitudes toward the land they possessed. The majority of farmers realized the fact that land was a precious commodity. And on an island with a high population density such as Taiwan, possession of land could turn them into nouveaux riches overnight. In the 1950s and early 1960s, there existed between farmers and their land a sort of covenant that was sacred in nature. After the mid-1960s, farmers treated the land they cultivated as a transferrable commodity. In contrast with their predecessors decades ago, the farmers after the mid-1960s have become alienated from the land to which their ancestors were so deeply bound. They adopted what may be called the "nomadic mentality" as opposed to the "agrarian mentality."

Needless to say, the changing attitudes toward land among Taiwan's farmers in the past twenty years are not an independent phenomenon.

They represent a facet of the new type of farmers' personality. The survey we conducted in 1985 attests that more than half (64.4%) of the farmers questioned subscribed to individualism in their relational orientation. It is understandable that Taiwan's farmers, with such a strong individualistic orientation, treat land as a commodity.

III. Farmers' Attitudes toward Living Conditions

From objective indicators one can readily observe the physical improvement in rural Taiwan, such as well-paved roads and beautiful farmhouses. Yet, these improvements hardly assure that farmers are more satisfied than before. From a policy point of view, data for subjective feelings about living conditions can supplement the limitations of objective indicators.

Various objective indicators, such as family income, household facilities, medical facilities, etc., show that living conditions of people in Taiwan, both farmers and nonfarmers, have improved greatly. Whether these improvements are due to the success of agricultural policy or are the result of overall economic development is a debatable topic. It is assumed that the subjective feelings of farmers toward their major living conditions will provide some clues for answering this question. This subjective feeling is an overall evaluation of level of living, which is sensitive to the effect of relative change in living conditions in various sectors. For example, current farm family income is much higher than before, but still far lower than nonfarm family income. Thus even while the objective indicators show a great increase of farm family income, farmers remain subjectively unsatisfied.

From input and output analysis one might be able to quantify the contribution of agricultural policy to the increase in agrarian productivity or farm family income, but it is difficult to quantify the policy impact on overall living standards. By using a subjective evaluation method this section is trying to explore farmers' level of satisfaction with their living conditions, to compare this kind of feeling in different developmental stages, and to identify the impact of agriculture policy on farmers' living conditions.

As pointed out earlier, the focus of the early developmental programs in rural Taiwan was on the increase in agricultural productivity, followed later by a focus on support to industrial development. Due to either financial constraints or policy bias, one of the consequences of such policies was imbalanced development. This imbalance in development is also reflected in the farmers' responses about their level of satisfaction with their living conditions. In general most farmers were satisfied. Among the thirteen items representing living conditions, the items rated "very satisfied" and "satisfied"—ratings of more than 80% satisfactory—were food and diet (80%), clothing (81.4%), neighborhood relations (84.3%), and relations with family members (86.5%). Overall only 7.2% were not satisfied with their living conditions (very dissatisfied 0.2%, and dissatisfied 7%). There were six items with which more than 10% of the farmers were dissatisfied, namely transportation (10%), working conditions (12.5%), job opportunities for family members (13.7%), family income (18.4%), medical care (29.3%), and recreation (20.5%). However, most of these farmers thought these items had improved in the previous ten years or so. Somewhat more than 10% of the farmers thought working conditions and job opportunities had become progressively worse.

The above description indicates that most farmers were satisfied with their living conditions and thought all the indicators had improved in recent years. Using open-ended questions, we further asked farmers about their perceived reasons for the improvement. Their answers were then placed in six categories. The first reason was social change (40.2%). Industrial development and the increase of nonfarm working opportunities had increased their family income as well as general standard of living. The second most common reason given was family factors (22.2%), either an increase of the work force in the family or hard-work and thriftiness of family members. The third reason was increased productivity in agriculture (17.4%), such as mechanization or diversified farming. The fourth reason was government policy (14.4%), such as implementation of various rural development programs. The fifth reason was price levels, perceiving that there had been good market prices for their products (2.7%). The final category includes all other reasons, and accounted for only 3.2% of the responses.

For farmers the main reason for their improved standard of living was the increase in job opportunities and income. As long as their income increased, their living conditions would improve accordingly. Social change and family factors were more important than agricultural productivity or government agrarian policy in contributing to improved living standards. In contrast, among the 39 farmers reporting worsened living conditions, the main reasons were factors leading to direct declines in agricultural production, e.g., high wages for farm help, small farm size, poor harvest. Other reasons were marketing problems and price, or family factors such as education for children, or increasing number or poor health of family members.

It seemed that social change was seen as the main cause of improvement in farmers' living conditions, while deterioration was attributed to high costs of agricultural production and low prices for agricultural products. But this by no means indicates that agricultural policy does not contribute to improving farmers' standard of living.

Since the land reform, agrarian development in Taiwan has made tremendous progress. It contributed to the development of the national economy as well as the improvements of farmers' lives in the 1950s and 1960s. As a result of economic development and social change, the rate of growth in agriculture began to slow down. Unit labor productivity could not be significantly raised within the structure of small-scale farming. Therefore the contribution of increased agricultural productivity to the improvement of farm family income was relatively small in comparison with the land reform period.

Table 1 shows that for the 1953-64 period the proportion of respondants who felt that living conditions had become better was the highest among all the periods compared; the later the period the lower the proportion. Nevertheless, 40% still perceived improvement in the 1981-84 period. For this same period, however, the percentage of people who reported a lowered living standard was higher than in any of the previous stages. And where improvement was reported, it was concentrated in areas where agriculture employs the lowest proportion of the work force. This data indicates that there has been steady improvement in farmers' living conditions since the land reform, but that the golden age for Taiwanese small farmers came in the period immediately after the reform and is now past. This view is supported by farmers' answers on the reasons for improvements in living conditions. They indicated that social change was more important than agricultural production in contributing to improved living conditions. In other words, government policy had its greatest impacts on agriculture in improving farmers' living conditions in the 1953-64 period. Since 1964, although farmers' living conditions have continued to ameliorate, the main contributing factor has been industrial rather than agricultural development. This inference can be attested by the fact that in recent years only two-thirds of farm family income came from farming directly.

Table 2 on page 365 shows further that from farmers' self-evaluation of agriculture, 39.3% thought agriculture was much better than other industries during the 1953-64 period. Only 5.3% so responded in the 1981-84 period. For those who took the negative view, only 28.1% thought that agriculture was worse than other industries in 1953-64, but this rose to 83.5% by 1981-84.

As pointed out in the first part of this paper, developmental squeeze was characteristic of early agriculture policy. And since 1972, subsidy and protection have been the foci of attention. It seems ironic that farmers

TABLE 1   Farmers' Perceptions of Their Living Conditions

Changes in Living Conditions	Agricultural Areas*			
	Low (%)	Medium (%)	High (%)	Total (%)
1981-84				
Better	50.7 (75)**	34.8 (49)	34.7 (52)	40.1 (176)
No change	24.3 (36)	32.6 (46)	31.3 (47)	29.4 (129)
Worse	25.0 (37)	32.6 (46)	34.0 (51)	30.5 (134)
Total	100.0 (148)	100.0 (141)	100.0 (150)	100.0 (439)
1972-81				
Better	58.9 (86)	60.7 (85)	59.1 (88)	59.5 (259)
No change	26.0 (38)	23.6 (33)	25.5 (38)	25.1 (109)
Worse	15.1 (22)	15.7 (22)	15.4 (23)	15.1 (67)
Total	100.0 (146)	100.0 (140)	100.0 (149)	100.0 (435)
1964-72				
Better	60.8 (87)	65.7 (92)	61.6 (90)	62.7 (269)
No change	23.1 (33)	15.7 (22)	19.2 (28)	19.3 (83)
Worse	16.1 (23)	18.6 (26)	19.2 (28)	17.9 (77)
Total	100.0 (143)	100.0 (140)	100.0 (146)	100.0 (429)
1953-64				
Better	72.5 (100)	66.4 (85)	66.9 (95)	68.6 (280)
No Change	10.9 (15)	17.2 (22)	12.7 (18)	13.5 (55)
Worse	16.7 (23)	16.4 (21)	20.4 (29)	17.9 (73)
Total	100.0 (138)	100.0 (128)	100.0 (142)	100.0 (408)

Source: Adapted from Liao, Huang, and Hsiao 1986, 320-21.

*Agricultural areas were classified into three categories according to the proportion of the labor force engaged in farming. Low = under 43%, Medium = 43-56%, and High = more than 56%.

** The figures in parenthesis are base Ns.

had good feelings toward the squeezing policy but bad feelings toward the "protective" policy. This does not mean that farmers like to be squeezed and do not want to be protected. It is meaningful to analyze

TABLE 2   Farmers' Evaluation of Agriculture Compared to Other Industries

Compared with other industries agriculture is:		Agricultural Areas*			
		Low (%)	Medium (%)	High (%)	Total (%)
1981-84	Better	8.9 (13)**	1.4 (2)	5.33 (8)	5.3 (23)
	So-so	13.0 (19)	10.0 (14)	10.7 (16)	11.2 (49)
	Worse	78.1 (114)	88.6 (124)	84.0 (126)	83.5 (364)
	Total	100.0 (143)	100.0 (128)	100.0 (149)	100.0 (430)
1972-81	Better	5.6 (8)	7.2 (10)	10.1 (15)	7.7 (33)
	So-so	28.0 (40)	18.8 (26)	23.5 (35)	23.5 (101)
	Worse	66.4 (95)	73.9 (102)	66.4 (99)	68.8 (296)
	Total	100.0 (143)	100.0 (138)	100.0 (149)	100.0 (430)
1964-72	Better	35.0 (49)	20.1 (27)	24.0 (35)	26.4 (111)
	So-so	42.1 (59)	35.1 (47)	36.3 (53)	37.9 (159)
	Worse	22.9 (32)	44.8 (60)	39.7 (58)	35.7 (150)
	Total	100.0 (140)	100.0 (134)	100.0 (146)	100.0 (420)
1953-64	Better	48.5 (65)	36.5 (46)	33.1 (46)	39.3 (157)
	So-so	33.6 (45)	30.2 (38)	33.8 (47)	32.6 (130)
	Worse	17.9 (24)	33.3 (42)	33.1 (46)	28.1 (112)
	Total	100.1 (134)	100.0 (126)	100.0 (139)	100.0 (399)

Source: Adapted from Liao, Huang, and Hsiao 1986, 322-23.

*Agricultural areas were classified into three categories according to the proportion of the labor force engaged in farming. Low = under 43%, Medium = 43-56%, and High = more than 56%.

**The figures in parenthesis are base Ns.

this question from a social-psychological point of view in addition to economic analysis.

It is true that total agrarian productivity has kept increasing and farmers' living conditions have been continuously improving since land reform. But income from farming has been relatively lower than that from nonfarm industries. This has convinced farmers that agriculture has declined relative to other sectors, while expectations for living standards have risen with the objective environmental changes.

On the one hand small-scale farming is an important characteristic of Taiwan agriculture due to limited farmland and overpopulation. Before World War II the developmental level of the whole island was very low and peasant economy was its major feature. At that time farming was a way of life rather than a means of subsistence. Current profit-making ideas were not pervasive among farmers. Increase in unit-area productivity rather than unit-labor force productivity was emphasized. But due to rapid socioeconomic changes, nonfarm job opportunities have greatly increased. Therefore, a competition for labor between agriculture and nonagriculture has emerged. Consequently farmers' concerns have shifted from unit-area productivity to unit-labor-force productivity. But because of the difficulties in expanding farming scale, it is hard to raise unit-labor-force productivity. Hence this occupation remains relatively low-profit compared to nonfarm jobs. In the early stages of development, most of the population were engaged in agriculture under conditions of universal poverty. They had no other job opportunities as alternatives, hence the level of dissatisfaction was relatively low. Farmers took it for granted that they were destined to be the way they were. But as industrialization and urbanization continue to deepen, the income differences between farming and nonfarm jobs have enlarged. In addition, working conditions for nonfarm jobs are much better.

Today, the materialistic needs of the general public are much higher than before. Farmers, like everyone else, want to improve their living conditions. However, farm income alone is not sufficient for them to adopt similar life styles as those who are engaged in nonfarm jobs. Unless there are good incentives, few people, especially the young ones, will want to go into farming today.

Conclusion

The rapid socioeconomic changes in postwar Taiwan have resulted in attitudinal changes among farmers. The market-orientated character of production and the decline of primary groups as a cohesive force are pervasive these days. The changing farmers' attitudes toward agriculture can be briefly summarized as follows: from traditional to modern, from farming as a way of life to a means of subsistence, from devotion to farming following land reform in the 1950s to alienation from the land since the expansion of industry in the 1960s. These changes are similar to the experience in Japan and France.

In their attitudes toward adopting innovations, Taiwan's farmers show modern characteristics rather than traditional ones. Their attitudes toward farming have been variable with the profitability of agricultural production. In the 1950s, following the implementation of land reform programs, farmers were eager to adopt innovations to improve farming due to large increases of income from farming operations. During the period of agricultural crisis in the mid-1960s and 1970s, however, farmers showed little inclination to improve or invest in their farmland. After the various remedy programs promoted a recovery, farmers' attitudes toward farming again became positive.

Not all these attitudinal changes are heading in the direction of modern agriculture. Farmers still possess some traditional values which might be detrimental to the development of modern agriculture. In order to facilitate further agricultural development, it is necessary to encourage them to acquire new attitudes favoring joint-farming or cooperative farming. Furthermore, it is also important to keep the integrity of the farmland, so that the land will not be subdivided into smaller pieces when inherited.

Since 1964, although the farmers' living conditions have continued to improve, the contributing factor has been industrial rather than agricultural development. This implies that to solve future agrarian problems, it will be necessary to take into consideration other sectors' development, not merely dealing within the agricultural sector per se.

In studying farmers' perceptions of their problems, heavy tax and inappropriate policy measures were the foci of attention during the 1960s, while low price levels for agricultural products and farmers' welfare problems have been emphasized since the 1970s (Liao 1984). This indicates that farmers' aspirations and expectations have risen with the improvement in the general socioeconomic situation. The previous problem was "poverty" and the current problem is "inequality." This implies that agrarian policy should be flexible enough to match the pace of social and economic change in order to meet the needs of farmers.

The farmers' changing attitudes imply the need to put more emphasis on agriculture in development programs. Because of the relative disadvantage of agriculture compared to industry, development projects should give priority to increasing farmers' welfare, to improving education, etc., rather than focusing mainly on increasing aggregate growth rates. As Ruttan and Hayami (1988, 71) put it, "successful achievement of continued agricultural development over time involves a dynamic process of adjustment to original resource endowments and to resource accommodations."

Bibliography

Council for Economic Planning and Development. 1988. *Statistical Data Book*. Taiwan: Executive Yuan.

Department of Agriculture and Forestry, Taiwan Provincial Government. 1987 and 1988. *Taiwan Agricultural Yearbook*.

Directorate-General of Budget, Accounting, and Statistics. 1987. *The Report on 1985 Agricultural and Fishery Census, Taiwan-Fukien District*. Taiwan: Executive Yuan.

Fukutake, Tadashi. 1967. *Asian Rural Society: China, India, Japan*. Tokyo: University of Tokyo Press.

Gallin, Bernard. 1964. Rural Development in Taiwan: The Role of the Government. *Rural Sociology* 29(3):313-23.

Hsiao, Hsin-huang Michael. 1981. *Governmental Agricultural Strategies in Taiwan and South Korea, A Macrosociological Assessment*. Taipei: Institute of Ethnology, Academia Sinica.

Huang, Chun-chieh, and Cheng-hung Liao. 1987. Between Tradition and Modernity: Value Orientations of Farmers in Taiwan. In *Confucianism and Modernization*, edited by Joseph P. L. Jiang, 233-54. Taipei: Freedom Council.

Liao, Cheng-hung. 1984. Rural Problems. In *Social Problems in Taiwan*, edited by K. S. Yang and C. C. Yeh, 133-56. Taipei: Chi Liu Publishing Co.

Liao, Cheng-hung, Chun-chieh Huang, and Hsin-huang Hsiao. 1986. *The Development of Agricultural Policies in Postwar Taiwan: Historical and Sociological Perspectives*. Taipei: Institute of Ethnology, Academia Sinica. In Chinese.

Liao, Cheng-hung, and Chun-chieh Huang. 1988. *Value Changes of Farmers in Taiwan*. Research Report of the Department of Agricultural Extension (NSC 77-0301-H002-02). Taipei: National Taiwan University. In Chinese.

Mendras, Henri. 1970. *The Vanishing Peasant: Innovation and Change in French Agriculture*, translated by Jean Lerner. Cambridge, Mass.: The MIT Press.

Rapper, Arthur F. 1953. *Rural Taiwan in Progress*. Taipei: JCRR. In Chinese.

Rogers, Everett M. 1958. A Conceptual Variable Analysis of Technological Change. *Rural Sociology* 23:138-45.

Ruttan, Vernon W., and Yujiro Hayami. 1988. Induced Innovation Model of Agricultural Development. In *Agricultural Development in the Third World*, edited by Carl K. Eicher and John M. Staatz, 59-74. Baltimore and London: The Johns Hopkins University Press.

Wu, Tsong-shien. 1964. *Diffusion of Agricultural Innovations*. Taipei: Department of Agricultural Extension, National Taiwan University. In Chinese.

Yang, Martin M. C. 1970. *Socioeconomic Results of Land Reform in Taiwan*. Honolulu: East-West Center Press.

Afterword

Joel D. Aberbach, David Dollar, Kenneth L. Sokoloff

Despite the detailed and inward-looking examinations of various aspects of the record of economic growth offered in this volume, it must be remembered that Taiwan was far from the only economy in East Asia to undergo such an economic and social transformation during the period. Indeed, the spread of industrialization through much of the region is one of the most salient developments of the late-twentieth century. This geographic diffusion of economic growth began a century ago in Japan, took root in the so-called Four Tigers of South Korea, Taiwan, Hong Kong, and Singapore by the middle of the 1960s, and continues to expand and encompass more and more countries—including China. This broader context must be understood if one is to put the modern social and economic transformation of Taiwan in a proper perspective.

What stands out from a comparison of the experience of Taiwan to those of the other East Asian economies is not only how widespread the process of industrialization has been, but also how similar the patterns of economic growth are—almost wherever the phenomenon has taken hold. Despite notable differences across countries in factor endowments, institutions, and policies, including the structure of government, the size and diversity of population, wealth, attitudes toward the role of women, education, the prominence of the military, the existence of a colonial legacy, as well as the degrees of industrial and financial concentration, the qualitative result of attaining rates of economic growth that are an order of magnitude more rapid than any previously observed seems remarkably robust across the region. From 1965 to 1989, per capita income in East Asia grew at an average 5.2 percent per annum. Largely due to the fact that it began to grow slightly earlier than its counterparts, Taiwan averaged the fastest pace over the entire period, 7.3 percent per annum, but countries as diverse as South Korea (7.0), Indonesia (4.4), Thailand (4.0), Hong Kong (6.3), and Singapore (7.0) also did remarkably well. Although high rates of capital accumulation made important contributions, most of these dramatic advances in per capita income appear to be attributable to extraordinarily rapid total factor productivity growth.

The chief characteristics that seem to distinguish those economies that have industrialized from those that have not as of yet (like North Korea, Burma, and Laos), are the extent of orientation toward trading in world markets and the effective existence of private property rights. Moreover, just as in Taiwan and South Korea, East Asian economies such as China and Vietnam stagnated when national economic policies were based on import-substitution and desires for self-sufficiency or when private property was not secure. They began to grow rapidly only after recognizing private property and contractual agreements (market-mediated transactions), as well as encouraging shifts of resources to industries in which they had an international comparative advantage—through policy changes such as cutting subsidies and altering exchange policies.

International Comparative Advantages

In Taiwan, the pace of growth began to accelerate shortly after the economy liberalized and adopted more export-oriented policies about 1960. In South Korea, the analogous changes in policy and in the stage of growth were a few years later. This initial phase of industrialization was marked, in both countries, by especially rapid productivity advance in labor-intensive industries—where they each enjoyed an international comparative advantage and ready access to enormous markets. Indeed, as indicated by the work of Fang-Yi Wang on Taiwan, the record of better performance by the export-oriented can be detected among firms within industries. Although Wang's study is relatively unique in being conducted at the firm level, the finding that productivity growth over time was higher in export-oriented industries has been widely reported by many scholars for a number of East Asian economies.

The generality of this association between productivity and export orientation is indeed striking, because of the variation in policy and circumstance across countries. South Korea resorted at times to industrial policies that targeted certain conspicuous capital-intensive industries for special support, but Taiwan pursued growth policies that were relatively neutral in their effects across industries, or aided industries already well positioned in the market because of international comparative advantage.

That both, as well as many other East Asian economies, have higher records of productivity growth in the export-oriented industries is suggestive of the sources of the rapid technical change in these economies. Specifically, the greater potential returns to improvements in technology implied by the competitiveness of these countries in world markets (for labor-intensive products) might have induced greater investment in the acquisition and adaptation of foreign technologies and inventive activity in general.

Another, though nonexclusive, possibility, however, is that the pattern is an artifact due to East Asian economies typically having their initial international comparative advantage in labor-intensive commodities because of their relatively large populations. In less-developed countries with relatively limited technical skills among the general population, industries producing labor-intensive goods may find it easier for technological reasons to increase productivity than their more capital-intensive counterparts do. This might reasonably be the case, because organizational improvements have the potential for yielding major gains in the productivity of what previously would have been handicraft operations, or because capital-intensive industries require greater levels of technical expertise among workers or management to increase efficiency.

Both of these interpretations of the positive association across industries between productivity growth and export orientation are consistent with the observation that, as they became more developed over time, Taiwan, South Korea, Hong Kong, Singapore, and other newly industrializing countries in East Asia have gradually upgraded the composition of their exports, as well as their subset of industries in which productivity growth was most rapid, from the most labor-intensive to the increasingly skill- or capital-intensive. Whatever the processes that underlay the evolution of these paths of technological capabilities and the composition of industrial output, they have encouraged a sorting of nations by time at which economic growth and human capital accumulation began to accelerate. The more recent newcomers to industrialization specialize in the simplest of labor-intensive products, with the progressively older cohorts favoring (or being more successful at) progressively more sophisticated or higher-value added activities. These developments have served to slightly reduce the degree of direct competition between the ever-growing group of prodigious exporters of manufactured products in East Asia.

A major question for the future is whether the mobilization of the truly extraordinary resource base in China will seriously undercut the prospects for other East Asian economies. Fortunately for Taiwan, it seems along with Hong Kong to be among the best positioned of East Asian newly industrialized to actually take advantage of the mainland coming on line. Not only does its population have close cultural links to the natives of rapidly growing southeast China, but the generation of rapid economic growth has yielded a factor endowment much different from that in China—with high levels of human capital, entrepreneurial skills, and relatively well-integrated financial markets. The two economies seem likely in the near term to complement each other rather than compete as substitutes, and the returns to economic cooperation should help ease the formidable political problems.

As is already evident to the reader, an intellectual tension concerning the efficacy or impact of government policy runs through the contributions to this volume, and indeed through much of the scholarly and popular discussion of economic development in East Asia. Some believe that the pace of economic growth is much enhanced by an activist government, which not only maintains general conditions conducive to commerce and investment but also mobilizes and directs resources to the benefit of politically selected industries. Others, including at least two of us, disagree with this view, and instead hold that an economy is normally better off if the government confines itself to maintaining the general conditions conducive to commerce and investment. We argue that when Taiwan is recognized as only one of many successful industrializers in East Asia, especially when compared to an economy such as South Korea (with a record of a generally more intrusive government), its experience tends to contradict the interventionist school. Taiwan has done at least as well as South Korea in per capita income and productivity growth since they both began to industrialize, and might have turned in a superior performance if the latter had not virtually abandoned the policy of targeting specific industries for special subsidies in the 1970s. Moreover, as we have suggested above, the more restricted role of the Taiwanese government in managing the economy may be partially responsible for the more equal distribution of income and the less concentrated industrial structure in that country. Despite this perhaps strongly offered interpretation, we acknowledge that the evidence is only beginning to accumulate and must be systematically analyzed, and that many prefer the alternative perspective. Contemporary authors and readers can assess the logic of the competing hypotheses and the weight of the evidence available to date, and improve their understanding of the issues, but it may not be until the next generation that the questions are ultimately resolved.

—August 1993

Index